D0408535

TEACHING MAINSTREAMED STUDENTS

TEACHING MAINSTREAMED STUDENTS

Thomas M. Stephens
The Ohio State University

A. Edward Blackhurst
University of Kentucky

Larry A. Magliocca
The Ohio State University

1807 175 YEARS OF PUBLISHING 1982

JOHN WILEY & SONS
New York • Chichester • Brisbane • Toronto • Singapore

LC
4015
S73
*

Copyright © 1982, by John Wiley & Sons, Inc.

All rights reserved. Published simultaneously in Canada.

Reproduction or translation of any part of this work beyond that permitted by Sections 107 and 108 of the 1976 United States Copyright Act without the permission of the copyright owner is unlawful. Requests for permission or further information should be addressed to the Permissions Department, John Wiley & Sons.

Library of Congress Cataloging in Publication Data

Stephens, Thomas M.
Teaching mainstreamed students.

1. Handicapped children—Education.
2. Mainstreaming in education. I. Blackhurst, A. Edward. II. Magliocca, Larry A. III. Title.

LC4015.S73 371.9 82-2593
ISBN 0-471-02479-1 AACR2

88649

Printed in the United States of America

10 9 8 7 6 5 4 3 2 1

This book is dedicated to Professor Jack W. Birch of the University of Pittsburgh. Dr. Birch was an early advocate of mainstreaming exceptional children at a time when it was unpopular. He has been in the forefront of the research, service, and teacher preparation of special educators. Through his leadership, commitment, and many years of service, Jack Birch has influenced thousands of people indirectly. We had the good fortune to be influenced and to have had our professional careers shaped directly by him.

About the Authors

Combined, the professional experiences of the authors in the field of education exceed 50 years. Both Dr. Blackhurst and Dr. Stephens earned their doctoral degrees at the University of Pittsburgh. Dr. Magliocca earned his doctorate at The Ohio State University and his master's degree in special education and rehabilitation at the University of Pittsburgh.

Thomas M. Stephens is professor and chairman of Exceptional Children at The Ohio State University. An author of many professional articles and textbooks, Stephens has been a classroom teacher, a school psychologist, a state consultant, and an educational administrator.

A. Edward Blackhurst is Professor of Special Education at the University of Kentucky where he had previously been chairman of the Special Education Department. An author of numerous professional publications, he has been a classroom teacher and a teacher educator. Dr. Blackhurst has been active in the Council for Exceptional Children, having served as president of the Teacher Education Division.

Larry A. Magliocca is director of the Tri-State Midwest Regional Resource Center which serves special educators in Ohio, Illinois, and Indiana. He has been a classroom teacher, a supervisor, and a school administrator. An author of professional publications, he is also the managing editor of *The Directive Teacher*, a magazine for teachers of special students.

Preface

This book is intended as an introduction to mainstreaming for students who are preparing to be regular classroom teachers. We have written with undergraduate and other preservice students in mind. Our assumption is that most users of this text will probably not have had much, if any, coursework in special education. Further, we expect that this book will be useful in those courses that are devoted to the mainstreaming concept.

We call readers' attention to our use of the word *mainstreaming* throughout this book. Although the language used in the federal legislation refers to placement in the *least restrictive environment*, we believe, along with Lester Mann,[1] that the "practical intent" of the two terms is the same. Similarly, we refer to the *mainstreamed student* as the student of concern. We find this phrase useful in that any exceptional student—handicapped or gifted—could be receiving some services within the regular class.

We believe that mainstreaming continues to be widely misunderstood by many educators and noneducators alike. For this reason our focus is on those students who are most likely to be placed in regular classrooms for part or all of their school days. Among the handicapped, those labeled *mildly handicapped* are most represented in our thinking. These are children who essentially have learning and behavior problems tending to interfere with their school adjustment—those students who are diagnosed as *educable mentally retarded*, *learning disabled*, and those with mild behavior problems. This group may also include, for purposes of our discussion, the visually impaired, the hearing impaired, the physically handicapped, and the language impaired. In other words, we have tried to address the needs of those students with mild disabilities for educational purposes.

It may seem strange to some that we have also considered gifted students in this textbook. However, with historical perspective it should become obvious to most serious students that not only did school treatment adversely influence education for the handicapped but it also hampered progress for able students. By assuming that intelligence is essentially genetically determined, some people still believe that "genius" can overcome all barriers. Ironically, able students are also neglected by those who favor equality of opportunity; politically progressive thinkers are known to use distorted egalitarian arguments in opposing individualized instruction for gifted students.

[1]Lester Mann, Divagations, *Journal of Special Education*, 1981, **15**(2), 98-99.

In organizing the contents, we sequenced our discussion as follows:

- An historical perspective (Chapter 1).
- Students who potentially represent the mainstreamed population Chapter 2).
- Factors comprising the mainstreaming concept (Chapter 3).
- Activities provided by classroom teachers (Chapters 4, 5, and 6).
- Competencies needed by teachers (Chapter 7).
- Rationale and procedures for working with parents (Chapter 8).
- An opportunity to apply knowledge of mainstreaming through a simulated case study (Chapter 9).

The back matter—six appendices and a glossary are aids that the reader can refer to. We hope that they are useful to you in your studies and career.

Although our purpose is to provide all necessary elements needed in an introductory course, we do recognize that courses in mainstreaming exceptional children are taught by university personnel who have had experience and professional preparation in special education; their backgrounds will permit them to supplement this text where they believe it is appropriate.

As teacher educators and former classroom teachers, we respect the great demands placed on all teachers in today's schools. We are also aware of the anxieties and concerns that parents have when they send their children to school. We hope that our efforts here have assisted both teachers and parents and, perhaps through them, have contributed to the welfare of students and children.

Thomas M. Stephens
A. Edward Blackhurst
Larry A. Magliocca

Acknowledgments

Our publisher, John Wiley & Sons, has been exceedingly patient with us. With the guidance and help of our editor, Carol Luitjens, we finished a text that three busy and none too efficient people should probably not have agreed to write at all. The support from colleagues, family, and friends has been invaluable. Much of the typing was done by Kay Weidner with the assistance of Robin Arnold and Minnie Pollard. Deborah M. Telfer and Leslie Sugiuchi, graduate students at The Ohio State University, provided many hours of proofreading and library work. To all of these dedicated individuals we extend our appreciation for their efforts and help.

Dr. Marjorie E. Ward advised us regarding many of the books listed in Appendix B. Dr. Sandra H. McCormick generously permitted us to include her work in Appendix F. Both of these professors are our colleagues at The Ohio State University. We thank them for their contributions and interest.

Dr. Phoebe A. Wienke, Principal of Tremont Elementary School in Upper Arlington, Ohio, allowed us to include in Chapter 2 that school's Statement of Philosophy.

Claudia J. Lewis, graduate student at the University of Kentucky, provided the photography. The very special attention she gave to this task is evident throughout the book.

We thank the students, faculty, and administrators of Fayette County Schools, Lexington, Kentucky, for their willingness to participate as subjects for the photographs that appear in the text.

Finally, we express our great appreciation for the advice and counsel of our reviewers, Joan Wolf and Virginia Lucas.

T.M.S.
A.E.B.
L.A.M.

Contents

TEACHING MAINSTREAMED STUDENTS

ONE

The Origins of Mainstreaming

- What is mainstreaming?
- What are the historical forces that led to mainstreaming?
- What are the legal requirements for mainstreaming?
- What implication does mainstreaming have for teachers?
- What attitudes are detrimental to successful mainstreaming?

Mainstreaming is the education of mildly handicapped children in the regular classroom. It is a concept that is compatible with the least restrictive environment provision of P.L. 94-142 requiring that all handicapped children be educated with their normal peers whenever possible. Mainstreaming is based on the philosophy of equal educational opportunity that is implemented through individual planning to promote appropriate learning, achievement, and social normalization.

Mainstreaming has captured the attention of educators and the general public as few educational topics have. Discussion and controversy have developed around mainstreaming as a result of coverage of the mass media and numerous articles in magazines and research journals. This public discussion has been filled with confusing concepts and assumptions from its advocates as well as its critics.

The major confusion of this public debate has been the mistaken notion that self-contained special education classes should be closed and that all exceptional students should be placed in regular education classrooms. The concept of mainstreaming was promoted with great fervor in the late 1960s and early 1970s; correcting this idea will take time. Although its advocates may have been well meaning, the concept of mainstreaming as an "all-or-none" placement in the regular classroom grossly oversimplifies the needs of exceptional students and creates acute apprehension on the part of regular classroom and special education teachers.

If mainstreaming is not the arbitrary practice of wholesale placement of exceptional students into regular classes, then what is it? We will elaborate on the definition of *mainstreaming* that we opened with in this chapter, but for now we will say only that the key to mainstreaming is to provide equal educational opportunities to mildly handicapped students by placing them in the educational environment that best fits their needs. Many times this can be the regular classroom, if not for the entire day, at least for part of the day. Other times the least restrictive environment may not include the regular classroom at all. The type of educational placement is determined by considering how best to promote learning, achievement, and social normalization.

Although a number of mildly handicapped students are educated in other school settings, the majority currently spend at least part of their educational day in the regular classroom. This book is about those students and for their regular classroom teachers. In this chapter, we describe the historical roots of mainstreaming, provide a detailed definition, discuss the implications that mainstreaming has for teachers, and conclude with a discussion of attitudes that are detrimental to successful mainstreaming.

HISTORICAL ROOTS OF MAINSTREAMING

Mainstreaming is a relatively recent development of special education. Birch (1978) indicates that the origin of the term *mainstreaming* is not known. The relative recency of the concept is reflected by the fact that the term is not yet defined in general dictionaries in the sense that it is used in special education today.

The seeds for mainstreaming grew from a number of different influences: the advocacy movement, litigation, research and evaluation studies, professional maturity of special educators, legislation, and changing public attitudes about what constitutes appropriate treatment of exceptional students. At different times one influence was in the forefront of awareness more than another; however, there is no doubt that the evolution of mainstreaming was the result of the interaction of these influences.

Probably no segment of education has shown such rapid and continual change over the past 90 to 100 years as special education. The majority of the changes that have occurred can be attributed to the social forces and attitudes that prevailed at each moment in time as illustrated by Reynolds and Rosen (1976).

The building of institutions for exceptional persons in the late nineteenth century was fostered by strong optimism that the judgment and intelligence of mentally subnormal persons could be dramatically increased by improving their sensory discrimination process. This initial unrealistic optimism was replaced quickly by a pessimism particularly reinforced by Galton's publication on eugenics. Galton hypothesized that handicaps were genetic defects that would be passed on from generation to generation. The fatalistic attitude of the unchangeability of the mentally handicapped reached U.S. Supreme Court Justice Oliver Wendell Holmes, Jr., who advocated compulsory sterilization for institutionalized mentally retarded people.

In the early part of the twentieth century, education for the severely disabled was primarily benignly neglected; the mildly disabled were either excluded from the public schools or placed in segregated facilities or classes. Public school systems excluded disabled children on the grounds they were "unteachable" and "harmful to others," or they pleaded lack of money for special programs. The compulsory school-attendance laws enacted by many states in the early part of the twentieth century were rarely extended to exceptional children.

The learning environments of schools ignored the individual's learning style and viewed variation as undesirable. This attitude was so prevalent that Hollingsworth (1926) felt it necessary to argue, in her classic publication on the gifted child, that precociousness in children was not something to fear but to be nurtured.

Although there were a few public school special education programs prior to that time, they began in earnest following World War II. Previously most special education occurred in residential schools serving the blind, deaf, epileptic, crippled, and retarded; and special educators served these children within these facilities.

From the 1920s to the 1940s, a few teacher-training programs were established around the country and a professional organization of special teachers, the Council for Exceptional Children (CEC), was formed.

The concern for the individual differences in learning has been of recent origin: only in the past 100 years in psychology, and only within the past 50 years in the United States by educators. Noting the group orientation of the schools and the past concepts of "protecting" exceptional persons in sheltered environments, it is easy to understand why the parents of exceptional children would have first sought special schools and classes for their children in relative isolation from mainstream education. During the latter half of the 1940s and particularly in the 1950s the accepted model of education for the handicapped was in the separate facility or class.

Sarason and Doris (1978) point out that special educators at that time would have viewed an effort to integrate the mentally retarded into mainstream education as unrealistic and probably not in the best interest of the exceptional individual. This attitude of parents and special educators supporting the development of segregated facilities and classes was to change.

RESEARCH AND ADVOCACY

By the mid-twentieth century several forces came together to precipitate change in the direction of mainstreaming. Studies began to emerge related to the education of exceptional students, and these studies provided fuel for the efforts of parent advocates.

The research literature that relates most specifically to the mainstreaming movement deals with the mentally retarded. The "efficacy" studies, as they began to be called, of the 1950s to 1970s questioned the academic value of special-class placement for the mildly retarded; more about these studies will be said later. The research literature of the 1940s is important in the area of mental retardation since it directly influenced the decision by parent advocates to seek special, isolated facilities rather than to demand integration within general education.

The classic study of Skeels and Dye (1939) and follow-up study (Skeels, 1941-1942) had a tremendous impact on the public's attitude toward the retarded. Through their research, they were able to show that environmental stimulation had significant positive effects on the development of the retarded child. This contrasted with previous attitudes that nothing could be done to assist the retarded, particularly those who were institutionalized.

Skeels and Dye (1939) provided a clear break from other research published in the 1930s. The attitude of many professionals, including noted authority Edgar Doll (1941), was that the condition of retardation was permanent and irreversible. The Skeels and Dye study of the positive effects of environmental stimulation of institutionalized retardates was a landmark. With the publication of the *National Society for the Study of Education, Part II* in 1940, not only did the education of the handicapped receive national recognition, but the studies of Kephart (1940) and Speers (1940) furthered the research into the influences of environmental factors on retarded persons. These early studies undermined the concept that attempts to diminish retardation were hopeless and educational programs would be wasted.

Several education approaches emerged during this period that are still important today. From his studies Samuel Orton (1937), a psychiatrist, formulated a hypothesis that neurological malfunctioning was the cause of a reading disability. Later, through his contact with educator Anna Gillingham, the Orton-Gillingham method of multisensory approaches to teaching was born.

Another early pioneer was Grace Fernald (1943). Her multisensory approach to teaching known as VAKT (Visual-Auditory-Kinesthetic-Tactile) is widespread today. Her teaching approach uses the four sensory channels simultaneously and was one of the first nationally recognized teaching methods for children we now call learning disabled.

The works of Orton and Fernald had an important influence during the 1940s. Combined with the growing advent of the mental-testing movement it convinced many persons of the importance of an individual approach to teaching exceptional students.

Other publications began to appear that stressed individual approaches to teaching the exceptional child. The works of Strauss and Lehtinen (1947) and Kirk and Johnson (1951) are two notable examples. But although their approaches were concerned with the individual characteristics of the exceptional student, they were heavily oriented to segregated self-contained classes for the handicapped.

Following World War II, there was an enlarged definition of *democracy* that demanded "freedom from fear and want." Parents began to form specific groups to better conditions for their handicapped children. One of the most powerful and influential parent groups was the National Association for Retarded Children (later changed to National Association for Retarded Citizens). Through their state chapters they lobbied state legislators to make special provisions for their children. They succeeded in getting legislation passed that contained provisions for the states to reimburse local school districts for the "excess cost" (over and above the costs of educating every student) of educating the exceptional child. From the end of World

War II to the 1980s, this excess-cost provision has enabled programs for the handicapped to increase approximately tenfold.

The advocacy movement for the handicapped also gained public acceptance due to the return of disabled veterans after World War II and the Korean War. Advocacy groups like NARC could apply political pressure to legislators, with the emotional acceptance of the public, to make special provisions for the handicapped. This was heightened by national campaigns like the "March of Dimes" for the physically disabled, which was inspired by President Franklin Roosevelt.

Special classes and special facilities burgeoned during the 1950s and 1960s, particularly in urban areas. With this growth began the publication of a broader array of educational research on exceptional persons. Drawing from the research of child development, applied behavior analysis, instructional technology, language and semantics, perceptual-motor development, and specific educational areas (e.g., vocational education), the research literature of special education proposed different methods, curriculum materials and media, and delivery systems for the handicapped. Concurrently, sociometric studies and efficacy studies of the comparative effects of special and regular education placement of the mildly retarded raised the question of the desirability of unrestrained growth of separate special-education programs. In certain ways, these two types of studies have drawn contradictory conclusions, as will be illustrated below.

Sociometric studies show similar results from the 1950s through to the 1980s. Mildly handicapped children have been less accepted, isolated, and more actively rejected than nonhandicapped classmates in the mainstream (Cassidy and Stanton, 1959; Goodman, Gottlieb, and Harrison, 1972; Gottlieb and Budoff, 1973; Kidd, 1970; Scranton and Ryckman, 1979; and Towne, Joiner, and Schurr, 1967). These studies also show that children in special classes have a loss of self-esteem with stigma attached to special class placement, lowered achievement expectancies, and restriction of social models from whom to learn interpersonal skills, beyond that presented by nonhandicapped peers.

In contrast, efficacy studies showed that some mainstreamed handicapped children fared better academically than similar handicapped children in special classes. Briefly, the efficacy studies examined the selective merits of regular versus special class placement for mentally retarded children. The studies followed this process: Equivalent groups of mentally retarded children were identified in a special class and in a regular class. These groups were given achievement tests and social adjustment tests in a pre- and post-test fashion. The data were analyzed through various statistical methods and in many of these studies the mentally retarded in regular classes performed better.

Several influential authorities reviewed these studies. First, Johnson (1962) reviewed a number of early works including Baldwin (1958), Cassidy and Stanton (1959), Jordon (1959), and Thurstone (1959) and concluded that special classes were of little academic value to mildly retarded children. Second, Dunn's (1968) review, "Special Education for the Mildly Retarded—Is Much of it Justifiable?," caused widespread reevaluation of the establishment of special classes. Although Dunn's conclusions were similar to those of Johnson (1962), they found the United States six years later in a different sociopolitical state of mind. Dunn concluded, as did Johnson, that special classes were academically ineffective for the mildly retarded, but he extended his criticism to other important factors. He pointed out that special classes had disproportionately large numbers of minority and disadvantaged children in them, minimal justification was required by general educators for special placement, and the monumental growth of special classes had thwarted the development of instructional options in regular classes. Dunn's article is frequently cited as the consciousness-raising article that began the mainstreaming movement in earnest.

Efficacy studies have been heavily criticized for using poor research methodology (e.g., Keogh and Levett, 1976; Kirk, 1964; MacMillan and Becker, 1977; Robinson and Robinson, 1976) and any attempt to generalize the conclusions of the studies should be done cautiously. One unfortunate result of the studies was the unwarranted assumption that all mildly handicapped children should be placed in the mainstream (e.g., Berry's call in 1972 for the wholesale return of the handicapped to regular classrooms). As Gickling and Theobald (1975) pointed out:

> Mainstreaming is cited so frequently that one might mistakenly think it a magic elixir rather than a particular orientation toward supplying special education for the majority of the mildly handicapped. It has been treated as if full participation in regular educational programs would overcome any adverse problems facing exceptional children. (p. 317)

Although the scientific validity of the efficacy studies could be questioned, there were some positive effects. These studies accentuated the need for the following practices:

1. A broader array of special services to support the exceptional child (now known as a "continuum of special education services")

2. Nondiscriminatory testing

3. Antilabeling movement

4. Participatory decision making in placement on the part of parents

The efficacy studies were soon to be replaced by more comprehensive evaluation efforts (Kaufman, Semmel, and Agard, 1974; Keogh, Kukic, and Sbordonc, 1975). The focus shifted to more fruitful avenues of search: What match do we need between the school environment and the exceptional child's needs to be successful?

The most important research of the last two decades that has productively expedited mainstreaming has been in two areas: differentiated programming and functional noncategorical approaches to educating the exceptional student. The research questions are rightfully being rephrased to ask, What specific program delivery systems and methods of instruction will affect the exceptional child's learning satisfactorily?

LITIGATION

It is important to note how the research and advocacy of the 1940s through the 1970s impinged upon the next influence on mainstreaming—litigation. By the early 1970s, there was general dissatisfaction with the special-education services provided, or the lack of services available, to the exceptional learner. Advocacy groups like the National Association of Retarded Citizens, the Association for Children with Learning Disabilities, and United Cerebral Palsy, Inc. became more sophisticated in lobbying and more concerned about the effects of labeling on their children. The stage had been set for the parent advocates to begin challenging the status quo in the 1970s.

A precedence-setting court case was the famous *Brown* v. *the Board of Education* (Topeka, Kansas) in 1954. This case established the right of "equal protection" of the Fourteenth Amendment. Although the decision was related to racial segregation, the idea of providing "separate but equal" methods of education was to inspire court challenges for exceptional children.

Three cases established the right to education for the handicapped. In the *Pennsylvania Association for Retarded Children (PARC)* v. *Commonwealth of Pennsylvania* case in 1971, 13 mentally retarded children were represented by PARC; the parties reached settlement through a consent decree and an out-of-court settlement. The State of Pennsylvania agreed not to apply any law that would postpone, terminate, or deny mentally retarded children a publicly supported education.

In *Mills* v. *Board of Education* (Washington, D.C.) in 1972, parents and guardians of seven Washington D.C. children brought forth a class action suit. The children had been excluded from public education; three were in public residential institutions with no education program; the others lived with their families at home. The four home-based children had been denied admittance to public-school programs and had been placed on waiting lists to receive tuition grants for private facilities. U.S. District Judge Joseph Waddy issued an order that required the Washington, D.C., Board of Education to provide educational services to excluded exceptional children even though the school district pleaded a lack of available funds. Not only did this case establish the principle of the inclusion of all exceptional children in future class-action suits, it also declared the constitutional right of all children to a publicly supported education and a guarantee of due process of, and equal protection, by the law. Because the *Mills* v. *Board of Education* decision was based on constitutional grounds, it was to set a strong precedent for future decisions.

Extensive litigation had now begun. Plaintiffs claimed that misclassification resulted in inappropriate placement, and that there was a general inadequacy of special education programs and inaccessibility of educational opportunities. In the face of these challenges, Turnbull (1978) notes "one of the most effective remedies . . . is to be included in a regular program in preference to a special program and that he [handicapped student] is to be educated in the regular school environment rather than in the special school." (p. 25)

LEGISLATION

Influential legislation at the federal level may be traced to the Elementary and Secondary Education Act of 1965 (P.L. 89-10) which provided massive amounts of money to educators. Inadvertently, a by-product of Public Law (P.L.) 89-10 was to disband the Division of Handicapped Children and Youth, which had just been organized a year and a half before. An amendment, P.L. 89-750, corrected this error by adding Title VI to the Elementary and Secondary Education Act. Title VI was a special education title which established the Bureau of Education for the Handicapped and the National Advisory Committee on Handicapped Children. Thus, the mechanism for prioritizing the needs of exceptional students was in place at the federal level.

In 1973, a civil rights act for the handicapped, the Vocational Rehabilitation Act of 1973, was passed by Congress. Section 504 of this Act is most important since it forbids discrimination in education and employment on the basis of handicap.

Although procedural safeguards and the "least restrictive" placement for the handicapped were passed in P.L. 93-380 which was developed in direct response to earlier court litigation, it was not until P.L. 94-142 was passed that the least restrictive placement had real impact. P.L. 94-142 contained provisions for congressional appropriations to the states for the education of the handicapped. To receive these important funds (legislated to include up to 40 percent of the additional costs of educating the handicapped child over the costs of educating nonhandicapped children), each state must submit an annual program plan assuring compliance to all provisions of P.L. 94-142. P.L. 94-142 has been the most comprehensive federal legislation for handicapped students ever enacted. Major provisions that relate to the process of mainstreaming include: (1) *free appropriate education*; (2) *individual education program*; (3) *least restrictive environment*; (4) *non-discriminatory evaluation*; and (5) *impartial due process hearing*.

P.L. 94-142 was passed in November 1975, with the target date for serving all handicapped children by 1980. Other provisions such as *child identification*, to find and serve all handicapped children, and the *com-*

prehensive personnel development requirements, to prepare all personnel to educate handicapped students, were included to ensure the rights and provisions of all handicapped children in the least restrictive environment.

The many influences that contributed to the mainstreaming movement were realized in P.L. 94-142. There is no doubt that amendments to this comprehensive legislation will be offered in the future as more experience is gained in implementing its provisions. Also, much of the success of this law will depend upon Congress authorizing the fiscal appropriations that the law stipulates. Taking all these factors into consideration, however, P.L. 94-142 still places the United States well into the vanguard of other countries in future planning and programming for its handicapped citizens.

Mainstreaming has been a grassroots movement propelled ahead by the loose alliance of many different people. From these grassroots origins, it is easy to see why the term *mainstreaming* has had and still has multiple meanings. Fortunately, it has outgrown the "faddish" stage wherein careful consideration was ignored and was replaced by sloganism (as in the late 1960s and early 1970s). Making the complexities of mainstreaming a workable process, in partial fulfillment of the ideals of this movement, is still in the future. Even with P.L. 94-142, the problem of a comprehensive support system of mainstreaming in our schools seems just out of reach. Providing for individual planning for each disabled student through the Individual Education Program (IEP), requiring a placement decision in the least restrictive alternative, and providing for due process and parental input are aggressive moves in the idealized direction. But the problem remains: Are the schools ready for what mainstreaming requires?

MAINSTREAMING DEFINED

The definition of *mainstreaming* given earlier in this chapter can now be discussed in more detail. The rationale for the different parts of this definition can be related to the historical development of the mainstreaming movement. Keep in mind that our definition of *mainstreaming* not only refers to educating the exceptional learner in the regular school environment but also to placement of the exceptional student in the least restrictive environment, depending on individual factors. With this caveat,

> *Mainstreaming is the education of mildly handicapped children in the least restrictive environment. It is based on the philosophy of equal educational opportunity that is implemented through individual planning to promote appropriate learning, achievement, and social normalization.*

The rationale for each major element of this definition will now be developed.

EDUCATION OF EXCEPTIONAL CHILDREN IN THE LEAST RESTRICTIVE ENVIRONMENT . . .

Throughout P.L. 94-142, the term *mainstreaming* is never mentioned. Instead, the legalistic term *least restrictive environment* is used. This phrase has several important advantages over the term *mainstreaming*.

What a least restrictive environment is, is a matter for individual determination. Some instructional and social environments will be less restrictive to growth and development of the individual than others. This depends on an array of individual variables including abilities, skills, and motivation. So the selection of an instructional environment for each student must be done separately. Education of the exceptional student must be delivered in the least restrictive environment and, as P.L. 94-142 goes on to specify, with as much involvement with nonhandicapped children as possible.

Second, the least restrictive environment provision implies a selection of placement for the exceptional learner from a number of options, commonly known as a "continuum of special education services." As the team of professionals and parents selects the least restrictive placement for an exceptional student, there should be several options under consideration. The continuum of special education services must include both segregated and integrated delivery services if the needs of all exceptional children are to be met. On the one end of the continuum, segregated services might involve a total program for certain students in a special school or residential facility if their learning and/or behavioral difficulties warrant this placement. On the other end of the continuum, special education could provide periodic or temporary assistance to students who spend most of their time in the regular classroom. There should be variations of these two extremes through other types of services (which will be discussed in Chapter 2). The important point to remember is that the least restrictive environment should be selected from a number of options on an individual basis.

THE PHILOSOPHY OF EQUAL EDUCATIONAL OPPORTUNITY . . .

Mainstreaming is a grass-roots philosophy. It provides the "why" for this social movement. When people ask, Why mainstream the handicapped? the most persuasive argument is a philosophical and moral one. The disabled, as citizens, should have the same rights and opportunities as others. Although many have attempted to justify the mainstreaming movement from a research basis, this has never succeeded in providing a definitive rationalization for mainstreaming. The justification of mainstreaming is sound and rational when viewed as a philosophy concerned with rights and equal opportunities.

The public schools are the gateway to American society in many ways. They are the primary route to personal, vocational, and social development of the individual. The diploma or equivalent received upon completion of secondary school programs becomes a gateway into the job market. Although some students may not take advantage of the opportunity (e.g., dropouts); it is quite another matter when exceptional students are systematically denied this opportunity.

The history of education for exceptional students is replete with this denial. Placed in segregated facilities which usually had been vacated by others for safety or other reasons these children were not given adequate space and the restrooms, gymnasium, food areas, classrooms, etc. were often in disrepair. Lack of money, teachers, and facilities, or the assump-

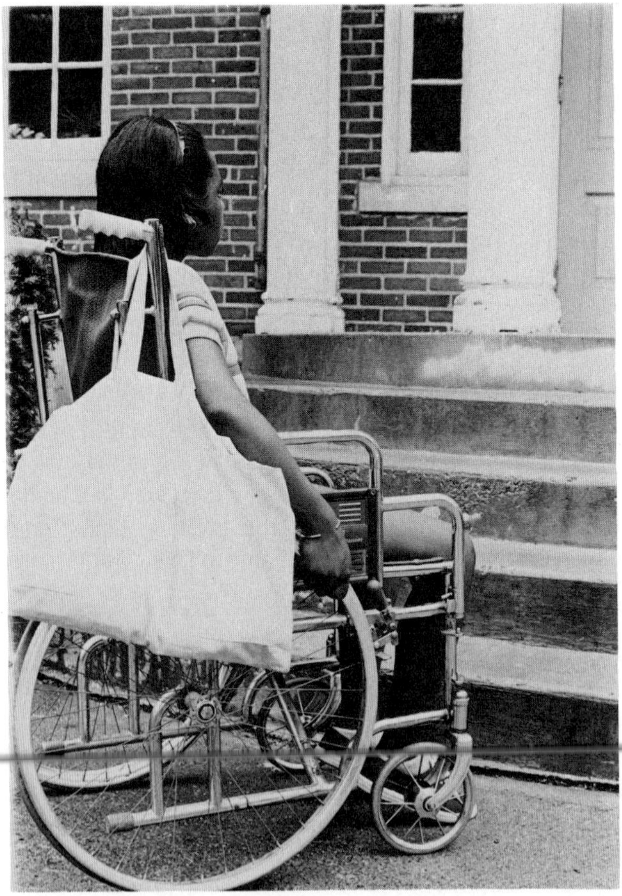

Laws now require that buildings be constructed without architectural barriers that prohibit access by people with physical disabilities.

tion that the disabled will be unable to profit from equal opportunities have all been given as reasons for this pattern of denial. Fortunately, through litigation and legislation, such blatant denial of opportunities are now forbidden. However, the real assurance of equal opportunity is through *access*—physical and psychological access. The disabled can be guaranteed equal opportunities of education by law, yet remain subtly subjected to discrimination.

Lack of physical access may relate to architectural designs of a building that impede access. Particularly relevant to the physically disabled, this involves architectural barriers to entrances and exits, and barriers within the building that prevent the physically disabled from moving from room to room or floor to floor, etc. Water fountains and restrooms may be impossible for them to use. Another physical barrier impeding access to sensory impaired students might be the lack of equipment or materials, making the learning process impossible.

Psychological access relates to the attitudes regular educators and special educators hold about the disabled. If the basic assumption is that different is undesirable, then psychological access for the disabled becomes impossible. By thinking certain activities are impossible, teachers make few efforts to make students do them. The disabled depend upon the educators' good will and effort to make access a reality.

An ingredient of effective mainstreaming is a belief that education of exceptional students is a desirable reality; professionals must be willing to work at it. The possibility of placement of the disabled with the nondisabled student revolves around making access to facilities a reality. The reality of successful placement of the eligible exceptional student in the regular education environment for part or all of the school day depends upon educators deciding (by their attitudes) whether the student's disability is a handicap.

. . . TO PROMOTE APPROPRIATE LEARNING, ACHIEVEMENT, AND SOCIAL NORMALIZATION

The focus must be on the individual student. Placement decisions must be based on the results expected of the learner. A mainstream or special placement should be decided upon through projected improvements in the student's learning, achievement, and social normalization; thus, the least restrictive to most optimal placement must manifest itself in improvements of the learner.

The process of learning must be the primary consideration. As an individual matter, learning requires interaction of the student with the learning task. The tasks must be carefully selected for appropriateness and clarity of expectations. If a task is too difficult or confusing, the disabled student will not make progress in his learning.

Much of the quality of the learning process will depend upon the establishment of directed antecedent and consequential conditions for the learning tasks. Teachers must be cognizant of the importance of cueing and prompting the student's progress in the learning task (as antecedents) and must be able to appropriately apply positive reinforcement to support particular progress (as consequences).

Learning also improves when there are opportunities to respond. If the teaching situation involves lectures or little active student involvement other than memorizing, the disabled student will find learning difficult. If there are many and varied opportunities for response, the learning process is improved.

Learning is perhaps the most important criterion for consideration for placement. It is the joint responsibility of the student and the teacher. The student must be able to participate many times with the help of adaptive materials or methods, or some assistance from the teacher. The teacher has the responsibility for ensuring the learning task is appropriate, the antecedent and consequential conditions of learning are present, and the learner receives feedback that will influence future performance. Thus the criterion of learning improvement must be given careful consideration.

Achievement is an important ingredient in American classrooms. The expectation that students will learn and demonstrate skills over a given period of time is a productive, goal-directed emphasis in our schools. The difficulty occurs when educators base those achievement expectations simplistically on age-related grade equivalents. If this is the achievement expectation, disabled students are frustrated; their emotional reaction to school and their own competencies will be blemished.

The achievement criterion must be derived from the disabled student's expected performance level. Individual factors like capacity, experience, and motivation determine performance levels. An estimate must be made that indicates student progress in the mainstream environment, with support and assistance from teachers and includes a reasonable expectation of success.

Achievement is not only an individual criterion. It is also comparatively based. Most teachers are aware that the achievement range of the students in their classes is quite large; that is, the teacher must expect a variety of student performance levels which require adjustments in method and necessitate instructional grouping. This instructional grouping should be made on the basis of skill needs rather than on achievement scores. How does the disabled student fit into this comparative achievement consideration?

The "group of one" rule applies in this situation. If the student's instructional needs are so unique from those of other children in the classroom that the teacher cannot group the disabled student with any other students, the chances of achieving successfully in the regular classroom are rather small given the disproportionate amount of time the teacher would need to devote to an instructional "group of one." The achievement criterion must be individually based as a reasonable expectation of progress, but it must also be considered in reference to the achievement-oriented regular classrooms.

Social normalization must also be given careful consideration. Many disabled students are mainstreamed for the purposes of social learning only; responsibilities for learning and achievement are left to the special educators. The stimulation of social learning by associating with nondisabled peers is powerful. Many school programs systematically expose all of their mildly disabled students to involvement with other students in art, music, and physical education classes, at recreation times, in cafeteria areas, etc.

Periodic mixing of children is one thing; social learning in the regular classroom is quite another. Research has consistently shown that the mildly disabled students in the regular classrooms are generally not well accepted; they are ignored or rejected by their nondisabled peers (Bryan, Wheeler, Felcan, and Herek, 1976; Bryan, P. and Bryan, J.H., 1977).

Mainstreaming to promote social learning experiences for the disabled student is different from simply mixing with nondisabled students in various activities. The important construct of self-concept enters into the decision. *Self-concept* is the label we use to describe that set of feelings we have about ourselves; these feelings are tremendously influenced by how others perceive us. Social normalization is an important consideration demanding the impact on the disabled student's self-concept. The goal, of course, is that a mainstream placement positively affects self-concept and provides more opportunities for social learning for the disabled than the special class is able to do.

Bruininks (1978) found that disabled students are less accurate perceivers of their social status within the classroom than are nondisabled students. If social normalization is to be a success for the disabled student, there are a number of facts to consider. First, the disabled student with assistance from the regular teacher must be able to meet implicit and explicit behavioral demands or expectations of the regular classroom. These expectations are developmentally related and easiest to identify when they are violated; the teacher will complain that the student is too disruptive of the learning of others in the classroom. Of course proper behaviors can be taught, but the regular education teacher would prefer a set of initial behaviors that were not grossly deviant.

Another important factor is the capacity of the disabled student to initiate, maintain, or reciprocate social interactions with others in some constructive way. For positive social learning to occur, the disabled student must be responsive on some level to nondisabled students. Certainly the regular educators greatly assist this process by preparing nondisabled students to be sensitive to the needs of the disabled, but there are a number of important individual characteristics that will determine how much will be learned by participation with nondisabled students.

Learning, achievement, and social normalization are important criteria for consideration of the least restrictive placement. The primary concern is that these three factors will result in progress for the disabled student.

In this definition, we have emphasized what we consider to be the most important aspect of mainstreaming. Mainstreaming involves careful individual planning for each exceptional student to ensure placement in the environment that promotes learning, achievement, and social normalization. The focus must be on the welfare of the individual student, the progress that can be expected, and the eventual role the exceptional person will play in society.

In the next section, the rights, roles, and responsibilities to support mainstreaming are discussed. All educators must know these new three Rs if they are to pursue their professional obligations to the exceptional student.

THE NEW THREE Rs: RIGHTS, ROLES, AND RESPONSIBILITIES

The rights, roles, and responsibilities that the teacher must be cognizant of are contained in P.L. 94-142. It must be pointed out that each state has variances from the federal legislation. Education is a states' right guaranteed by the U.S. Constitution and this cannot be abridged by the federal government. However, by the early 1980s, nearly every state has passed companion legislation at the state level that closely resembles P.L. 94-142. Therefore, our discussion of the new three Rs is possible in a general way. When there are questions about the exact nature of any of these areas in a particular state, the state regulations should be consulted.

RIGHTS

As indicated in the discussion of the origins of mainstreaming earlier in this chapter, a number of influences have contributed to the establishment of rights for exceptional learners. The most exacting influences are litigation and legislation. The litigation was initiated mainly by parents who wished to challenge the public school system's treatment of their children. From their point of view, there was arbitrary and prejudicial treatment of their children that was injurious to their welfare. Before too long, many of the court decisions were contained in federal legislation. Dimond (1973) termed this "the quiet revolution."

Lack of public resources to accomplish equal educational opportunities for the disabled is no longer a valid argument. However, this does not mean that the provisions of the laws will be carried out as ordered. P.L.

94-142 is a complicated law; it cannot be implemented quickly in an effective way. There must be a sense of commitment to the task by all educators, which cannot be legislated. More resources must be applied since the federal funds appropriated to implement the law only cover a small amount of the cost. The new requirements involve considerable skill on the part of regular educators, skill the majority have not yet learned. So it may be premature to signal "The End of the Quiet Revolution" as Abeson and Zettel (1977) proclaim, since legislating and implementing the legislation are two very different things.

Let us now examine this "bill of rights" for the exceptional learner:

The right to a free appropriate public education

The right to an individual education program

The right to a nondiscriminatory evaluation

The right to due process of law

The right to the least restrictive environment

A free appropriate public education is the key to P.L. 94-142. As a matter of national policy it is illegal to exclude the exceptional learner from a public education on the basis that the child possesses special needs. Within the law, it is stated in this way:

> It is the purpose of this Act to assure that all handicapped children have available to them, within the time periods specified, a free appropriate public education which emphasizes special education and related services designed to meet their unique needs. (P.L. 94-142, 1975, Sec. 3, c)

The important words are *free* and *appropriate*. Free means there should be no additional expenses to the parents or guardians of the child. Even in situations where a tuition-based program is needed, that is, when it has been determined that a public school program is not available, the costs will be assumed by the public agency. Expenses for related services (e.g. transportation) are also to be assumed at public expense. The appropriateness of the educational program is determined by the individual's needs and derived as part of the Individualized Education Program (IEP).

This is a reversal of a long-standing policy in public education in which disabled learners were automatically excluded from educational activities available to other children on the basis that programs were not available or the child was thought to be incapable of participating. Particularly the severely disabled are most to benefit since public schools historically have ignored the needs of the child and forced parents to find programs for their children at their own expense. Other parts of this legislation determine how this policy is carried out.

The Individualized Education Program is the revolutionary means by which this free appropriate public education is to be ensured. The IEP is the keystone through which the individual exceptional learner is considered by a group of people including the child's teachers and parents. The IEP requirement indicates the type of information that is to be in the IEP, the people who are to be present to plan it, and the type of services the child is to receive in the least restrictive environment.

The IEP is basically an agreement describing what and when special education services will be provided. It is a management device for indicating what will be provided for the child, when and by whom it will be provided, and that at least an annual review of the appropriateness of the placement of the child will be conducted.

The Individualized Education Program is the first time in federal legislation that an educational method has been specified. In this document are contained the ideals of educators for the past five decades. *Individualized* means the educational needs of the child will be determined rather than the needs of a category of children. *Education* refers to the special education and related services that are required for the individual child; this determination must be made on what education the child needs rather than limiting it to what the school district currently provides. *Program* refers to the required statement of what will be provided to meet the needs of the child as agreed upon by a group of interested persons.

Although the contents of the IEP are specified here, most school districts design their own forms. Many IEP forms contain more information than what is required by law. Whatever the form may be, it must contain the following information and the parent(s) must sign in agreement. All

The development of the IEP is a team effort that involves teachers, specialists, the school principal, and the child's parents. The child should also be involved, when possible.

such forms are confidential, but they must also be available for inspection by the designated state and federal agencies which act for the law.

THE INDIVIDUALIZED EDUCATION PROGRAM (IEP)

The Individualized Education Program is the management tool that specifies the child's unique educational needs, annual goals for the child, the services allocated to achieve the desired results, and how the effectiveness of the program will be determined.

If a child has an educational need that requires specially designed instruction, an Individualized Education Program as defined in Public Law 94-142 must be developed to link the child with the appropriate special education and related services.

The requirements of P.L. 94-142 are divided into two parts:

Participants of the IEP Meeting

- A representative of the local education agency or of the intermediate educational unit who is qualified to provide or to supervise the provision of special education
- The teacher(s) of the child
- The parents or guardians
- The child, whenever appropriate

Content of the IEP

- A statement of the child's present level of educational performance
- A statement of annual goals, including short-term instructional objectives
- A statement of the specific educational services to be provided
- The extent to which the child will be able to participate in regular education programs
- The projected date for initiation and the anticipated duration of such services
- Appropriate objective criteria, evaluation procedures, and schedules for determining, on at least an annual basis, whether instructional objectives are being achieved

In arriving at a statement of present educational level of performance of the student, P.L. 94-142 requires that all professionals who evaluate the child do so in a nondiscriminatory manner. A well documented problem has been the inappropriate use of standardized tests with certain groups of children. Intelligence tests particularly were abused in the placement of minority children, non-English speaking children, and children with certain types of handicaps, for example, language or motor problems. In testing situations, children of these groups were unfairly evaluated, since the test required that responses be made in ways that were not within their repertoire of behaviors; thus the tests were not really measuring intelligence validly for such children. Many of these children were placed in classes for the retarded based on the results of one of these biased testing sessions.

P.L. 94-142 has corrected this situation to some extent. First, no single test or procedure may be the sole determiner for making a placement decision. Second, the materials or procedures selected for evaluating the child must not be discriminatory and must be in the native language or mode of communication of the child. Through these safeguards, the type of information, the types of materials and procedures, and consideration for the child's response modes are regulated to eliminate abuses. One positive result has been the use of evaluation information more for the purposes of educating the child and less for determining abilities and categories of handicapping conditions.

The due process provision of P.L. 94-142 establishes a means for resolving disagreements; all parties involved—the child, the family, and the school—have a mechanism for communicating about the educational status of the child and equal consideration in disagreements about the identification, evaluation, and placement decisions. The intent of the due process provisions is to provide for review and adjustment of practices by either the parents or school personnel.

Several major provisions for due process are provided in the next section. They include: (1) the need for written notification before evaluation or change in placement; (2) the access to relevant records (also assured by the Family Education Rights and Privacy Act) and the right of parents to enter independent evaluation materials from certified professionals; (3) the provision of impartial hearings to resolve disputes and the right to appeal the findings of hearings, even into the federal courts.

DUE PROCESS

Due process rights are guaranteed to exceptional children and their families by Public Law 94-142, Education for All Handicapped Act of 1975, and by Section 504 of Public Law 93-112, The Vocational Rehabilitation Act of 1973.

Testing and Placement

- Parents must receive written notification prior to special testing and other evaluations of their child.
- Parents must receive written notification of initiation or refusal to initiate a change in educational placement of a handicapped child.

- Parents must have the opportunity to present their views regarding the identification, the evaluation, the placement, or the provision of a free appropriate education to their child.
- Parents must have the opportunity to present information from an independent educational evaluation of their child.

Records

- Parents must have access to all relevant school records of their child.

Impartial Hearing

- Parents must have the right to, or schools may initiate, an impartial due process hearing to resolve differences that could not be resolved informally. In conducting such a hearing, parents must:
  (a) Receive timely and specific notice of the hearing
  (b) Have the right to be accompanied and advised by counsel and/or by individuals with special knowledge or training with respect to the problems of handicapped children
  (c) Confront, cross-examine, and compel the attendance of witnesses
  (d) Present evidence relevant to the decision

Interactions with parents regarding the testing and placement of their children must be provided in language which they can understand. In this case, an interpreter has been provided to assist in communicating with a deaf parent.

(e) Obtain written or electronic verbatim record of the hearing and obtain written findings of facts and decisions

- The hearing is to be conducted by an impartial hearing officer who is not an employee of the school system involved.
- The decision of the hearing is binding on all parties pending appeal.
- Either party has the right to appeal the findings and the decision of the hearing to the state.
- During the hearing process, the child shall remain in the original program or in another program to which both parties can agree.
- At any step along the way either party may take the matter to court.

It is quite clear that the vast majority of parents or school personnel do not use the impartial hearing provisions. Perhaps the opportunity for impartial hearings is enough of a stimulus for communications and programming to avert this type of confrontation. It is important to note that where adequate communications mechanisms exist between school personnel and parents and where each listens to the needs of the other, impartial hearings are a rarity.

The right to placement in the least restrictive environment may be the most elusive of all the students' rights. It is a legalistic principle and more specific in interpretation than the term *mainstreaming*. It simply means that at the time of a placement decision for special education and related services, the decision must be made on the basis of the individual's present level of performance and needs and the first consideration for placement must be with nonhandicapped children as much as possible. The IEP requires a statement of the percentage of time the child will be in regular classrooms and the methods of determining the extent of this time is established through

> . . . procedures to insure that, to the maximum appropriate, handicapped children, including children in public and private institutions or other care facilities, are educated with children who are not handicapped and that special classes, separate schooling, or the removal of handicapped children from the regular education environment occurs only when the nature or severity of the handicap is such that education in regular classes with the use of supplementary aids and services cannot be achieved satisfactorily. (P.L. 94-142, 1975, Sec. 612, 5 B)

The law requires that a continuum of special-education services exist from which the placement decision may be made. The provision does not mean that all handicapped children will be placed in regular classrooms. It does mean that the placement decision should begin with consideration of the most normal setting and be based on the individual's needs.

ROLES AND RESPONSIBILITIES

New roles and responsibilities have emerged through mainstreaming for the regular classroom teachers. There are three areas for consideration: accommodation and adjustment of the learning environment, coordination with colleagues, and a cooperative relationship with parents.

Accommodation and adjustment of the learning environment is a primary responsibility of the teacher in working with the exceptional student. Accommodation in the regular classroom does not mean watering down or slowing down the rate of curricula presented to the student; this is generally an inadequate practice. The learning difficulties the exceptional student possesses are not simply derived from the speed at which the learning tasks are presented. The disabled learner has problems with language facility, learning styles, motivation, and usually displays inconsistent work and study habits.

The teacher must adjust a number of traditional instructional practices. There must be careful, specific directions to the student; many times these should be presented both visually and verbally. One must begin at the student's response level. If the student can only do one arithmetic problem at a time, start with one problem and a successful experience with the student and build from there. The need for frequent praising and reserving criticism is important in motivating a student who personally feels like a failure in school-related tasks. Clear directions, presenting the task at the student's response level, and providing reinforcement for effort are important ingredients in starting off right.

New concepts must be task-analyzed by the teacher. The generalization required by the instructional tasks should be provided in small accomplishable steps. When difficulties occur, the student should have the option of attacking the tasks through one modality or through a combination of modalities. Through this adjustment, the student may comprehend through a visual channel of learning what was difficult to understand simply from the aural channel. Previous learning must be reviewed and related to new materials. There should be opportunities for repetition of more difficult materials. For certain students who are experiencing difficulties in traditional methods the teacher might also provide several response modes—using tape recorders, making models or drawings—to show comprehension of a story rather than always verbally reporting it, and so forth.

The problem of evaluation and grading is another area of adjustment. Depending on the individual school district's grading procedures (e.g., letter grades, narratives, checklists), there must be provisions made for the disabled student so that penalization does not occur. Just as individualizing of instruction is important, so is evaluation in the form of grading. The grading system cannot be simply based on competition between students, but rather on individual accomplishment. If the grading system consists of letter grades, the teacher should carefully explain to the student what is required to receive a certain grade. In this way evaluation can be a fair reflection of what the individual student is doing. The parents of the disabled student must also be informed of the basis of the grading system; otherwise, some parents may misunderstand the student's progress as a grade in relation to other students in the class.

The teacher is also responsible for creating a climate of acceptance for the learning disabled students. Research has shown that without this type of intervention, the disabled student will feel rejected and isolated in the regular classroom. A primary task is the teaching of tolerance for individual differences. Rather than ridiculing someone for being different, the teacher must show, through modeling, simulation, and discussion, appreciation and respect for what makes one person different from another. More directive techniques for teaching acceptance for the disabled students and development of appropriate social skills in the disabled learner is presented in a later chapter.

Teamwork with other professionals takes on new importance in mainstreaming. The needs of the student demand that administrators, regular and special teachers, and supportive personnel work together. For the regular education teacher, this cooperation may be critical since expertise and resources may not be available otherwise. Although there are a multitude of people the teacher will be working with, three critical relationships involve the principal, special-education teacher, and school psychologist.

The principal has a key role in mainstreaming. Besides setting the affective tone, he or she also spells out the policies and procedures for mainstreaming. The regular teacher must depend directly upon the principal for clear efficient procedures for identification, referral, evaluation, and the implementation of the IEP process for programming. Sometimes, principals may not have clear mainstreaming policies or efficient procedures. Under these circumstances, the regular teacher must work with other faculty members to press for adequate policies and procedures. The consequences of not seeking correction will be a frustrating and inadequate program for the teacher and the mainstreamed student.

Teachers have a right to have competent colleagues in the mainstreaming efforts. A primary responsibility of the school administrator is not only to select and evaluate teachers and supportive personnel, but to arrange for staff development that improves the skills and attitudes of teachers. Teachers must insist on systematic in-service education provisions to update and improve their skills in working with exceptional learners.

Additionally, teachers must clearly understand what information must be available when referring a student. Should there be a collection of the student's work over a period of time? Should an identification on a scale of some type be applied to substantiate teacher judgement? Should the teacher request observation by other colleagues before making the referral? A legitimate role clarification for the regular education teacher is to know what kinds of information are necessary. A good general practice is for the teacher to keep samples of the student's work in various activities for use in any meetings involving planning for the student's special needs.

Closely related to the type of student information to be collected are the new requirements of record keeping under P.L. 94-142. Although regular education teachers have no official responsibilities for the types of records that must be kept, copies of the IEP, for instance, should be available at the teacher's desk for instructional planning. Each state agency is required to examine individual student records randomly selected by state specialists during periodic visits to all school districts. The principal should be consulted about information for student records that would be required of the regular education teacher.

The principal greatly influences the teamwork that occurs in a school by encouraging joint planning and management of student's programs, providing time and incentives for such coordination, and generally expecting cooperation as a part of the teacher's role. Since educational systems are set up as operational units in isolation (each classroom) it takes consistent and constant effort on the principal's part to make teamwork happen. Regular education teachers particularly must look to the principal to require special educators to work in support of the regular education teacher.

The critical person in relating as a team member to the regular education teacher is the special teacher. This is particularly true when the special teacher is a resource-room teacher. A resource-room setting involves movement of students through the resource room from the regular classroom usually on an hourly basis; thus, the resource teacher and the regular teacher share certain students in common. Because the special resource teacher will have an individually developed instructional program for every student, he or she should be able to provide a great deal of individual information about particular students. The resource teacher can be a source of materials and methods that work with students. Most resource teachers are trained thoroughly in assessment techniques and can provide information on present student performance in many areas including learning styles, work habits, and reinforcement preferences.

As a team, the regular teacher and special teacher can make considerable progress with students. The resource teacher should provide instruction relating to what the student is receiving in the mainstream. The resource teacher should provide specific instruction on learning tasks where difficulties are being experienced. This depends upon the regular teacher and the resource teacher planning cooperatively. All too often resource teachers are found to be working completely independently of what is happening in the mainstream; many times this results in the exceptional student floundering in the regular class.

One successful type of collaboration between regular and special teachers is the establishment of individual behavioral contracts. The individual contract is most effective when the exceptional student needs to be motivated to learn certain essential social and deportment skills. Particular behaviors are specified in the contract, with the conditions and frequency of occurrence and the positive reinforcers that will be earned. Contingency contracting in this manner should be planned between regular and special teachers to extend across the classroom areas. Many times the special resource teacher will have individual forms for use and assist the regular teacher in drawing up a contract that is appropriate for the individual student.

There are other types of specialists, depending upon the particular school setting, who can constructively assist the regular teacher. This commonly includes a speech and language therapist, an itinerant resource teacher, and various other special teachers. A speech therapist can provide suggested materials and methods for assisting certain students; many times a therapist can provide special materials that the regular teacher may use when it is requested. Itinerant resource teachers are particularly essential when physically or sensory impaired students are mainstreamed. This specialist will supply adapted instructional materials, equipment when needed, or supplementary teaching aids that fit the student's particular learning needs.

School psychologists play an important role for regular education teachers when their caseloads are not overwhelming. They are one of the first specialists in most programs to see a referred student. Many psychologists will set up observation periods within the regular classroom to identify the nature of the problem that prompted referral. When teachers request certain types of assistance, the psychologists usually have a wealth of material on behavior management strategies and adaptation of materials or methods; they also assist the teacher in contacting parents and explaining the child's needs. A primary responsibility of the school psychologist is the formal assessment required in P.L. 94-142. This will usually involve an individual intelligence test, an adaptive behavior scale, and direct observation of the student. Teachers should always request that the assessment information be interpreted in terms of its instructional assistance. In this way, assessment results will have usefulness for the teacher's task.

Parents are now the legitimate partners of the team in planning for the exceptional student; guaranteed by the provisions of P.L. 94-142. Before any formal assessment is done, parental permission in writing is required. It is important that the reason for referral of the student, samples and explanations of his or her work, and an invitation to the parents to observe the child in class be provided. There must be opportunities for the parents to ask questions, observe, and provide important information concerning the student at home.

The parent has an official role in the IEP process and should be given the opportunity to contribute in the assessment of the child's progress and asked to suggest favorable options of special education particularly if they have visited special-education programs. The parent must know what is to be done and why, and made to feel like a contributing partner in the whole process.

HANDICAPISM: AN ATTITUDE DETRIMENTAL TO MAINSTREAMING

The exceptional student is more like other children than different from them. The needs for maturing, stimulation, opportunities, and success are important to all children and just as important for the exceptional student. The common practice of identifying humans as of one two types, those that are normal and those that are abnormal, is an over simplification of human nature which is misleading and detrimental to the well-being of America's children. As teachers, the understanding that children are different by degree rather than by kind is an important underlying assumption for mainstreaming.

The exceptional person has abilities as well as disabilities. Rather than seeing the exceptional person as different in some ways from other people, the tendency is to think in terms of the disability rather than the person. When looking at the disability rather than the ability, it is easier to find reasons why one can not teach the exceptional child rather than seeking how to do so. When thinking solely of the child in terms of a label or disability, we deny that the child possesses individuality and abilities.

There are several distinctions that should be made with references to exceptionalities. We must distinguish between impairment, disability, and handicap.

Impairment refers to a mental or physical incapacity.

Disability refers to the reduction of function, or the absence of a particular body part or organ.

Handicap is a degree of disability that makes performance unusually difficult.

Many times a disability becomes a handicap when factors in the school environment arbitrarily limit a person's growth and development. The mobility of the physically impaired would not be a handicap if buildings were designed with access to its different parts for the people in a wheelchair. The crippled person may not be handicapped if architectural barriers are removed. The mentally or perceptually disabled child is not handicapped when teachers and administrators plan and implement education that meets his or her educational needs.

Cohen (1977) identifies a fear the disabled arouse in others. The disabled person is different or has something less than others and this difference is undesirable. Cohen feels this arouses our own vulnerabilities of being disabled. This type of irrational fear produces avoidance—if the person is out of sight, we will not have to think of them.

The historical treatment of the handicapped has been rejection and isolation by society in general and, in specific ways, by the public schools. This negative attitude by educators has been labeled the "two box" theory by Reynolds and Birch (1977)—children are considered as exceptional or normal. This attitude overlooks the variety of differences in every learner; some learners excel in certain areas and need the teacher's assistance in others. The "two box" attitude has contributed to the continuing oversimplification that average is normal. This thesis erodes the educational opportunities for the mildly disabled learner. The educators' attitude that exceptional is unteachable is the fundamental barrier to mainstreaming.

Bogdan and Biklen (1977) have coined the term *handicapism* to describe this unfair attitude which results in discrimination of the disabled. It is a parallel term to "racism" and "sexism." Handicapism's roots are prejudice, an oversimplified belief in the negative differences or incapacities of some group of people. Stereotypes equating *different* with *undesirable* are produced. As Bogdan and Biklen point out, handicapism is practiced with impunity to violate the learning opportunities of exceptional students as though it were justifiable.

Blatt and Kaplan poignantly portrayed the extreme results of handicapism in the book *Christmas in Purgatory* (1966). The institutionalized retarded suffered criminal neglect, depicted in written and pictorial detail, living out a meaningless existence in a human warehouse. Handicapism in our society is most evident in *Christmas in Purgatory*: The stereotype of the institutionalized retarded person as subhuman resulted in subhuman treatment.

On reflection 14 years later, Blatt assessed the treatment of the institutionalized retarded since his earlier publication (Stephens, 1980). He observed that the physical treatment of institutionalized persons improved but their existence within the institution was still meaningless. This attitude is indicative of an intransigent prejudice of a limited potential of this group of people.

Such institutions have been designed for subhumans, according to Wolfensberger (1975). All freedom of choice for people within the institution is taken away. They are lined up for showers, meals, and medication. They are allowed to have few personal properties, no privacy, and no meaningful educational or vocational programs. Witnesses (such as noted researchers, educators, and parents) have detailed their observations of assembly-line baths, bruised and beaten children, maggot-infested wounds, cruel and inhuman use of restraints, etc. (President's Committee on Mental Retardation, 1975). These signs point to an attitude of subhuman treatment of the more severely disabled.

The professional special educator's contribution to handicapism is also pointed out by Blatt (Stephens, 1980) as a prime motivator to write *Christmas in Purgatory*. He recalls a luncheon discussion with colleagues on the merits of deinstitutionalization, systematic removal of the retarded to smaller, treatment-oriented facilities, and was shocked to discover that the professional custodians genuinely accepted the inhuman treatment of such people. Nothing could or should be done for them. This attitude of professionals ignited his effort to expose the inhuman conditions to the society-at-large. Blatt's powerful message may be: Look at what our attitudes have allowed us to accept.

The outcome of handicapism in the public school system continues to restrict access to educational opportunities for the exceptional learners. Since the public schools represent the gateway to the economic and social benefits of the larger society, handicapism may affect the life-time productivity of the exceptional child. Changes in traditional attitudes must come.

Handicapism implies the exceptional learner is unteachable and unsocializable. Access to facilities, special activities, extracurricular activities have been arbitrarily denied. Programs in vocational-technical education, distributive education, and career counseling, physical education, and opportunities others take for granted were considered unnecessary.

Concern for the feasibility of mainstreaming the disabled is not only voiced by general educators. Ashley (1977), a learning disability specialist in a New York State program, cited three factors causing mainstreaming to be one step forward, two steps back: (1) the difficulties in developing individualized education programs; (2) the time-consuming, costly mechanism of due process; and (3) the increased money needed to serve the handicapped that would come from other programs. This rationale in the public-school sector is very similar to that of professionals in institutions; the overriding concerns are how difficult the task is rather than how it should be done.

Does legislating a "bill of rights" for the disabled mean an end to unwarranted segregation and denial of equal educational opportunities? Sarason and Doris (1978) place mainstreaming in a historical context relating to the problems of societal changes, "Deeply rooted attitudes, reinforced by traditions, institutions, and practices, are not changed except over long periods of time. And mainstreaming is no exception. . . ." (p. 5) Irrespective of the problems of implementation, though, they identify mainstreaming as a moral issue; and seeing mainstreaming as a moral issue will have profound effects on whether the task is taken seriously. In their words, ". . . differences in moral stance have very practical consequences." (p. 39)

Has handicapism disappeared? Generally the answer is no. The number of children served has increased, the types of services to the disabled have increased, and the parents' role in the decision-making process of providing programs has increased, but the mainstream educational system is slow in adopting this new perspective.

SUMMARY

- *Mainstreaming* is a grass-roots movement to establish the educational rights of exceptional children in the least restrictive environment.
- *Handicapism* is institutionalized prejudice that interferes with equal education opportunities for the exceptional students.

- Mainstreaming resulted from the confluence of such different origins as advocacy movements, research and evaluation studies, political pressures, a greater societal concern for the civil rights of its citizens, litigation, and legislation.
- Public Law 94-142 has been the most comprehensive and influential legislation to affect the education of exceptional children.
- Under P.L. 94-142, major rights of exceptional children have been established such as a free and appropriate public education, an Individual Education Program (IEP), nondiscriminatory education, due process of law, and education in the least restrictive environment.
- Educators have new roles and responsibilities to exceptional learners under the new legislation. These include accommodation and adjustment of the learning environment to assist the exceptional student; to work as a team member in planning with the principal, specialist, and parents; and to communicate and involve parents of exceptional children in the educational program for their child.

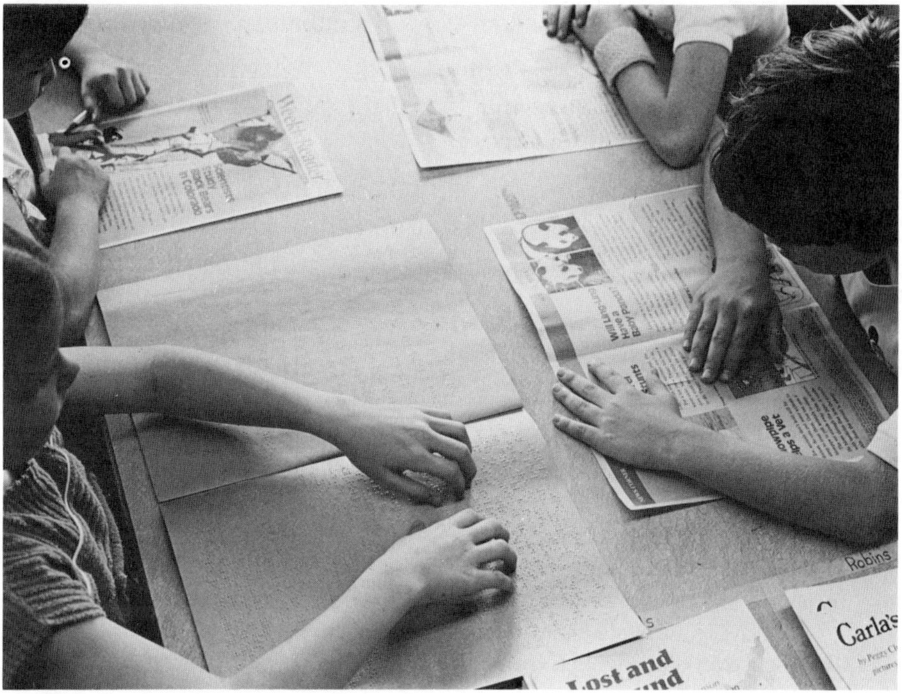

TWO

Mainstreamed Students

- How are students selected for mainstreaming?
- What are the characteristics of students who may be mainstreamed?
- Are there indicators that signal the need to refer students for special education services?
- What implications do the characteristics of mainstreamed students have for teaching practices?
- How should teachers be involved in the referral process?
- What criteria should be used for selecting students for mainstreaming?

Teachers who learn that they will be responsible for mainstreamed students are frequently apprehensive about this responsibility because they do not know what to expect from the students who will be integrated into their classes. In this chapter we describe the kinds of students who can and should be mainstreamed, and how they should be selected. A perspective on how to facilitate mainstreaming is presented, and we conclude with a discussion of student referral.

STUDENTS WITH PROBLEMS—OR PROBLEM STUDENTS?

It is interesting to note that many of us (particularly those of us above the age of 30) had experience with "mainstreamed" students during our public-school careers. Prior to the advent of sophisticated special education services, it was very common to have classmates who exhibited problems of one form or another. Most of us can remember, perhaps, a student who used thick eyeglasses, or wore a hearing aid, had an artificial limb, was confined to a wheelchair, presented behavior problems, or was "not too good with the books." For the most part, no special attention was paid to these students and, with minor adaptations on the part of teachers, they progressed through the school program—some with more success than others.

As special education programs came to be more available and sophisticated, students such as the ones just mentioned, were singled out, diagnosed as "handicapped," and enrolled in special education programs. By labeling these students as "handicapped children," it seemed that we called attention to the fact that they were "different." Such perceptions have, unfortunately, surfaced as negative attitudes which are reflected in less than optimal teaching practices with these students.

When teachers discuss students who are mainstreamed in their classes, it is not uncommon to hear the term *handicapped kids* used in conjunction with difficulties that the teachers might be experiencing. Unfortunately, the use of such terminology seems to set up a negative image.

When thinking about mainstreamed students, we would like to propose a perspective that is positive. This perspective was articulated by Linda Roberts. Linda has cerebral palsy and was mainstreamed through most of her public-school career. In a panel presentation to prospective teachers she made the following point:

> When you think of the words, *a child with a handicap*, which word comes first? The word, *child*, comes first. Remember that you are dealing with a child that has a handicap rather than a handicapped child. Try to remember that he's a child, first. Therefore, when things don't go as you like them to, when things go wrong, try and think, "Is this happening because he is a child, or because he is handicapped?" I think that this might give you a different outlook, because children *do* fall; they run and skin their knees and things do happen to them because they're human beings. I think that even I need to remind myself of this, because things do go wrong. Problems arise and I need to stop and think, "Is this happening because I'm handicapped or because I'm a human being?" I think that this is helpful to think about—to put things in their proper perspective when they go wrong. (1980)

We would like to see Linda's perspective used when viewing mainstreamed students. If their problem interferes to some extent with their education, rather than apply the label *handicapped* or *problem student*, implying that these students have intense, long-lasting problems, approach the *problem* with *problem*-solving techniques in order to provide the *student* with an appropriate educational program. As Linda Roberts points out, we should view these children as students first, and any problems that they might exhibit as secondary to the fact that they *are* students. Our task then becomes one of overcoming the problem in order to teach the student.

HOW STUDENTS ARE SELECTED FOR MAINSTREAMING

Many students who are to be mainstreamed are identified prior to the time that they enter school. This is particularly the case with those who have sensory problems such as poor vision or hearing or physical problems such as paralysis or cerebral palsy. Other students are placed in mainstream settings because of some trauma or disease that occurs after they have been admitted to school. These might include students who have contracted diseases such as multiple sclerosis, cystic fibrosis, muscular dystrophy, or other chronic illnesses. Others may have lost their sight or received serious physical injuries as a result of an automobile, or other, accident.

The majority of mainstreamed students, however, are first identified by regular classroom teachers. These are students who may be experiencing difficulties in either learning or adjusting to school situations. For the most part, primary-level teachers suspect that a problem is present when a particular student appears to have difficulty mastering academic tasks. Following attempts to remediate the problem, teachers might refer the student to appropriate school officials to assess and determine the nature and severity of the problem. Often such students are identified as a matter of course. Sometimes, schools conduct formal screening programs to identify those who may be in need of special services.

When a student is referred for special education services, P.L. 94-142 requires that the parents be notified, and signed permission for testing must be obtained for further diagnosis of the problem. After permission is obtained, the student may be seen by a variety of diagnostic specialists, depending on the nature of the suspected problem. Specialists may include the psychologist, speech-language pathologist, audiologist, ophthalmologist, physician, educational diagnostician, and others.

If a determination is made that the student is eligible for special education services, the parents are invited to a conference at which an individualized educational program (IEP) is designed for the child and a decision is made about the appropriate educational placement. Included in the placement decision are the amount and type of education that the student should receive in the regular classroom, if such is appropriate. When regular class placement is called for, the teacher should be involved in the development of the IEP and discussions about the type of experience that is most appropriate for that student.

Mainstreamed students may be placed in the regular class for a variety of experiences and durations of time. Some students may be in the regular class for virtually all of their education. This may be the case for children with physical disabilities who are capable of academic achievment at grade level. Other children, such as those with visual impairments, may receive the majority of their education in the regular class but may go to the resource teacher for assistance in taking tests and for learning how to read and write braille. Still others may go to the resource room for education in the basic tool subjects of mathematics and reading and return to the regular class for science, social studies, physical education, and participation in lunch and other social activities. Each experience is different and should be planned to meet the individual needs of each student.

It should be emphasized that not all students with problems will go through this formal process of diagnosis, IEP development, and placement. Virtually every classroom setting includes children who exhibit problems of one form or another. Some of these are transient, such as initial adjustment to school or a behavior problem in response to a divorce or some family trauma. Others may be more severe, such as loss of a limb, which might require some initial physical therapy and the fitting of a prosthesis, but no other long-term special education services are required.

The remainder of this Chapter provides material that will aid in understanding various students who may be mainstreamed. Space limitations do not permit a complete, in-depth exploration of all of the factors that could be considered in a discussion of this topic. Readers who are interested in additional study about the characteristics of mainstreamed students should either enroll in an introductory special education course or read a text that is used in such a course.

Students with problems in communications, hearing, vision, ambulation, health, learning, and behavior and gifted students are discussed in this chapter. For each area, basic information is provided describing the educationally relevant characteristics of the students. Effects of each problem on educational practices are addressed, and indicators are given for teachers about when to refer children with suspected problems for special services. Each section concludes with a description of some of the implications that each problem area has for instruction. Except as indicated, documentation for any of the statements made in the following sections can be found in the text *An Introduction to Special Education* (Blackhurst and Berdine, 1981), along with additional information on particular topics.

STUDENTS WITH COMMUNICATION PROBLEMS

It has been estimated that approximately 10 percent of our population experiences problems in communicating. In fact, communication problems are probably the most pervasive of those discussed because they often affect all types of students. Some forms of communication problems are relatively mild and disappear as a result of maturation and learning. Others are much more severe and may require the services of a speech-language pathologist for remediation.

Causes of communication problems vary widely. Some children, such as those with cleft palate, are born with deformed articulation mechanisms that cause their speech to be distorted. Children born with cerebral palsy may lack the muscle control and coordination needed to make the rapid muscle movements required for speech. Some children who have hearing problems can not hear the sounds that they are making. Consequently, they produce speech sounds that are distorted. Other children may have suffered brain damage impairing their ability to understand others or to express themselves. Some children have simply developed faulty speaking habits as a result of poor speech learning or exposure to poor speech models. Finally, there are some communication problems that exist for no apparent or readily identifiable reasons.

Regardless of the reason for a particular communication problem, it is important for teachers to understand a basic fact about communication: Speech and language are not synonomous. This differentiation has important implications for teaching and also for the type of treatment or therapy a person with a communication problem might receive. Language is an arbitrary system of symbols that we use to convey meaning about things and events in our environment. The symbols that we typically use to convey this meaning are words and word combinations. Language has a receptive component and an expressive component. It can be expressed visually (as in sign language) or tactilely (as in braille). Speech is the oral production of the sounds of the language.

It is possible for a student to have good language skills (understanding) and very poor speech. Similarly, it is possible for another student to be able to articulate various speech sounds but have poor language skills. If a student has poor speech, teachers should not infer that the child also has poor language skills. This is often one of the mistaken assumptions made by teachers when they first encounter a child with cerebral palsy.

LANGUAGE PROBLEMS

There are three primary types of language problems that are encountered in school-age children. Receptive language problems are those related to the understanding of language. If a student does not understand spoken language that is appropriate for the particular age or intellectual ability level of similar students, then a receptive language problem is present. For example, a normal first grader should be able to understand the command, Take off your coat and put it in the closet. If the student does not respond to this request, the teacher should investigate further to see if the child does not seem to understand other spoken information or whether something else might be causing the child not to respond.

Expressive language problems are those related to the production of language. All of us understand more than we can express. We have all had the experience of being able to read a word without difficulty, but not being sure how to pronounce it. This illustrates that our receptive language is greater and more sophisticated than our expressive language. In fact, receptive language must be developed first in young children before they can develop expressive language. It is when the gap between receptive and expressive language becomes great that the student has an expressive language problem.

The third type of language problem exists when a child has a mixed receptive and expressive language difficulty. This occurs when the child's receptive language is below intellectual ability level and the expressive language is lower still.

Language problems are far more severe than speech problems. Although we are more aware of speech problems because they are typically more noticeable, language problems create greater difficulty in school because we are dependent upon language for virtually all of our learning. Can you imagine what it is like to learn how to read when you cannot understand the teacher's instructions? Teachers should be particularly alert for potential language problems and identify them before their effects become so serious that the students are hopelessly behind in their education.

SPEECH PROBLEMS

There are three primary types of speech problems exhibited by school children. These are problems of articulation, voice, and fluency. Students with articulation problems may substitute, omit, distort, or add sounds to words. A substitution is indicated when a child pronounces *rabbit* as "wabbit." Omissions are pronunciations such as "ireman" for *fireman*. Saying "shell" for *sell* is indicative of a distortion; while "warsh" for *wash* signals the addition of a sound.

In looking at these symptoms of articulation problems, it should be remembered that all of us occasionally make articulation errors. Such errors are particularly evident in preschool children who are learning to speak and children who are in the primary grades. In order for an articulation problem to be severe enough to create concern, the misarticulation must be frequent and recurring. It must also not be part of the child's particular culture. For example, people with regional dialects may sound like they have an articulation problem to people from other parts of the country (e.g., the New Englander's "yahd" and the Appalachian child's "y'all"). These articulation differences are not generally considered to be articulation problems unless they meet criteria specified in the following section.

A number of voice problems can be identified. Some children have pitch problems in which their voices may be too high, too low, or monotone. While these may not seem too troublesome on the surface, some girls with very low voices and boys with very high voices may be teased by other students, causing emotional problems. Remember that adolescent boys frequently have trouble with pitch breaks, and this should not ordinarily be cause for concern.

Loudness is another voice problem existing in some children. Although this is typically not too great a concern, some children can develop "screamer's nodes" on their vocal cords which will result in a harsh sounding voice. Those who speak too softly may create social problems for themselves. Problems in voice quality are also identified in some children. These may include voices that sound excessively nasal, breathy, harsh, or hoarse. In many cases, when these voice qualities are severe, they can be diminished through speech therapy.

The third major type of speech problem is disfluency, the preferred term for stuttering. Most children go through a period where they are somewhat disfluent in their speech production. This is when they are learning the rules of grammar and have to stop and "edit" their speech production. This developmental disfluency almost always disappears as children become more proficient with their speech production. Many of us exhibit normal disfluencies as we speak, inserting "uhs" into our conversation as a means of pausing to decide what to say next. Disfluencies that present problems occur when there is a repetition of words, syllables, or sound. This may be illustrated by the child who asks, Can-can-can-can I g-g-g-g-go t-t-t-to the b-b-bathroom?

Severe disfluencies that exist over long periods of time are very troublesome to children and are quite difficult to cure. These generally require the services of a speech-language pathologist. However, it is important for teachers to assist in the therapy program. This can best be done by attempting to treat the child just like the other students. Particular efforts should be made not to call attention to the child's disfluency. Do not encourage the child to "slow down" or to "try that sentence over."

REFERRAL INDICATORS

Keeping in mind that young children may exhibit some speech and language difficulties as part of their normal maturational and learning process, there are a number of clues that classroom teachers can look for in making a decision about whether to refer a child to a speech-language pathologist for a suspected speech or language problem. These are phrased in the form of questions that teachers can ask about their students.

- *Can I understand the student*? Obviously, if speech is very difficult to understand or language is nonsensical, then the student has a problem.
- *Does the student sound strange compared to others in the class*? Speech mannerisms that are so different from other class members that they call attention to the speaker could cause problems. This is particularly the case when the speech characteristics cause the other students to tease the speaker.
- *Does the student engage in peculiar physical gyrations when speaking*? Some students move their mouths, tongue, noses, hands, arms, heads, and other parts of their bodies in unusual ways when they talk. Such mannerisms are distracting and call negative attention to the students; consequently, these should serve as the basis for a referral.
- *Do I enjoy listening to the student*? Here reference is not to the message that the student is communicating. Rather, we are referring to the actual quality of the voice. Some of the characteristics that might be included here are hoarseness, breathiness, nasality, harshness, and whining.
- *Is the student damaging the communication mechanisms*? This is a judgement that is difficult for a teacher to make. However, if it sounds like the student is straining the voice or if straining brings on extended coughing or clearing of the throat, a problem in this area might be present.
- *Does the student suffer when attempting to communicate*? Again, this is a difficult decision to make. There may be indicators, however, that would tend to confirm such judgment. For example, teachers should be

on the alert for signs of embarrassment and/or physical discomfort on the part of the speaker. Reluctance of some children to participate in oral discussion may also be due in part to communication problems.

If the answer to one or more of the above questions is, yes, then you might have the basis for a referral. In a number of cases, subsequent diagnosis may indicate that a problem really does not exist. However, it is better to be on the safe side and refer a problem before it becomes too severe. In many cases, informal discussions with the speech-language pathologist and brief observations in the classroom by that person can verify whether a formal referral is warranted.

IMPLICATIONS FOR TEACHING

In cases where a student is accepted for speech or language therapy, the majority of treatment occurs in therapy sessions conducted by the speech-language pathologist. In some instances, this person will enlist the teacher's help in following up on activities in the classroom. When this happens, it usually requires very little extra effort or modification of classroom practice on the part of the teacher. For example, the teacher may be asked to structure situations where the student can use skills gained in the therapy sessions. Reinforcement can also be provided by the teacher when the child exhibits appropriate speech or language behavior.

It is important for teachers to avoid calling attention to children with speech problems in the classroom. This is particularly the case with

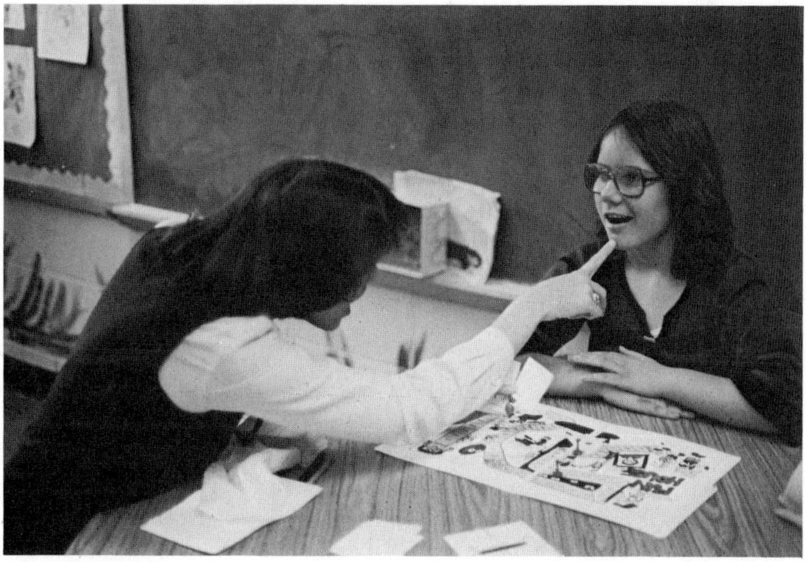

The speech-language pathologist provides therapy for those students who need assistance with speech or language problems.

children who are disfluent. When one calls attention to speech problems, it has a tendency to reinforce the problems and make them worse. For example, don't encourage disfluent students to "slow down" or "try that sentence over again."

Perhaps the major contribution that classroom teachers can make in overcoming communication problems is in the area of language development. This is particularly the case in the primary grades. There are currently available some very useful instructional materials, such as the Peabody Language Development Kits, that provide instruction in expressive and receptive language. Interestingly, these materials are equally beneficial for those students who are progressing normally in the development of their language skills.

It should be emphasized that your best resource is the speech-language pathologist. Any questions about particular children or specific instructional procedures should be directed to that person.

STUDENTS WITH HEARING PROBLEMS

There are approximately 49,000 deaf children and 328,000 hard of hearing children in our nation's schools. Although many of these children are educated in special classes and others are in residential schools for the deaf, the trend is for children with hearing problems to be educated in regular classrooms.

Students with hearing impairments fall into one of two classifications: deaf or hard of hearing. A deaf student is one whose hearing impairment is so severe that he or she cannot understand linguistic information with or without a hearing aid. A hard of hearing student is one who has residual hearing that is sufficient to enable the processing and understanding of linguistic information. Usually, hard of hearing students require the use of hearing aids to hear such information.

Many hard of hearing children can function quite adequately in regular classes with the assistance of hearing aids. A large number of deaf children can also be educated in regular classes with the assistance of supportive services. This is particularly true when deaf children are taught to read lips (speechread) at an early age.

There are five primary types of hearing loss: conductive, sensorineural, mixed, functional, and central. Conductive hearing losses are caused by problems with the middle ear. This is the portion of the ear with the tiny bones shaped like a hammer, anvil, and stirrup which conduct sound waves from the ear drum to the inner ear. Conductive losses may be the result of blockage of the ear canal by earwax or foreign objects, bony growth around the bones of the ear, or infection. Otitis media is the most common infection of the middle ear. Fortunately, most forms of conductive hearing loss, including otitis media, are temporary and can be cured through medication or surgery.

Sensorineural hearing losses occur in the inner ear and are caused by damage to the cochlea or the auditory nerve that transmits electrical impulses to the brain. Some children inherit these problems; others are born with them as a result of some infection, such as German measles, contracted by their mothers during the first three months of pregnancy. Frequently they are caused by viral disease. Sensorineural loss can also be caused by some medications, aging, and by loud noise. This latter condition is seen frequently among rock musicians who have been exposed for long periods of time to highly amplified sound. Sensorineural hearing losses are quite severe and are not medically or surgically treatable.

Mixed hearing losses are a combination of conductive and sensorineural losses. Functional hearing losses are psychological in origin. There is no physical reason for their existence. Except with adults who may be "faking" a hearing loss in order to gain insurance or disability benefits, functional hearing losses seem to appear most frequently in children between the ages of nine and thirteen. We do not know what causes functional losses, but it is expected that they occur to gain attention, explain poor performance, or avoid responsibilities. Some may be precipitated by some sort of emotional or psychological problem.

Central auditory disorders are the result of damage to the brain. Specific causes are hard to pinpoint and treatment is long and difficult.

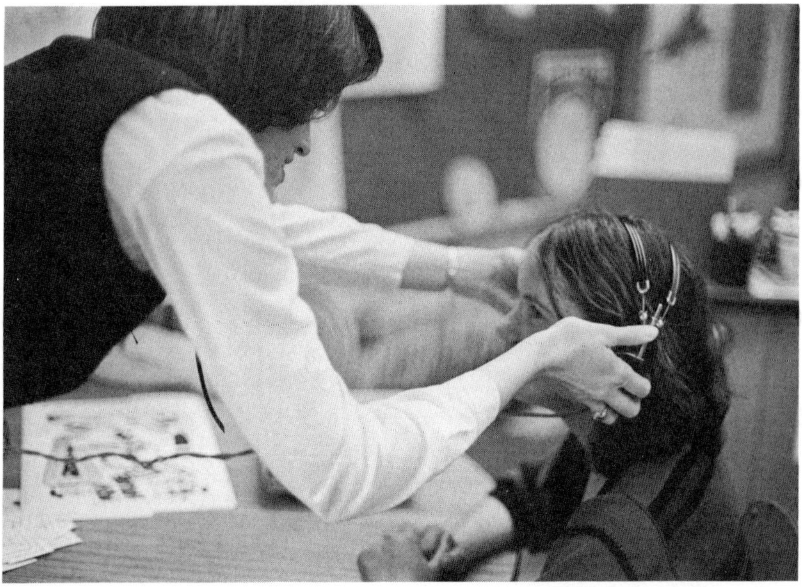

Routine audiometric screening can help to detect those students who may have a hearing problem.

EVALUATING HEARING LOSS

Most school systems conduct routine hearing examinations for their students. These audiometric screening tests present the children with a series of tones over a range of frequencies at a set level of loudness. Students are asked to raise their hands when they hear the tones. Those who do not hear sounds at two or more of the frequencies are referred to audiologists for a more detailed evaluation.

Audiologists perform a variety of audiometric tests to determine the type and amount of hearing loss. Audiologists can determine which of the frequencies a person is having difficulty hearing, and the amount of hearing loss (measured in decibels). Hearing losses are described as mild, moderate, severe, or profound. Normal hearing falls in the 0 to 20 decibel range. Mild losses are 20 to 40 dB, moderate losses are 40 to 60 dB, severe losses are 60 to 80 dB, and profound losses are greater than 80 dB. Some people hear some frequencies normally and have difficulty hearing other frequencies—often higher frequency sounds. Because the letter *s* is a high frequency sound, students who have this type of problem cannot hear the *s* sound in words. Try reading this paragraph without saying the *s* sound. This should give you some idea of what it would be like not to be able to hear high frequency sounds. It would certainly distort your understanding of spoken words.

EFFECTS OF HEARING LOSS

Most people, when posed with the hypothetical question of which would be worse, blindness or deafness, choose blindness. However, Helen Keller, who was afflicted with both, often stated that deafness was the more serious disability. The reason for this is that deafness impairs the ability to communicate. Not only is it difficult to hear what others are saying, but the development of both speech and language skills are hindered. Consider the following descriptions of how different levels of hearing loss affect the ability to hear speech.

A person with normal hearing generally has no difficulty hearing speech in any conversational setting. A student with a mild loss misses only soft or whispered speech. The student will hear most vowels, but will miss many consonants. This student often says Huh?, and wants the television turned up loud. The student with a moderate hearing loss will have difficult hearing in most conversational settings, particularly when there is a lot of background noise. The student may hear television, radio, and records if they are turned up loud. The person with severe hearing loss misses all but very loud speech, cannot function in conversation without help such as written messages or sign language, and cannot use the telephone.

Not only does hearing loss impair the ability to communicate, it can also cause problems in areas that most of us take for granted. For example, people with hearing problems have difficulty using conventional alarm clocks. They do not hear door bells or fire alarms. Announcements in airports are incomprehensible. Warnings such as police sirens, car horns, and shouts of impending danger also go unheeded. As you can see, a hearing loss can have serious consequences besides impeding the development of communication skills.

Although it is difficult to accurately assess the intellectual abilities of hearing-impaired children because of their language difficulties, studies have shown that there do not seem to be any major intellectual differences between hearing and hearing-impaired students. Because of the language problems that such children have, however, many are below grade level in reading ability. This is primarily the case for those with more severe hearing losses, though. Most students with mild hearing losses can be expected to keep up with their hearing classmates in their academic work.

Hearing losses can also affect the vocational, social, and emotional adjustment of those who have them. Because of the need for spoken language, many occupations are closed to deaf people. Some school-aged hearing-impaired students have trouble with peer relationships. Some of their peers may tease them and some adults may be impatient with them. Such instances may cause social withdrawal and feelings of isolation.

REFERRAL INDICATORS

Children with severe hearing losses are most often identified prior to the time that they enroll in school. Milder hearing losses and those that develop later are most often identified as a result of the audiometric screenings mentioned earlier. When schools do screenings, however, they are frequently done every other year and only in the primary grades. Teachers of older children should particularly be on the lookout for signs of hearing loss, and all teachers should watch for signs of hearing loss between screenings. It is possible, for example, to have a student contract an illness shortly after a screening has been completed that might result in otitis media which would lead to a hearing loss. If this is not detected, the child might lose out on precious school time waiting two years to be identified at the next screening.

There are a number of "horror stories" in the educational literature about children who were thought to be mentally retarded, learning disabled, or emotionally disturbed, but were later found to have a hearing problem. The lesson to be learned from this is not to jump to unwarranted conclusions about a child's behavior, and to include an audiological assessment for students who may appear not to understand the teacher's directions. Following are a number of questions that teachers might ask when making a determination of whether to refer a student for a hearing evaluation.

- *Does there appear to be a physical problem associated with the ears?* The student may complain of earaches, discomfort in the ear, or strange ringing or buzzing noises. You should note these complaints and so be alert for signs of discharge from the ears or excessively heavy waxy buildup in the ear canal. Frequent colds and sore throats are occasional indicators of infections that could impair the hearing.

- *Is there poor articulation of sounds, particularly omission of consonant sounds?* Students who articulate poorly may have a hearing problem that is preventing them from getting feedback about their vocal productions. Omission of consonant sounds from speech is often indicative of a high-frequency hearing loss.
- *When listening to radio, TV, or records, does the student turn the volume up so high that others complain?* While it is much in vogue among young people today to turn up the amplification of rock music almost "to the threshold of pain," this determination will sometimes be difficult to make. Teachers can often get clues, however, by observing students listening to audio media that are not producing music, such as instructional records and sound-filmstrips.
- *Does the student cock the head or turn toward the speaker in an apparent effort to hear better?* Sometimes such movements are quite obvious and may even be accompanied by the "cupping" of the ear with the hand in an effort to direct the sound into the ear. In other cases, actions are much more subtle. Teachers often overlook such signs, interpreting them as symbols of increased inquisitiveness and interest.
- *Are there frequent requests to repeat what has just been said?* Although some students pick up the habit of saying, Huh? as a form of defense mechanism when they are unable to provide what they perceive as an acceptable response, such verbalizations may also indicate a hearing loss. When a particular student requests repeated instructions frequently, teachers should further investigate the possibility of hearing loss.
- *Is the student unresponsive or inattentive when spoken to in a normal voice?* Some students who do not follow directions or do not pay attention in class are frequently labeled as "trouble makers," which results in negative or punitive treatment. Often, however, these inappropriate school behaviors are actually caused by the inability of the student to hear. They can also be caused if the sounds that are heard appear to be "garbled."
- *Is the student reluctant to participate in oral activities?* Although reluctance to participate orally may be symptomatic of problems such as shyness, insecurity with respect to knowledge of subject matter, or fear of failure, it may also be due to a hearing loss. The child might not be able to hear the verbal interactions that occur in such activities.

Gearheart and Weishahn (1976) have identified a number of other potential indicators of hearing loss such as acting out behavior, stubbornness, withdrawal, dependence on classmates for instruction, disparity between expected and actual achievement, and seemingly better performance in achievement when the student is functioning in small groups. It should be evident from these descriptions, plus many of the ones listed above as questions, that there are numerous explanations for behavior that is observed in the classroom. For almost all of these, one could generate explanations of a psychological or educational nature to explain the behavior. Similarly, in each case, the behavior could be traced to a hearing loss. The message here is very clear: Rule out a hearing loss as the cause of problems before looking for other explanations.

One final point should be emphasized with respect to referral. The appropriate person to refer a child suspected of having a hearing loss is the audiologist. In the event that such a person is not part of the school staff, referrals should be made to the speech pathologist, who will be able to make appropriate arrangements to see that a qualified person evaluates the child. Under *no* circumstances should the first referral be to a hearing aid dealer. Many hearing aid dealers do not have trained audiologists on their staffs. The audiologist is specifically trained and qualified to make a determination of whether a hearing aid will help a particular student and should be the person to recommend referral to a hearing aid dealer. In consulting with parents who may be concerned that their child has a hearing loss, you should emphasize to them, also, that their first contact should be with a certified audiologist if they want to have a hearing evaluation performed. Many parents (and subsequently their children) have been misled by unethical hearing aid dealers who have fitted children with unnecessary and expensive hearing aids.

IMPLICATIONS FOR TEACHING

Although an exceptionally able student with severe or profound hearing loss may occasionally be assigned to the regular class for a portion of his or her instruction, the majority of the students with hearing problems that are assigned to the regular class will have losses that are mild to moderate. Some of these students will wear hearing aids, others will not. For the most part, teachers will not have to make any dramatic changes in their instructional programs to accommodate the special needs of these students. Most of the adaptations that are necessary are relatively simple and can be accomplished with a minimum of effort. As will be seen in the remainder of this section, the main problem that teachers may encounter is the modifications of some of their habitual teaching techniques—such as talking to the class when facing the chalkboard.

The charge to the teacher is, of course, to structure the classroom in order to maximize the probability that the student with a hearing problem can hear as well as possible. This generally entails having the student sit at the front of the classroom. A student with a hearing problem in only one ear should be seated to the side of the classroom so that the *good* ear faces the teacher.

Efforts should be made to keep light out of the eyes of these students. Light in the eyes can make it difficult to speechread. This might involve placing the student on the side of the classroom next to the windows (unless the light coming through the windows shines in the student's face, or the better ear is next to the windows).

The student should be encouraged to watch the faces of the speakers during communication. This will facilitate speechreading and will assist the student in picking up nonverbal cues. Wherever possible, communication should be done at eye level, when the teacher is working one-to-one with the student.

As implied earlier, instructions and verbal teaching should be done facing the student. Avoid "talking to the chalkboard." If you frequently use the chalkboard, you might consider substituting an overhead projector. It can be used in the same way, yet you face the students when you are teaching. Try not to place yourself between the windows and the student when speaking. Glare from the windows will make speechreading difficult.

Do *not* exaggerate the pronounciation of your words. Speak naturally. Exaggeration of pronunciation distorts the mouth and lips, which results in the inability to correctly speechread. Similarly, keep exaggerated gestures to a minimum. Although these may be of assistance in dramatizing points, they tend to distract from your face when someone is trying to speechread.

Trouble Shooting Hearing Aids. Contrary to popular opinion, hearing aids do *not* make sounds clearer; rather, they make sounds louder. If a person has a hearing problem that can be helped by making sounds louder, a hearing aid can be effective. But if a person has the type of hearing loss in which sounds are distorted, all the hearing aid will do is make the distorted sounds louder. This is a major reason why you may see some people who you know are hard of hearing not wearing hearing aids. Again, people with hearing problems should see an audiologist prior to visiting with a hearing-aid dealer to determine whether a hearing aid will improve hearing.

There are four primary types of hearing aids. The body aid is strapped to the body with the earmold connected by a long wire. Young children are frequently fitted with a body aid which is strapped to their backs to that they cannot tinker with the adjustments. The eyeglass aid has the controls secreted in the arms of the eyeglasses. The ear-level aid fits behind the ear, and the all-in-the-ear aid is used as its name implies. Regardless of the type of aid, all have similar components. The earmold fits into the ear and serves as the amplifier of the sound. Each has a miniature microphone that picks up the sounds. Volume and tone controls are provided and the hearing aids are powered by small batteries.

Although major repairs on hearing aids should be attempted only by the manufacturer, there are a number of things that teachers can check if a hearing aid appears to malfunction. Obviously, it is advisable to consult with the child's parents for specific instructions that might be relevant to a particular hearing aid. Spare batteries should be kept at school and those who wear body aids should keep at least one spare cord at school.

Sometimes a hearing aid will squeal, which is annoying to the child and to others in the class. The squeal is often due to an earmold that is placed incorrectly in the ear or is the wrong size. You can check to see if the earmold is correctly placed if squealing does occur. If the problem seems to persist, it may be that the child is outgrowing a particular earmold, and the parents should be notified that a change may be necessary. Although it is the responsibility of the student and the family to keep the aid clean and functioning properly, there are occasions when the earmold may become plugged with earwax. The earmold can be cleaned with a pipecleaner dipped in lukewarm soapy water. The earmold can be immersed in water that is of room temperature; however, it should not be immersed in boiling water. Hearing aid manufacturers do provide a special earmold cleaner for this purpose. Alcohol should never be used to clean earmolds because it will damage the plastic.

Sometimes the aid will not work or will work intermittently. If this occurs you can replace the battery, making sure that the positive and negative poles are placed correctly. Any corrosion on battery contacts can be removed with a pencil eraser. The cord on body aids may be wiggled to see if it is not making contact properly and replaced, if necessary. These cords frequently become worn and break, so you should be particularly alert for this possibility.

The student may report that the signal is weak or scratchy. You can check on this by listening to the aid. Sometimes a different battery can remedy this problem. Most often, however, it is necessary to have the aid serviced by the manufacturer.

Young students are particularly curious about classmates who wear hearing aids. An interesting teaching unit can be developed about hearing in which opportunities are provided for other children to listen to the effects of a hearing aid. Often, an aid can be borrowed from a hearing aid dealer for this purpose. You can facilitate listening by providing a stethoscope for the students to use to hear the aid so that they do not have to put the earmold into their ears. They will probably be surprised at the way in which the aid picks up background noise. This feature helps to explain why some students find the use of aids to be somewhat distracting and why others may turn off their aid when there is considerable noise or commotion.

STUDENTS WITH VISUAL PROBLEMS

Students with visual problems comprise the smallest group of students who might be mainstreamed. Estimates vary, but it is generally agreed that approximately 55,000 children of school age have visual problems that require special education and related services. We usually think of two types of visual problems: partial sightedness and blindness. For educational purposes, the major factor that differentiates these two conditions is the ability to use ink print in education. That is, partially seeing children can use printed materials and other visual aids in their education; blind children must rely upon braille and auditory and tactile materials for educational purposes. Most partially seeing students can function entirely within regular classrooms with the use of adaptive materials and devices that can help them utilize their remaining vision. Many blind students can also function for most of the school day in regular classrooms, going to a resource teacher for special instruction in braille and for specialized services, such as test administration, that must be done on an individual basis.

Visual problems are caused by a variety of factors. Some children are born with them, others acquire them as a result of disease or accidents. One of the leading causes of blindness has been retrolental fibroplasia (RLF) which is caused by the administration of pure oxygen in the incubators of babies who are born prematurely. Glaucoma, cataracts, muscle disorders that result in severely crossed eyes, and retinal and optic nerve disorders also cause visual problems.

EFFECTS OF VISUAL PROBLEMS

Physically, students with visual problems do not appear to be any different from other students. Because blind students are restricted in their mobility and are sometimes overprotected by their parents, some do not have physical skills that are as highly developed as their seeing peers. Educational programs for these children should include physical education and other opportunities to move freely in their environment to develop physical skills.

Although it is difficult to estimate the intellectual ability levels of children with visual problems using standardized tests that require vision for successful completion, other testing methods have generally shown that there are no major differences in ability between students with visual problems and those who can see normally. Similarly, there appear to be no major differences in other intellectual abilities such as divergent thinking, which is often used as an indicator of creativity.

In school achievement, students with visual problems often lag below grade level. This is not due to the visual problem, per se; rather, other factors have been pointed to as causing such lags. These include later entrance to school, excessive absence from school for those who need medical and surgical care, slowness in acquiring information due to the necessity of having to use large-type books or braille, and inappropriate educational programs.

Perhaps the major effect that a visual problem has on a student relates to the area of concept development. As you can imagine, it would be very difficult to develop concepts related to color, space, and other abstractions when a child is not able to use visual referents. Most educational programs for students with visual problems heavily emphasize concept development.

The effect of visual problems on social and emotional adjustment will obviously vary with each individual. Some students will accept their problem and make an excellent adjustment, others will have difficulty. It is generally thought that when students do have adjustment problems, these are often the result of the attitudes and reactions of the seeing people in their environment. For example, some research seems to indicate that partially seeing students are often more isolated by their seeing peers than are blind students because the former do not elicit the same feeling of concern that do the latter. Another reason for social-adjustment problems is that many students with visual problems have been educated in segregated programs. Thus, they lack normal contacts with sighted peers. This segregation leads to misunderstandings of both groups and contributes to inappropriate and unrealistic concepts that prevent the attitudes and social adjustments needed by both sighted and visually handicapped students.

EVALUATING VISUAL PROBLEMS

Fortunately, most public schools conduct periodic visual screening programs to identify those students who may have visual problems that will require some form of remediation—primarily the prescription of eyeglasses. As with students who have hearing problems, severe visual problems such as blindness are almost always identified prior to admission to school. When students do not pass the visual screening tests in school, they are referred to a vision specialist for additional examination to determine the nature and extent of the visual problem.

There are two major professionals who are qualified to evaluate vision. The optometrist is a person who is qualified to conduct eye examinations and prescribe corrective lenses. The ophthalmologist also conducts examinations and prescribes lenses; however, this person can also prescribe medication and conduct eye surgery. The ophthalmologist is a medical doctor who has specialized in diseases of the eye. Opticians are not qualified to administer eye examinations; these people grind lenses and fit eyeglasses according to the prescription rendered by the optometrist or ophthalmologist.

Most people are considered to be legally blind if the eye examination leads to a finding of visual acuity that is worse than 20/200 in the better eye after correction. This means that the person can see at 20 feet what a normally seeing person can see at 200 feet. A legally blind person may also have a field of vision that is restricted to an arc of 20 degrees or less. This would be the case of a child who can only see directly ahead, as if looking through a tightly rolled tube of paper. Partially seeing students are those whose corrected visual acuity is between 20/70 and 20/200.

It may surprise you to learn that many legally blind people do have some usable vision. However, their vision is so bad that they need special education and related services. As was mentioned at the beginning of this section, the criterion for determining the type of educational programming that is appropriate is dependent primarily upon the child's ability to use ink print and other visual materials for education.

REFERRAL INDICATORS

Teachers need to be on the alert for visual problems in the school because these can obviously affect learning. Most problems, fortunately, can be corrected relatively easily through the prescription of eyeglasses. Here are some questions that should be noted when observing students for potential visual problems. These are recommended by the National Society for the Prevention of Blindness (1969):

- *Do there appear to be any physical problems with the eyes?* You should be alert for any physical signs such as excessive redness of the eye and the area around the eye, crustiness on the eye and eyelids, crossed eyes, swollen eyelids, and any other physical characteristics that appear different from those of other children in the classroom.
- *Do the eyes appear to be irritating the student?* This judgment can be made if students rub their eyes excessively or push their eyeballs with the fingers or knuckles. Some students will complain about "itchy eyeballs" and will seem to spend an inordinate amount of time rubbing and scratching at them through the eyelids.
- *Does the student hold written materials close to the eyes to see them?* Some students will hold the material close to the eyes, others may hold the materials up to the eyes but off to one side. Still other students may tilt their heads at awkward angles when attempting to read.
- *Does the student squint?* Students who are myopic (near sighted) can see things a bit clearer from a distance when they squint. This is a good indicator that the student may be having difficulty seeing things that are on the chalkboard or are a distance from the student's seat.
- *Does the student constantly request classmates or the teacher to explain what is going on?* Many students who do not see normally, do not realize that they have a visual problem. These students ask for assistance in reading or explaining visual work. Often, this is done quite surreptitiously, so you should be particularly alert for this sign.
- *Does the student "tune out" when information is presented from a distance?* You should be on the lookout for visual cues that would indicate that the student loses interest or becomes distracted when board work is called for in class. These cues may be evident in facial expressions and body language.

- *Is the student clumsy in new environments?* Many students with visual problems have learned to adapt to their environments and can travel quite proficiently. When these students are placed in unfamiliar surroundings, however, they may experience difficulty as evidenced by bumping into things and tripping over obstacles that other students are able to avoid.
- *Does glare seem to bother the student?* Glare from the sun entering the windows is annoying to all of us. Students with visual problems, however, appear to be particularly bothered by glare from sunshine or other light sources. Some of these students have difficulty seeing things at different times of the day. For example, a condition known as retinitis pigmentosa is a condition in which students may function relatively well during the day; but they may have considerable difficulty at night or in semidark settings such as when preparing to view films. This condition is also known as night blindness.

If the answers to any of these statements are positive, you might want to investigate further and consult with the school nurse or other appropriate school personnel who are responsible for conducting the vision screening programs. These people can assist in making a decision about whether the student needs to be referred for a more comprehensive vision evaluation. Remember, it is better to "over-refer" than to neglect a referral. As with any problem that a student might be having, the sooner it can be identified, the quicker the problem can be solved, and the less the student will miss in school.

IMPLICATIONS FOR TEACHING

Students with visual problems can be taught the same materials and from the same curriculum as their normally seeing classmates. With perhaps the exception of the use of braille with blind students, the major implications for teaching students with visual problems revolve around modifications in the teaching environment. Unless teaching in a very large school, there are generally too few students with visual problems to warrant hiring a full-time resource teacher for these students. Instead, most school districts that provide services in vision employ itinerant teachers who travel from school to school and provide supportive services such as obtaining special instructional materials for use by regular classroom teachers. These specialists can also provide invaluable consultation about teaching techniques. In the remainder of this section, we provide an overview of some of the ways that students with visual problems can be served in regular classes.

Low Vision Aids. Some students find that they can use magnifiers to assist in their academic work. These may either be held in the hand or placed on stands, which leave the hands free for holding the book and

Print materials can be magnified and projected on a TV screen according to the size that is most comfortable for partially-seeing students to read. Machines such as this and other low-vision aids can be obtained by the vision specialist.

turning the pages. There are now machines available that can magnify the print of regular texts and project it on a screen similar to a television screen. The students can adjust the size of the image in order to facilitate their reading.

Note that some students will hold materials very close to their eyes while reading. Contrary to popular opinion, this will not harm the eyes. Actually, students should be encouraged to read in whatever way they can. Any particularly appropriate or inappropriate reading habits or procedures will be identified by the report of the specialist who has made a diagnosis of the visual problem.

There are now several machines that are available to facilitate learning on the part of blind students. The "talking calculator" does just that. Using synthetic speech, it repeats the numbers and symbols of the buttons that are pressed and then repeats the answer to the problem that was calculated. The optacon is a device about the size of an audio cassette recorder that has a small camera that is used to scan printed materials. The optacon translates the visual image into a tactile image that is "read" by the fingers. This device can be used to facilitate reading of materials that are not available in braille. Another device, which is still quite expensive, and is available on only a limited basis is the Kurzweil Reading Machine. This computer-based device converts printed materials of all types into synthetic speech. Available now mostly in libraries, schools for the blind, and research laboratories, the Kurzweil Reader will undoubtedly become more available as demand grows. Still another device is "paperless braille." This machine stores braille on audio cassettes which are used to retrieve the information on a keyboard that has rods that are raised up and down in the configuration of the braille cell. It is obvious that these machines, and others like them, have the potential for greatly improving both the education of students with visual problems and the ability of these people to access information more readily.

Special Instructional Materials. There are literally hundreds of special instructional materials that have been developed for students with visual problems. These range from raised-form globes and maps, to records and tapes, to raised drawings, to braille-embossed clocks, to large type books, to braille "Weekly Readers." Excellent lists of such materials can be obtained from the American Printing House for the Blind, 1839 Frankfort Avenue, Louisville, Kentucky 40206 and the American Foundation for the Blind, 15 West 16th Street, New York, New York 10011.

It should be noted that it is possible to obtain most standard school texts in either braille or large type. With respect to large type, many partially seeing students can read adequately with 18 point type. When possible, however, it is best to permit the student to choose a type size that is particularly comfortable. Large-type books correspond in virtually every detail to the regular texts used by normally seeing students. The itinerant or resource vision specialist can assist in obtaining special instructional materials that are appropriate for a particular student.

Orientation and Mobility. There are specialists who provide mobility training for students with visual problems; consequently, this is not the classroom teacher's responsibility. However, there are some things that regular classroom teachers can do to facilitate and reinforce appropriate mobility skills. Some students may use some of the new technological devices to assist them with mobility. These include a laser cane and various types of sensors that send out sound waves that are bounced back to the user in much the same way as radar. The user can then identify obstacles based upon different frequencies of sound. Other students (usually adolescents) may use a cane or have a guide dog. Still others may insist on independent travel.

Regardless of the preferred mobility mode, teachers can help the students to develop and hone their mobility skills. The students should be encouraged to move around the classroom and school building just as do the seeing students. They should also be sent on errands as are the other children. When errands are assigned, instructions must be made very specific. Some teachers hesitate to rearrange their classrooms for different subject areas and purposes because they believe that this might be confusing to blind students. Such hesitancy is unwarranted. Teachers should move their classrooms to suit their instructional purposes. The important thing is to make sure that the blind student is well oriented to the changes. Assigning a "buddy" helps in cases such as this.

Other students should be instructed in the appropriate ways to assist blind students in mobility. They should not grasp the hands and "pull" the person along. Instead, they should be taught to offer their arm to the blind student, who will grasp the upper part of it between the elbow and shoulder. The grasp will be with the thumb on one side and the fingers on the other, not with the arm hooked around the arm of the guide. The blind student will then walk about one-half pace behind and to the side of the guide and will be able to move quite swiftly and confidently from place to place. This is a good thing to practice in class and it can be quite instructive to have classmates wear blindfolds and simulate ways to lead each other from place to place.

Finally, in dealing with students who have vision problems, do not avoid words that relate to the visual process. Some people feel embarrassed by using words such as *see* or *look* to blind people. By attempting to avoid such terms, conversation frequently becomes convoluted and awkward. It is best to speak in normal conversational conventions when working with blind children. They want to be treated as normally as possible. In doing so, you will not be surprised to hear a blind student say, "See you later," at the end of the day.

STUDENTS WITH PHYSICAL PROBLEMS

Some 328,000 children under the age of 19 years have physical problems that are severe enough to warrant special instructional programs for them in the schools. When considering physical problems, we generally deal with two types: problems that affect ambulation and those that affect health. Both types will be discussed briefly below.

AMBULATION PROBLEMS

Many of the students who are confined to wheelchairs have suffered spinal-cord injury from automobile accidents or accidents associated with sporting events. Some of these students may have paraplegia, which is paralysis of the lower extremities; others may have quadriplegia, which is paralysis of all four extremities. Occasionally, a student may appear who has hemiplegia, which is paralysis of one half of the body, or monoplegia, which is paralysis in only one limb.

A number of students may be able to move about with the assistance of braces, crutches, and/or canes. Often these students have developed ambulation problems as a result of contracting poliomyelitis. (Even though this disease can be prevented through vaccination, some children are not vaccinated and still contract the disease.) Other children may have contracted muscular dystrophy or spinal muscular atrophy. Still others may have been born with problems such as spina bifida, a congenital defect in which the bones of the spine do not grow together properly, or osteogenesis imperfecta, the "brittle bone" disease in which a child is prone to multiple fractures. Conditions such as juvenile rheumatoid arthritis, club foot, amputations, and birth defects in which children have been born with missing or deformed extremeties also fall into this category.

One of the largest groups of children with ambulation problems consists of those with cerebral palsy. Cerebral palsy is caused by disease or injury that results in damage to the portion of the brain that controls motor movements. Usually this occurs either prior to or during birth. Spasticity is the most common type, with the child's movements being tense, jerky, and poorly coordinated. Athetosis results in "writhing," purposeless movements of the limbs. Because the throat, diaphragm muscles, lips, and tongue are effected, speech is very difficult to understand in children with athetosis. Ataxia is a form of cerebral palsy that results in balance problems. Children with this condition frequently stagger and fall. Rigidity cerebral palsy causes limbs to be rigid and hard to bend. It appears as if they have "lead pipe" stiffness. Tremor cerebral palsy results in small rhythmic movements of the limbs. Most children who are afflicted with cerebral palsy have more than one type.

HEALTH PROBLEMS

One of the most common health problems, which fortunately can be controlled through medication, is epilepsy. Although there are many types of convulsive disorders, the most common that are observed in schools are petit mal, grand mal, and psychomotor seizures. Petit mal seizures are characterized by momentary suspensions of activity that may last five to ten seconds. The student may appear to be staring, with a frozen posture and perhaps a fluttering of the eyelids. Students with petit mal seizures are often accused of daydreaming or sleeping in class. The condition results in short lapses of consciousness that cause the student to miss part of what is going on. Grand mal seizures are more conspicuous. With grand mal seizures, the student may fall to the ground, thrash about, lose bowel or bladder control, and cry out or make noises. Most frequently, this is accompanied by unconsciousness and the student will not remember what occurred during the seizure. If it is severe, the student may complain of being very tired and may want to rest. In other cases, the student will want to resume normal activities almost immediately.

Psychomotor seizures are characterized by repetitive, stereotyped movements which may seem to be purposeless and inappropriate. Often, the sequence of a psychomotor seizure goes from suspension of activity, to repetitious movements, incoherent or irrelevant speech, followed by rage or anger and confusion. Students who have psychomotor seizures are often accused of having temper tantrums.

Another health problem encountered in schools relates to students with metabolic disorders. These may include those with diabetes and hypoglycemia. In the former case, some students may be required to take periodic insulin injections. In both cases, diet is rigidly controlled. Occasionally, it is necessary for children with diabetes or hypoglycemia to take snacks on a regularly scheduled basis.

Some students may have respiratory problems, such as those caused by asthma or cystic fibrosis. Others may have degenerative diseases such as multiple sclerosis, muscular dystrophy, heart disease, and a host of others. With very few exceptions, however, the great majority of students with ambulation or health problems can be educated in regular classrooms with assistance from specialists in this area. Some may not need any supportive services; others may require the services of a physical or occupational therapist or part-time instruction by a speech-language pathologist or special education resource teacher. It is important to remember that although many students may have physical problems, their intellectual ability and potential for achievement are quite likely to be no different from those of children in the classroom who do not have such problems.

REFERRAL INDICATORS

Most physical problems will have been identified prior to school admission or as part of regular physical examinations that are not part of the school routine. This is particularly the case with very evident problems associated with ambulation difficulties and health problems that have fairly obvious physical symptoms such as allergic reactions. Teachers should always be on the alert, however, for physical signs that might be indicative of serious health problems. Some questions that teachers should be on the alert for are listed below.

- *Does the student appear to tire easily when engaged in physical activities?* Students who appear to lose stamina easily, appear to be short of breath as a result of relatively minor physical exertion, or seem to avoid physical activity may have a physical condition that warrants medical attention.

- *Does the student complain of dizziness, shakiness, fatigue, headache, nausea, excessive perspiration, hunger, and/or fatigue?* These symptoms are often the result of an insulin imbalance and can be indicative of either diabetes or hypoglycemia.

- *Does the student appear to daydream, have a wandering mind, engage in inappropriate repetitive movements, or engage in temper tantrums?* All of these can be symptomatic of mild convulsive disorders. Keep in mind, however, that all can also be symptomatic of other problems. If there is any question, it is always better to rule out any physical problem before looking for psychological or other reasons for this (or any other) form of behavior.

- *Does the student sneeze, cough, have runny eyes, or have shortness of breath when engaged in a particular kind of activity?* Some students have allergic reactions to things in their environment that are unknown to their parents. These could include allergies to substances used in the school program such as paints, industrial arts materials, dust or pollens encountered at certain times of the year in physical education classes, foodstuffs served in the cafeteria or encountered in home economics classes, etc. If there seems to be a regular pattern of reactions, it should be called to the attention of the student's parents.

Many schools have school nurses and other itinerant medical personnel that can serve as a valuable resource for teachers who may wonder if a particular physical problem observed in the classroom is severe enough to warrant referral. In all cases, however, it is better to err on the side of over-referring than to take the chance of missing a particular problem. In the overwhelming majority of cases, the child's parents will be grateful that you are observing their child carefully and have the child's best interests at heart.

IMPLICATIONS FOR TEACHING

One of the first things you should do if you learn that a student with a physical problem is going to be enrolled in your class is to find out as much as possible about the student's problems, needs, and special considerations for treatment. This information can be obtained from the student's parents, the school nurse, medical records, and/or the physical therapist, if the student is receiving services from this person. The following checklist can be used as an aid in seeking information that has potential implications for educational practices or classroom management.

Medical Information

1. Nature of the problem
2. Medications taken, frequency, dosage, who administers it
3. Side effects of medication, problems if it is not taken
4. Restrictions in activities
5. Procedures to be followed in medical emergency, people to contact, physican, preferred hospital, emergency numbers

Communication

1. Nature and extent of any communication problems that might be present

2. Methods of communication used by student to make needs known
3. If speech is difficult to understand, procedures commonly used to communicate with student; things to avoid in communication
4. If there is physical involvement of the hands, what method the student uses to write (can the student type?)

Travel

1. Mode used to get to school, time of arrival
2. Assistance needed getting off school bus and into classroom
3. Preferred ways to lift and transfer student from wheelchair to chair, cautions in lifting and transfer, extent of assistance needed

Self-Care

1. Unique needs of the student with respect to eating, dressing, toileting, drinking, etc.
2. Special equipment needed to assist in self-care or to facilitate schoolwork
3. Considerations needed for any special positioning required such as seating, frequency of movement, positioning aids, and any specific positions that are particularly appropriate for various activities

In addition to making a determination of the type of services that the student will be receiving from specialists such as physicians, physical therapists, occupational therapists, and special education teachers, you should check with the parents to find out how much the student knows about his or her physical problem. This has obvious implications for the type of interaction that you will have with the student. Also, do not hesitate to ask for the student's preferences with respect to doing things in the classroom or for suggestions about how to make classroom tasks simpler and more pleasant to do.

Using Wheelchairs. Many mainstreamed students are confined to wheelchairs. Because most of us have had little contact with wheelchairs, we tend to be wary of these devices. In this section, we explain some of the main components of a wheelchair and provide some tips for working with a student in a wheelchair.

It may surprise you to learn that there are many different types of wheelchairs. Designed to meet the needs of their intended users, some are self-propelled, others are automatic. Some even have treads on them like tanks and are designed to climb stairs. Options include detachable armrests, footrests that have straps on them to secure the feet, adjustable leg rests to put the leg in different positions, and a variety of attachments such as lap boards, pads, head restraints. The most common type of wheelchair is illustrated here. As you can see, the two large wheels have a separate rim which is grasped for turning. The two front wheels are small and pivot 360 degrees to facilitate turning. Wheelchairs are made of lightweight metal with canvas seat and back.

In using wheelchairs, several principles should be kept in mind:

- When the wheelchair is at rest the brake should always be on. This is particularly true when attempting to transfer the user from the wheelchair to a seat.
- When going up an incline, the pusher should be behind the wheelchair. Similarly, when going down, the wheelchair should be reversed and the attendent should precede the wheelchair down the hill.
- If it is equipped with a seat belt, the seat belt should be fastened at all times, unless advised to the contrary by the parents.

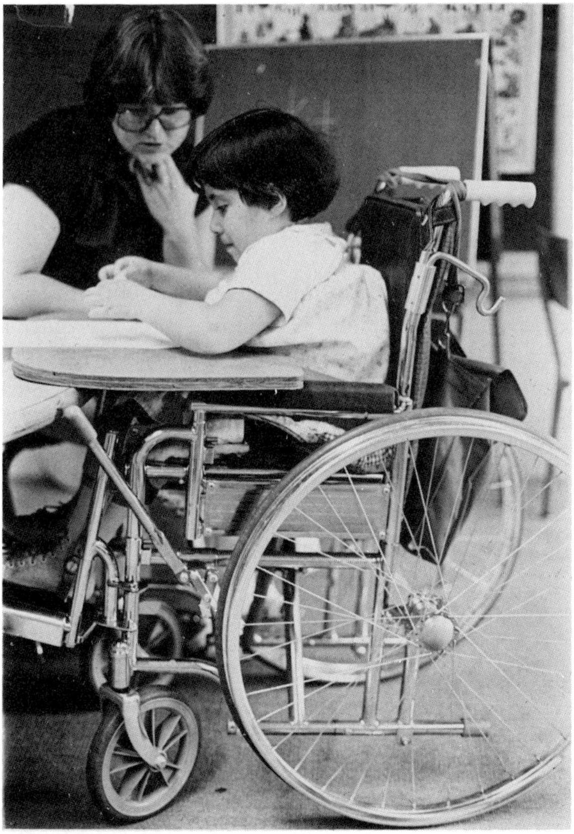

Wheelchairs can have special features such as this detachable lap board, which serves as a desk top.

- In positioning your classroom equipment, seats, dividers, and other furniture, you should allow for a passageway of at least 32 inches to permit wheelchair access.
- As a general rule of thumb, items put on the walls such as switches, posters, bulletin board materials, chalkboard problems, etc., should be no more than 40 inches from the floor. This may be less for smaller children.
- Most wheelchairs need a minimum of 29 inches to fit under desks and tables. It may be necessary to either raise or lower desk surfaces to meet the needs of an individual student. The student's height preferences should be taken into account if such adjustments are to be made.
- A real courtesy to a student in a wheelchair is to arrange to have a chalkboard constructed that will enable the student to wheel the chair under the chalkboard. You can imagine how difficult it would be to use a regular chalkboard from a seated position.

You should be alert for potential problems with wheelchairs. For example, watch for any tears in the seat or back fabric, rubbing noises when the chair is in motion, wobbly feelings when pushing the chair, and signs of discomfort on the part of the user which may indicate that the student is outgrowing the chair or that an adjustment is necessary. Venn, Morganstern, and Dykes (1979) provide a series of useful checklists which teachers can use to evaluate the fit and function of prosthetic devices (artificial limbs), orthotic devices (braces), and wheelchairs.

Dealing with Seizures. Most students with convulsive disorders are on medication and are relatively free from seizures. Occasionally, however, changes in physical functioning (particularly at puberty) or psychological factors may precipitate a grand mal seizure. This can be rather frightening for the teacher and the students if they have not encountered them previously. Obviously, it can be quite embarrassing to the student who has the seizure. Teachers should be prepared for such an eventuality if they have a student with a convulsive disorder in their classroom. Unfortunately, some parents do not inform school officials that the child has such a problem. Consequently, a seizure may occur in students when it is unexpected.

Many people experience a warning that they are going to have a seizure. This may take the form of experiencing an "aura" just prior to the seizure. The aura may be the sensation of a peculiar odor, a sound, or a feeling that something is amiss. If a student who is prone to epilepsy reports this, he or she should be taken to a quiet place and be permitted to lie down. More frequently, there is no warning or the warning is insufficient. When this occurs, the student will fall to the floor. You should clear the immediate area and permit the student room to thrash. The head can be protected from injury caused by banging on the floor by cradling it or placing a blanket under it. If the head is cradled, it should not be held rigidly; rather, the head should be moved with the child. The head should also be held to one side to allow saliva to drain and to prevent choking.

The student should be kept on his or her side, if possible, and not be placed on the stomach since this will impair breathing. Contrary to what many people think, you should *not* put a tongue depressor or other hard object in the mouth to "prevent the student from swallowing the tongue." The student will not swallow the tongue, and a hard object may only cause the student to bite the lips or tongue or choke on it. Never put your fingers in the student's mouth to see if the tongue is free. You might get them bitten off.

The student will be more comfortable if you get down on the floor rather than stand up and watch the seizure. After the student has regained consciousness talk in a calm manner. Acknowledge the seizure but do not make a big issue out of it. If the student wants to rest, permission should be granted to do so. You should follow the parents' guidelines in the event that a seizure occurs. If a convulsion lasts longer than five minutes, or if the student seems to go from one grand mal seizure to another, a physician should be contacted. This may be indicative of a condition knows as status epilepticus, which can be fatal if allowed to continue.

The other students in the class should be prepared to deal with seizures. As a form of health lesson, the condition can be discussed, procedures for treatment can be dealt with, and various students can be given tasks to do to assist, such as moving furniture, notifying the school nurse, or other agreed-upon medical emergency procedures. Students should be instructed to try to treat the student in as normal a fashion as possible following a seizure.

Students who have petit mal or psychomotor seizures should be dealt with accordingly. Those with petit mal seizures may have to have instructions repeated several times because they may miss content during a seizure period. Those with psychomotor seizures may appear to have a tantrum. It may be desirable to remove these students from the classroom for a short period, unless the student resists this.

Adapting Instructional Materials and Resources. A number of assistive and adaptive materials and equipment are available to aid in the education of students with physical problems. For example, automatic page turners, book stands, special typewriters with templates over the keyboard to facilitate their use with pointers, and electronic boards with letters and symbols capable of being printed on paper tape or pronounced by speech synthesizers are available to assist in communication. A variety of walkers, wheelchair appliances, scooters, lifts, and automobile drive controls can assist in travel. Other special utensils include spill-proof cups, specially designed eating utensils, expandable forceps for reaching and grasping, specially designed grooming aids and gadgets to assist in dressing. These, and many other devices too numerous to mention, are described by Lowman and Klinger (1969) and Melichar (1977).

Although most of the above mentioned items are commercially available, it is possible to make a number of relatively easy modifications in the classroom which will greatly facilitate instruction at a minimum of expense. For example, children who have difficulty controlling the movement of their hands and arms will find that clip-boards will help to hold paper in place so that they can write. The use of large round pencils instead of thin square or octagonal ones are easier for cerebral palsied children to use. Workbooks can be taken apart and used one page at a time, which is easier for some children to handle than the bound books. Templates can be made out of metal or plastic that will fit over the keys of an electric typewriter. Holes in the templates correspond to the keys. A student with limited finger control can use a pointer to type any written work that is required. Numerous other ideas can be found in the text by Anderson, Greer, and Odle (1978).

Modifying Classroom Routines. It may be necessary to modify some of your typical routines to compensate for the specific needs that some students with physical problems might have. For example, those with heart defects may not be able to participate fully in physical activities. Students with diabetes or hypoglycemia may need to have periodic snacks to keep their metabolism balanced. This practice might be contrary to classroom rules regarding eating. Some students with restricted mobility may not be able to participate in physical education classes; although many do enjoy becoming score keepers and managers for athletic functions.

Usually, physical therapists, occupational therapists, and special educators who have specialized in working with students with physical problems can be quite helpful in providing advice about ways to modify the classroom environment and about adaptations that can be made in equipment. The important thing to remember in working with students who have physical problems is that the great majority of them are capable of functioning at or beyond grade level. These students learn in the same way that other students do. Because a student may have difficulty in talking due to cerebral palsy, do not assume that this student may be less intelligent or may not be aware of what is happening in the classroom. For the most part, the only adaptations that need to be made in accommodating students with physical problems are those associated with the adaptation of the physical environment to make it accessible, the modification of instructional materials so that they can be used by the students, and some slight alteration in the regular classroom routine.

STUDENTS WITH LEARNING OR BEHAVIOR PROBLEMS

By far, the largest number of students who are mainstreamed into regular classrooms are those who have mild learning or behavior problems. Approximately 7 to 8 percent of our school-age population falls into this category. Translated into numbers, this amounts to somewhere in the vicinity of 4.5 million students. It should be noted that we have specified that students who would be mainstreamed have *mild* problems in these areas. Those students who have severe learning or behavior problems should be educated in other settings, such as self-contained classes or special programs that provide short-term residential treatment for students with behavior problems and are closely coordinated with services to parents and short-term placements in regular school as the students progress.

Unfortunately, some school officials have misinterpreted the mainstreaming mandates and have closed all special classes and placed all special students in the school in regular classes. In our opinion, this is a mistake when there are students in the regular classroom that have moderate to severe problems. This approach is wrong for at least two reasons. First, regular classroom teachers simply do not have the time to provide the intensive individual attention that many of these students need. Second, it is unfair to both the mainstreamed student and to the others in the class to allow continual disturbances in the class by children who cannot control their behavior. We believe that school officials should provide alternative educational placements for children with severe learning or behavior problems, and that teacher should resist accepting such students in their classrooms until the behavior can be brought under control. Mainstreaming into regular classrooms was designed to accommodate those who have *mild* problems that interfere with learning. Consequently, the emphasis should be placed upon providing services to these students.

EVALUATING STUDENTS WITH LEARNING OR BEHAVIOR PROBLEMS

Students with suspected learning or behavior problems are typically evaluated by a school psychologist and/or an educational diagnostician. The former is qualified to administer tests of intelligence and personality; the latter administers educational diagnostic tests.

As a result of the evaluation, students with mild learning or behavior problems are typically diagnosed as *educable mentally retarded, learning disabled, emotionally disturbed,* or *behavioral disordered*. It is unfortunate that such diagnostic labels are applied to these students because the use of the labels immediately suggests negative images and expectations for performance on the part of people who are responsible for their education. At present, it is necessary to place students in diagnostic categories if they are to be eligible for special education services. But this labeling is done primarily for administrative purposes and has virtually no implications for ways in which the students are to be taught. Smith and Neisworth (1975) succinctly summarized the issue of labeling and categorizing students this way:

> The categories are educationally irrelevant. . . . Categorical groupings overlap; children do not fit neatly into single categories. . . . Categories label children as "defective" implying that the cause of the educational or developmental deficiency lies only within the child. . . . Special educational instructional materials and strategies are not category specific. . . . Preparation of teachers along traditional categorical lines results in redundancy of course work and barriers within the profession. (pp. 8-9)

The point that should be particularly emphasized is that there are very few teaching strategies or materials that are uniquely useful to a given category of students. Thus, regardless of whether a student might be diagnosed as mentally retarded or learning disabled, teachers would use the same techniques to teach them if their educational needs are the same.

It is for these reasons that we have avoided the use of labels. We believe that it is sufficient to indicate that there are some students who experience difficulties in learning academic materials and there are others who have problems in adjustment. The reasons for these problems are many and varied. For the most part, we cannot pinpoint the reasons for problems in learning and behavior. Some problems might be inherited, some may be due to environmental factors, others may be due to disease or injury, and still others may be due to poor teaching. Regardless of the cause, however, the students are still taught in the same way; consequently, we encourage you not to dwell on causes of a particular student's learning or behavior problem. Your time can be better spent in developing ways to teach the student and in overcoming the problems that the student exhibits.

REFERRAL INDICATORS

We have grouped learning and behavior problems together because the two are so frequently related. It is quite common, for example, to see students who have difficulty in learning develop behavior problems as a result. Conversely, students who have adjustment or behavior problems can develop learning problems because their behavior problem interferes with their learning. In fact, educators are continually amazed at the similarities in educational performance and behavior that are observed in students who have different diagnostic labels. This does not mean that all children with learning problems are also going to have behavior problems or vice versa. It does mean, however, that the two do seem to occur simultaneously in an inordinate amount of cases.

Following are some potential indicators that a student needs to be referred to the school psychologist and/or the educational diagnostician for further evaluation.

- *Is the student significantly behind the other students in achievement?* To be eligible for special education services that are formally approved by the parents and the schools, a "significant" discrepancy in achievement must be noted. The question then becomes one of determining what a "significant" discrepancy is. As a general rule of thumb, many believe that a significant discrepancy exists if the student is two or more years behind grade level. Although this might be a criterion for formal admission to a special education program, it is our contention that *any* discrepancy in achievement is cause for concern and that efforts should be made to remediate such discrepancies. At any rate, you should be on the alert for lags in achievement in level of functioning that might be evidenced by everyday performance, unit tests associated with basal materials, and results of standardized achievement tests that are now quite common in our public schools.
- *Does the student "act out" or engage in aggressive behavior?* Many students will have "problem days" in which they engage in acting out, aggressive, or hyperactive behavior. Usually, however, such disturbances will be transient and can be dealt with as they occur. A real problem may exist when a student persists in such behaviors over a fairly lengthy time span and when the behaviors occur in more than one situation. For example, many young boys are quite aggressive on the playground. When they return to class, however, they settle down (some faster than others). A student with a behavior problem, however, usually will exhibit the problem in different classes, on the playground, and in other settings. To be truly classified as a behavior problem, an assessment of the child's behavior in different settings must be completed. This is known as "ecological assessment."
- *Is the student withdrawn and reluctant to play with other students?* Many people have the mistaken impression that the withdrawn student is easily overlooked and escapes the detection of teachers. Actually, most withdrawn students will have virtually no communication with anyone in the classroom and are easily identified; other students usually have one or two friends and will participate as they become comfortable with a situation. Withdrawal may indicate some form of behavior problem that needs to be evaluated further by appropriate diagnostic personnel to determine the nature of the problem and the possible factors in the environment that are maintaining it.
- *Is the student unmotivated and disinterested in schoolwork?* Frequently, what we call "poor attitudes" and "poor motivation" are symptoms of difficulties that various students may be having in learning or adjusting

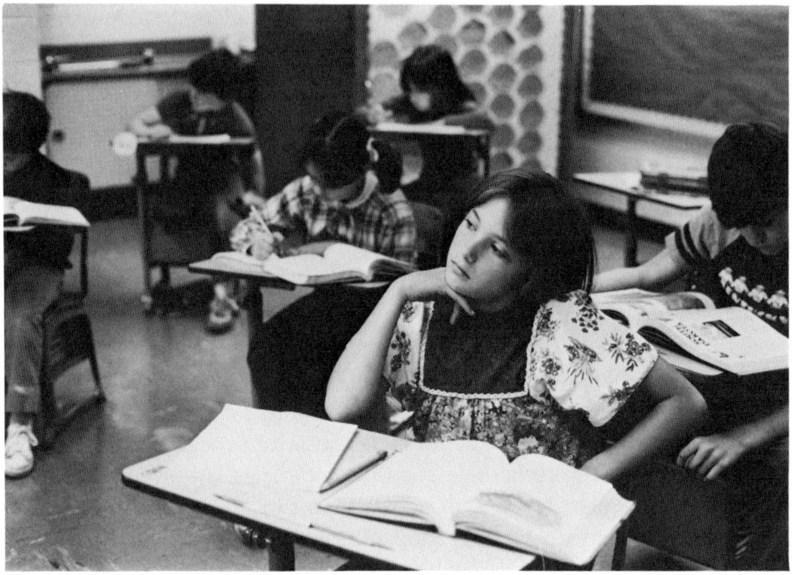

Students who do not remain "on task" may be in need of special attention. Remember, however, that most students are "off task" some of the time.

to school situations. Often, these factors can be remediated through the development of contingency management systems that very effectively enhance interest and motivation for school tasks.

- *Does the student appear to have difficulty paying attention*? Some students have learning problems because they have difficulty attending to instructions and in completing a task. Such students need to be identified to determine procedures that can be initiated to remedy these attention difficulties.

- *Does the student have either an expressive or receptive language problem*? Language problems were discussed earlier under the section on communication. It should be emphasized, however, that language problems can interfere greatly with learning; consequently, teachers should be on the alert for such problems.

- *Does the student have difficulty remembering?* Many students with learning problems are able to remember things once they have successfully learned them. However, these same students may have difficulty in remembering things that were presented immediately before they were asked to recall them. In other words, they may have good long-term memory but poor short-term memory. Whether this is the case can be determined through diagnostic examinations. It is important to identify such students so that appropriate techniques can be initiated that will compensate for poor short-term memory.

Positive answers to the above questions may indicate that a student has a learning or behavior problem. Other indicators may be things such as short attention span, poor initiative for planning, difficulty in dealing with abstractions, oversimplification of concepts, difficulty in evaluating their own efforts, difficulty in transfer and generalization, poor incidental learning, and proneness to frustration. As we have mentioned in previous sections, however, many students may exhibit some of these characteristics at various times. It is only through additional assessment that the severity of the problem can be determined and appropriate educational programming planned.

IMPLICATIONS FOR TEACHING

Unlike the other problem areas that we have covered, we will not provide any pointers for teaching students with learning or behavior problems in this section. Because most of the students who will be mainstreamed will exhibit learning or behavior problems, we have chosen to devote several chapters to instructional implications. We do want to reinforce three concepts that have considerable importance, however. First, you should make good use of the resource personnel who are available to support your efforts in working with these students. Second, learning is facilitated if you have a relatively structured classroom. Finally, learning can be improved and behavior problems can be diminished if you use systematic approaches to instruction. Descriptions of how this can be done are provided in Chapter 5.

GIFTED STUDENTS

Although P.L. 94-142 does not include provisions for gifted students (except for those who might have a disability), we are including a discussion of gifted students in this textbook because most gifted students are mainstreamed into regular classrooms.

Gifted students are those who give evidence of having very high performance potential in areas such as intellectual, creative, academic, psychomotor, leadership, or in the visual or performing arts. Comprising approximately 3 percent of the school population, these students often become our future leaders, artists, doctors, performing artists, and All-American athletes.

Contrary to what many people think, gifted students are not the "weirdo's" that are frequently depicted as frail, obnoxious bookworms with horn-rimmed glasses. Research has shown that gifted students are, in general, better adjusted, brighter, and healthier than other students. Similarly, most gifted students enjoy school and do not create problems. As can be seen from the description above, giftedness is not just limited to very high intelligence, although students with this characteristic are the ones that most teachers think about when this subject is raised.

Some gifted students exhibit problems that can interfere with their education, however. Students who are able to function at grade levels higher than the one in which they are placed may become bored with school. They may have little tolerance for activities of their classmates that they believe to be juvenile or inappropriate. Some may appear eager to dominate the classroom discussions because of their superior fund of knowledge and curiosity about the nature of things. Not all gifted students are like this, of course, but those who are create interpersonal problems for themselves which may interfere with their happiness and learning.

EVALUATING GIFTED STUDENTS

When one thinks of evaluating gifted students, use of IQ tests comes automatically to mind. While IQ tests can be useful in the identification of the intellectually gifted, these are not appropriate for use in identifying other forms of giftedness, such as creativity. It should also be pointed out that the results of IQ tests are most valid for white, middle-class English-speaking students. Students from other cultures and social classes do not often fare well on such tests, even though they may be intellectually gifted.

Other methods of evaluation are used with gifted students. These include peer evaluation and parent evaluation using behavior checklists or questionnaires, grades and other academic records, interest inventories, achievement tests, and tests of creativity. Most authorities recommend that a case-study approach be used in evaluating gifted students because no single test or combination of tests will reveal the special gifts and talents of all students.

REFERRAL INDICATORS

One thing that teachers need to be aware of when considering students who might be gifted is that research has shown that teachers may fail to recognize as many as half of the gifted students in their class. Teachers also have a tendency to identify students who are high achievers and are "model" students as gifted when actually they are not. Several questions can be asked related to the identification of gifted students that might indicate that a referral is appropriate. These include the following:

- *Does the student excel academically and appear to learn and retain information with ease?* This is the most evident referral indicator for a gifted student who is performing up to the level of the teacher's expectations. Such students typically read at an early age, have superior comprehension and an advanced vocabulary, and see relationships that other students may miss. They may be highly proficient in mathematics, able to formulate hypotheses in science, and show considerable imagination and originality. Students such as these are fairly easy to spot as having superior intellectual ability. Gifted underachievers are much more difficult to identify.

- *Does the student have a seemingly insatiable curiosity about a particular topic?* Gifted students will often develop an interest in a particular topic, such as computers or astronomy, and will pursue an exhaustive independent study of the topic of interest. They will seek out resources, library references, and people who are knowledgeable about the topic. In some cases, other responsibilities may be neglected as they pursue their interests.
- *Is the student harshly critical of himself or herself, classmates, and teachers?* Because gifted students often set very high expectations for themselves and others, they may tend to be somewhat intolerant of others who do not live up to their expectations. They are also often hard on themselves when they encounter failure. Sometimes, the criticism that is levied against others is done without tact and consideration for people's feelings.
- *Does the student seem to be a noncomformist with wild and silly ideas?* While this may be the mark of simple nonconformity in some students, it can also be indicative of students with high levels of creativity. Such students frequently develop new or novel ideas toward problem solving. They may show intellectual playfulness and have a somewhat offbeat sense of humor. Risk taking and independent thinking are marks of creative students. They may prefer loosely structured and open-ended learning activities that permit them to express their own ideas. Often, such students will become impatient with classroom routine.
- *Does the student exhibit particular talent in physical education, art, music, or dance?* Students with these characteristics usually come to the teacher's attention. However, it is important that teachers be alert for signs of superior ability in these areas. Often, students may hide their talents or the talents will be overlooked by teachers.
- *Is the student consistently elected to class offices or looked to for leadership by the other students?* Leadership ability is a highly valued commodity in our society. Many students who are gifted in leadership ability are never really recognized by school officials so that their particular talents can be nurtured. Although they may become the school leaders, much can be done to reinforce and encourage further development of these skills. Students with leadership ability are characterized as empathic, sensitive, and charismatic. They also have good decision-making skills and the ability to communicate and express themselves orally.

IMPLICATIONS FOR TEACHING

Throughout this book, we have been addressing the topic of the least restrictive environment for students who exhibit problems that may interfere with their education. In many cases we have proposed the placement of these students in regular classrooms as much as possible. In actuality, however, the regular classroom may be the *most* restrictive environment for gifted students. They may be bored with instruction on topics that they have already mastered. Or they may need to have exposure to advanced materials and instruction that are not available in their regular class. Some might profit from independent study that is not feasible within the routine of the regular class. In cases such as these, it is easy to see that the regular class placement may not meet the instructional needs of gifted students.

The fact remains, however, that the great majority of gifted students will probably receive most of their education in regular classrooms. It is important, therefore, for teachers to be alert to possible modifications that can be employed to facilitate learning of these students. In general, there are three primary approaches to teaching gifted students: enrichment, skill building, and investigation.

Enrichment is the provision of materials that will enable the student to go beyond what is typically covered in the class. Frequent access to the library can greatly facilitate enrichment activities. Use of autoinstructional packages can also be helpful. Volunteers from the community, known as mentors, often enjoy working with gifted students. Mentors are experts on a given topic who are willing to share their knowledge with others. Field trips are good enrichment devices (as they are for all students).

Skill building involves the development of research and problem-solving skills. The use of instructional materials, games, simulations, brainstorming sessions, and other techniques that encourage logic and deductive thinking strategies can be quite valuable. The teacher's goal should be to provide opportunities to use the scientific method of inquiry and to encourage complex thinking skills such as analysis and synthesis.

Investigation is pursued through independent study and small-group instruction. It is important to note that independent study should be designed so that the student is pursuing new material. Some students deviate from traditional forms of independent study that result in the production of a paper in favor of other forms of media such as the production of a film, articles for the school newspaper, or research projects.

For some gifted students, cross-grade placements facilitate acceleration. For others, part-time instruction in a special class is useful. Contrary to what many people believe, grade skipping is also an effective means of acceleration; and research has shown that grade skipping does not have ill effects on students if they have sufficient social and emotional maturity. It is important for teachers to determine that necessary concepts and skills are not missed as a result of acceleration.

STUDENT REFERRAL

In the previous sections, attention was directed to referral indicators. Because the referral process is so critical, several additional points need to be made about this topic. Moran (1978) has identified four things that the regular classroom teacher should address when referring students for special services. Each of these will be discussed in the following sections.

COMMUNICATION OF STUDENT STATUS

Most school districts have special forms and standard operating procedures for making student referrals. Obviously, these should be followed carefully. It is not enough, however, simply to refer a student for testing because of a suspected problem. The teacher has the obligation to collect data based upon observation of the student's performance to be used to support the rationale for the referral. For example, it is insufficient to indicate, "I am referring Ann for testing because I suspect that she has a learning disability." Rather, the following specific information should be included in the referral request:

1. Current grade levels in the subject matter areas that are the teacher's responsibility (reading comprehension, word recognition, arithmetic computation and reasoning, spelling, etc.)
2. Any major skill deficits that might account for discrepancies in any of the grade levels (inability to identify initial consonants or to add double-digit numbers without carrying; reversal of manuscript letters b, d, p, q, and s, etc.).
3. Behavioral characteristics that might interfere with academic work (delay of two to three minutes before beginning a task after assignments are made, working on a task for no longer than five minutes, placing head on desk when a problem is encountered that he or she cannot compute, etc.).

By including this type of detailed information, the specialist who receives the referral is equipped to make a more intelligent decision about the need for further diagnosis. The type of diagnosis that would seem to be indicated is also facilitated.

REPORT OF INTERVENTIONS ATTEMPTED

Sometimes, a student has learning problems because an inappropriate teaching technique or material is used. Before making a decision to refer a child, the teacher has a responsibility to attempt to remediate the suspected problem. Reports of such attempts should be included in the referral report. It is also appropriate to provide a brief description of the typical classroom environment of the child. For example, the teacher might include a statement such as the following in the report:

> Instruction is provided in my first-grade class in an "open" setting. Students are permitted to work independently on projects that are set up as interest centers following completion of their work. John is in the lowest reading group, which consists of five boys and one girl. This group is working on the primer level of the Houghton-Mifflin basal reading series. The DELTA reading program, which is skill-referenced, was used with John in an attempt to remediate his deficiencies in initial consonant recognition. Other members of the reading group met criterion with the DELTA series; however, John did not.

It is also helpful to the specialist to know whether the teacher provides any particular incentives to the class or operates any form of contingency managed instruction.

FORMULATION OF THE REFERRAL QUESTION

It is incumbent upon classroom teachers to justify the referral. This can be done by raising questions that indicate that instruction cannot proceed unless the questions are resolved, and that the questions cannot be answered by the teacher by intervening with the child in the course of everyday interactions. In formulating the referral questions, three criteria should be met:

1. The questions should be answerable. The question, "Is Jane's lack of attention due to emotional disturbance?" is far too general and, in fact, may not be answerable. But the question, "What procedures can I use in my classroom to help Jane stay on task?" is much more specific and will lead to the development of some specific recommendations.
2. The question should be as specific as possible. "Could there be a medical or physical reason why Max closes his eyes and appears to nod off two or three times per hour?" is a much more specific question than "Why does Max seem to be so sleepy in class?"
3. The question should derive directly from what is known about the student. This relates, in part, to information obtained from the observations previously mentioned and from other background information that the teacher may have collected about the child. Moran (1978) provides an example of a good set of referral questions that illustrate these points:

> Are there medical or physical reasons for slow movements, lack of energy, and low classroom productivity? Is visual acuity adequate for

> making discriminations among similar letters such as *a*, *e*, and *o*? Do visual memory deficits in spelling, spatial disorganization in computing problems, and lack of sight vocabulary constitute a specific visual disability? Does Jim need special reading techniques? Or should insistence on reading give way to alternative kinds of instruction? What motivational strategies are suggested by Jim's test behavior? (p. 92)

It should be obvious that this list of referral questions will be much more helpful to the diagnostic specialist (and subsequently to Jim and his teacher) than the question, "Does Jim have a learning disability?"

PREPARATION OF THE STUDENT FOR REFERRAL

One of the factors that is most neglected by teachers in the referral process is preparing the student for what is to happen. We all know that test scores can be dramatically affected by less than optimal testing conditions, poor rapport with the examiner, and apprehension on the part of the students. These factors will be in evidence in almost any testing situation. Our job as teachers is to do what we can to minimize the effects of such factors on the child's test performance. Moran provides four guidelines that teachers should follow in preparing the student for an evaluation:

1. Provide a statement of purpose for the evaluation. For even the youngest child, an explanation is warranted. In this explanation, the problem should be acknowledged simply. Students know when they are having difficulty with a particular subject area. This needs to be acknowledged, with no blame assigned. The teacher should stress this in a positive fashion so that the evaluation is looked at as a means for finding a solution to the problem. The examiner should be referred to as a helper so that any potential threat to the student is removed.
2. A description of the procedures should be provided to the student. Although teachers must be careful not to provide information that could invalidate standardized tests that might be administered, a simple explanation of what might be involved should be provided. (e.g., "You will probably be asked to answer some questions. You may have to write some things on paper or show how things fit together.") You should avoid giving the impression that the student will be "playing games" with the examiner. Tell the student that it is part of school work and not play. Also convey the possibility that there might be some unfamilar things presented and that some of it may be difficult. Point out, however, that as long as the student tries to do good work it does not matter if all of the questions are answered.
3. Provide a guarantee of feedback to the student. This may be somewhat at odds with typical procedures that are followed by some teachers.

However, if we are to view education and learning as a cooperative process between teacher and student, it is necessary. Naturally, technical or emotionally loaded terms should not be used; however, the teacher should be able to indicate areas of strength and weakness to the student.

4. Describe implications of the evaluation. Students typically wonder what will happen as a result of the examination. Because outcomes cannot be predicted, it is sufficient for teachers to describe the staffing process. That is, tell the child that people who have been involved in the testing will meet to discuss ways to help him or her. As a result of this meeting some changes might be made in the student's educational program; however, any changes would come after consulting with the child's parents and getting their permission to make the changes.

By following the guidelines just described, you will improve the likelihood that a good evaluation will be conducted by the various specialists to whom students are referred. This will ultimately result in better information for you to use in planning an appropriate educational program. In addition, you will help the students to be less fearful of evaluation efforts, which will yield test results that have a higher degree of validity.

PLACEMENT CRITERIA

After an appropriate diagnosis of a student's problem has been made, a decision must be reached about whether to place the student in the regular classroom for part of the academic program and for what subjects and what duration of time. We do not yet have firm guidelines to aid in making this difficult type of decision. As school districts gain more experience with mainstreaming, such guidelines will emerge.

An initial investigation of a number of school districts reporting success in mainstreaming was conducted by Schubert and Glick (1981). They discovered seven criteria for placing students in regular classrooms that were common to these successful schools:

- Students should be capable of doing some work at grade level.
- Students should be capable of doing some work without much assistance, special materials, or adaptive equipment having to be provided by the regular classroom teacher.
- Students should be capable of "staying on task" in the regular classroom without as much help and attention as they would receive in the special classroom or resource room.
- Students should be capable of fitting into the routine of the regular classroom.

- Students should be able to function socially in the regular classroom and profit from the modeling of appropriate behavior by their classmates.
- The physical setting of the classroom should not interfere with the student's functioning (or, it should be adapted to their needs).
- Scheduling should be able to be worked out to accommodate the students' various classes; and the schedules should be kept flexible and be easily changed as the students progress.

These criteria should be kept in mind as students are evaluated for potential mainstreaming. Students who are unable to meet these criteria should be educated in other programs, such as a self-contained special class. If students are placed in self-contained classes, however, one of the goals for their instructional program should be to develop the skills that are necessary to meet the criteria for mainstream placement into regular classes. Similarly, as these skills are developed, efforts should be made to integrate the students into the regular classroom for brief periods of time in order to practice the skills so they may eventually spend extended periods of time in regular classes as they mature and learn.

SUMMARY

- Mainstreamed students should be viewed as students with problems interfering with their education that can be solved, rather than as "problem students."
- The regular classroom teacher plays a critical role in first identifying students who may be eligible for special education services.
- Speech and language are not synonymous; language problems have more severe consequences than speech problems, although the latter are initially more noticeable.
- Students have communication problems when their speech differs from others to the extent that it calls attention to itself, interferes with the intended message, or causes either the speaker or the listener to be distressed.
- The most serious effect of a hearing problem is on the development of communication skills.
- Students suspected of a hearing loss should be referred to an audiologist for an evaluation of their hearing.
- Students with hearing problems should be seated with their best ear toward the teacher.
- For instructional purposes, blind students must use tactile or auditory materials, but partially seeing students can use large-type print in their education.

- The American Printing House for the Blind is a valuable resource for materials that can be used in the teaching of students with visual problems.
- Most students with physical problems can be educated in regular classes by adapting the physical environment to make it accessible, using assistive and adaptive equipment, and making slight alterations in the regular classroom routine.
- Most mainstreamed students will be children who have learning or behavior problems.
- Every effort should be made to reduce the use of labels such as *educable mentally retarded, emotionally disturbed, learning disabled,* and *behavior disordered* because these have little relevance for actual teaching methods.
- The regular class may not be the least restrictive environment for gifted students.
- Teachers often have difficulty identifying gifted students.
- In addition to describing the nature of the problem and the teaching alternatives that were attempted, teachers making referrals for evaluation also have the responsibility of preparing the student for testing.
- Criteria for mainstreaming students into regular classes are just beginning to evolve; however, a major factor to be considered is that students should be capable of functioning and learning while they are in the regular classroom.

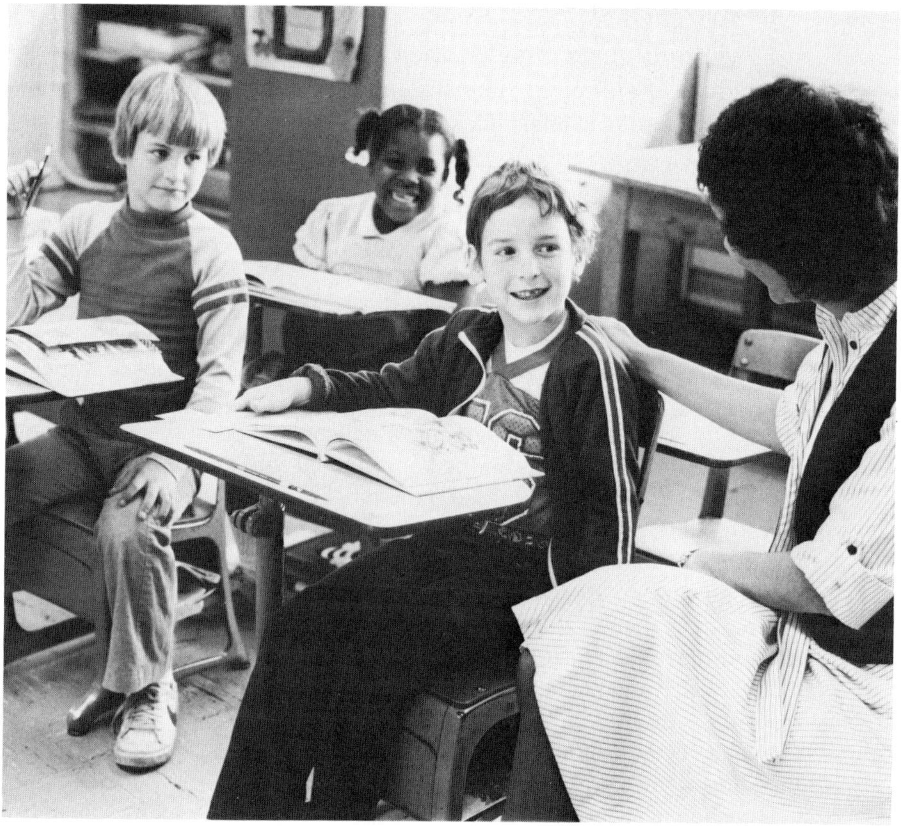

THREE

The Elements of Effective Mainstreaming

- What basic skills should teachers have as a prerequisite to teaching mainstreamed students?
- How do teachers organize their classrooms to provide more individual attention to mainstreamed students while maintaining instructional responsibilities to the group?
- How are individual teachers' efforts to mainstream helped or hindered by the school's organization?
- What basic organizational elements benefit all learners in schools?

In special education, the common historical practice has been to categorize students as to their exceptionalities. The purpose of this practice is mainly for targeting and tracing funds to special education services. While this practice facilitates the management of educational programs, it also contributes to pejorative labels for the handicapped student population. Labeling students as mentally retarded, emotionally disturbed, speech impaired, and so forth is not instructionally useful. Further, it contributes to a perception of these students that prevents teachers from viewing them as worthwhile individuals. As teachers get to know mainstreamed students unencumbered by their diagnostic labels, they realize that these labels have little relationship to their instruction.

The key to developing effective teaching skills with mainstreamed students is to determine their individual learning characteristics. The special educator should assist students with extraordinary instructional problems when they are assigned to regular classrooms.

Teachers should have had as a part of their preparation training in classroom organization and pupil management. Chapters 5 to 7 provide a detailed discussion of these elements.

ELEMENTS OF TEACHING

Many classroom teachers are apprehensive and often have feelings of inadequacy when faced with mainstreamed students (Graham, Burdg, Hudson, and Carpenter, 1980; Hudson, Graham, and Warner, 1979). Are these feelings and attitudes realistic? What are the similarities and differences between teaching mainstreamed students and other children?

Lack of confidence on the part of classroom teachers is probably based on a number of interrelated factors. First, special educators in the past have willingly assumed the responsibility for these students. As a result of their eagerness, there has been little need for collaboration between general and special educators. Second, there has been a mystique about special education instruction that has convinced many regular educators that they have little understanding of these sometimes "exotic" techniques. This mystique has grown out of concentration on the unusual, experimental practices of special educators and researchers. Third, regular educators have instructional responsibilities for larger numbers of children. There is an understandable tendency to equate numbers of children with complexity of the teaching task. To a certain point, the number of children assigned to each teacher is not a problem; it is their lack of sound classroom organization and pupil management skills that convinces some educators that the number of children in the classroom is a primary barrier. Fourth, mainstreamed students sometimes have behavioral difficulties accompanying their learning problems. These behavior problems may simply annoy the classroom teacher, or in extreme situations, they may disrupt the entire class. Although applications of behavior modification principles often will alleviate these problems, many teachers plead that they have neither the time nor the skill to use these tactics. Consequently, the use of structured, positive classroom environments based on easily applied behavioral principles to remedy behavior difficulties is often ignored. Fifth, misinformed people sometimes exaggerate the concept of mainstreaming. A prime example is contained in a March 20, 1977, article in the *New York Times* by Albert Shanker (President of the American Federation of Teachers). He frightened many readers by describing the following mainstreaming possibilities:

> . . . the handicaps we are talking about . . . include . . . . Hydrocephalic children who were born with holes in their hearts, who turn blue periodically and have water on the brain. . . . Children with bones so brittle that if they are touched the wrong way, their bones could break. . . . Children with separations in their spines who are paralyzed from the waist down. . . . Children who need to be taught toilet training, self-feeding. . . . Autistic children . . . including children who are schizophrenic . . . (p. E-7).

Rhetoric of this type can cause consternation in most educators; it is grossly inaccurate and damaging to the concept of mainstreaming.

Successful mainstreaming depends upon accurate placement decisions and sound instructional practices. These practices are based upon a systematic teaching of skills—if failure in the mainstream is to be appreciably reduced, skills must be taught systematically. This instructional approach determines the *what* and *how* of teaching. The teacher's prime responsibility in a skill model (Stephens, 1977) is to be the link between the student and learning by determining what to teach and by controlling the conditions that lead to appropriate responses. This systematic approach to instruction possesses certain characteristics. It reflects what skills are valued, how they are learned, and how to determine when learning has occurred.

The skill model of instruction tends to alleviate the many inadequacies teachers experience in attempting to instruct the mainstreamed student. It is functional and noncategorical, directly relating to daily life in the classroom. This approach depends upon teachers making direct observations of students' behaviors, assessing students' current skills in reference to a detailed set of learning outcomes (i.e., curriculum), systematically teaching a specific skill towards a level of desired performance, and changing methods based on the student's performance. Note that the skill model of teaching is not dependent on a categorical handicap (i.e., mental retardation, learning disability, or behavior disorder). It is based on students' needs and performance in reference to a specific set of learning objectives or curricula.

Skill instruction is facilitated through two complementary processes—organizing and managing. The organizing process is anticipating, planning, and arranging so that students will have the best opportunities to learn. The managing process involves the skills of observing, presenting, adapting, and decision making during systematic instruction.

THE BASICS OF ORGANIZING

Although there are many organizational factors within the skill model, only a select number of imperatives are presented here. These factors set the conditions of learning. Without careful thought and planning, the condition of learning cannot be well ordered by the teacher; the results are "hit-and-miss." The mainstreamed student is most likely to fail under poorly structured conditions.

Curriculum, as a set of desired learning outcomes, is a primary organizing method. In organizing to do any task the first question should always be; What am I trying to accomplish? In education, we are trying to ensure student mastery of curriculum, most notably reading, mathematics, and writing. In the skill model, curricula of all types are specified as behavioral (i.e., observable) student objectives. Figure 3.1 presents an example of part of a math curriculum from a Burlington, Vermont school program (Armstrong, Stahlbrand and Pierce, 1980).

This curriculum specifies not only what is to be learned, but how it is to be learned. Through sequencing and hierarchically arranging the learning outcomes, an entire skill area is distilled for efficient utilization in materials selection and development, record-keeping, and mini-grouping of students.

Individualization of the teaching process, that is, adjusting the learning tasks to fit various idiosyncratic needs of the learner, becomes possible under these conditions. Since much individualization depends upon the use of instructional materials, the curriculum provides the framework for organizing, selecting, and developing them. This is done by referencing materials to the numbering system of the curriculum.

Under the numbering system of the curriculum, each behavioral objective of the curriculum is given a letter or some other ordering descriptor and a number. The letter usually refers to a unit of the curriculum, for example, in reading, sight-word skills would have a separate number, and

MATH CONTINUUM SKILLS SHEET

NAME ______		Probe #1 ______	Date ______
GRADE ______		Probe #2 ______	Date ______
TEACHER ______		Probe #3 ______	Date ______
SCHOOL ______		Probe #4 ______	Date ______
		Probe #5 ______	Date ______
Entry Level ______	Date ______	Probe #6 ______	Date ______
Exit Level ______	Date ______	Probe #7 ______	Date ______

A: BASIC NUMBER CONCEPTS

K (1) (2) (3) (4) (5) (6) (7) (8) (9) (10) (11) (12) (13) (14) (15) (16) (17) (18) (19) (20) (21) (22) (23) | 1 (24) (25) (26) (27) (28) (29) (30) (31) (32) (33) (34) | 2 (35) (36) (37) (38) (39) (40) (41) (42) | 3 (43) (44) (45) (46) (47) (48) (49) (50) (51) | 4 (52) (53) (54) (55) (56) (57) | 5 (58) (59) (60) (61) (62) (63) (64) | 6 (65) (66) (67) (68) | 7 (69) (70) | 8 (71) (72) (73) (74) (75)

B: ADDITION

1 (1) (2) (3) | 2 (4) (5) (6) (7) (8) | 3 (9) (10) (11) (12) (13) (14) | 4 (15) (16) (17)

C: SUBTRACTION

1 (1) (2) (3) | 2 (4) (5) (6) (7) (8) | 3 (9) (10) (11) (12) (13) (14) | 4 (15) (16) (17) (18) (19)

D: MULTIPLICATION

3 (1) (2) (3) (4) (5) | 4 (6) (7) (8) (9) (10) (11)

E: DIVISION

3 (1) (2) (3) | 4 (4) (5) (6) (7) (8) (9) | 5 (10) (11) (12) (13) | 6 (14) (15) (16) (17)

F: FRACTIONS

2 (1) (2) (3) | 3 (4) | 4 (5) (6) (7) (8) | 5 (9) (10) (11) (12) (13) (14) (15) (16) (17) | 6 (18) (19) (20) (21) (22) (23) (24) (25)

G: DECIMALS

5 (1) (2) (3) (4) | 6 (5) (6) (7) (8) (9) (10) (11) (12) | 7 (13) (14) (15)

Figure 2.1 Math continuum skills sheet. (From Armstrong/Stahlbrand and Pierce, 1980. Reprinted from *The Directive Teacher*, Vol. 2, No. 5, Summer/Fall, 1980. Copyright © 1980 by Faculty for Exceptional Children, The Ohio State University.)

the individual objective within the unit would be numbered. Thus, various materials may be stored and easily located when needed.

Proficient individualization for differing learning styles is possible within such a system for drill and practice, and alternate strategies for teaching certain skills. When a student experiences difficulties learning a certain skill, the teacher has the option of presenting the task through several modalities (visual, oral, tactile) or through one modality (utilizing games, learning stations, or other materials so that the student may practice the skill; or providing materials that stress a different cognitive process in learning the task and varying student response requirements).

Evaluation is expedited. If the objectives of the curriculum are known in advance, evaluation involves detecting any discrepancy between the student's performance and the desired performance. Student performance data are recorded using the same curriculum numbering system. When a teacher has a group of students, this type of organizing system is vital. The teacher easily retrieves the evaluation information by placing the sheet on curricular charts for measuring progress and detecting problems. Such information is an important basis for managing instruction; the teacher's decision must be accurate and timely.

The basis of organizing for mainstreaming requires a flexible, differentiated structure that assists teachers in anticipating, specifying, and adapting the learning environment for students. It also provides information for communicating with administrators, ancillary personnel and other teaching personnel. In communicating with parents, information on student progress is invaluable for a realistic objective appraisal.

If teachers are not organized, mainstreaming success from an instructional point of view is unlikely. Such teachers will either become hopelessly bogged down in details or will revert to group instructional methods providing little individual help for mainstreamed students.

THE BASICS OF MANAGING

Teacher behavior and instructional decision making are influenced by the type of organization developed. For instance, if the teacher has organized instructional materials by objectives, deciding which materials fit the learner's needs is possible. This is a fundamental basis for differentiating instruction. Without organization of curricula and materials, individualizing instruction is difficult.

Many teachers believe student directiveness occurs by repeating "Now, pay attention" often and loudly. But in a skill model of teaching, more effective methods for obtaining student attention and effort are employed. Attending student behaviors are influenced by teacher behaviors. Teachers must strive to create an attending set in students. Using interesting approaches to tasks and varying the approaches is part of the answer. Giving clear, understandable directions, focusing students' attention on the important parts of the task, providing specific cues and prompts, and following up on the students' performances are also important. Goal-directiveness in students is considered highly important for learning for all students (Borg, 1977). A great deal of inaccurate, incomplete work can be avoided when teachers apply these skills systematically.

Occasionally teachers must prompt students, actually taking them through each task step by step. Teachers may also apply social modeling through appropriate directed pairing of learners. When cues or directions are not working, more structuring for some students becomes necessary.

If the curricular system is clear and workable, and if students learn to use cues efficiently over time, their learning will become more self-directed. Unfortunately, too many teachers (in poorly managed environments) assume learners are at the self-directed level or must be at this level in order to survive.

Moving from teacher-dependent to independent functioning occurs through the systematic application of positive reinforcement. The simplest and most often overlooked reinforcer for students involves providing knowledge of results in a positive manner. Many students are uncertain about the accuracy of their performances and teacher feedback helps them to change incorrect responses and continue correct ones.

Sometimes the management strategy that is used is criticism or sarcasm. This affects students' performances and feelings about themselves. The classroom becomes a dreaded place; many behavior problems are begun and nurtured by teachers in this way. Using positive reinforcement consistently changes the environment. Sometimes it may be something tangible; more often it is a pat on the shoulder, a smile, or some words of praise. Using such a management strategy means changing some negative teaching behaviors and carefully selecting any punishment that must be used.

The last of these selected management basics is the opportunity to respond. Remember learning only happens through students' efforts. It is the result of active participation of students with the learning task. Mainstreamed students often will thrive when the learning tasks involve active and frequent responding.

Without having the learner actively respond, a number of things may happen. Students can become inattentive, only superficially learning the material and forgetting it immediately. Many times, as learners, we demand opportunity to respond, not only because it is more interesting, but because we distrust our own learning. Thus we ask "to try it ourselves;" or we explain our need to "try it myself before I'll know it."

Active responding is not just important for maintaining interest in tasks but for practicing, assimilating, and transferring learning from one task to another. These opportunities will exist if they are planned before teaching. Thus, managing and organizing complement and support each other.

ORGANIZATION ELEMENTS

Teachers work in an organized system. The most apparent organization is represented by the school building in which they teach. On a larger scale, the school district organization influences how the staff in each building operates. Teacher efforts with mainstreamed students are greatly affected by this hierarchical organization. Some teachers complain that their work with students is frustrated by school policies and procedures favoring and supporting more segregated educational programs. Problems that teachers identify in working with mainstreamed students often can be traced to inadequate organizational support of their efforts.

What can individual teachers do about this situation? First, recognize key organizational elements supporting effective mainstreaming. Once identified, teachers may work in concert with others to develop these organizational necessities. Second, teachers seeking employment should examine the school organization to see if these elements are in place. Their absence will make teaching more difficult.

An effective organization demands articulated development within each school building. The starting unit must be the individual school building since each has its own characteristics based on the staff, principal, students, and available ancillary personnel and resources. The interrelationships and interdependencies of those persons within that environment determine important outcomes of effective mainstreaming: Are students learning? Are achievement and socialization occurring in a beneficial manner?

Four elements of school organization that affect mainstreaming are:

- An enabling philosophy
- Participatory leadership
- Continuum of special education services
- Communication mechanisms

A critical consideration is that interrelationships between various elements determine the long-term effects of the particular system. When specific elements of an organization are ineffective, the system begins to falter. This usually results in lower effectiveness for the entire system.

An "enabling" philosophy is a beginning point. It is hoped that all school systems have a philosophy of education that is meaningful to their personnel. Crucial to mainstreaming efforts are commitments to the primacy of the individual, participation, and adjustment within the school environment to permit individual participation by students.

Schools are required to have a written philosophy as a part of their accreditation procedures. In effective organizations, this philosophy is reexamined periodically by the entire staff. It becomes a "living" document which expresses a consensus of purposes. It provides the answer to "why" a school does one thing and not another. It is not unusual to find very different philosophies in schools within the same district.

The following is a statement of philosophy from the Tremont Elementary School in Upper Arlington, Ohio.

Statement of Philosophy, Objectives and Commitments[1]

Philosophy: The staff of Tremont Elementary School strives to provide learning experiences which offer opportunites for the personal, social, and academic development of the children entrusted to us.

Objectives: The staff of Tremont Elementary School will:

1. Provide learning experiences in sequence for each learner (students and staff members).
2. Use positive reinforcement of appropriate/desired behaviors in academic, personal, and social areas.
3. Evaluate students continually in academic and social areas with fall and spring assessments in the basic skills (math, language, and reading) as one component of the process.
4. Communicate with parents and students the academic and social progress of each student and describe activities appropriate for each student to reinforce and extend this progress.
5. Involve adults other than Tremont staff members with continued learning experiences for students and staff.

Commitments

1. Children need a positive environment in which to learn and progress. Characteristics of a positive environment include but are not limited to: love, security, success, and an acceptance of individual differences. The staff of our school will insure that such an environment exists and continues.
2. Teachers will design learning experiences appropriate to individual learning styles and create classroom environments which stimulate and facilitate the learning process.
3. Our school will provide opportunities to develop academic skills needed to function successfully in our society.
4. Children will have the opportunity to appreciate and develop skills in physical, artistic, and musical activities.
5. Children will have opportunities to develop self-respect, respect for others, and respect for property. The staff will provide for this growth. Further, we believe that a child's self-concept and motivation are the most critical factors in his/her success.
6. Assessment will consider the broad range of children's learning and behavioral needs. Further, we believe children should be

[1]Courtesy of Dr. Phoebe Weinke, Principal, Tremont Elementary School, Upper Arlington, Ohio.

evaluated in relation to their progress through a curriculum which has been individually prescribed to provide for the various needs of each child, including enrichment and remediation.

7. It is essential to have a Library-Learning Center which provides materials, activities, and personnel to assist in the learning process of all children.
8. The principal of our school will provide leadership in developing a school environment which enables children to meet appropriate behavioral standards. Such standards will be established in terms of realistic expectations and limitations and will be developed cooperatively by teachers, students, and parents working with the principal. Further, when children do not comply with such expectations, they will be confronted with consequences which are related to the violations and designed to improve subsequent behavior.
9. The principal of our school will provide educational leadership and support for parents, students, teachers, and related school personnel as they work together on school programs.
10. We will use the services of school auxiliary and university personnel, parent volunteers, students from our school and the district, and other community resources to enrich and enhance the total educational experiences of our children.
11. Meaningful home-school communication is essential for maximum educational development of each child. Classroom and school visitations, written and verbal communications, formal and informal reporting will be part of our continuing parent-school relations.
12. Staff members will serve as positive models for our children. Our school environment is enriched when we respect and care for each other.
13. Staff members benefit personally and professionally from positive interaction with their peers. Such interaction will foster attitudes of mutual respect and appreciation for the individuality of each staff member. Further, our staff is committed to professional growth through our own cooperative efforts, in-service participation, and formal education.

In addition to commitment to individual learners in the enabling philosophy, there should be joint responsibility for all students. Contained in the above statement is no distinction between *special* students and *regular* students. All students in the school deserve adequate attention and consideration. This sense of joint responsibility requires that professionals work together as a team. Each professional supports and aids others on the team so that personnel work *with* each other.

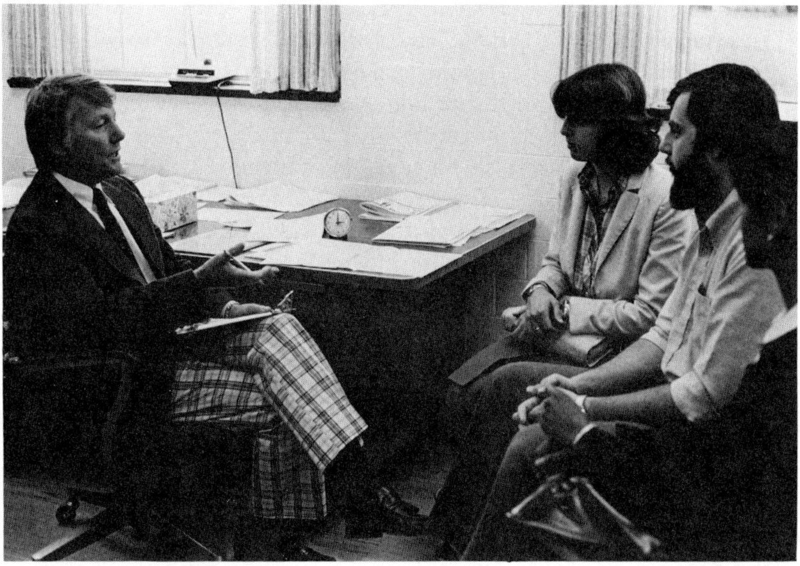

The school principal plays an important role in mainstreaming efforts. If that person is highly committed to the concept of mainstreaming, chances for success will be increased.

Leadership is important to all organizations. A central leadership role is provided by the principal. For overall planning and to make participatory decision-making work, the principal must be "on top" of the situation. The sense of purpose and commitment to mainstreaming will hinge on the principal's involvement. Participatory leadership, however, involves a certain style of administration. A colleagial relationship between principal, teachers, and ancillary personnel must exist; in addition, personnel must have some capacity to influence decision making concerning programming, scheduling, services, and so forth. This approach requires a principal who is sure of the purpose of the program and allows the faculty to share in making critical decisions.

Participatory leadership extends to important policy decisions. Policies provide the framework for decisions within all school systems and provide general decision rules, that is, when confronted with a certain condition for deciding a course of action a policy specifies what should be done, dramatically influencing how mainstreaming will be carried out. The decisions made under these policies dictate what adjustments can be made in the regular education environment and which resources will be made available to make these adjustments. Supportive policies are formulated to assist teachers in their mainstreaming tasks by reducing barriers to implementation, resolving conflict situations fairly, distributing the workload, providing the assistance and resources to accomplish the task, and many others.

When the entire staff has input into formulating policies, there is more of a sense of commitment to these policies. When certain policies do not seem to work well, there should be less complaining and more effort toward finding a better policy. Many problems may be worked out as compromises through this policymaking process. Everyone may not get exactly what is ideal for them but the overall functioning of the school is enhanced. Specifically with mainstreamed students, such problems as scheduling, testing, instruction, and transportation must be discussed by everyone involved. There may be no one "right" policy, but the pros and cons can be discussed until a consensus is reached. This is the essence of effective participatory leadership that supports the mainstreaming effort.

With supportive policies in place that help teachers do their jobs, the specific way they are able to carry out their mission is through definitive procedures. Procedures should provide a clear answer to who should do what, when. For example, in developing a new IEP questions might include what types of information will the regular teacher need during the IEP meeting; who should obtain parental permission for evaluation; who will be involved in the meeting; and what services for the student seem most appropriate. Most school systems develop a procedural manual defining who is to do what and when. At a minimum, every teacher should know the procedures for screening, referral, evaluation, and placement of students.

A continuum of special educational services is an important part of the entire organization. Systematic, variable programming is required for mainstreamed students in all parts of a program. There is a need for consistent treatment from one teacher to another (e.g., between regular teacher and special teacher). In this manner the skill development of the student can progress in an orderly manner. Systematic programming requires that teachers and other personnel agree on what skills are to be taught, in what order, and where the student stands in relation to this task. Along with systematic programming, the programming should vary to meet many different learning characteristics of students. There should be agreement, particularly among specialists, about the types of services to be provided and to which students. All of this must be coordinated to avoid duplication and wasting of resources.

In fact, a continuum of special education services is required by P.L. 94-142. Simply stated, the school must have available an array of services for placement purposes. These services include the most restrictive services (e.g., special school, special class within a regular school) to less restrictive services (e.g., consultation services to regular teachers, tutors). Placement of mainstreamed students should be made through a process that considers this array of services and selects the most appropriate ones. The decision about placement of a student must be made from many choices, not the one choice of the one type of placement available.

A continuum of special education is very important to the regular teacher as well. Once mainstreamed students are placed in regular classrooms, consulting help should be available. Consultive help might include special methods or materials, suggestions for working with an individual student, and tutoring services. An adequate continuum ensures against teachers having to do everything on their own. The continuum anticipates instructional needs and provides the resources.

A predecessor of the continuum is the cascade model (Reynolds and Birch, 1977). The cascade system contains six alternatives in descending order of consideration for placement: (1) part-time special class; (2) full-time special class; (3) special day school; (4) residential school; (5) hospital school; and (6) residential programs. The residential programs, or institutions, were considered the most expensive provision for the fewest children. Reynolds and Birch (1977) point out, however, the early cascade model was too "place" oriented. Now the place is less important than the instructional diversity needed to serve students. Thus, the continuum concept has emerged. It emphasizes an array of instructional services available at each school.

The continuum should consist of school psychological services, diagnostic and prescriptive services, resource-room services, and communication services. The continuum plan should be developed at the individual school, the size of the continuum staff depending on the size of the school population. Each school should set up its own continuum committee, chaired by the principal, to facilitate the teaming of special and regular educators.

Pupil services are administered by school psychologists, counselors, social workers, and the school nurse. Since the trend is to de-emphasize norm-referenced testing for placement of children, pupil personnel workers can spend more time on individual student cases, working with families and teachers. The goal is to maintain more students in regular classes, to the maximum extent possible by assisting the instructional staff.

Diagnostic and prescriptive services involve specialized personnel who provide individual instructional assessment and consultation to all teachers working with mainstreamed students. Often a special teacher works as the assessment specialist, the observer of referred children, a demonstration teacher, and consultant. At different times during the year, this teacher provides individual tutoring for certain children and in-service education to groups of teachers.

Communication services involve specialists in the areas of language and reading. Speech and language therapists provide direct services to target students and consultation to teachers to improve appropriate language activities. Remedial-reading specialists are often included within communication services because they also provide corrective instruction in reading.

Resource-room services include provisions for short- or long-term instruction on a daily basis. The extent of services is based on students' needs with the intent to help maintain students in regular classes as much as possible. Along with resource-room teachers, another kind of teacher works in the *structured learning environment*. This involves services to students who need one-half to three-fourths of their days in a structured, highly individualized program of instruction and behavior management.

The amount of time the student spends in the structured learning environment diminishes as each student shows progress in academic and behavior learning. The re-assessment for this type of placement is usually made every nine weeks by the Continuum Committee.

Adequate resources have always been a problem for special education; however, it is not simply the quantity of resources but how these resources are used. Certainly, the first determination for adequate resources is based upon the needs of special education and related services. If a continuum of special education services exists, the next step is to identify the most pressing problems affecting mainstreamed students. Are the instructional options adequate to meet needs? Are the types of options being deployed helpfully?

Special educators provide their expertise as part of the continuum of special education services. They have the "know-how" to get the job done when problems arise. Their approaches involve identifying competencies that are needed and devising an in-service plan for personnel to learn these competencies. Many times expertise depends on the ability to identify other people outside the school building, such as itinerant specialists or community agencies. For example, if a cerebral palsied child is mainstreamed, what particular adjustments in the program should be anticipated and how can these be made efficiently? Continuum specialists will be aware of limitations of the cerebral palsied student that regular educators must know; they will be able to suggest or provide special materials or equipment. The continuum of special education services provides expertise to work with all types of exceptional students and often provides in-service training to teachers as needed.

Another important organizational element for supporting mainstreaming is the provision of communication mechanisms. A frequent complaint of mainstreaming participants is that there are few ways available to them to coordinate their efforts with other colleagues. In such situations, a regular classroom teacher may be instructing the mainstreamed student one way while the resource special teacher chooses another. Sometimes their efforts are at cross-purposes to each other. Such problems can be avoided by their communicating with each other—informing, planning, and coordinating their efforts. Teachers and specialists must have time to meet and discuss the progress and problems of different students. Many schools depend mainly upon written communications as the chief means of exchanging information while face-to-face contact is left to chance. Under these circumstances coordination in any meaningful way is difficult and haphazard.

P.L. 94-142 implies that communication is necessary for effective mainstreaming. A well designed organizational context supports the mainstreaming of handicapped children in a systematic way assisting the student to receive educational services in the least restrictive environment systematically and efficiently. Without good communications, mainstreaming is haphazard, depending more on the "good will" of educators than on a planned effort.

Parents provide insight into the fragmentation of our mainstreaming programs since they deal with several different school personnel during the year. Schleifer (1979) shows an example of the fragmented approach to mainstreaming in an interview of parents, in *The Exceptional Parent*. The parents complained that their learning-disabled daughter was mainstreamed into a school program with the following type of problems:

> There are days when I feel that the IEP is just something the school psychologist has to work up to satisfy the law. . . . I've come away not knowing whether psychologists or teachers really know what the other one is doing or how it all fits together. . . . The school people have the program pieces, but they never put them together. (pp. 10-11)

In discussing the organizational elements of mainstreaming, one is impressed with the complexities of the undertaking. What appears as a single process is far more involved. It may be that planning in some types of organizations is not difficult, but in education the traditional method is for everyone to "do their own thing." But in education these organizational elements must be coordinated if all students are to be served efficiently and effectively.

SUMMARY

- Successful teaching is based on sound instructional methodology.
- A functional approach to teaching exceptional learners is needed instead of the emphasis on diagnostic categories.
- Organizing and managing instruction are two prerequisites for teaching mainstreamed students effectively.
- The skill approach promotes efficient individualizing of instruction.
- Successful management instruction requires proficiency in students' directiveness, positive reinforcement, and in giving students opportunities to respond.
- The school is composed of a system of interdependent people.
- Effective mainstreaming requires an enabling philosophy, a continuum of special education services, participatory leadership, and adequate communication mechanisms.

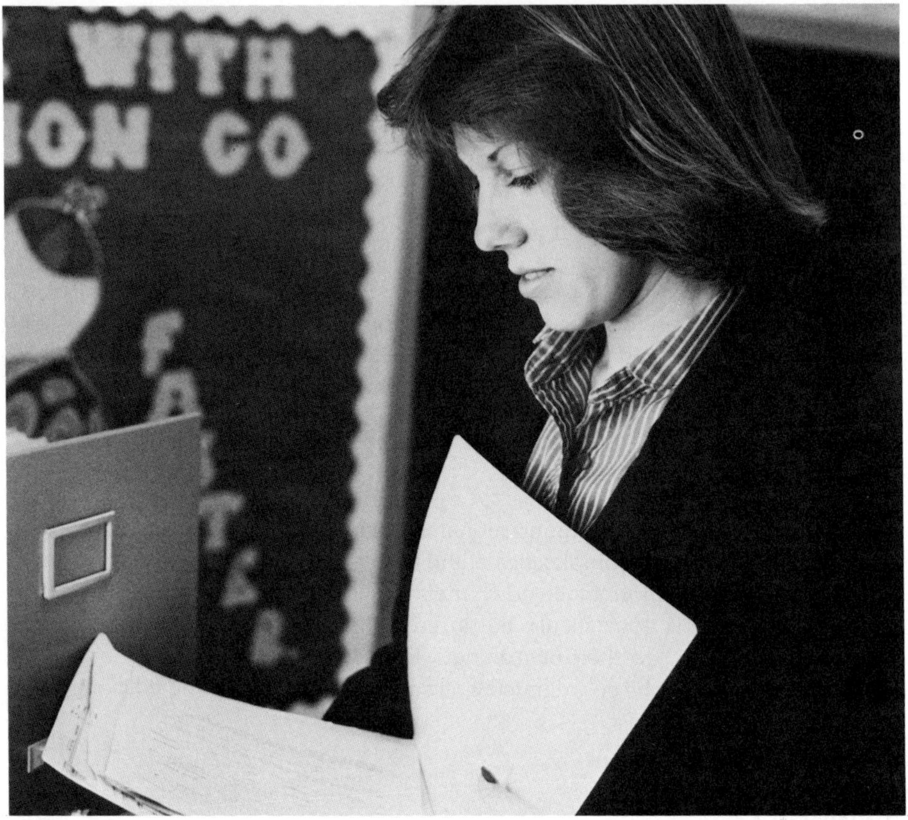

FOUR

Obtaining Assessment Information

- What sources of information are available to classroom teachers?
- Which of these provide instructionally valuable information?
- What value do test results have to teachers?
- What are the ways for teachers to obtain assessment information through direct observations?
- What are some models for assessing and teaching students in the mainstream?

In the history of education, an elusive but important goal—*individualizing instruction*—stands out as an ideal for which many teachers strive. But realization of the importance of recognizing differences among individual students did not come quickly. First, an awareness that there were significant differences among children of the same ages led to the study of child development and the creation of tests and other means for measuring differences. Second, it soon became necessary to determine if structuring teaching to accommodate those differences mattered. Efforts have continued to this day to individualize instruction. These efforts reflect an important change in educational philosophy in the United States from the nineteenth to the twentieth century.

During the nineteenth century, the philosophy of the lockstep system assumed that all students should progress at the same rate and should learn in the same ways. By the early twentieth century, the lockstep fell into disfavor because those who did not attain predetermined goals were required to repeat the grade. Attempts at individualizing instruction, when it did occur, usually involved grade acceleration; although rapid learners were accelerated by grade levels, they were still only being moved from one lockstep system to another.

By the 1920s several plans were used in attempts to break this closed system of education. Most prominent among these were the Winnetka and Dalton Laboratory plans. The Winnetka plan (Washburne, 1925) was a rearrangement of the curriculum permitting each student to progress on an individual basis. Thus, a student might be doing work in several different grades. The Dalton Laboratory Plan (Parkhurst, 1925) divided curriculum into projects with each student entering into a contract to learn each task. This latter plan was criticized as being too individualistic and soon fell into disfavor.

As public education was made available for those children who had been previously denied schooling, the pursuit of individualized instruction became more intense. The press for full educational opportunities, change in American thinking from Social Darwinism (Hofstadter, 1955) to the importance of environmental influences, and the availability of technology for educating handicapped children (Martin, 1972)—all of these factors combined to increase the public's favor of individualizing instruction. Foremost among this progress was the improvement of tools for assessing students.

These tools were first used to classify students by the condition of their handicap or problem. The term *diagnosis* was used in reference to the tests as well as to the result of testing. But neither the instruments nor the classification schemes were precise—often people were misdiagnosed as mentally retarded when, in fact, English, the language used in testing, was not their primary or native tongue. In other cases, those with learning difficulties were mislabeled as mentally retarded because they did not have sufficient reading proficiency for taking group-administered aptitude tests.

Although tools of psychological testing are less than perfect, when properly used and interpreted they provide important information for educational planning for students. *Educational* uses of tests usually cover school placement and prediction of future school success, serving as a basis for educational and career counseling. Such information is usually more valuable to school administrators, counselors, and others who are engaged in non-instructional roles in the schools than it is to teachers.

But assessment instruments and procedures can also be valuable for instructional purposes. *Instructional* activities demand precise information that relates to students' daily work. Such information is used for planning teaching activities and short-term instructional objectives.

SOURCES OF ASSESSMENT INFORMATION

As a teacher you have access to a range of information about your students. For mainstreamed students, you can expect most assessment results to be provided by others within the school program. However, you should be familiar with the various sources of assessment and have knowledge of their instructional value.

Four sources of assessment information are considered here: students' records, test results, permanent products, and direct observations.

STUDENTS' RECORDS

Cumulative records typically contain students' school histories, pertinent illnesses, significant absences, family members' names, home address, date of birth, and test results. When examining students' cumulative files, be aware of several factors. First, recognize the confidentiality of this information. Review the file at school being careful not to permit unauthorized personnel to have access to it. You should, of course, be familiar with the school's policies concerning the use of, and safeguarding of, such information.

Second, be careful with whom you discuss the information; a student's file represents a segment of his or her privacy and it must not be taken lightly. Third, students and their parents have a right to review all contents in the file; be certain that all information that you place in it is accurate and necessary for the student's education.

Finally, use caution when interpreting information in the file and limit the degree of reliance you place on it. Sometimes such information is used to confirm our biases against a student. An attitude of this sort develops when we look for reasons to confirm *why* students have problems.

For teaching purposes cumulative files rarely contain very much helpful instructional information. Having *educational* rather than instructional significance, the information is used to make decisions regarding school placement, referral to community agencies, and special services.

Since cumulative files are often repositories for a wide range of information concerning students, you may find it helpful to use a form for gathering information about mainstreamed students. One such form is shown in Figure 4.1.

Note that the form in Figure 4.1 provides a convenient way for calculating current chronological age and spaces for noting chronic health problems, information concerning family members and where parents can be contacted, school placement history, and standardized test results. All of this information has educational relevance—it can be useful for planning. But, it has no instructional usefulness—it is not important for daily instruction.

By being attentive to details, you can glean clues to potentially useful information about mainstreamed students from cumulative file information. For example, the chronological age can be important when comparing students' developmental progress; even differences in months are often significant among children. For example, six months represents 4 percent of a 12-year-old's life but only 3 percent of a 15-year-old's. So do not disregard increased life experiences when comparing siblings and other students.

Other important clues may include significant gaps in students' schooling, chronic illnesses which may have limited students' experiences and their energy levels, single-family homes, age differences among siblings, family mobility, and erratic standardized test results. Although such information may be a plausible explanation for performance and behavior problems, it rarely will provide instructional assistance. You may use these clues for explaining to parents or others *why* children need special assistance. But, you will need more functional information if you are to help improve their functioning.

TEST RESULTS

Tests are the most widely used sources of student assessment information. These may be commercially obtained or teacher constructed. Even though standardized test usage has increased markedly in contemporary American schools, teacher-devised tests still represent the most frequently used assessment tool.

Student's Name ____________________

Home Address ____________________ ____________________

____

Today's Date ____ ____ ____
Year Month Day

Birth Date ____ ____ ____

C.A. ____ ____ ____

Significant Health Problems

Condition ____________________

Date of Onset ____________________

Treatment ____________________

____

____

Family

Parents: Father ____________________ Mother ____________________

Phone (s): ____________________ ____________________

Address (es): ____________________

____

Names Ages

Siblings: ____________________ ____________________

____________________ ____________________

Figure 4.1 A form for summarizing students' records.

Characteristics of Tests. Any test, standardized or nonstandardized, has certain characteristics that set it apart from other activities that occur in school:

- Students are made aware that their responses are being evaluated.
- The test items have been carefully devised.
- Students are expected to respond to the stimuli without assistance.
- Responses are evaluated following a prearranged format.
- Conclusions regarding students' performances are made as a result of their responses.

When these five activities are combined the result has great potential for obtaining important information about mainstreamed students. But the

School Placement

Year	Placement	School
________	________________________	______________________________
________	________________________	______________________________
________	________________________	______________________________

Standardized Testing

Test	Date	Results
_______________	______________	____________________________________
_______________	______________	____________________________________
_______________	______________	____________________________________
_______________	______________	____________________________________

Comments: ____

____

____

____

____

____

____

____

Form completed by ____

Figure 4.1 (continued)

nature of the information and its use varies with the type of tests and how the results are used.

Individual standardized tests are typically administered by someone other than classroom teachers, but teachers should recognize the assumptions underlying these tests. Test construction and test interpretation are technical areas that will require specialized personnel such as psychologists, psychometrists, special teachers, and counselors.

In most schools standardized tests are used as both predictive and diagnostic tools. When used as diagnostic measures, tests can reveal students' areas of strengths and weaknesses. Such information is useful for remedial instructional purposes. When tests are used to predict students' performances, they have less instructional value but still may provide educationally valuable information.

Tests as Predictors. Predictive measures are valuable because their scores can be compared with those of identifiable groups. In order to interpret aptitude measures, we must draw upon the standardized properties of the ideal, bell-shaped normal curve as shown in Figure 4.2. Of course scores are rarely distributed exactly as in the normal, bell-shaped curve. But, given a large test sample, the scores will approximate this distribution.

About 68 percent of the typical student population will test within one standard deviation of the mean. On a test such as the Wechsler Series, with a mean of 15 IQ points, about 34 percent of the population will score between 100 and 85 and another 34 percent will score between 100 and 115.

For example, the test results of Charles, a mainstreamed student, show that his overall reading achievement score is 4.6 and intelligence testing shows a 95 IQ. What do these scores predict? Before answering this question, we need more information about the student.

Chronological age of the student at the time of testing serves as the basis for comparing his score with the average grade score for his age as shown in Figure 4.3. We know two facts about Charles: (1) his age (8 years, 3 months); and (2) the average grade score for his age (early third grade). The second fact is less definite since we did not bother determining his *exact* age at the time he entered first grade. So *early third grade* is based upon his approximate age when entering first grade.

Assuming certain conditions about the test and the testing situation, we can now predict that Charles' measured reading achievement (4.6), at the time of testing, was about one year above what would be average for his age. In making this prediction we have assumed that Charles tried his best while taking the test, that he followed the directions, that the test was prop-

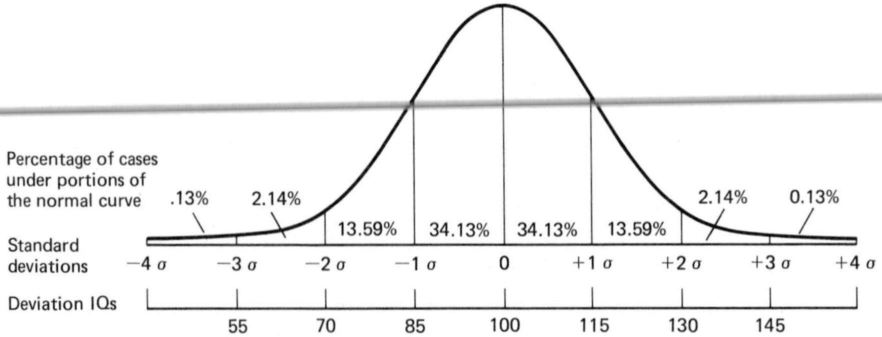

Figure 4.2 The theoretical bell-shaped normal curve.

erly administered, and that Charles' significant characteristics were represented in the sample population upon which the test was standardized.

All standardized tests are not appropriate for all students. Such matters as the composition of the representative sample population upon which the test was standardized and the validity of the test's contents should be included when considering the appropriateness of predictive measures.

Charles's IQ score of 95 is also a predictive measure. This score suggests that his overall intellectual development is about average. In more precise terms, it is 95 percent of average development (i.e., 95/100). An IQ score of 100 represents the average. By dividing 100 into the score you will obtain a rate of intellectual growth. Of course, these types of scores and calculations are not precise and should be used merely as suggestive of students' measured potential. Even when other considerations are accounted for, all tests contain some error. Allow for an error margin of about five IQ points. Thus, in Charles's case we can say that his rate of intellectual development is, at this time, *about average*.

IQ is a predictive score because general intelligence tests focus on *potential* abilities. What is measured, of course, is what the student now knows and *can* do. Measured performance serves as a basis for predicting one's aptitude. Results of these tests are typically used for educational and vocational counseling and as one factor, among others, for determining eligibility in special instructional programs.

Remember these cautions when interpreting aptitude test scores:

- All tests are not well standardized, some are better than others.
- No test is designed for all students, check to determine if students with characteristics similar to the target students were included in the standardization population.

Charles took the reading test on September 15, 1980. He was born June 10, 1972. His chronological age at the time of testing was 8 years, 3 months:

	80 - 9 - 15	Test date
Minus	72 - 6 - 10	Birth date
	8 - 3 - 5	Age

If Charles is an average reader, his grade score will be near beginning third grade:

	8 - 3	Chronological age
Minus	5 - 0	Age at first grade entrance
	3 - 3	Average grade score for age

Figure 4.3 Determining average grade score for age.

- Measured aptitude and present rates of development are changeable, significant intervening factors in children's lives can increase or decrease their measured intelligence.

Some standardized tests, while not specifically designed for use in teaching, do provide ways for teachers to "tease" out instructional information. For example, the California Achievement Tests have provided, for many years, an easy format for analyzing each student's areas of strengths and weaknesses. In addition, this type of test provides global scores, such as grade scores.

Achievement tests often provide a format for analyzing the content. As a result of conducting an analysis of a student's performance, teachers can determine which areas need special attention. Analyses of standardized tests in this way have serious limitations. First, subcategories are represented by small item samples; small samples result in lowered validity and reliability coefficients. Second, the analysis is less valuable as the length of time between taking the test and the instruction increases; instruction should closely follow testing. Third, because of the way in which predictive tests are constructed, those items missed by students may require mastery of lower-ordered skills and concepts that are not measured in the test. In these cases it is necessary to analyze the higher-level skill, dividing it into its subcomponents for instruction.

Measures of intelligence have also been used for instruction. Some tests of intelligence, such as the Wechsler Series (1974), provide formats for analysis. But when aptitude measures are used as a basis for teaching, they are limited by many of the same problems as are the achievement tests.

Tests as Instructional Tools. Remedial and corrective instruction was used early in the 1920s to help students with academic learning problems. This practice grew out of clinical education and out of the testing movement following World War I (Stephens, McCormick, Sutherland, and Genshaft, 1980). Diagnostic testing was a natural outcome of the clinical education movement and from it emerged medically related diagnostic terms for classifying and identifying academic learning problems (Thompson, 1966).

Prior to the late 1950s, clinical work was emphasized instead of classroom applications. But by the end of the decade, students of normal abilities who displayed learning difficulties were given special help in some public schools. During that same period and prior to the use of the term *learning disabilities*, perceptual-motor classifications emerged. Kephart (1940) pioneered in relating motor functions to learning-process problems. He considered such perceptual-motor functions as laterality, directionality, body image, form perception, and figure-ground perception. Language problems were also considered to be process disorders very much in the way that perceptual-motor problems were (Bush and Waugh, 1976).

Diagnostic-prescriptive teaching became popular in the mid-1960s (Peters, 1965). It was an outcome of more precise measurements and improved instructional technology. In education, diagnosis is typically followed by a prescribed instructional program. So the term *diagnostic-prescriptive teaching* was soon applied to most systems of instruction for students with learning difficulties.

Assessment practices concerning learning process disorders continued into the 1970s in the United States, but the assumptions underlying these practices came under increasingly heavy criticism. Critics raised issues concerning the use of standardized measures for identifying handicapped learners, the validity and reliability of these tests, and those assumptions upon which tests were developed and used. By the early 1970s criticism of tests used to assess learning disabilities became widespread. Process approaches to measurement were critically analyzed by Ysseldyke and Salvia (1974) and intervention strategies based upon the process model were attacked by Quay (1973), Mann (1971), Stephens (1976, 1977), and Hammill and Larsen (1974, 1978).

Since testing is an important part of a systematic instructional program, process or ability training is believed to be based upon teaching strategies in relation to the diagnostic profile. Among these, the Frostig Program for the Development of Visual Perception (Frostig and Horne, 1968) has been widely used and studied.

Another test that greatly influenced programs for the learning disabled is the Illinois Test of Psycholinguistic Abilities (Kirk, McCarthy, and Kirk, 1968). This test, referred to as the ITPA, yields a diagnostic profile for use in teaching. A series of articles, however, has raised serious questions as to the ITPA's usefulness (Hammill and Larsen, 1974, 1978; Lund, Foster, and Perez, 1978).

By the 1980s, measurement and treatment of children with academic learning problems were represented by two schools of thought. The first includes the *process* or *ability training* advocates; the second model has been termed *skill training* (Stephens, 1977). Advocates of ability training emphasize remediating those underlying processes believed to be contributing to inadequate learning (Frostig, 1970; Johnson and Myklebust, 1967; Kirk et al., 1968). Skill training begins by identifying those precise responses that are in error. Correct responses are then taught. Assumptions are not made regarding causes of learning problems because remediation is not based upon causality (Engelmann, 1969; Lovitt, 1975; Stephens, 1977).

Assessment practices are also affected by how academic learning problems are viewed. Typically, those who take an ability-training stance view learning deficits as symptoms of the *real causes* of incorrect responses and so the learning processes are treated. In the ability-training view, a direct approach to academic instruction is typically considered to be supplemental to the necessary teaching. Skill trainers deal directly with academic learning problems. Those responses that are incorrect are analyzed and specified. Corrective instruction for skill trainers consists of changing those responses that are directly related to the academic learning problems.

Ability and skill-training views of academic learning problems are often not compatible. Even though identification of students who have learning difficulties are usually identical regardless of how the problems are viewed, the information needed by instructional personnel differs greatly, depending upon how the problems will be treated. So the value of testing procedures and instruments will vary with the treatment to be used.

While ability or process oriented educators have relied upon standardized tests for their instructional information, skill trainers use nonstandardized tests, permanent products, and direct observations as a basis for instructional approaches.

PERMANENT PRODUCTS

Students' permanent products represent a rich source of assessment information. These may consist of written examinations, audio and visual recordings, completed tasks such as jigsaw puzzles and handcrafts. Products of this sort are not, by themselves, necessarily valuable. To be useful assessment sources, they must be scoreable, dated, and representative of the student's work.

Cooper (1981) describes three ways in which teachers score permanent products:

- Frequency of occurrence (e.g., six problems were correct)
- Rate of occurrence (e.g., he read 100 words per minute)
- Percentage of occurrence (e.g., 90 percent of the problems were correct)

If you plan to use permanent products as assessment or evaluation data, each should be dated and placed in a file for future reference. Equivalent products viewed over an academic year can be helpful for showing a student's progress. A series of products over time is particularly effective in showing parents the gains made by their child. Some mainstreamed students do not show measureable gains on standardized tests or do not appear to be learning. But when data are collected systematically from their daily efforts, their rate of learning can be impressive.

The collecting, scoring, and filing of permanent products alone does not represent their full usefulness. An *analysis* of the responses is needed for obtaining valuable instructional information.

Ashlock (1976) provides useful guidelines for acquiring what he terms *diagnostic* information. He recommends that the teacher present an accepting attitude toward the child to obtain cooperation. Teachers should not instruct when collecting diagnostic data: Do not point out errors or prompt the child to correct the initial responses. Be thorough, even to the point of observing students' work during instructional sessions. When assessing permanent products, look for patterns of errors in order to locate consistent use of incorrect procedures.

You may also find it helpful to conduct an analysis of the student's thinking that resulted in a specific product or response. This can be done by simply asking the student to "work the problem aloud for me." Or, "find the sentence in the story that told you the answer." When conducting an analysis of this type, you can identify and record points at which students have difficulty.

DIRECT OBSERVATIONS

Observing students involves obtaining and recording a sample of their performances under specified conditions. If such observations are to be useful the occurrences must be recorded. Responses may be counted, described, or timed.

Directly observing students' performances is most effective when you have established procedures to follow. Steps for observing behavior are: (1) describe the target behavior; (2) identify a target (student, subject matter) to observe; (3) select samples (students, responses) from the target; (4) specify the conditions under which the observations will take place; (5) select a method for recording your observations and begin observing.

1. *Describing target behaviors.* Target behaviors should be well defined and described so that two independent observers closely agree on the observations. When describing target behavior, the question to be answered is: will the occurrence of this behavior be readily recognized by another independent observer?

2. *Identifying a target behavior to observe.* The target may be a behavior among several students or behavior of one student. Behaviors might include performances on tests (number of items correct), volunteering during class discussions, or other school related behaviors.

3. *Selecting samples of the target behavior.* Sampling may be across students (e.g., every third student is observed); across time (e.g., observations will occur daily for 15 minutes beginning at 9:45), and across frequencies (e.g., record every third response).

4. *Specifying conditions under which the observations take place.* Those conditions to be specified may include time of day, subject matter, location in the room or school, activity, day of week, and so forth.

5. *Recording observations.* The method of recording is typically related to the type of target behavior. These may include: counting responses, duration of responses, and counting and recording duration of time expended.

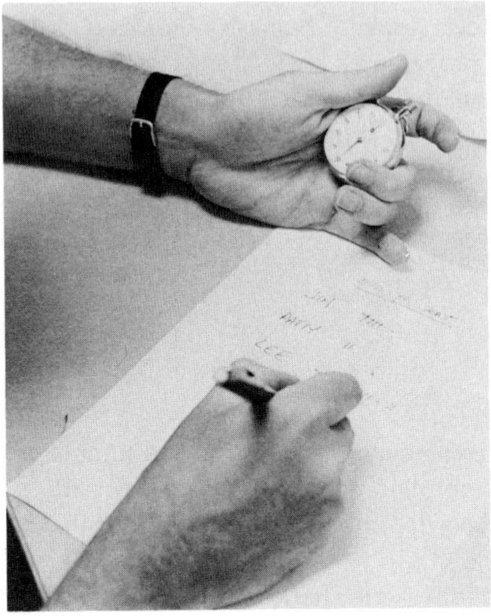

Tabulating the number of times a behavior occurs at various intervals of time is a useful way to record observations.

When directly observing performances, such as the number of times students participate in a group discussion, a simple method for recording should be used. Such methods involve:

- Counting responses, tallying the number of times a target behavior occurs
- Continuous recording, describing in writing everything as it happens
- Duration recording, using a stopwatch or a wristwatch with a sweeping second hand to note elapsed time of the target behavior during the observation period
- Interval recording, observations divided into equal time periods quantifying the results

Calculating Percentage of Agreements. Cooper (1981) recommends that two independent observers should reach at least 80 percent agreement in order to have reliable observations. Percentage of agreement is calculated by using this formula:

$$\text{P.A.} = \frac{N\ \text{agreements}}{N\ \text{agreements} + N\ \text{disagreements}} \times 100$$

Duration Observations. Some behaviors are best recorded in duration terms (e.g., tantrums). When using duration observations, *both* frequency of occurrence and length of occurrence must be in agreement. In this example, X indicates agreement of both observers on amount of time consumed and frequency of tantrums; whereas, V represents disagreement on one of both dimensions.

Frequency and Length of Time
X
V
X
X
X

Totals: 4 agreements, 1 disagreement
P.A. = 80 percent

Interval Observations. During an observation, two different observers recorded their observations as shown (X represents agreement, V disagreement).

Intervals	***Length***
1	X
2	V
3	X
4	V
5	V

Totals: 2 agreements, 3 disagreements
P.A. = 40 percent

Rate of Response Measure. A rate measure, rather than a frequency count, should be used when session time is not constant. Rate of response is calculated by converting frequency count to rate by using this formula:

$$\text{rate} = \frac{\text{frequency of occurrence}}{\text{duration of session}}$$

Two independent observers confirmed five observations (P.A. = 100 percent) of a target behavior, volunteering responses (hand raising), during class discussion. The rate of response is shown in the last column.

Session	***Frequency***	***Duration Minutes***	***Rate of Response Minutes***
1	16	15	1.1
2	19	15	1.3
3	18	20	.9
4	22	10	2.2
5	43	25	1.7

ASSESSING FOR INSTRUCTION

After mainstreamed students have been evaluated for educational placement and IEPs have been developed, you will need information for making instructional decisions for short-term purposes. This information is typically provided by specially trained teachers and other school personnel who are prepared for that purpose. However, as a well prepared classroom teacher you may want to acquire some assessment competencies for use with all students who present learning problems.

In this section, some information and suggested activities are provided to assist you in achieving assessment knowledge and some degree of competency. First, however, we will present some instructional models to help provide you with an understanding of how assessment information is related to instruction.

MODELS FOR ASSESSMENT AND INSTRUCTION

Educational researchers develop models to understand reality and to explain theory. Instructional models are also useful to teachers and other practitioners because they provide a set of procedures to follow, such as goal setting and ways to achieve those goals.

Diagnostic Prescriptive Teaching. Contemporary instructional models in special education have been dominated by diagnostic prescriptive teaching although some authorities, such as Peters (1965), propose similar approaches for all students. In diagnostic prescriptive models, student assessment precedes instruction which is followed by evaluation. A schematic view of one such model, Directive Teaching (Stephens, 1976), is shown in Figure 4.4.

Similar to most diagnostic prescriptive models, four steps are followed and repeated in Directive Teaching: (1) assessing; (2) planning; (3) instructing; (4) and evaluating.

1. *Assessing.* Prior to beginning new instructional tasks, units, or experiences (depending upon the context's nature and goals) teachers obtain relevant information about students' performances on those types of skills, concepts, and tasks to be taught. In addition, they may find it necessary to assess reinforcement preferences, expressive and receptive modalities, and the classroom environment as described in Chapter 6.
2. *Planning.* Instructional plans should be based upon the assessment information. During this phase, teachers determine those instructional tasks to be taught within the IEP's framework, the level of performance expected on each task (terminal criteria), and the instructional material

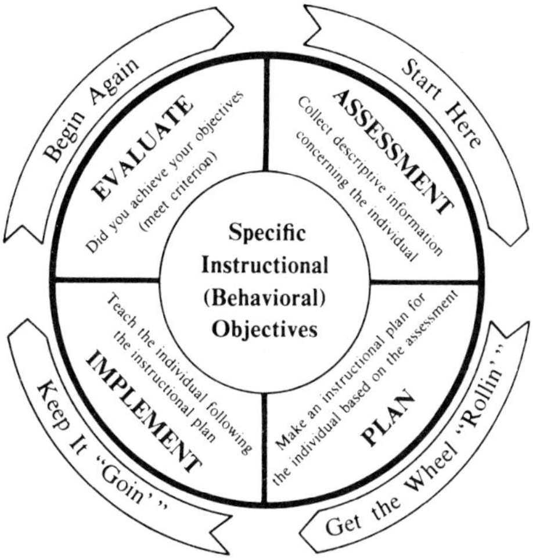

Figure 4.4 The Directive Teaching Model. (From Stephens, *Implementing Behavioral Approaches in Elementary and Secondary Schools*. Copyright © 1975 Charles E. Merrill Publishing Company, Columbus, Ohio.)

to be used. Since IEP's level of specificity may vary from school to school, planning at this point may often involve the placement team including the parent. In situations where IEPs are less detailed, planning of this sort is done by instructional personnel using the IEP content as a guide. Planning may also by necessity specify incentives (rewards), ways to deliver reinforcement, and required schedules of reinforcement to maintain student interest and performance.

3. *Instructing.* During the instructional phase, plans take the form of teaching strategies. These strategies serve as guides, although experienced teachers will deviate from strategies when it seems appropriate. It is during this step in Directive Teaching that instructional planning and student assessment efforts pay off in effective teaching.

4. *Evaluating.* By comparing students' performances with the terminal criteria as stated in the strategy, teachers determine the levels of learning that have occurred. When students' performances equal or exceed criteria the tasks have been learned or mastered. At this point, other tasks are selected and the cycle begins again.

Diagnostic-Prescriptive Tools. With evolving diagnostic-prescriptive practices, tools for using these models have continued to be perfected and some have been adapted from other theories. Often teachers and other users must make exacting decisions about when to use which specific techniques. Again the Directive Teaching Model serves as the example:

Tools in Directive Teaching

Step 1 **Assessing student performance**
Tools:
Direct observation, criterion-referenced tasks, skill statements, performance criteria.

Step 2 **Instructional planning**
Tools:
Behavioral objectives, task analysis, commercial materials.

Step 3 **Instructing**
Tools:
Stimulus control, cueing, social modeling, chaining, social reinforcement, contingency management, worksheets, games, and other commercial materials.

Step 4 **Evaluating Effects of Instruction**
Tools:
Direct observation, criterion-referenced tasks, skill statements, performance criteria, record of progress.

Those tools shown above for use in Directive Teaching reveal the extensive knowledge and skill required by those who use diagnostic prescriptive teaching. Other models may be even more demanding such as those in which instruction must be based upon data generated during the assessment phase (Kunzelman, 1970). Some commercially available programs have reduced the level of training and the frequency of teachers' decision making, as in the DISTAR program (Englemann and Bruner, 1974). While these are usually effective for their stated purpose, they are, by necessity, often less flexible and tend to reduce teaching to a more automated function.

OTHER ASSESSMENT CONSIDERATIONS

When assessing students for instruction consideration must be given to their ages, prior learning, levels of achievement, and the nature of the material to be taught. Age is a central factor for formal instruction because of its relationship to interests and to physiological and transient psychological adjustment problems. By the primary grades, for example, children who have basic learning problems have demonstrated their difficulties through poor school performance. However, children who are just beginning formal schooling may exhibit very basic learning problems that are not readily apparent. Such problems *may* be suggested by motor discoordination and other physiological signs. At times poor attitudes toward learning are seen in preschoolers. Often such behaviors serve as ways for children to hide their learning difficulties—by resisting learning experiences they can avoid the pain of their expected failure. When attitudinal problems are exhibited at these early ages, parents and other adults will tend to focus on the resistance. Thus, they unwittingly help these children to avoid the needed learning experiences.

Gaps in students' earlier learning are often barriers to effective instruction. Those who assess such students may find the results uneven and at times baffling because these students' skills and concept developments reveal confusing patterns. Such gaps may also have a cumulative effect. For example, when the defect is rooted in a basic learning behavior, such as attending to details, many higher-order learnings that require attending skills will be impaired. Those students who have spent several years accumulating poor attention habits may be incapable of following instructions in a group situation and will require special tutoring as well as special attention when they are placed in groups.

The potential for learning gaps is great and presents important assessment issues. Some authorities, recognizing the significance of basic learning processes, emphasize remediation of the basic learning deficits. Others, taking into account the magnitude of correcting these problems as well as the many underlying assumptions inherent in this type of diagnosis, approach them by dealing with the overt responses instead of the basic processes. Readers who are interested in this important controversy may wish to examine some of these references: Mann (1971, 1979); Quay (1973); Stephens, Hartman, and Cooper (1973); Wiederholt and Hammill (1971); Ysseldyke and Salvia (1974); White (1979); Parmenter (1980); Frostig and Maslow (1979); Hardyck and Haapanen (1979); Salvia and Ysseldyke (1978).

Academic content also may limit assessment methods; contents vary in their amenability to certain teaching and assessment tactics. For example, arithmetic computation permits the use of task analysis because of its explicit hierarchy of skills. By comparison, most language assessment is not amenable to task analysis. But, there is not a one-to-one relationship between an academic subject and assessment and teaching tactics. It is for this reason that assessing student performance is both complicated and challenging.

ASSESSING BASIC ACADEMIC SKILLS

Basic academic learning includes prerequisite skills and concepts as well as language and arithmetic achievement. Regardless of mainstreamed students' ages and grade placements, basic academic skills are essential if students are to learn content subjects.

Developmental Learning. At basic learning levels, developmental learning theory can be particularly helpful in teaching young children. Stephens and Wolf (1981) present a generic model based upon developmental learning theory for assessing and teaching beginning learners. Their model specifies six phases in the learning sequence: (1) discriminating and differentiating; (2) labeling; (3) copying and imitating; (4) reproducing to mastery; (5) practicing; and (6) applying.

These six phases are not mutually exclusive; that is, learners could perform more advanced tasks prior to having mastered easier ones. For example, without having acquired correct labels (Phase 2) they could be copying and/or imitating responses. The extent to which the sequence is not necessarily followed probably varies with the content, learner, and prior experience. But while they might perform the more advanced tasks, they are not performed readily or at a mastery level. Difficulties in doing such tasks easily are believed to be due to lack of mastery at the lower phases.

Phase 1 involves attention to details, configurations, and other aspects of specific phenomena that set it apart from others in the learner's environment. The learner matches similar stimuli and differentiates them from dissimilar ones.

Phase 2 requires learners to use names and other language symbols that correctly identify stimuli learned during the mastery of the first task. This phase includes concept formation as well as skill acquisition.

Phase 3 occurs when responses are copied, traced, or imitated in the presence of stimuli or immediately following exposure to stimuli. Often, when children respond correctly in the absence of models the performance is mistaken for mastery. In fact, learning is in process but will require the remaining three phases or steps for mastery.

Phase 4 involves reproduction where children respond from memory or in the presence of visual, auditory, or other sensory cues. These cues may be represented by directions to perform incomplete equations and any other appropriate stimuli. Throughout this phase, as in the earlier one, feedback to learners usually takes the form of correction and/or encouragement.

Phase 5 consists of practicing the newly acquired skill and/or concept. Although practice occurs under supervision, it is of a more general type than in the previous phases; feedback is often not immediate and correction is often not as detailed as in the earlier phases. The practice will vary with the nature of the content to be mastered, its importance to the learner and the teacher, and the ultimate application of the skill or concept.

Phase 6 takes place under the general direction of the instructional agent; although mastery may have been demonstrated during the five previous phases, application still will demand instructional evaluation. This evaluation may be formal as in the use of school marks, or it may be solely utilitarian such as observing the behavior being demonstrated.

Implications for Assessing. These six phases and their sequencing have important implications for assessing young and low-functioning students. Their task performances can be examined with this sequence in mind. When students encounter difficulties in learning a specific concept or task, their performances on lower-level phases may reveal defects in their learning which need to be corrected before they can master the more advanced responses. An application of this learning model is shown here:
Class of behavior: READING
Skill and Concept to be learned:

Tell Meaning of Root Words Before and After Suffix Is Added

Phase 1 **Discriminating and differentiating**
Children identify common root words with suffixes.

Phase 2 **Labeling**
Children name root words and suffixes.

Phase 3 **Copying and imitating**
With examples, children tell meaning of root words after suffixes are added.

Phase 4 **Reproducing to mastery**
Children tell meaning of root words before and after suffixes are added without models.

Phase 5 **Practicing**
Children practice identifying root words and reciting their meanings before and after suffixes are added with correction as needed.

Phase 6 **Applying**
Children indicate meanings of root words before and after suffix is added without assistance and across settings.

Prerequisite Skills and Concepts. Almost all learning requires prerequisite understanding, skills, and concepts. But the concept of prerequisite learning is particularly important for beginning learners because they typically have few personal and experiential resources upon which to draw. In this context, basic, prerequisite responses are those performances that usually precede reading, writing, and arithmetic skills.

Content at this level can be categorized as: attending skills, auditory skills, visual skills, and speaking skills.

Attending skills include responding to auditory and visual stimuli appropriately. These behaviors involve listening to teachers and to other children as well as to television and other electronically mediated stimuli.

Auditory skills involve correctly discriminating sounds, words, and other auditory stimuli.

Visual skills require correctly discriminating shapes and other visual stimuli.

Speaking skills require the correct use of oral language.

Implications for Assessing. Mainstreamed students who have difficulty in these basic prerequisite responses often demonstrate inattention, difficulties in following oral directions, misreading of visual cues or failure to notice them, or use of poor-quality oral language. Particularly with young children, you should consider these areas of behavior when determining where to begin assessing. These prerequisite responses are observable and thus lend themselves to direct observations.

ASSESSING SOCIAL BEHAVIOR

All educational practices are based upon assumptions concerning what learning can occur and how it is facilitated. Mainstreaming beliefs are no exceptions. Gresham (1981) identified three assumptions about mainstreaming which he believes are false. First, many mainstreaming advocates assume that students' social interactions will increase when placed in regular programs (Peterson and Haralick, 1977); second, mainstreaming will result in an increased social acceptance by the nonhandicapped peer group (Birch, 1974); and third, mainstreamed students model their behavior after nonhandicapped peers through increased exposure to them (Birch, 1978).

Gresham reviewed a large body of research that refutes these three assumptions. Instead he has shown that mainstreaming efforts are likely to increase social isolation unless the mainstreamed students are prepared in those social skills needed for effective social interactions and peer acceptance. Yet, in spite of the research supporting his conclusion, few schools have a systematic instructional program of social-skills instruction. Such programs are needed if the promise of mainstreaming is to be met. With this need in mind, imperative classroom social skills are presented here followed by ways to assess them.

Imperative Social Skills. Social skills assessment and instruction should occur before and during mainstreamed students' integration into regular classrooms. While the assessment may be a shared responsibility of special educators and classroom teachers, instruction should be provided as an adjunctive activity by tutors or resource-room teachers. However, regular class teachers may find it useful, in some instances, to provide such instruction to all elementary-school-aged children.

A curriculum for social skills was developed from a taxonomy containing 4 major categories and 30 subcategories (Stephens, 1978). From this framework 136 social skills for elementary-school-aged children were identified (Milburn, 1974). Figure 4.5 shows the major categories and subcategories of that taxonomy.

Major Categories, Subcategories, and Number of Skills in Each	Abbreviations		
ENVIRONMENTAL BEHAVIORS	ER		
Care for the Environment	ce	*N* skills	5
Dealing with Emergency	de	*N* skills	3
Lunchroom	lr	*N* skills	3
Movement around Environment	mo	*N* skills	4
		TOTAL ER	15
INTERPERSONAL BEHAVIORS	IP		
Accepting Authority	aa	*N* skills	5
Coping with Conflict	cc	*N* skills	6
Gaining Attention	ga	*N* skills	6
Greeting Others	gr	*N* skills	7
Helping Others	hp	*N* skills	7
Making Conversation	mc	*N* skills	8
Organized Play	op	*N* skills	4
Positive Attitude Toward Others	pa	*N* skills	3
Plays Informally	pl	*N* skills	5
Property: Own and Others	pr	*N* skills	4
		TOTAL IP	55
SELF RELATED BEHAVIORS	SR		
Accepting Consequences	ac	*N* skills	3
Ethical Behavior	eb	*N* skills	4
Expressing Feelings	ef	*N* skills	2
Positive Attitude Toward Self	pa	*N* skills	4
Responsible Behavior	rb	*N* skills	7
Self Care	sc	*N* skills	3
		TOTAL SR	23
TASK RELATED BEHAVIORS	TR		
Asking and Answering Questions	aq	*N* skills	4
Attending Behavior	at	*N* skills	3
Classroom Discussion	cd	*N* skills	6
Completing Tasks	ct	*N* skills	4
Follows Directions	fd	*N* skills	3
Group Activities	ga	*N* skills	5
Independent Work	iw	*N* skills	3
On Task Behavior	ot	*N* skills	6
Performing Before Others	pf	*N* skills	5
Quality of Work	qw	*N* skills	4
		TOTAL TR	43

Figure 4.5 A social skills taxonomy. (From *Social Skills in the Classroom.* Thomas M. Stephens, Cedars Press, 1978. Copyright © Cedars Press, Inc., 1978. All rights reserved.)

As can be seen in Figure 4.5, the number of skills vary for each category; these represent the importance that classroom teachers placed on the different social behaviors (Milburn, 1974). For example, *interpersonal behaviors* are viewed as more important than *environmental behaviors* since the former category contains 55 skills whereas the latter has only 15 skills. One sample skill for each major category is shown below:

Class of behavior: ENVIRONMENTAL (Care for the Environment)
Skill: *Uses classroom equipment and materials correctly.*

Class of behavior: INTERPERSONAL (Gaining Attention)
Skill: *Gains attention from peers in appropriate ways.*

Class of behavior: SELF-RELATED (Ethical Behavior)
Skill: *Avoids wrong-doing when encouraged by peers.*

Class of behavior: TASK-RELATED (Group Activities)
Skill: *Works cooperatively with a partner.*

Two steps are necessary for assessing systematically students' social skills: First, define the social skills; second, assess the students' performances against the defined skills.

Defining Social Skills. Notice the wording of each of the sample social skills. In each, the student's behavior is described. Descriptions of behavior represent the first step for studying behavior objectively. In defining social skills, make them observable and avoid speculative inferences about inner processes. Even though students think, feel, and have emotions that are not always evident, we can study these inner conditions indirectly by observing their consequences—that is, the student's behavior.

Define the behavior in positive terms—what students will do when they have acquired the skills. As an example, look again at the skill under ethical behavior: *Avoids wrong-doing when encouraged by peers.* The wording describes what students will do when encouraged by their fellow students to do something that is not right. They will: *avoid wrong-doing.*

Sometimes it is helpful in assessing to indicate *where* the behavior will take place, *when* it will occur, and under which circumstances; wrong-doing will be avoided *when encouraged by peers.*

Using Defined Skills When Assessing. Social behavior varies with circumstances and because there are degrees of "right" and "wrong" behavior the performance lends itself to a rating approach. With such ratings, we are not assessing what students *know* but rather what they do. Thus, a system of relative measurement is appropriate. For example, in the *Social Behavior Assessment* (Stephens, 1980a), the rating scale is as follows:

0 = Behavior not observed or not applicable for the student
1 = Behavior is exhibited at an acceptable level
2 = Behavior is exhibited at a lower than acceptable level
3 = Behavior is never exhibited

Rating of students' social skills may be done through direct observations—either what you have seen the students do (your knowledge of their behavior) or, how students behave in a contrived situation. An example of the contrived approach is: *Have the student role play with the teacher playing the role of name caller. Ask the student to show what he/she would do in the name-calling situation.* Teachers should exercise caution when conducting this type of role playing. In the example above, watch the severity of name calling so that it is not excessive.

A summary of an assessment rating for interpersonal behaviors is shown in figure 4.6 for David, a nine-year-old mainstreamed student who receives special instruction one hour each day in a resource room. Ratings of his interpersonal behaviors are also shown in the figure.

In this summary of David's interpersonal behaviors, you can see that his ratings are at mastery in two areas: accepting authority (AA) and plays informally (PL). He is close to mastery in two other areas: organized play (OP) and property—own and others (PR). His ratings are three points from mastery in: making conversation (MC) and positive attitude toward others (PA). Those areas in which he is four or more points removed from mastery are: 4 points from mastery—greeting others (GR); 5 points from mastery—gaining attention (GA); 8 points from mastery—helping others (HP); 10 points from mastery—coping with conflict (CC).

Ratings of this sort form the basis for teaching social skills. Instructional strategies in teaching social behavior are discussed in Chapter 5.

ASSESSING READING SKILLS

Reading skills are widely recognized as the single most important area for school success. Mainstreamed students who have reading difficulties should receive assistance as supplemental instruction from instructional aides in order for them to be successful in regular classes. Although the supplemental reading instruction should not be the regular classroom teacher's responsibility, information concerning instructionally valuable reading assessment can be shared between the two teachers.

In this section, a framework for considering beginning reading skills is described in relation to criterion-referenced assessment. When criterion-referenced assessment is used it is necessary to have specific skills in mind

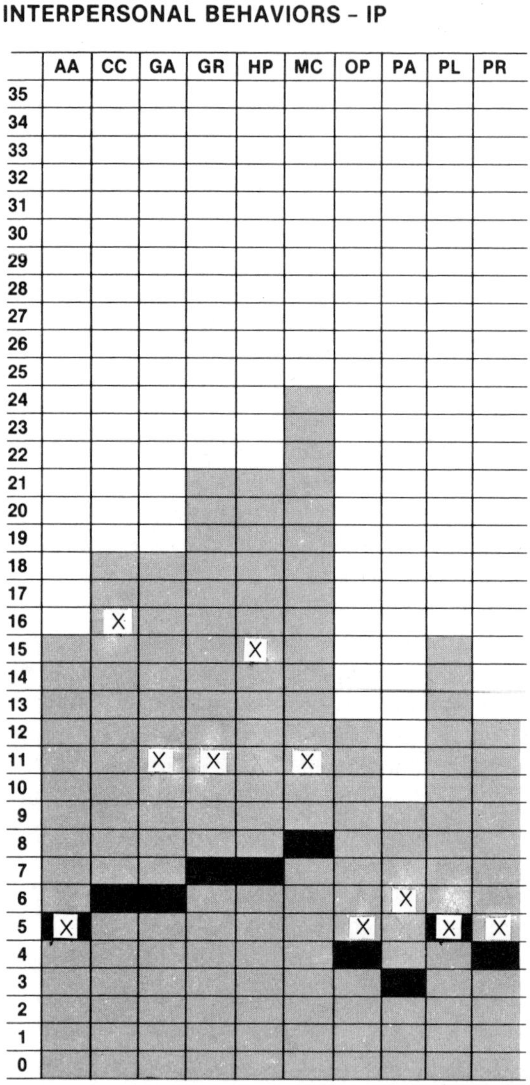

Figure 4.6 A social skills assessment rating summary. (From Thomas M. Stephens, *The Social Behavior Assessment Scale*. Copyright © 1979 by Cedars Press, Inc. All rights reserved from The Social Behavior Assessment Scale.)

and a task-based curriculum. In categorizing beginning reading skills, Stephens (1973) used 7 major categories and 48 subcategories (see table on page 117).

Major Categories and Subcategories in Stephens' Reading List (1973)

Comprehension	Structural Analysis	Visual Discrimination	Auditory Discrimination	Phonetic Analysis	Sight Words	Oral Reading
Classifying and categorizing	Contractions	Likenesses/differences	Environmental sounds	Blends	Preprimer	Oral reading
Drawing conclusions	Compound words	Matching symbols	Identifying rhymes	Final consonants	Primer	Clarity
Identifying speaker	Punctuation	Recognizing letters	Matching sounds	Consonant variants	First	Intonation and expression
Inference	Prefix/suffix	Recognizing numbers	Repeating sounds	Digraphs	Second	
Interpretation	Singular/plural	Repeating visual patterns	Following instruction	Diphthongs	Third	
Labeling	Syllabification			Phonetic words in context		
Location skills	Uppercase/lowercase			Long vowels		
Main idea	Word building			Short vowels		
Matching						
Opposites						
Recall						
Sequencing events						
Following written directions						
Word meaning						

To assess and teach these skill areas, 267 skills are specified in terms of student behaviors (Stephens, Hartman, and Lucas, 1978). Assessment tasks are also available for each skill (Stephens, 1973b). Two criterion-referenced assessment tasks are shown below:

Example A (AUDITORY DISCRIMINATION: matching sounds)

Skill: Point to pictures that begin with *N*

Assessment: Present the sound of *N* to students. Then show 10 pictures, one at a time, and ask students to point to the picture if it begins with the *N* sound.

Materials: Pictures of: (1) the numeral 9; (2) a net; (3) a frog; (4) a needle; (5) a pencil; (6) a dog; (7) a musical note; (8) a pig; (9) a horse; (10) a cup.

Criteria: mastery 10/10, instructional 9/10 to 6/10, frustrational below 6/10.

Example B (STRUCTURAL ANALYSIS: syllabification)

Skill: Listen to a word and say the number of syllables it contains.

Assessment: Read each word as you show it to the students. Ask them how many syllables are in the word.

Materials: Word cards: (1) butter; (2) return; (3) magic; (4) disregard; (5) hospitable; (6) presented; (7) however; (8) kindergarten; (9) ornament; (10) discontented.

Criteria: mastery 10/10, instructional 9/10 to 6/10, frustrational below 6/10.

Both of the above examples contain the skill to be assessed in terms of students' responses, suggested materials, and fixed criteria for determining if the student has already mastered the skill or if performance is at the instructional level. When performance is at frustration, teachers are encouraged to assess the student on lower-level skills.

Reading performance may also be assessed through direct observation by noting and recording reading errors. This approach is less systematic than the criterion-referenced one but can be effective with students who have obvious reading problems.

A NOTE ABOUT ASSESSING READING COMPREHENSION

Reading skill instruction is directed toward the ultimate goal of comprehension—that is the purpose of having reading skills—to understand printed materials. One tactic that teachers can use to estimate students' reading levels and to stimulate thinking is described below.

The Cloze Technique. Since students must be able to comprehend the texts and printed materials they use, the "cloze test" (Kennedy, 1974) can help match students to books they can read successfully. A cloze test for each textbook you are using, from fourth grade up, can be developed in this way:

1. Randomly select a meaningful sample passage of about 250 words from a representative section.

2. Type a duplicating master of the passage, leaving every fifth word blank until you have 50 blanks.

3. Do not omit any words from the first and last sentences.

4. Do not omit the first word in any sentence, any proper noun, or any number. Omit the next word instead.

For example, the start of a clozure test might read as follows:

A Clean Environment

Pollution is one of our worst problems today. Every spurt of smoke ______ a chimney puts some ______ in the surrounding air. Stopping ______ has become one of ______ major problems which . . . and so on.

In evaluating a student's performance in an informal cloze test, use these guidelines:

1. If 50 words are omitted each correct answer counts 2 percent.

2. For testing purposes count only the exact word omitted as the correct answer.

3. Do not have the student use a book on which the score is less than 40 percent correct. Select an easier book.

Beyond its use as a testing and discussion technique, cloze passages can provide excellent comprehension practice. In this kind of situation, synonyms or other suitable words may be accepted. Teachers can encourage discussion about the words to be used in the blanks, since in most instances there is no right or wrong answer.

ASSESSING ARITHMETIC SKILLS

Arithmetic performance can be analyzed by identifying computation error patterns (Ashlock, 1976). Pattern analysis requires finding consistent use of incorrect computational procedures in contrast to isolated errors. The nature of arithmetic computation is such that permanent products can be collected for analysis and filed for future assessment or evaluation.

Arithmetic also has been assessed using criterion-referenced measures. Stephens (1973a) identified 317 arithmetic skills to be mastered through the third grade. These skills are arranged into 4 major categories and 19 subcategories (see the table below).

Measurement	Numbers, Numerals, and Numeration Systems	Operations and Their Properties	Sets
Geometry	Cardinal numbers	Addition	Comparing
Length, height, distance	Numeral	Division	Ordering sets
Money	Odd/even	Inverse operations	
Temperature	Ordinal numbers	Multiplication	
Time	Place value	Subtraction	
	Rational numbers		
	Roman numerals		

Criterion-referenced assessment tasks are also used for each skill. Their format is similar to those shown for reading assessment, containing a skill statement, suggested procedures, materials, and criteria levels.

ASSESSING LANGUAGE USAGE

Phares (1980) investigated how 62 regular classroom teachers and 62 teachers of children in elementary grades who were learning disabled rated 56 language usage skills. These 56 skills were identified by Stephens (1979) through a content analysis of six language usage texts for elementary-school-aged children. In her study Phares verified the importance of the 56 skills by having two high-school English teachers rate these skills; the two high-school teachers agreed (P.A. 94 percent) that these skills were prerequisites for success in high-school English.

Phares also found no significant differences in the ranking of the 56 skills by both groups of teachers. Her findings revealed that they are most concerned with students learning the language fundamentals necessary for daily speaking and writing.

Figure 4.7 shows the categories representing the 56 language usage skills.

Language Usage: Skills and Concepts			
PARTS OF SENTENCES—	PS	VERBS—	ve
Subject Part—	sp	Definition—	vd
Verb Part—	vp	Being—	vb
Helping Verbs—	hv	Action—	va
Statements with Parts		Tense—	vt
Understood—	sp	Principle Parts—	vp
		Agreement with Subject—	va
AGREEMENT OF VERBS		Special Verbs—	vs
AND SUBJECTS—	AG		
		PREPOSITIONS—	pe
Singular and Plural—	sp		
Subjects in Question—	sq	Definition—	pd
		Objects—	po
NOUNS—	no	Infinitives—	pi
Definition—	nd		
Possessive Forms—	np	ADJECTIVES AND	
Nouns and Verb Forms—	nv	ADVERBS—	AA
		Uses, Adjectives—	au
PRONOUNS—	pr	Uses, Adverbs	ua
		Negatives—	ne
Definition—	pd		
Objects—	ob		
Subjects—	su		
Forms—	pf		

Figure 4.7 Taxonomy language usage: skills and concepts. (From Thomas M. Stephens, 1979.)

Some sample skills as related to the taxonomy in Figure 4.7 are shown below:

Category: NOUNS, possessive forms
Skill: Plural nouns ending in *S* form their possessives by adding an apostrophe.
Example: *ladies'* dresses

Category: PARTS OF SENTENCES, subject part
Skill: A subject is the person or the thing being discussed.
Example: The *boy* ran home.

Category: VERBS, action
Skill: A verb of action goes somewhere or does something.
Example: Bill *walks* to school.

Assessment of language usage skills may be achieved through examining written work and by directly observing students oral language. It is the *application* of these skills that are assessed rather than the students' recitation of them.

ASSESSING SPELLING SKILLS

Content for assessing spelling skills should be drawn from the commercial spelling program used in the school. Draw your sample from the listing of words shown in the back of each grade level spelling book. If a commercial spelling program is not in use, employ a list of basic spelling words.

Words written by students should be analyzed to determine types of errors made.

Two types of spelling errors can be identified: (1) phoneme/grapheme association; and (2) spelling generalizations (Stephens, Hartman, and Lucas, 1978).

Phoneme/Grapheme Examples

1. Say and write initial consonant when words are said aloud.
2. Identify and say words that rhyme when told aloud a series of three words.
3. Say and write consonant blends when words are said aloud.

Spelling Generalization Examples

1. Most nouns form the plural by adding *s* to the singular.
2. An abbreviation is always followed by a period.
3. Final *e* is dropped before a suffix beginning with a vowel but is kept before a suffix beginning with a consonant.

ASSESSING STUDY SKILLS IN CONTENT AREAS

Success in subject areas is critical for mainstreamed students. Thus, students should be selectively placed in regular classes on the basis of their likelihood to be successful. This placement principle should be observed across all grade levels; if the probability of the student's success is low then alternative placement or supportive help will be necessary. An important type of supportive help is represented by instruction in study skills.

Content of Study Skills. Five broad areas make up study skills:

1. Library use
2. Reference skills
3. Reading and using illustrative materials
4. Writing tools
5. Study patterns

Library use involves behaviors that are essential for using libraries properly. These include using a library catalogue finding specific references, and seeking help from librarians.

Study skills, including the use of the library, are important for the development of mainstreamed students.

Reference skills include using dictionaries, encyclopedias, indices, and other reference sources. These may be specific to a particular subject such as a listing of capital cities or they may be nonspecific such as a dictionary. For primary and early elementary students, such preliminary skills as alphabetizing and using a glossary should be considered.

Understanding illustrative materials such as maps, graphs, tables, and charts are often critical to success in specific subjects. Geography, mathematics, and social science courses often require these skills.

Writing tools are represented by note-taking skills, outlining, and summarizing skills.

Efficient study patterns follow formulas such as the SQ3R method (Robinson, 1970). This formula consists of:

1. *Survey.* Glance over the headings in the assigned reading matter.

2. *Question.* Form questions about each heading or segment.

3. *Read.* Find the answer to each question.

4. *Recite.* Use your own words in answering each question.
5. *Review.* Check notes and memory and recite the major points covered.

Direct observations and examining students' written materials can be used when assessing study skills. In addition, students can be questioned about how they *say* they study. This latter approach, of course, only determines students' knowledge of how to study rather than their studying behaviors.

SUMMARY

- Assessing mainstreamed students' performances is an essential step toward designing instructional activities.
- Instructional information differs from educational items on the basis of usage; information for instruction is useful for daily applications. It must also be specific and related to instructional objectives.
- Sources of assessment information include students' records, test results, permanent products, and direct observations.
- Instructional models provide practical procedures for assessing students.
- Basic academic skills include prerequisite behaviors, concepts, language, and arithmetic content.
- Suggested ways to assess social behavior, reading skills, arithmetic skills, language usage, spelling skills, and study skills.

FIVE

Using Assessment Information for Teaching

- What are classroom teachers expected to do when teaching mainstreamed students?
- How can instructional planning improve teaching?
- How does the IEP relate to the planning?
- Are regular teachers governed by the IEP?
- How is assessment information used in planning?
- Should students be involved in planning?
- What are some instructional techniques for teaching mainstreamed students?

Formal education is among the greatest inventions of humankind. Through it we have progressed from primitive living to highly refined verbal communications, less ignorance, more civil rights, and a continuing high level of technological development. Throughout the history of education, the teacher has been the central figure, guiding students and encouraging them in their learning. Teaching is an indispensable condition in the formal education process because what teachers do contributes to what students will learn. For mainstreamed students, in particular, what teachers *do* is important. First, they must plan their instruction in relation to the IEP and second, they must use those plans effectively.

PLANNING FOR INSTRUCTION

Planning is a particularly important behavior for successful teaching. In special education, the basic planning tool is the IEP. Remember, it contains two parts: the total service plan, and the implementation plan. The total service plan is shown in Figure 5.1. You may wish to refer to Chapter 9, Exercises 3, 4, and 5 (pages 285-287). These exercises show how an IEP is developed.

Content to be taught typically comprises the implementation portion of the IEP as shown in Figure 5.2. The implementation plan is used by special education personnel for achieving long-term goals of the total service plan.

Special education teachers are required to use the IEP as the basis of their instruction because the IEP represents all special education services and instruction. But the IEP is not designed or intended to be a daily lesson plan for the special teacher. Stated objectives may be more or less specific, depending on the makeup and preferences of the placement committee. The basic purpose of the IEP is to provide a written statement and to delineate the overall special program appropriate for a student; in that sense it is a management tool. Teachers may wish to treat IEP objectives as classroom goals and develop more specific objectives for the student's monthly, weekly, or daily lesson plans. The IEP should be designed so as

Search and Serve No. ______________ Projected Length of Total Program ______________

Present Placement: Projected Date of Comprehensive Review ______________

Name of Student ______________

Date of Birth ______ Age ____ Grade ____

County ______________

School ______________

Present Number of Hours Per Week in Regular Classroom ________

PLACEMENT ADVISORY COMMITTEE MEMBERS PRESENT

Date of Placement Advisory Committee Meeting ______

Signature	Position	Signature	Position

Summary of Present Levels of Student Performance:

Evaluation Instruments or Procedures Used:

Description of Placement Recommendations (Program Area and Service Configuration):

Prioritized Long Term Goals	Specific Educational and/or Related Services (include type of physical education program)	Personnel Responsible (Name and Title)	Hours Per Week	Recommendations: Specialized Methods, Materials and Equipment

Figure 5.1 Individualized education program: total service plan.

to encompass all of the special education portion of the student's schooling and to delineate, through either time or subjects, the student's mainstream placement.

Regular classroom teachers are not governed by the IEP. Except for the stated time in the regular program shown in the IEP, they are expected to provide mainstreamed students with the same quality of instruction as that given to the other students. This is a confusing area of mainstreaming.

Where do the regular classroom teacher's responsibilities for individualizing instruction begin and end? The regular teacher's lack of time, skill, and appropriate resources are common curriculum-related problems. For regular classroom teachers, adjusting the curriculum becomes problematic, not only in terms of content but also in length of assignments and tests used in regular classes. Reading materials may be too difficult for those students who have been placed in the mainstream for instruction in certain content areas. In these cases, the regular teacher is expected to circumvent the reading problem in teaching the subject matter. Those materials listed in Appendix F will be helpful for such problems.

Many regular teachers oppose modifying classroom requirements for mainstreamed students. Their opposition is reflected in issues surrounding

Date of Entry into Program ______________

Date Written Individualized Education Program Completed ________

Date Written Individualized Education Program Initiated ________

Projected Program Termination Date ______________

Projected IEP Review Date(s) ______________

______________________ ________
Signature(s) of Parent or Guardian Date

______________________ ________
Signature of Child (if appropriate) Date

____
Signature of County Director of Special Education or Designee

____
Signature of Implementer(s)

____
Signature of Implementer(s)

Annual Goals From (P.A.C.)	Short Term Objectives (Include Criteria for Mastery)	Specialized Strategies and/or Techniques	Specialized Materials, Equipment and/or Resources	To be completed as program is implemented.			
				Date Started	Date Ended	Date(s) Reviewed	Achieved Mastery for Each Short Term Objective

Figure 5.2 Individualized education program: implementation plan.

grading criteria, insufficient time, the necessity for students to do independent assignments, and students' inadequate study skills (Treblas, McCormick, and Cooper, 1981).

No specific rule can resolve those issues surrounding the regular classroom teacher's responsibilities for mainstreamed students. As a general guideline, regular classroom teachers should be expected to do *at least* as much in modifying instruction for mainstreamed students as they do for all other students. Beyond that, more significant adjustments will have to be made within the IEP by special teachers.

Under what conditions do IEPs control instruction? Teachers are sometimes confused about this. But this confusion can be clarified by recognizing those areas required by law, or regulation, to be included in the IEP. These are:

- Student's current level of performance
- Annual goals and short-term instructional objectives for the student
- Specific educational service to be provided
- Amount of time student is to spend in regular classes, or experiences to occur with nonhandicapped peers
- Dates and duration of services
- Criteria and evaluation procedures
- A review, on at least an annual basis, for determining if the objectives are being met

Note that regular class instruction is only in relation to the specific time and experiences in the regular class. The assumption is that those instructional activities in regular education will be determined by the *regular curriculum*. Thus, those goals, objectives, and instructional strategies to be used by the regular educator need not be incorporated into the IEP.

In her description of an effective mainstreaming strategy, Demers (1981) recommends an excellent rule to follow when assimilating mainstreamed students into the content areas—*place the student in the regular program after achievement in that content area is at least within the middle range of the regular class*. This rule allows for some loss in performance when students are placed in the mainstream without their slipping into a failure situation.

However, if an IEP requires modifying regular class curriculum or instructional methods within the mainstream class, then short-term objectives for regular class instruction must be shown in the IEP. Under these circumstances, the regular teacher's activities with the mainstreamed student is governed by the IEP.

Regardless of your status as a regular or special teacher—whether you use the IEP as a planning document or not, assessment information should be the basis for planning instruction.

PLANNING FROM ASSESSMENT INFORMATION

After students' IEPs are developed teachers will still need to have an ongoing system of assessment for short-term instructional decisions. This information may be obtained, as discussed in Chapter 4, from students' files, test results, permanent products, and direct observations. This system of assessment, planning, teaching, and evaluating is based upon sound instructional decisions throughout the process. Such decisions will invariably have to be made by teaching personnel.

Much forethought should be given to instructional decisions because a considerable investment in time and effort, on both the teachers' and students' parts, occurs as a result. Although individual teachers will vary the process used to arrive at decisions, there are some basic considerations that are likely to improve decision making.

At least six sequential factors should be considered when arriving at instructional decisions:

Placement → Goals → Objectives →
Instructional Time → Availability of Resources →
Student's Achievement.

Placement. First, consider students' educational placements. Review their IEPs. This review should be done even if you are not the special education teacher; you will want to have a clear understanding of how the special instruction relates to your responsibilities.

If you are responsible for some part of the special instruction, examine the IEP in terms of your role. Or if you are a regular classroom teacher with mainstreamed students in your class, look at their IEPs *in relation* to your role. Is any part of the special instruction designed to supplement your teaching? That is, will supplementary tutoring or instruction be provided in subject or skill areas in which you are teaching these students? If the answer is yes, you should plan your regular instruction *after* having discussed with the special teacher what exactly is being done with these students.

Goals. Carefully examine the instructional goals contained in the IEP. In Figure 5.1, these are found under the heading *Prioritized Long Term Goals*. The IEP format used in your school may differ—but somewhere in the IEP, goals will be shown. The manner in which these goals are prioritized can be important. For example, consider these long-term goals:

1. Reduce maladaptive social behavior.

2. Increase word attack skills.

3. Raise reading performance.

Note, in the above example, the first long-term goal is critical to the next two and can be related to the first and second goals in the instructional planning. The special education teacher responsible for reading and social skills instruction may wish to interrelate goals 1, 2, and 3 by selecting social behavior instruction that involves reading. Since reducing maladaptive social behavior has the highest priority, it should consume a corresponding amount of the special instructional time for that student. An efficient approach is to interrelate social skill instruction with reading.

An Example[1]

Objective:

THE STUDENT GAINS ATTENTION FROM A PEER BY SAYING THE PEER'S NAME IN A VOICE APPROPRIATE TO THE SETTING AND BY TELLING WHAT HE/SHE WANTS.

Social Modeling

1. Identify a need for the behavior through classroom discussion. Teacher may begin by posing questions, such as, "If you need to talk to one of your classmates, how could you do so without disturbing anybody else?" "Why do you think we should have a rule about yelling across the room?"

2. Identify specific behaviors to be modeled. When you want to get the attention of a classmate:

(a) Call him/her by name in an appropriate tone of voice, and
(b) tell him/her what you want.

3. Model the behavior for the class. Teacher may first demonstrate the incorrect way to gain attention of the person to whom he/she wants to speak.

Example

(a) Teacher may address student—snapping his/her fingers—"Hey you, come here. I want to use your pencil."
(b) Teacher whistles and gestures with hand to student, "Come over here, you."

Next, the teacher explains to students that these ways of getting attention are inconsiderate and disturbing. Teacher calls on students individually to demonstrate a better way of:

(a) borrowing a pencil,
(b) asking student to come to the teacher's desk.

4. Allow each student to practice the behavior. Set up situations for each student to properly gain a classmate's attention.

5. Recognize those students who demonstrate appropriate behavior in role playing.

6. Maintain appropriate behaviors for gaining attention from peers through social reinforcement.

Note: For those students for whom peer attention is highly reinforcing and who resort to inappropriate means of seeking it, in addition to being taught appropriate ways to gain attention by addressing others, it may be necessary to provide opportunities for obtaining peer attention in the natural enviornment. For example, the student can be taught to demonstrate something to the class or can be called on to perform something he/she does well.

Related Reading Texts
Publisher: Ginn
Title: The Dog Next Store
Series: Reading 360, First Edition, 1969, page 264.

[1]From *Social Skills in the Classroom* by Thomas M. Stephens. Columbus: Cedars Press, 1978. Pages 167-169. Reprinted with permission of the author and publisher.

In the above example, the teacher can incorporate reading experiences into the social behavior instruction. Although this instruction will not eliminate the need for goals 2 and 3, it does provide additional opportunities for students to practice reading skills. Dreyer (1977) provides a useful reference for teachers who want to interrelate their instruction in this way.

Objectives. Short-term objectives are shown within the implementation plan of the IEP (See Figure 5.2). Objectives are statements of intent describing a proposed change in a learner and showing what the learner will be like after successfully completing a learning experience (Mager, 1962).

Objectives vary widely not only in content but also in format. Precisely stated objectives written in performance terms are more useful in planning than are general statements written in nonbehavioral terms. Consider these objectives:

STUDENT WILL READ QUESTIONS WITH PROPER EMPHASIS.

STUDENT WILL RAISE VOICE PITCH WHEN A QUESTION MARK APPEARS AT THE END OF A SENTENCE.

Which of these objectives indicates exactly what the student will do after achieving the objective? Which is observable? Since the second objective meets both requirements, it can facilitate instruction because the teacher knows exactly which behaviors the student will demonstrate when learning has occurred. The social behavior objective shown earlier is also an example of a measureable objective.

Instructional Time. Planning must include time considerations. How much instructional time is available for teaching the mainstreamed student? Since the amount of time on task is often directly related to learning, the answer to this question will reveal how much can be reasonably achieved by the teacher.

Resources. In planning instructional activities, teachers also consider the human and material resources available to them. The presence of a teacher's aide, peer tutoring, and other assistance can be factored into the plan. These human resources should be related to the objectives and the student's schedule. Special education teachers should have a wide variety of instructional materials available to them. They should consider the student's interests and motivation as well as level of functioning when selecting appropriate materials to meet an objective.

Sometimes teachers will find it necessary to modify existing materials or develop their own to achieve certain objectives. Regular classroom teachers may find that the use of nontextbook materials will help diversify instruction for mainstreamed students as well as for the other students. In the following example, a high-school social studies teacher uses a newspaper item to build the class's interest as well as to differentiate instruction. This approach permits teachers to be responsive to the wide range of reading levels often found among older students.

An Example

Using a daily newspaper as the instructional medium, a high-school social studies teacher clipped out an article from the financial section that provided considerable information about *farm subsidies.*

1. She briefly introduced the topic and related it to textbook readings that had been previously covered. She asked leading questions to encourage student participation. During the discussion she wrote terms that were being used on the chalkboard.
2. She introduced the news item and placed on the chalkboard other terms that students would encounter in the article. She then reviewed with the class the words on the chalkboard and orally gave definitions and examples of each.
3. Although all students were given the same news item to read, she differentiated the assignments: (a) one group of students was asked to record other terms related to the topic that were not on

the chalkboard; (b) others were asked to identify issues concerning the farm subsidy program; and (c) the last group was asked to write questions derived from the article's content.

4. After students were given about 20 minutes to read the article and complete their assignments, the teacher conducted a short discussion concerning the assignment. With students' assistance, she added to the list of terms on the chalkboard. Selected students presented the issues that they had identified and read a few of the questions they developed. The session ended with two students volunteering to lead discussions at the next class meeting. One student would lead a discussion advocating continued farm subsidies; the other agreed to lead a discussion of reasons for abolishing farm supports.

Achievement. Planning should recognize students' achievement levels. Test scores and teachers' assessments, as described in Chapter 4, are sources for this information. As a general rule, reading materials in the content areas should be at least one grade level below that indicated by test scores.

Other basic skill achievement information permits teachers to develop plans that build on students' strengths. Where actual performance is significantly lower than test scores suggest, teachers should plan with that lower functioning in mind. In this way, students are not being forced to work at their frustration levels for prolonged periods of time. In some situations it is appropriate to circumvent that skill barrier by providing alternative means to learn, for example, using a recording to provide information that is contained in a reading assignment, or teaching a student who has a severe arithmetic deficiency to use a hand calculator.

INVOLVING STUDENTS IN PLANNING

Try to involve students when planning their learning experiences. Special education teachers should use the IEP as the framework within which planning can occur while other teachers should use the curriculum that is typically provided for the mainstreamed students and their age-grade peers. The nature and extent of student involvement will vary with age, maturity, motivation, and understanding.

It is probably easier for teachers *not* to involve their students when planning instruction (and there *are* several other ways to build student interests). In doing so however, they may be sacrificing learning for efficiency. Remember this widely accepted learning principle: *students' interests are accelerated with an increase in their involvement.* Involving students in planning their learning experiences provides them with a feeling of ownership in the teaching-learning process, in addition to building interest by involving them in planning. Personal responsibility and commitment to

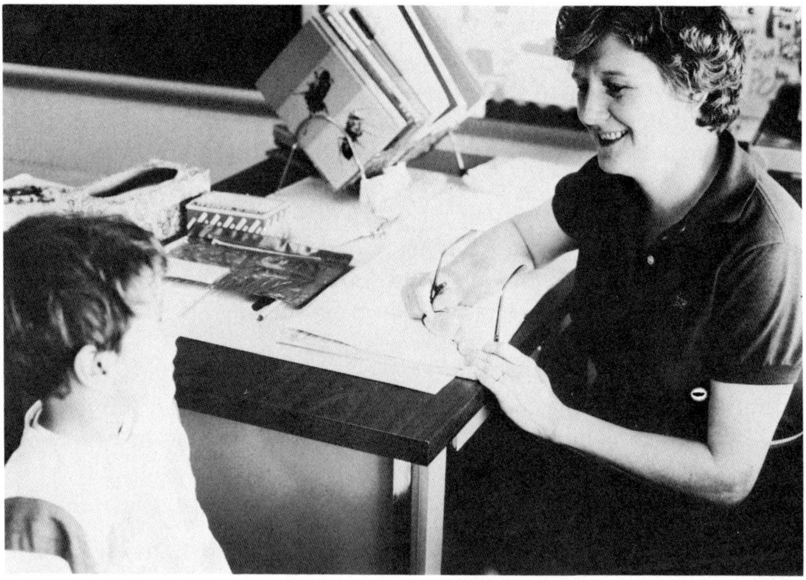

Effective teachers involve students in planning for their instruction.

learning tend to grow. Students may learn *how* to learn and you may be able to identify greater options for achieving instructional objectives.

Considerations. Certain factors among students and teachers should be considered when determining the extent of students' involvement in planning. Students vary widely in their readiness to be involved in instructional planning and this variability is not necessarily related to their ages and types of handicapping conditions. Level of understanding and their motivation to participate are two important considerations.

To some extent all students, regardless of their readiness, should participate in planning. Provisions for interaction among students and teachers is, in a sense, one aspect of sound classroom management. Stephens (1980) suggests that teachers answer four questions to determine how well they encourage interactions: *Are students involved in planning? Do constructive interactions among students take place? How frequently? Are students encouraged to participate and to ask questions?* Guidelines regarding student involvement are contained in Appendix E, page 329.

When involving students in planning, teachers should have clear guidelines in mind. Instead of asking *What do you want to learn today*? provide information about objectives to be achieved, feedback as to progress in learning, and choices that might involve alternative activities for achieving objectives, or even objectives to work toward when such options are reasonable.

One way to help students make intelligent decisions about their learning activities is to show them how to collect ongoing performance data as shown in Figure 5.3. They can maintain this information themselves and record new performance data on a regular basis. In Figure 5.3, Jerry M. recorded his performance data in four subject areas. At the end of each unit of study, he recorded the results of the end-of-the-unit test. One can readily identify, as Jerry did, that reading and language were his most difficult areas. Because arithmetic and spelling were his stronger areas, Jerry recognized the importance of assigning more time to the weaker areas. He was also able to see that, like most students, he had both strengths and weaknesses in his academic work.

Charting of academic performance can also be used to encourage students by displaying gains that they are making. Had Jerry's profile form included preunit test results as well as postunit results he could have seen the gains made following each unit of work.

Planning within Groups. Group planning is most desirable for those students who participate in discussions and who seemingly learn social behavior from group participation. Those students who are reluctant to participate in groups and tend not to imitate group behavior may initially need one-on-one planning sessions with teachers.

Speculating about students' readiness to engage in planning is unnecessary: Assess their planning readiness by providing them with age-appropriate, short-term goals and ask them for suggestions in reaching those goals.

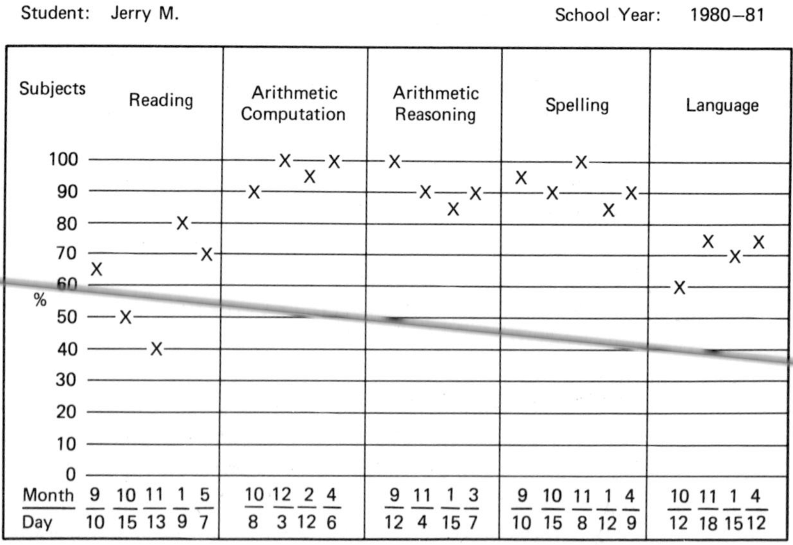

Figure 5.3 Profile form for recording performance information.

An Example

Teacher: (addressing a group of eight-year-olds) How many of you would like to do better in your spelling work? (seeing a high positive response) Well, it is good that so many of you children want to learn how to spell better. I am going to pronounce some words, as I say them you try to write them. This is not a test and it is not likely that you can correctly spell all of these words, but do your best.

Teacher: (following the spelling "test" and providing correct spellings) How many of you misspelled some of these words?

Teacher: (following discussion) There are some things that you can do to learn to spell better. Here is one way. (teacher describes and demonstrates a practice exercise) How many of you want to use this way to learn how to spell better? (noting a high positive response) Alright, let's talk about ways you can practice spelling words.

In the above example, the teacher engaged a group in planning. By carefully guiding the students, it was possible to determine their level of responsiveness. Those students who did not participate and seemingly did not follow the discussion will require small group or individual planning sessions with the teacher.

Note that once students had indicated their willingness to learn how to spell better, the teacher began discussing ways they could learn to spell. At this point, it is important to establish the fact that some individuals learn differently than others. The concept of individual differences should be taught. For example, with young children have them point out obvious differences among individuals and lead them to recognize that an investment of time and effort may be more necessary for some than for others in certain subject areas. Through discussion lead them to see that differences are expected within natural environments. This concept is most important among young children who often believe that differences denote inferiority instead of uniqueness.

After students select the ways they want to learn, they should be taught how to evaluate what they have learned from these activities. Once more teachers will find charts useful for students to record their progress. These records might include a space for students to write the amount of time used in each activity. Later, with the charts completed, students can be shown how to select activities to achieve specific goals. As students begin to differentiate activities and examine such factors as time consumed, achievement (e.g., number of words correctly spelled), and the effects of different approaches, they will be able to become more independent learners.

Teacher-pupil planning has the potential for long-term effects. Such activities should be thought through by teachers to achieve the best results. The critical point to recognize here is that when such involvement occurs, students are more likely to view learning as an activity that requires *their participation* rather than something that happens *to them*.

TEACHING MAINSTREAMED STUDENTS

In this section, you view Jeff from two perspectives—that of the regular classroom teacher and that of the special education teacher.

JEFF IN THE MAINSTREAM

It is the beginning of a new school year and you now face 25 students who have been placed with you for instruction. One of them, Jeff, is a mainstreamed student. You look at his IEP.

You note, from the Total Service Plan portion of the IEP that Jeff is expected to be in your class 15 hours each week. The remaining time he receives special supplementary instruction in reading and adaptive physical education. Clearly, the IEP suggests that he will receive all other instruction from you.

For the next few days you resolve to observe him during the time he is with you to determine how much help he may need, and to talk with the resource room teacher and the adaptive physical education teacher to find out what more you should know about him and what additional experiences you might provide for him during the three hours each day that he is in your class.

Following your observations and discussions with the two teachers you conclude that Jeff is not *that* much different from some of your other students. Reading and poor physical coordination are his major problems and he will receive special instruction in those areas. You are determined to help him adjust in your class and you select ways to work around his reading difficulties.

JEFF IN SPECIAL EDUCATION

You are the special education teacher responsible for one of the resource rooms. Jeff spends each day with you. On Monday, Wednesday, and Friday, he is in your resource room from 9:45 A.M. to 11:45 A.M. But on Tuesdays and Thursdays, he leaves at 10:45 A.M. for adaptive physical education. Since he is with you primarily for reading instruction, you examine the long-term goals and find those that relate to reading.

The goals are general:

IMPROVE READING WORD ATTACK SKILLS, INCLUDING SIGHT WORDS.

ENCOURAGE HIM TO DEVELOP AN INTEREST IN READING.

His IEP was developed over the summer months, before you were employed. You note that the standardized reading test score is at a late first grade level, even though Jeff is almost 10 years old and has consistently tested in the average range of intelligence.

You conduct an informal reading assessment with special attention to the two goals. From your assessment, you establish short-term objectives that you will try to achieve within the next two weeks. Here are your objectives for Jeff:

Phonetic Word Parts. Point to the letter combinations *ing, in, en* in a word when given the sound orally and shown a word card.

Point to the letter combinations *at, ake, all* in a word when given the sound orally and shown a word card.

Point to the letter combinations *ot, old, ould* in a word when given the sound orally and shown a word card.

Say the sound of *ing, in, en* when shown the letter combinations on a word card.

Say the sound of *at, ake, all* when shown the letter combinations on a word card.

Say the sound of *ot, old, ould* when shown the letter combinations on a word card.

Say the sound *ing, in, en* when shown the letter combinations in a word.

Say the sound *at, ake, all* when shown the letter combinations in a word.

Say the sound *ot, old, ould* when shown the letter combinations in a word.

Reading Interest. Listen to a story as it is read.

Now you develop the teaching strategies to meet those objectives.

You plan to use a task analysis approach. The manner in which you have established your objectives for teaching the phonetic word parts reflects that strategy. Being a strong believer in using natural reinforcers, you also plan to reward Jeff for his efforts by reading portions from an adventure story to him toward the end of each daily session. You are also using this same reward for the other four children who will be in the resource room at that time. Thus, you are wisely working toward the second goal and helping him to meet the second objective.

After identifying the instructional materials you will use and recording them on the IEP, you are now ready to teach Jeff. But wait!

Teaching is more than techniques, rewards, and establishing objectives. It also involves *human interactions*—helping students learn about themselves and others, and learning how to learn. So early in the first week, you have a group discussion with Jeff and the four other students.

You encourage them to talk about themselves, their hopes and expectations. Gradually, you explain what you are about—that you can help them learn but you cannot learn for them, that they can help themselves as much as you can help them, that each person is different and may learn in different ways, that there are a few rules to follow, and that you want them to work together and help each other.

You also *tell* them something about a story showing them the book as you talk. Stopping at an exciting place, ask what *they* think will happen next. Accepting all answers but not giving away what really happens then ask, "Would you like me to read some more of this story?"

Because they *do* want you to read more, you read what *really* happened and then say: "Toward the end of each time we are working, if each of you have tried hard, I'll read a little to you. Tomorrow, I'll let you help me choose which book you want me to read from next week." You have begun to teach!

SPECIFIC INSTRUCTIONAL TECHNIQUES

Teachers have only recently started to use scientific methods. When we began using scientific knowledge in teaching, there were naturally differences regarding the importance it should assume, procedures to follow, and models to copy. In the light of such differences, the best way to begin your practice is to *master one model thoroughly*. Thus, your ideas will be consistent and your knowledge will develop in an orderly way. As you become more competent, you can use your system as a model for testing new concepts and for arranging new knowledge. When the new ideas seem more desirable than the old, or if the old model cannot accommodate to new situations, you can change your model accordingly. If you begin otherwise, by trying incompatible applications or by using conflicting concepts, you will become confused and ineffective as well as physically exhausted. Remember it is always better to be wrong than confused—errors can be corrected but confusion is unending. It is with this belief firmly in mind that we consider task analysis and five related techniques for teachers that can help students learn.

These techniques are sequential and are used to meet certain performance outcomes.

Step	***Technique***	***Result***
1	Task Analysis	Tasks are divided into subtasks.
2	Shaping	Responses are shaped toward terminal behavior.
3	Demonstrating	Responses are demonstrated for student.
4	Imitating	Student imitates response.
5	Producing	Student produces response.
6	Practicing	Student practices response.

Step 1: Task Analysis. Return to the objectives established for Jeff. Now, notice these:

- *point* to the letter combinations,
- *say* the sounds when shown the letter combinations word card.

And these:

- when given the sound *orally*,
- when *shown* the letter combinations.

And these:

- when shown a *word* card,
- when shown the *letter* combinations on a card.

Note in the first set, Jeff must first *point* and then *say*. In the second set he is given the sound and then shown the letter combinations. In the third set, he is shown a word first and then shown letter combinations. His expected responses have been divided—broken down in such a way that will increase his chances of responding correctly. You are proceeding from easier tasks to harder ones.

It is wise to begin instruction with tasks of moderate difficulty (Valett, 1970). First, have students try completing the task. Note where they have difficulty and begin your analysis around that point. Second, divide tasks into natural units—remember that the smallest units may not be instructionally valuable ones, for example, divide words into sound-syllables units, not simply by letters.

Step 2: Shaping. Shaping is the process of reinforcing responses that make up the terminal behavior. This process involves the use of task analysis since the terminal behavior is divided into subtasks before shaping begins. In successive steps, with reinforcement occurring after each step or response, the behavior is shaped toward the outcome performance.

An Example[2]

Scotty, a ten-year-old, is uncooperative when requested to perform certain academic tasks. Observations of his reactions to reading instruction are shown in Figure 5.4. His positive and negative reactions are summarized by two plus (+) signs and one minus (−) symbol. It should be pointed out that the word level of the story was two years below his demonstrated reading level (early 5th grade), otherwise, the example could lead one to infer incorrectly that the reading level of the story was too difficult for Scotty.

Recorded observations indicate that Scotty willingly listened to the story and behaved appropriately. He also engaged in a discussion concerning the story with his teacher. He was unwilling to read aloud, however, when pressed to read he kicked and shouted. In other words, there are elements of reading instruction in which Scotty already participates without objection; but oral reading, which is viewed by his teacher as important, is not willingly engaged in by Scotty. In order to change Scotty's responses when requested to read aloud, certain procedures should be followed by the teacher.

Mr. James, the teacher, should first establish the social learning task. It can be shown as:

Task	***Criterion***
Read aloud a story at an easy third grade level.	Reads the story aloud without objections.

He must then answer the question: Which behaviors will progressively lead toward the fulfillment of this task? These behaviors are then viewed as short-term goals which serve to meet the final outcome. Because criterion for completion of the task is specified in behavioral terms, Mr. James will know at which point Scotty has successfully completed the task.

A succession of tasks was devised in order to encourage Scotty to read orally. Note that at each point Scotty was reinforced. In this example, verbal praise ("Very good" and "That's fine") are used as rewards, while a wink is paired with these as a potential reward.

Task number 7 is the desired outcome and is arrived at by carefully reinforcing previous steps while gradually modifying demands of each succeeding task. The management strategy that was used in teaching each task will not be described here but some of the factors that Mr. James recognized as important are mentioned.

Scotty was given a choice of three books from which he was permitted to choose one. The books were written at a third grade reading level but the interest level was aimed at ten and eleven-year-old boys. Each text contained a series of stories that represented chapters involving the same main characters, making it easier for Scotty to

Tasks	***Criteria***	***Rewards***	***Rate***
1. Listen to a story that is read.	listens without disruptive behavior	"very good" wink	at completion of task
2. Listen and hold book while story is read.	same as 1, plus holds book	"that's fine" wink	at completion of task
3. Same as 2, plus answers questions about the story.	same as 2, plus tries to answer questions	same as 2	at completion of task and after each answer
4. Same as 3, plus locates answers to the question in the story; (after each paragraph a question will be asked).	same as 3, plus locates answers in the story	same as 3	at completion of task and after each answer
5. Same as 3, plus locates and reads answers to the questions after each paragraph.	same as 3, plus locates and reads answers	"very good" wink	after reading correct answer
6. Alternates with teacher in reading paragraphs of the story.	takes turn reading willingly	"that's fine" wink	after reading each selection
7. Reads entire story aloud.	reads the story aloud without objections	wink "very good"	after every paragraph; midway through the story; and at completion

recall names of leading characters and their experiences. The serial format helped to maintain his interest. Mr. James also used pictures in the text as "coming attractions" by encouraging Scotty to examine the pictures in the forthcoming story at the close of each session.

Each social learning task was designed to be achieved in one session if possible, although the sequence did not prevent devoting as many sessions as necessary until criterion for each task was met. In instances when criterion was not achieved, the subsequent session was devoted to that task. Scotty was expected to achieve a task only after the preceding one had been demonstrated. At completion of the sixth step, winking by Mr. James had acquired power as a reinforcer and was used as one in the final session.

[2]From *Directive Teaching of Children with Learning and Behavioral Handicaps* by *Thomas M. Stephens*. Columbus, Ohio: Charles Merrill, 1970. Pages 148–150.

REACTIONS TO INSTRUCTIONS

Child:	Scotty	Age:	10–2
Date:	November 15	Setting:	Resource Room
Observer:	Mr. James	Time of day:	From 9:15 to 10:05

REACTIONS TO INSTRUCTIONS

Activities		Reactions
Oral reading: Scotty was asked to read a story that I read to him yesterday.	–	He said he didn't want to read, when I said: "I read to you yesterday. It's your turn today," he shouted "No" and began to kick the table.
Listening: I read a new story to him.	+	He became quiet and listened.
Discussion: Scotty talked about the story in response to my questions.	+	He accurately answered three questions about the story and was pleasant.

Figure 5.4 Observations of Scotty's reactions to reading

Step 3: Demonstrating Responses. With modeling as the teaching method, arrange conditions so that the response to be learned is presented correctly as the students attend. Responses may be demonstrated by students or by the teacher. But, it is important that they are demonstrated correctly each time.

An Example

When presented with numeral cards 1 to 100, student will arrange them in natural order.

Teacher: Billy will demonstrate what we are to do. Here are the numeral cards (handing the pack to Billy). Billy will take cards 1 through 12 (Billy selects the 12 cards). He will then place the lowest numeral here (pointing to the ledge).

Billy: This is numeral 1 (as he places it on the ledge).

Teacher: He will now place the next lowest numeral here next to the 1. Teacher proceeds through 12 in the same way.

Step 4: Imitating Responses. Another part of modeling involves encouraging students to imitate responses that were demonstrated. Under your direction, provide students with opportunities to respond. Give reinforcement or correction immediately.

Responses may also be initiated when teachers present models to be traced or copied, or when students are asked to repeat what was said or done.

An Example

Teacher: Now that Billy has arranged his numeral cards correctly from 1 to 12, here is a set of cards for each of you. Find the same cards that Billy used and place them in the same order on your desks as they are on the ledge.

Step 5: Producing Responses. In Step 5, students respond without models present. By responding under the teacher's direction, they can be corrected before incorrect responses are repeated, thus avoiding the cycle of practicing and reinforcing errors.

An Example

Students will say the sound of *at, ake,* and *all* when shown the letter combinations in a word.

Teacher: (teacher provides seven cards, three cards with the letter combinations *at, ake,* and *all* on them, and four cards with letters *b, c, f,* and *m* on them. Holding a *b* card in front of *at* combination card) This is the word *bat.* Say *bat.* (teacher waits for a response) The first letter *b* (holding the *b* apart) gives the word the *b* sound. The *at* (holding up the *at*) gives the word the *at* sound. Say *at.* (teacher waits for a response)

Step 6: Practicing Responses. Students are given opportunities, through assignments, to practice responses. Initially, practice should occur under the general direction of the teacher or with students or aides who have already mastered the task, since students may need some help during practice activities.

At first, opportunities to practice responses should be provided under supervision.

An Example

For practice, the teacher has prepared two large cubes (plastic, wood, or cardboard blocks). On two sides of one cube, each of the endings (*ake, at, all*) have been printed. The letters *b, c, f,* and *m* are printed on sides of the other cube.

Students take turns tossing the cubes and reading the combinations. The game continues until each child has read each of the three combinations twice correctly.

Practice may also be provided through assigned seatwork, games, and homework. Seatwork should always be composed of tasks that the students have already learned, since seatwork often requires them to work alone with a minimum of direct assistance.

Consider several factors when assigning seatwork. First, decide if it is for simple or mixed practice. If students have not yet *mastered* the task, then seatwork should be simple. That is, it should consist of the same level and type of task and require the same type of response (e.g., addition of two place numerals by two place numerals in vertical form with sums below 100).

After students have demonstrated the skill in practice in singular form, mixed practice activities should be assigned. Mixed seatwork assignments consist of tasks that vary somewhat from the original or from a more simple format (e.g., addition of two place numerals in vertical *and* parallel forms with sums below 100). Students who demonstrate difficulty in generalizing to new conditions should be taught the various forms of responding before such items are used in combination. As the students become more proficient, mixed practice seatwork activities may vary greatly, such as combining addition and subtraction problems in both parallel and vertical forms.

Other factors to consider when planning seatwork activities are clarity of instructions, length of assignments, and the relationship of the activities to the terminal behavior. Seatwork has two purposes: (1) to provide opportunities for students to practice skills; and (2) to serve as an evaluation of students' learning. Assignment of tasks that are solely intended to occupy students' time are always inappropriate. Teachers should always provide feedback to students on assigned work. If the activity has not already been learned and is not directly related to the terminal performance, do not assign it!

Games provide another way to provide practice in academic skills. These can create interest and provide students with opportunities to work in small groups. There is a wide assortment of educational games available commercially. In addition there are games that can be developed by teachers to meet specific instructional objectives (Stephens, 1973).

SUMMARY

- Assessment information is used most effectively when teachers proceed in a systematic way.
- Planning should begin by examining the IEP.
- Involve students in planning.
- Develop short-term instructional objectives.
- Instructional objectives should be precisely stated in performance terms.
- Adopt a teaching system that seems effective.
- The teaching system proposed in this chapter involves task analysis and shaping responses. These responses should be demonstrated for the student to imitate, then produced and practiced by the student.

SIX

Classroom Organization and Student Management in the Mainstream

- How can teachers organize their classrooms for managing and teaching students in the mainstream?
- What are the elements of classroom management?
- How can teachers provide direct control of students?
- What are some proven methods and practices for improving student behavior?
- How can teachers evaluate their classroom conditions?

CLASSROOM ENVIRONMENT MANAGEMENT

Classroom management skills form the basic ingredient for successful teaching; all teachers must be effective classroom managers. When mainstreamed students are placed with age-grade peers, classroom management factors become even more critical. Under these mainstreaming conditions, teachers must adapt physical, psychological, and instructional aspects of the classroom to meet mainstreamed students' learning needs. These adaptations can be made successfully by using behavior management techniques. Consider first environmental controls that can be used to improve classroom management.

Control of classroom environments can lead to better learning. Controls relate to classroom grouping procedures and organizational arrangements. Some authorities have also described the importance of planning instructional time in order to facilitate learning (Stephens, 1976). In classrooms, three essential factors for successful teaching are related to environmental controls: structuring the physical environment, structuring the use of time, and organizing students for instruction. *Structure*, in this context, refers to the form of a given activity.

It is important that seats and desks properly fit students, particularly primary and elementary school-aged children. Mainstreamed students often have trouble doing neat written work so their desks and seats must fit properly for maximum support and comfort. Students should always be able to place both feet on the floor with their knees about even with the seat. Desks should be of sufficient height so that they can look down at the desk tops and be able to place their entire arms, from elbow to hands, horizontally on the desks. But the desks should not be so high that students must reach up to use their desk tops.

Desks and chairs that do not fit contribute to discomfort, squirming, fidgeting; thus students may leave their seats frequently. Both posture and behavior can be improved through careful attention to how well desks and chairs fit students of all ages.

Teachers can and do manipulate structures to achieve specific instructional goals. For example, teachers who want to increase students' interactions with other students often arrange seating so that they face one another. Conversely, if you wish to reduce such interactions, seat the students in rows with their backs to each other. The latter arrangement increases teacher interactions with students and discourages students from responding to each other.

Let students know why you have arranged the seating in certain ways. By sharing your objectives with them, you will more likely be successful. For example, say, "I asked you children to sit in rows because you will learn how to calculate these types of problems quicker if you are able to look directly at me while I show you how to do these on the chalkboard." Teachers can organize their instructional time to increase (or decrease) the likelihood that more students will respond and to facilitate learning by increasing it for certain activities and decreasing it for others. Classroom events can be structured so as to encourage or discourage the learning of certain skills and concepts. By encouraging students to engage in particular activities, you are placing a higher value on learning those responses. And by omitting or reducing other activities, you are lowering the probability that students will learn those particular behaviors.

STRUCTURING PHYSICAL FACILITIES

Classroom furniture should be arranged to provide for various learning activities. Figure 6.1 shows a functional use of classroom space and furnishings in a self-contained elementary school room. Provisions are shown for individual work, small group instruction, independent work, time out, and individual rewards.

Figure 6.1 shows that classroom areas are furnished to meet specifically identified instructional needs. At the elementary grade levels these needs may consist of tutoring and individual assessment areas, interest and learning centers, a job board area, and an area for small group instruction.

At the upper grade levels a continued need may exist for many of these same types of activities. Although job boards have been used at junior and senior high-school levels (Stephens, 1975), they are often more effective at the elementary grade levels. Also, more group discussion often occurs at upper grade levels and the arrangement of seats and desks should reflect the emphasis on that activity.

Tutoring and Assessment Area. Mainstreamed students, as well as others who are in need of specific and individual instruction, can receive help quickly in a designated tutoring and assessment area.

A table and two chairs, one for the student and one for the teacher, represent the necessary furniture for tutoring and assessment. It is wise to arrange the seating so that you can sit alongside the student, for assisting and observing students easily. When you need to record information, sit with your writing hand away from the student.

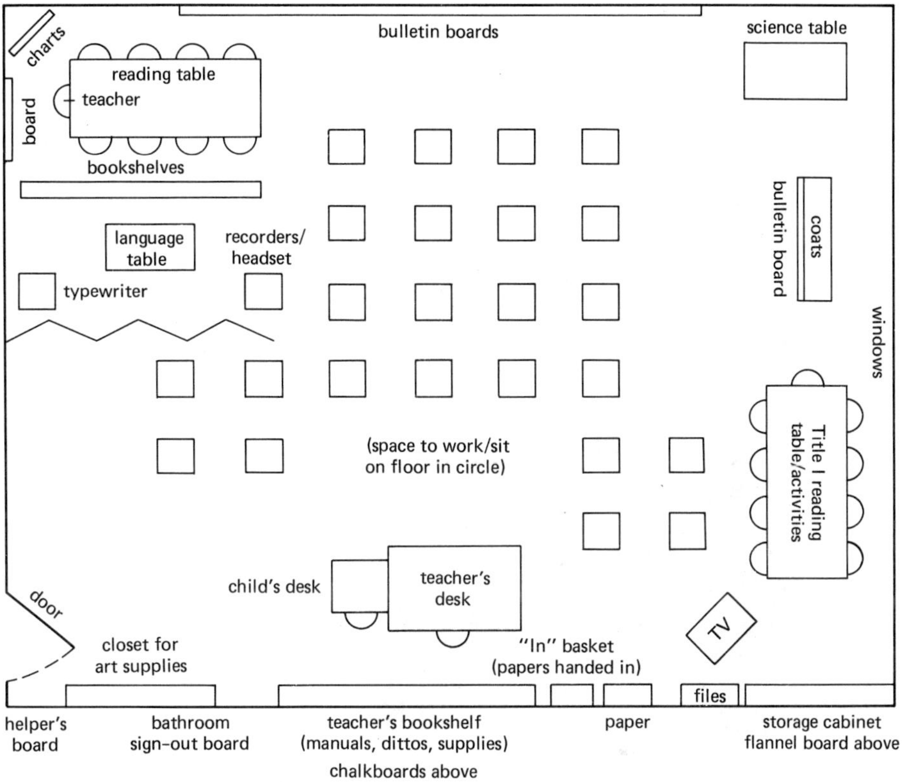

Figure 6.1 Floor plan for self-contained elementary classroom (From Morsink 1981).

Carrels of sufficient width for both student and teacher to be seated side by side are ideal for tutoring and assessing. Carrels are typically panelled on three sides and contain a built-in desk or sufficient space for a table. Students and teachers face the inside panel, thus reducing visual and auditory distractions. Some carrels have built-in lights, shelves, drawers, and some have insulated panels for reducing sound. You can create carrels by placing a table between two cabinets with chairs facing the wall. Cabinet exteriors can be decorated or used as displays to increase their attractiveness.

Individual tutoring and assessment may also be conducted at the teacher's desk. This arrangement, however, does not provide sufficient privacy for students, particularly at the upper grade levels when they are often concerned about peer opinions.

Learning Centers. Learning centers provide assigned tasks for individual students and small groups for practicing skills that have already been learned. These assignments may be in the form of educational games, seatwork assignments, and other paper/pencil tasks. Learning-center time

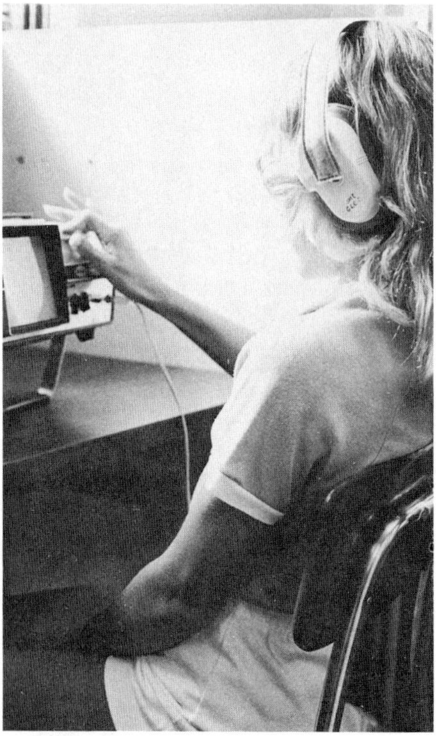

This student is doing an assignment at a carrel to reduce distraction.

should be scheduled and may serve as a station for small groups of students who have already received teacher directed activities. Tables, window-ledges, and other special areas in the room may be designated as learning stations.

Small Group Instructional Area. Small group instruction is necessary at all grade levels and with most subject matter. It provides you with an opportunity to work closely with students and to attend more fully to their instructional needs. Also, students have more opportunities to interact with other students and with teachers within small groups.

Specific areas in classrooms may be designated for small group work. Such an area may consist of a table or desk and chairs. Or, if the room is carpeted, students may lounge on the floor when the activities permit.

At the lower elementary grade levels, small-group work may consist of short-term, specific skill instruction. In such instances, students may come in groups of two to five to a designated area referred to as a *skill table*. Teachers than proceed to provide quick and specific instruction on a single skill. One advantage for conducting this type of instruction in a designated place is that you can keep your supplies and teaching strategies there.

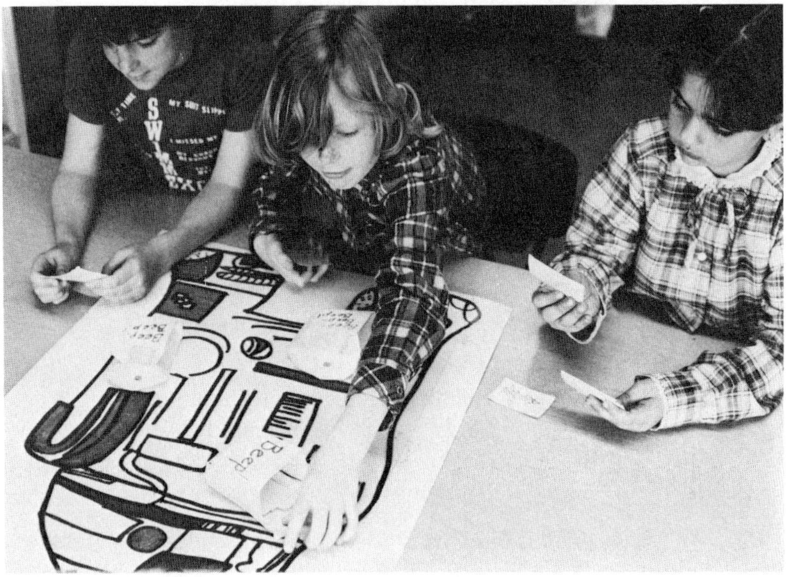

Interest centers that contain educational games can be very useful in teaching mainstreamed students.

As students respond, make a notation next to each child's name, concerning those items missed. This information can then be used for teaching in tutoring sessions or in another small group and it can form the basis for reorganizing groups for needed skill instruction. In the above example, the teacher used flashcards with each card numbered on the back. Each card also had the upper left hand corner clipped off so that the cards could

An Example: *Short-term Skill Instruction*

Objectives:

The student identifies both words that make up a compound word.

Teacher: Take turns reading each word aloud and tell me the two words that it is made from. If you don't know the word say *next to me* and the person on your left will try the word. If someone reads the word incorrectly, I will read it correctly and that person may then say the two words. All right, I will begin: *Airplane*, air and plane."

airplane	redbird	playhouse	housefly
someone	bluebird	something	outdoor
into	onto	playtime	hatbox
doorman	doorstep	daytime	overeat

quickly be placed right side up. Each student's responses were recorded as shown in Figure 6.2.

Incentive Areas. Physical facilities should also include areas of the room for rewards and punishment. Reward areas may consist of displays where students' work can be shown, a job board, and interest centers. A punishment area may contain a space for time-out. *Do not use the same space for both punishment and rewards.*

Interest Centers consist of certain areas in classrooms containing items for students to explore. These may consist of a wide variety of items such as:

Art forms	Film strips
Goldfish	Educational games
Maps	Art materials
Books	Displays
Magazines	Artifacts

These centers provide students with activities during slack classroom times and have been used effectively with students ranging from kindergarten through senior high school. In a contingency contracting system their use will be contingent upon certain previously specified behaviors and performances.

Job boards (Stephens, 1977) show classroom duties that may be purchased by students. In a token system (Steinbeck, Payne, Steinbeck, and Payne, 1973) the jobs represent some of the events that may serve as rewards.

Use *time out* to remove a disruptive child from participation in the classroom. During time out, do not let the child have access to rewards or earn credit toward rewards as in a token economy system (Leitenberg, 1965). At the elementary level the time-out area may simply be a corner of the classroom. A disruptive child is assigned for a brief time interval (not to exceed 10 minutes), screened off from the rest of the class, and not permitted to engage in any activity. It is important that areas of the room that are used for other purposes, such as for tutoring and individual work, are *not* also used for punishment.

TASK: Reading Compound Words from Flashcards

Name	Date	Number of Words missed	Notes
Mary	11/3	7 12	
Fred	11/3	14 9 8	Immature sounds
Jerry	11/3	None	
Sue	11/3	None	

Figure 6.2 A recording form for small group instruction.

CLASSROOM TIME

All teaching occurs within such time structures as hours of school attendance, time devoted to academic subjects, meal and recess times. Some of these time segments are established at the school building level. Others, however, permit you considerable leeway in the amount of time devoted to specific classroom activities.

You can also increase the amount of time students devote to certain activities by rewarding their on-task behavior and through other means. *On task* refers to the amount of time students use for particular assignments. This time can be increased in several ways. For example, by assigning specific chairs and desks to students, time used in selecting seats may be reduced (it also provides a way to assign students to seats and desks that properly fit them).

On-task time should be considered in relation to the amount of time available for an assigned activity. For example, if a mainstreamed student has 30 minutes allotted to an assignment and fails to complete it on time, any of three factors may be contributing to the failure: The student may not possess the prerequisite skills and/or concepts to do the task; the student may not have any incentive for doing the assignment; or the student may have had insufficient time to complete the task. Sometimes all three factors contribute to failure. But these three factors are not always easily seen, as depicted in the following anecdote.

An Example

Mr. Fifer noted that Harold was turning in unfinished assignments at the close of each general math class. Since Harold was a mainstreamed student, Mr. Fifer discussed his observations with Harold's special education, resource room teacher. Based upon what the two could determine, Harold was being assigned math tasks that were within his "instructional range" and he seemed enthusiastic about his math class.

His resource room teacher observed Harold during his assigned seatwork time in Mr. Fifer's class. The observations for five consecutive days were as follows:

Day	*Total Time Allotted*	*On-Task*
1	30 minutes	13 minutes
2	24 minutes	12 minutes
3	18 minutes	6 minutes
4	20 minutes	15 minutes
5	32 minutes	14 minutes
Totals	124 minutes	60 minutes
Averages	24.8 minutes	12 minutes

A stopwatch was used when observing Harold, halting it each time he went off-task and starting it each time he began working. On-task was described as those activities that clearly were related to the assignment (e.g., looking at the textbook, writing responses, erasing, and calculating). Examples of off-task behaviors included sharpening pencils, talking to other students, staring into space and doodling.

Instructional Time. Some teachers increase the usefulness of their classroom time by planning instruction within time blocks, using effective ways to initiate instruction, scheduling rewarding events, and terminating instruction in ways that increase learning.

Regardless of the setting, you can plan how much time to allocate for each instructional activity. First, consider the total amount of time available for an entire period, day, or session. At elementary grade levels where teachers are responsible for the same group of students all day, planned time should encompass the entire day. Starting with students' arrival in the classroom and continuing until they are dismissed at the close of the school day, a time plan for a typical school day may appear as follows:

8:45	Students arrive
8:50	Attendance, announcements, and collection of lunch money
9:00	Opening exercises
9:05	Establish day's goals
9:10	Reading
10:10	Recess and restrooms
10:30	Arithmetic
11:30	Spelling and writing
12:00	Lunch
12:45	Science or Health
1:30	Social studies
2:30	Art or Music or Physical education
3:15	Closing exercises
3:30	Students leave

In settings where students are not with the same teacher all day, such as in resource rooms or at the upper grade levels, a schedule should be established for those times students are present. Specific times should be shown for each activity. The amount of time assigned for specific activities depends upon such factors as the subjects to be taught, ages and attention spans of students, and the objectives to be achieved. With mainstreamed students the Individualized Educational Program (IEP) will include the amount of time assigned for achieving each objective.

Initiating Instruction. Setting occasions for students to begin formal learning can increase instructional time and contribute to more rapid learning. Environmental cues for encouraging students to participate in learning activities is a way to increase instructional time. All people have within their environments stimuli that cue them for responding in certain ways. For example, safe automobile drivers automatically slow their vehicles when they see a caution signal ahead. Similarly, polite people thank others for small courtesies (e.g. holding doors, stepping aside, or helping them in some way). Both the caution signal and the assistance serve as *cues* for people who were conditioned to respond in certain ways.

Since cues are learned, teachers should purposely teach their students how to respond when selective stimuli are present. This type of instruction can improve classroom management and will thus facilitate the mainstreaming of handicapped students.

Instructional time is often lost in situations where students arrive prior to the beginning of class, such as is common at the lower grade levels when announcements and/or collection of money must occur. You can use a bonus system for encouraging students to practice skills and for setting occasions for proper classroom behavior. A bonus basket may also be used as shown in this example.

An Example

Mr. Blum saves all seatwork which he has assigned to his class. Each assignment is coded and filed separately along with an answer key. Prior to the beginning of each school day he places about 30 different sheets from his file into the *bonus basket.* A number is placed at the top of each sheet representing the amount of points students may earn for completing that assignment. Numbers range from 1 to 50 depending upon the level of difficulty for each assignment.

Students are then informed that when they arrive in class, or at any other time during the day when they have time, they may select a worksheet. After the assignment has been completed they place the sheet in another basket.

Students who purchase the job of *bonus basket director* score the sheets using the answer keys that are on file. Sometimes Mr. Blum permits trustworthy students to correct their own sheets, thus providing immediate knowledge of responses to the students.

Special events, such as opening exercises, assist students to prepare for instruction. Opening exercises serve to separate loosely structured time from what is to follow. An opening event is a means of gaining the entire group's attention. These may consist of patriotic or group activities such as singing, saluting the flag, reading a poem or "a thought for the day."

Teachers may also use a signal for eliciting students' attention. Flashing the room lights, playing the piano, or blowing a whistle are types of signals. Students should be instructed as to what they are to do when the signal appears. Information, however, is not a very effective way to change students' behavior. Thus, *telling* them what they are to do when the signal appears will often not be enough. Sometimes teachers are inconsistent in what they expect and may resort to nagging students who fail to adhere to signals. Students' attention to cues can be increased by following this sequence:

1. Inform students as to how they are expected to respond when the signal for obtaining their attention is issued.
2. Have selected students repeat the instructions in their own words.
3. Repeat the signal and have students *perform* their expected reactions.
4. Occasionally provide positive consequences when the entire group responds to the signal correctly.

Providing students with information concerning what they are to accomplish and showing them a time sequence will increase their cooperation. Such information may take the form of student objectives (e.g., "Today each student should have completed two practice sheets in reading before noon). When it is possible for you to conduct individualized instruction, objectives should be specified for each student. Remember target students must always have objectives that are tailored for them.

One way to personalize instruction is to post under each student's name a menu of relevant and related objectives. Students may select those they wish to achieve during a given segment of time. They may also select from the reward menu events they wish to earn. In this way they *write their own contract* and develop self-control.

Reward Time. All students need encouragement—some more than others. When encouragement takes the form of activities or other rewards that consume time, this time should be controlled through careful planning. Effective reward structures in classrooms do indeed take some time. Yet, they are essential for encouraging students to achieve instructional objectives.

Reward time may be scheduled for all students at specific times. Or, rewarding events may be scheduled for individual students at different times. When reward time is scheduled for all students, those who are ineligible or those who elect not to participate must continue with classroom work.

You should incorporate some reward time into the classroom schedule irrespective of the presence of mainstreamed students. There is little doubt that planned breaks of rewarding events tend to increase students' interest in learning as well as their motivation.

Reward time should be scheduled at least once per day. With younger children, or those performing at very low levels, it is often necessary to schedule rewards more frequently. Scheduled rewards may occur at times in the school program when students have already participated in learning. Avoid scheduling rewards early in the school day or early in an instructional period. Planned reward times should generally not exceed 15 minutes. Stephens (1976) allotted 10 minutes for a short reward time at mid-morning and another prior to class dismissal time for students with learning and behavioral disorders.

> Mini-Reward Time. This is a time for drinks and restroom breaks. It can also be used as a reward time with a structured independent game for groups or individual children; use it as a time for each child to choose a job from the job board to be done at the end of the day. (p. 46)

> Maxi-Reward Time. This is the time when the children are rewarded with a major reward or task for behavior contracted earlier in the day. (p. 48)

Individual students may also elect to purchase reward time between tasks. With this plan students should simply notify you (or the student in charge of rewards) and a timer is set for the time purchased. They then can proceed to that area of the room containing their preferred reward (e.g., interest center). When the timer rings they must discontinue the rewarding event and return to an assigned task.

Reviewing and Evaluating Instruction. Time should be planned for students to review and evaluate their activities. In reviewing, students may orally report what they did and what they think was learned. Sometimes a brief group discussion can be conducted by teachers or students regarding what the class learned. At other times, it may be more appropriate if you ask students to give short, individual reports. In the latter situations, have all students take turns in reporting their progress but not, of course, in the same day. Be sure to include your mainstreamed students in the review activities.

At least three benefits are derived from students discussing their learning. First, they can reexperience the learning by using language to describe it. Second, their descriptions serve as verbal models for other students. And third, the importance of learning and being able to identify what is learned are both highlighted.

Students should be encouraged to evaluate their own learning since they should judge themselves by what they have accomplished. Self-evaluation can be part of the review time. They should be trained to evaluate their activities in comparison to stated outcomes.

Student: This morning I wanted to get all of these problems in dividing common fractions correct. I can divide these types of problems but I wanted to get them all right. I got all 15 of these problems correct.

Student: My goal today was to spell correctly five words from my "error list." I studied them this morning and again after lunch. Jack gave me this test and I got them all right.

Student: All day I tried to finish each assignment on time. I did finish all six. Tomorrow I am going to try to get all assignments done on time again and get them all right too!

Sometimes students do not achieve their objectives and careful guidance from the teacher is needed.

Student: I wanted to get 100 percent on all of my work today but I missed some of my reading seatwork.

Teacher: You seem disappointed.

Student: I feel dumb, like I'll never get everything all right.

Teacher: You came close, getting everything right is very hard to do. You got all but one thing right. Keep up the good work. See if you can get *almost* everything correct again tomorrow.

Discussions may also focus on evaluating the group's performance and/or behavior. When evaluation is directed at the group, begin the day or period by helping them to identify a behavior or academic task that they will make a special effort learning.

Students often demand 100 percent accuracy on tasks they have identified. It may be necessary to help them recognize that accomplishments

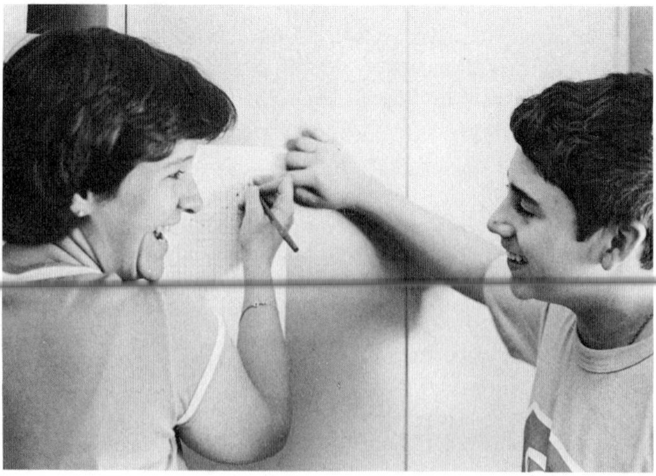

Visual records of performance help students to evaluate their progress.

are often incremental and mastery does not always come quickly or easily. Self-charting is one way to help students view progress on an incremental basis. Show them how to develop a chart so that they can record their progress each day. Gains and losses provide natural opportunities for teachers to guide students, to help them to acquire patience, and to rejoice in their small, steady, and significant achievements.

Terminating Instruction. Closure is important for learning; so schedule time for ending a school day or period. While only a short amount of time need be used for this purpose, good study habits can be taught at this time and preparation for the next instructional day can take place.

Although large portions of students' time are spent in solitary study, there is little attention given to that aspect of learning. Mainstreamed students, in particular, often require structure and direction for their assignments. These can be provided as a part of terminating instruction. But be careful to avoid lecturing or nagging as a means of instructing students in study skills. Follow these procedures:

1. Provide verbal instructions, be certain that all students follow these directions.

2. Practice the behavior; that is, have the students actually rehearse studying. For example, if you want them to use outlining in studying, have the students outline a passage from their texts. Discuss their completed outlines, pointing out similarities and differences.

3. Provide help, during the practice, for correcting any mistakes. Remember immediate correction is the best way to remediate. Following correction, have them practice the activity again using steps 1 through 3. Continue in this way until the practice session is perfected.

Once study skills have been acquired, use positive reinforcement from time to time to encourage students in their use.

After reviewing the day, take a little time to recognize students for their accomplishments that day, and remind them about what they are expected to do in preparation for the next school day. Questions students may have regarding that preparation should be answered and the group should then be dismissed.

In settings such as resource room programs, where individual students leave at different times, other ways of terminating instruction can be used. Notes in students' learning packets, brief checkout sessions with the teacher, or regularly scheduled teacher-pupil conferences may be used to instruct students in study habits, to encourage them in their efforts, and to emphasize the importance of completing their individual assignments.

ORGANIZING STUDENTS FOR INSTRUCTION

The Individualized Education Program (IEP) will indicate when and where to assign mainstreamed students for instruction. But you will often find that subgrouping within the class is necessary. Subgrouping within your classroom for academic instruction should be based upon students' specific academic performances, the amount of special assistance needed, the rate of completion of daily assignments, interpersonal skills, achievement levels, and other similar types of behavior. As a general rule, subgrouping for instruction should be based upon relevant skill performances rather than on aptitude or other predictive measures.

Within standard classroom-size groups, you can also create stations for individuals and for small groups. These stations may consist of interest centers, learning centers, or other content centers that will extend learning beyond direct teacher instruction. Rawson (1971) in recommending the use of classroom stations also suggested that subgroups should seldom exceed six students and, as a rule, the more severe students' learning problems are, the smaller the group should be.

Temporary Grouping. All subgrouping within classrooms should be temporary. Students should be assigned to small groups for specific instruction. As their skills improve, they should be reassigned within the classroom to other groups. Teaching within small groups may focus on academic skills and concepts and/or social skills and attitudes. Information for assigning students to the various subgroups should be derived from your observations of individual students.

A skill oriented curriculum permits the coding of each skill. Students can be assigned to temporary groups on the basis of skills they are to learn. By coding the skills, teachers can cross-index students' names with the skill number. Each skill number is recorded on a vertical file folder. As assessment information about individual students is collected by the teacher, students' names are placed in the appropriate skill files. When that skill is to be taught, teachers may assign those students whose names are in the coded folder to the instructional group.

Student files set up by teachers for instructional purposes have been described by Stephens (1975). An alphabetical file by students' last names forms the core of the filing system. Cross-referencing by instructional variables is done by using color tabs and/or numbers. These tabs are clipped on each student's folder and are easily removed when students are assigned to other subgroups.

Subject matter teachers in the upper grade levels tend to subgroup less often than do teachers in the lower grade levels. This practice is usually due to the limited time in which students are in their classrooms. However, mainstreamed students and others who are having difficulties in mastering some aspect of the content should be subgrouped for specific purposes. Such purposes may include:

- Clarifying instructions for an assignment with which the teacher anticipates selected students will have trouble.
- Checking or evaluating the progress of students on a unit of study.
- Introducing new concepts or words with which students are expected to have difficulty.
- Increasing learning of identified areas of difficulty by short, intensive instruction.

Individual Instruction. Instruction of mainstreamed students will often require one-to-one teaching for short but regularly scheduled times. When this type of instruction is included in the IEP, it will be provided by a specialized teacher rather than by the regular classroom teacher. Some of the *reasons* why this instruction is provided are:

- The mainstreamed student's performance is far below other students in a specific skill or subject area.
- Adaptations are necessary due to physical factors such as adaptive physical education, braille instruction, mobility training, and speech and language training.
- The mainstreamed student needs special counseling due to personal adjustment problems.

Although regular teachers are not expected to provide special instruction to mainstreamed students, they are expected to work cooperatively with specialists. Such cooperation may require regular meetings of both teachers in which observations of the student's progress are shared. Also, cooperative planning between the two teachers will often be necessary. This planning may include divisions of labor concerning which aspects of subject matter will be taught, by whom, and ways to supplement, and thus strengthen, each other's instruction.

In situations where mainstreamed students present behavior management and adjustment problems, teachers will find it useful to develop a common behavior reinforcement approach. The commonalities from one setting to the other might include types of rewards (social reinforcers), rates of rewarding, and the type of reinforcement plan (direct reinforcement or contingency contracting).

PROVISIONS FOR INTERACTIONS

Classrooms represent a life-environment where students and teachers spend a relatively large portion of their time. As in all living areas, the inhabitants experience the range of human emotions; thus, along with their didactic instruction, students also have opportunities to learn from each other. Learning from ones' peers requires many opportunities to interact with them.

You can encourage mainstreamed students to interact with the others in three ways:

- Involve all students in planning.
- Provide opportunities for constructive pupil-pupil interactions.
- Provide opportunities for pupils' questions.

INVOLVING STUDENTS IN PLANNING

Schedule time for the entire class to discuss future activities. When it is feasible, provide options for students. These planning sessions can involve planning activities, setting goals, and establishing rules for classroom behavior. As the teacher you are expected to guide students but be careful not to dictate. When there are no options available, do not open such areas for discussion—let students know which items are not negotiable and why they are not.

Goal-setting discussions can involve establishing behaviors and/or levels of achievement to be attained by groups or individual students. Once agreed upon, these goals should be explicit—in either written or oral form.

Constructive Pupil Interactions

Picture this classroom scene:

> Twenty-five boys and girls ages 10 and 11 years are busily engaged in a variety of tasks. There are five students working in one corner—their desks are arranged in a semicircle around a table. They are sketching on a large sheet of unlined paper. Their assignment—to organize four interest centers within the classroom. There is heated discussion but Mary Alice, their elected chairperson, is managing to keep them on task.
>
> About 12 students are doing individual seat assignments. Occasionally one will signal for help by placing a large red marker on the desk. Two students, who have been designated as "teachers" because they have already mastered those seat assignments now being done by the 12 students, move about the room assisting those students who signal.
>
> In another group of six students, the teacher is conducting arithmetic instruction. He is introducing the task of dividing two-place numbers. As

he teaches, Mr. Jimney elicits from the pupils the answer that is required for each step. By doing this, he is teaching them how to think with numbers as well as to do the mechanics of division. He encourages students to ask questions of one another—later he will select a student from the group to serve as "teacher" while some of those who have not mastered this task do individual seatwork.

The above classroom scene provides ample opportunities for constructive interactions both among students and between teacher and students. Such interactions may occur while students are performing assignments, individually and in groups, and during classroom discussion. In Mr. Jimney's classroom there are three mainstreamed students all of whom receive special assistance outside his classroom. Yet, each student is an active participant in this fifth grade class. Fellow-students are aware that they receive some special assistance, but they view such help as an ordinary part of schooling. Because they are not referred to as "special students," the mainstreamed students are accepted by their peers as a part of the class.

DIRECT CONTROL OF STUDENTS

Teachers can influence academic performance and improve classroom behaviors by exercising direct controls over mainstreamed students. Such controls may be applied by teachers, peers, or by the mainstreamed students themselves through self-control procedures. In all of these instances, teachers are responsible for the use of direct control approaches.

You must have direct control of students in your classroom because, as the teacher, you are responsible for what students learn while in your classroom; you are responsible for protecting students from the disruptive classroom behavior of others; and you are responsible for protecting your students from any physical and psychological harm that could occur in the classroom.

Mainstreamed students tend to be academically, socially, and psychologically vulnerable. By exercising direct control over their classroom behaviors and over that of the peer group, you can shield them until they are better able to cope with classroom stresses. Since children are legally minors they may not be fully responsible for their own actions. Teachers need to instruct them in the necessary behaviors for coping with the classroom environment.

METHODS OF DIRECT CONTROL

As a classroom teacher, you have available to you some tactics that have been demonstrated to be effective in improving social behavior, maintaining appropriate behavior, and stopping or extinguishing undesirable and

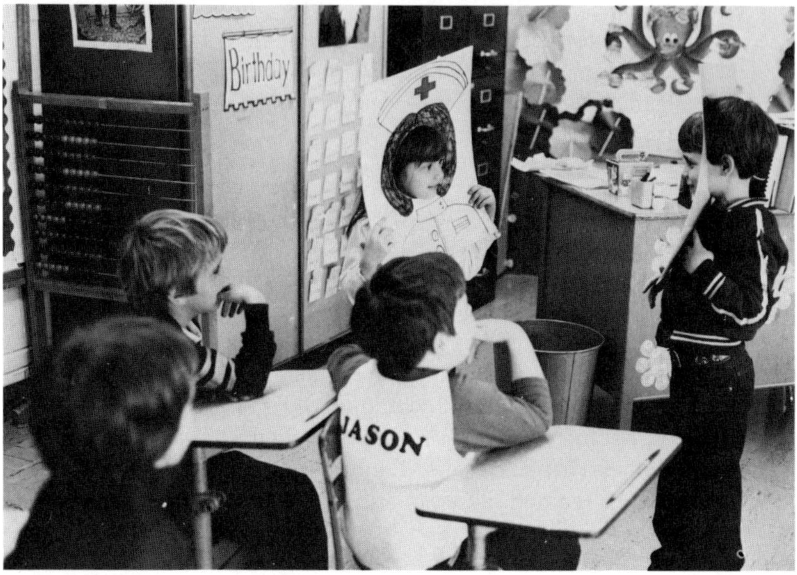

Social modeling and role playing are useful techniques with mainstreamed students.

maladaptive behaviors. Such tactics are derived from five similar, but not identical, practices: social modeling, social reinforcement, contingency management, stimulus control, and extinction.

Social Modeling. Bandura (1969), an early pioneer in learning through imitation, makes a distinction between *initial learning* and *using learned responses*. He and his associates have demonstrated through many research studies that social modeling tactics are effective in teaching new behaviors to children through overt modeling and through vicarious modeling.

Learning through social modeling consists of providing opportunities for students to imitate behaviors they have observed. These opportunities may be provided with live people or with visually or auditorily mediated models.

Live Models. You are a powerful and influential person in your students' lives. You can serve as a model for a wide range of social behaviors that your students will often unwittingly imitate. In addition to inadvertently serving as a model for your students, you can also systematically use modeling tactics. Modeling tactics for classroom use include role playing and behavior rehearsing.

Technically, role playing differs from behavior rehearsing in one major respect. In role playing, students assume roles that are not necessarily similar to their own. Through acting, students are helped to anticipate social situations and are encouraged to use strategies for coping with those circumstances. Behavior rehearsing provides students with opportunities to learn and practice responses that they need to use immediately.

When teaching appropriate behavior through social modeling, teachers should follow these steps:

1. Set up the act to be observed.
2. Give students instructions to observe specific behaviors. Inform them of which behaviors they are to observe.
3. When possible have students record or tally responses.
4. Enact the behavior.
5. Discuss the enactment, having students report their observations.
6. Repeat these procedures when necessary.

With older students it is usually necessary to move them gradually into such activities. Initially, it may be necessary to begin with pantomime where students simply act out a word or situation without speaking. Other students try to determine what the pantomimist was trying to communicate. After a few sessions of this game, teachers gradually move toward verbalizations and into rehearsing. Steps for shaping reluctant students toward social modeling are:

1. Devote a few minutes to pantomime relating to the subject matter under study. Do this two or three consecutive days at the same time each day.
2. Using the same time slot, indicate that in pantomiming students may now give verbal clues, such as the first letter that a word begins with, initials of a person's name, and a verbal description of the act that is being performed.
3. Gradually change the subject matter. In Step 1, select topics that relate to academic subjects. Then in each successive session select a topic that is more related to the personal interest of students until topics are central to students' social behavior.

Vicarious Modeling. Models may be provided vicariously through various media so that students can learn to imitate the models' behaviors. Printed material provides a rich source of models. When using such material, you should identify some reading matter containing characters, attitudes, values, and situations for use as models for your students.

Auditorily produced models may also be useful in situations where you are trying to provide language for students to imitate. Tape and cassette recordings will allow you considerable flexibility in developing language models for students to emulate.

Three possible effects of modeling may occur regardless of the types of models used. First, students may acquire new behaviors. Second, existing behaviors may be strengthened. And third, inappropriate behaviors may be weakened.

Factors which affect students' learning through modeling include their motivation; the characteristics of the human models; the types of behaviors being modeled; and the learners' readiness for acquiring the behavior.

Motivation. The extent to which students are motivated to observe models determines how willing they will be to profit from the instruction. Motivation may be increased through the use of social reinforcement and through contingency management tactics.

Characteristics of models. Students' motivations may also be increased by the model's characteristics. Age, sex, and other physical attributes of models contribute to students' interests. Models who are viewed as prestigious, attractive, and powerful will also motivate observers.

Behaviors. Those behaviors to be imitated are learned more readily when they are not too complex. When complexity is inherent in the responses, they should be divided into simpler components. Students tend to imitate behaviors they have observed as being rewarded. Such rewards may be implied or overtly administered during the modeling session.

Characteristics of learners. Students must be capable of discriminating responses to be learned. Film-mediated models provide an advantage for teaching since these may be repeated, stopped, and reviewed as needed. Observations are often facilitated when the teachers instruct students in advance of the modeling as to which behaviors they are to observe closely.

Students must also be able to imitate the desired behaviors. Responses that are too difficult physically, or require experiences that they have not had, often cannot be imitated even though students wish to perform them. It is also valuable for students to have opportunities to practice the behavior immediately following its observation.

An example of teaching behavior through social modeling is shown in Figure 6.3

Social Reinforcement. Direct positive reinforcement has been demonstrated to be an effective way to develop new behaviors in the classroom through shaping responses that make up those behaviors. It has also been used successfully to maintain behaviors which have already been acquired.

When using social reinforcement, you should immediately reward students for a desired response. Rewards may consist of any event or object students value. In one study the systematic use of teacher attention and praise were used to increase the studying behavior of seventh and eighth grade students (Broden, Hall, Dunlap, and Clark, 1970). In addition to praise and attention, teachers have used privileges, tokens, recognition, and signs of approval for rewarding student behavior.

SKILL: When given an academic assignment, the student will attempt to resolve problems he or she has with the assignment alone before asking for help.

Social Modeling

1. Identify a need for the behavior through a classroom discussion. If we encounter a problem with school work, what are some ways we could try to work it out before asking the teacher for help? Why should we try other things before going to the teacher? Have students contribute ideas to the discussion. Write key words on the board.
2. Identify specific behaviors to be modeled; for example, when the student is having difficulties with an assignment, he might:
   a. Look at the assignment again and think about it
   b. Reread the instructions or try to remember instructions that were given verbally
   c. Look for examples of similar work and see how it was done
   d. Go back and reread earlier material and assignments that preceded the present one
   e. Seek other solutions appropriate to the immediate situation (e.g., consulting with peers if permitted).
3. Model behavior for the class (e.g., take the part of a student with a difficult assignment). Demonstrate application of various problem-solving efforts, describing out loud to students the actions being taken. Ask students to identify the problem-solving behaviors. Praise the students who make appropriate responses.
4. Have class practice the behavior. Provide each student with an assignment and ask students to tell and show what steps they might take before asking the teacher.

Figure 6.3 An example of teaching classroom behavior through social modeling. (From *Social Skills in the Classroom* by Thomas M. Stephens. Columbus, OH: Cedars Press, 1978, p. 559. Reproduced with permission of the publisher.

Two steps are involved when using positive social reinforcement. First, identify a specific behavior to be increased. Second, when the behavior is observed, issue rewards to those students who exhibit the behavior. Initially, you should reward the desired responses frequently. As they occur more often, target behaviors should be rewarded less often. In this way, the responses become strengthened and they become an integral part of the students' behaviors.

Figure 6.4 shows an example of teaching strategy using direct reinforcement. Notice that the same social behavior that was taught through social modeling (shown in Figure 6.3) is maintained through social reinforcement in Figure 6.4.

SKILL: When given an academic assignment, the student will attempt to resolve problems with the assignment alone before asking for help.

Social Reinforcement

Identify and praise by name, outloud, target student when observed attempting to resolve a problem with school work before asking for help. Call attention to specific behavior. For example; "Robin, you certainly did a nice job of trying to work out your math problem on your own, first. I see that you asked for help *after* you tried it by yourself." "Greg, I noticed that you went back and reread the directions before asking for help." "Melissa, you are doing a wonderful job of trying to answer your reading questions on your own. I am happy to see you are trying to work problems out by yourself."

Praise others around the target student who appear to be trying to work independently before asking for help.

Figure 6.4 An example of maintaining a classroom behavior through social reinforcement. (From *Social Skills in the Classroom* by Thomas M. Stephens. Columbus, OH: Cedars Press, 1978, p. 560. Reproduced with permission of the publisher.

Feedback to Students. To be effective feedback should quickly follow the completion of a student's work or response. When quick feedback is not possible, use classroom posting of performance feedback—this has also proved to be an effective method for improving students' work (VanHouten, Hill, and Parsons, 1975).

An Example

In her general mathematics class, Ms. Smith posts percentages for the entire class as well as for teams within the class. In addition, students maintain their own individual records of performance. The classroom posting, on a prominent bulletin board, shows:

ASSIGNMENTS CORRECT FOR CLASS YESTERDAY ______ %

ASSIGNMENTS CORRECT FOR TEAMS YESTERDAY:

TEAM A ______ %

TEAM B ______ %

TEAM C ______ %

TEAM D ______ %

TEAM E ______ %

BEST CLASS PERFORMANCE SO FAR ______ %

Contingency Management. You can develop and maintain social behaviors in classrooms through another positive reinforcement approach: *contingency management*. This refers to tactics where students' behaviors are consequated. In contingency management situations, students are told which behaviors are high in priority and what positive consequences will occur as a result of their performing those behaviors. For example, you may say, "Jack, after you have completed this assignment, you may select a table game." Or, the tactics may be elaborate such as a written contract indicating the terms of behavior and rewards. Often tokens are used to "pay off" students for their behavior. The tokens are exchanged for rewards. Sometimes students may be taught procedures for using self-induced contingency systems. As they learn self-management tactics, you can shift the control of pupil behaviors to the students.

Important features of contingency systems include the needs for immediate reinforcement, rewards for small approximations of complex behaviors, rewards for accomplishments rather than for obedience, students knowing why they are being rewarded, and there being a range of possible rewards.

An example of a contingency management strategy is shown below for encouraging a student to listen to directions by repeating them.

An Example

Marla doesn't listen to directions. Her teacher decides to make a contract with her to increase her listening behavior. "If you can repeat the assignment directions I give you when I ask you to, you may have three extra minutes at our map-drawing interest center (an item which is reinforcing to her). The contingency is in effect five times during the first day. Each time the teacher asks Marla to repeat directions which were just given. Marla repeats the directions fairly accurately four times out of five and receives 15 extra minutes. The teacher then cuts down gradually on the number of times Marla is asked to repeat the directions until Marla is listening without being reinforced. The teacher keeps Marla aware of the need for listening by praising her when she listens to directions.[1]

[1]From *Social Skills in The Classroom* by Thomas M. Stephens. Columbus: Cedars Press, 1978. Page 516. Reproduced with permission of publisher and author.

A contingency approach is also effective with an entire class. You can quickly assess students' reward preference by asking, "How many of you would like to be excused from homework (or quit 10 minutes early) tonight?" If the response is heavily favorable then state the contingency: *During this discussion if 15 of you participate (or correctly answer, or make insightful contributions, etc.) the class will be excused from homework tonight.*

A variation on the above example is to write a series of numbers on the chalkboard from one to whatever number is reasonable. Then announce that each time someone does whatever is required (answer, participate, etc.) a number will be crossed off. When the target number is reached, the class will have earned the reward.

Stimulus Control. You can exercise direct control of students' behaviors through the use of cues and signals. Unlike rewards which *follow* responses, these are events that *precede* responses. But remember that cues and signals are effective only when students know *how* to respond when these appear. When systematically used, they can serve to control students' behaviors, placing students under stimulus control.

You can use visual and auditory cues to signal students as a means of managing their behavior. Sometimes it is necessary to teach students how they should respond to signals. You can do this by providing initial instructions when signals are to be used (e.g., "When I flash the room lights, all students are to return to their seats."). Conditioning may also be developed by following signals with rewards for those who respond correctly. Later the signals are used without explicitly rewarding the behavior.

Visual Signals.

Students raise their hands when they want to contribute during a discussion.

Teacher flashes room lights as a signal for students to return to their seats.

Students place red markers on their desks to signal that they need assistance during individual seat work.

When the room's clock indicates 3 o'clock, students begin preparing to leave.

Students place litter in the waste basket when they see it on the classroom floor.

When a visitor enters the room, Jack offers him a chair.

Mary speaks louder when the teacher places his hand to his ear.

Jeff speaks softer when the teacher places her finger to her lips.

Students select "bonus work" from the envelopes with their names printed on them.

Auditory Signals.

When the teacher asks of Jeff "Please come here," he promptly goes to her.

When the bell rings, all students prepare to leave the classroom.

Miss Jones snaps her fingers as a way to get the class's attention.

Mr. Nettle announces, "It's time to begin," when he wants the class's attention.

A note on the piano is a signal for all students in Ms. Rapport's class to be quiet and pay attention.

You may verbally or visually mediate signals to help students understand stimuli. For example, when teaching students to discriminate different words, show the words and simultaneously say them. In this way, your students will begin to attach language labels to visual clues. Or, by using visual mediation, you can help students attach images to already known language.

Extinction. It is usually not possible to teach groups of children without using some form of punishment. Teachers can evaluate their use of punishment in terms of frequency by following the 80/20 rule:

> The 80/20 rule is practiced at Thurber Elementary School. Teachers are asked to count the number of positive interactions they have with students. Counting may be done by transferring a paper clip from the right pocket to the left each time they do or say something to a target student.
>
> Counting may be conducted by a student or an observer. Each time the teacher interacts with a target student, a tally mark is made under the appropriate symbol (+ positive; − negative; 0 neutral).[2]

Implications of the 80/20 rule, as described above, are that you should not use punishment more than 20 percent of the time and that these should be offset by a high rate of positive reinforcement.

Extinction occurs when punishment or nonreinforcement is used to stop behavior. Unfortunately, teachers sometimes extinguish desirable behaviors. This can occur if you unwittingly punish or do not reinforce responses you really want.

Many tactics have been used as punishment in classrooms to extinguish behavior. Those discussed in this section are social punishment, isolation, removal of reinforcement, and ignoring.

Social punishment in the form of verbal reprimands can be effective in changing classroom behavior. Sometimes verbal reprimands are combined

[2]From *Directive Teaching of Children with Learning and Behavioral Handicaps* by Thomas M. Stephens. Columbus, OH: Charles E. Merrill Publishing Co., 1976. Page 203. Reprinted with publisher's permission.

with other forms of punishment. Physical closeness to or physical contact with target students, or facial expressions along with reprimands sometimes are effective in reducing inappropriate classroom behavior. When using verbal reprimands, you should issue the reprimands immediately following or in association with the inappropriate behavior. Students should be told what they have done or are doing that is inappropriate. Later, you should discuss with students alternative behaviors that are acceptable.

Isolation or time out, can be used to stop certain undesirable behavior. Essentially, time out consists of placing disruptive students in a setting where they are separated from their peers, where no attention is directed to them and where they are not eligible for earning rewards when a contingency is in force. Students should be isolated for short periods, not to exceed 10 minutes.

Criticisms of time out have dealt with ethical considerations (Martin, 1975) because, among other concerns, students lose the opportunity to learn. Time out has also been considered to be impractical and cumbersome (MacDonough and Forehand, 1973). However, brief time out is often effective in stopping misbehavior in the classroom. It should not be used with fearful or reticent children or for long periods of time.

Removal of reinforcement includes withdrawing privileges or tokens. This punishment tactic has not been widely studied except in relation to time out procedures. Isolation is a form of reinforcement removal since students do not have access to positive reinforcement.

Teachers in situations where tokens are used may fine students for each inappropriate behavior. Token loss is difficult to implement, however, when students have no tokens. One procedure that has been used in such situations is to give tokens to students noncontingently and then take them away for misbehaving (Kadzin and Polster, 1973).

Ignoring is another form of nonreinforcement. In using ignoring, teachers avoid providing attention to students when they are misbehaving. Sometimes teachers place a contingency on target behavior for a group's reward; the class is informed that if they ignore specified misbehaviors a group reward will be issued.

Dangers of Punishment. You should use punishment sparingly and only when positive approaches have proven ineffective. Frequent punishment can teach students to dislike schooling because they may come to associate unpleasant experiences with classroom activities. In addition, punishment may also teach students to be punitive, thus defeating one of the purposes of schooling—the nurturance of sensitivity toward others. Recognize that while punishment alone may serve to stop responses, it is important that students be taught appropriate behavior.

As a general rule, misbehavior should be ignored. If it is not possible to ignore or when this proves ineffective, try to reward a behavior that is incompatible with the misbehavior. When the misbehavior continues, one of the various punishment tactics will then be necessary.

A Note about Incentives. Incentives, when used in conjunction with sound learning principles, have great impact on social and academic behavior. All learners must gain some kind of satisfaction from their actions soon after the act or they will be unwilling to continue responding. This is a fundamental law of learning and it is true for all humans and for all complex behaviors. Incentives have been used by successful teachers throughout history—but not always systematically.

Incentives or rewards may take many forms, depending upon the needs of students and teachers. Social recognition, the satisfaction of a job well done, special privileges, peer approval, the promise of obtaining a good job, and school letters and awards have all been used, and with some degree of success. Teachers use many different rewards such as:

Bonus day. Those who turn in completed assignments for three consecutive days are excused from doing an assignment for one day.

Magazines. Those who complete their assignments in class may select magazines from the newsrack to read during the remainder of the period.

Special events. Those who complete 15 days of assignments may attend a special school event (pizza party, go out as a group to lunch, see a movie in school, go to the student lounge).

Table games. Those who complete their assignments may spend the remainder of the period in the game room or at the game corner.

Learn more. Those who complete their assignments may select any other assignment for extra credit or simply to test their skills.

Help others. Those who meet criterion may tutor fellow students who desire assistance.

How often rewards are given is very important too. At first, give rewards frequently. As the sought-after responses are developed, longer and longer periods should elapse between the performance and the reward. Coupons, tokens, or marking systems can be used to keep a record of how well students are achieving. The frequency of rewards can be changed by simply reducing or increasing the number of tokens needed to earn a reward.

Before using incentives, ask these questions:

1. What are my objectives?

2. How will these be reflected in student behavior?

3. What information do students need in order to acquire the behavior?

4. What is the most efficient and interesting way to present the information?

5. How will students practice their learning during the instruction phase?
6. Which incentives are present in the environment so that students will engage in learning activities?
7. Which acts must students perform in order to demonstrate their learning?

Answers to these questions will help to determine if the instruction has a chance of changing behavior. The following example describes the application of functional teaching using these seven questions.

An Example

Ms. McGhee had three mainstreamed students in her sixth grade class who displayed poor reading skills. Their IEPs assigned the students to daily tutoring outside the regular class. But Ms. McGhee also wanted to help improve their reading. So, at her request, the tutor assessed these students on criterion-referenced reading measures, and from these assessments Ms. McGhee and the tutor determined which reading skills each student had the prerequisite responses to learn.

She then made separate folders for each student and inserted reading worksheets that related to the skills the student was ready to learn. Her answers to the seven questions are:

1. Her objective was to improve reading performance of the three students.
2. Each student will:
   (a) Express more interest in reading by volunteering to read in a small group
   (b) Will meet criterion on at least 75 percent of the reading assignments within a two-week period.
3. Students need direct instruction in the specific reading skills.
4. It is efficient to present the information through individual student packets. To increase student interest, each will keep a chart showing the progress being made. Also, content of the worksheets will be geared to student interest.
5. The teacher will rotate among the students, having them read aloud paragraphs from the previous assignments in which criteria were achieved.
6. The students *want* to improve their reading. In addition, for each assignment that the students complete, regardless of performance, one credit is earned toward an extra gym period. As a bonus, for every assignment in which

criterion is achieved, five credits are earned. When 50 credits are earned by the students, the entire class gets an extra gym period.

7. The students will demonstrate the two behaviors shown on page blank.

In the above example the teacher used several strategies which should be noted. First, she identified target behaviors (reading skills) among the mainstreamed students. By using a credit system and in posting the credits earned, she provided interim reinforcement that will encourage students to continue their progress. Since the entire class is rewarded for the main-streamed students' performances, they gain their peer's approval for their progress.

Schedules of Reinforcement. Planned reinforcement can be related to the rate at which reinforcement is issued. Two general schedules of reinforcement are common: continuous and intermittent. When a schedule of continuous reinforcement is used, every time a desired response occurs it is rewarded. After a response is established, change the schedule so that positive reinforcement is not provided after every desired response. When this change is made, the schedule becomes intermittent, resulting in more stable behavior. Four types of intermittent schedules are:

1. *Fixed-interval schedules.* Once a response is established (which may require immediate reinforcement of every response) we can then reinforce it at certain clock intervals, every five minutes or every hour. Although the response rate becomes slower, the response is more stable and more immune to extinction, but another process sometimes intervenes. Immediately after reinforcement, the response rate may become lowered since no reinforcer is immediately forthcoming.
2. *Variable-interval schedules.* A low probability of response due to reinforcement on a fixed-interval schedule can be eliminated by using variable-interval reinforcement. Instead of reinforcing a response every 10 minutes, we can vary it so that it is now 1 minute, now 30 minutes, etc., but averages every 10 minutes. Use of this type of schedule results in a response that is very difficult to extinguish.
3. *Fixed-ratio schedules.* Under fixed-ratio schedules reinforcement occurs every X number of responses. This is a quite inefficient schedule, for it results in long pauses between reinforcements, especially if the ratio of responses to reinforcement is high. To avoid long pauses after reinforcement, a schedule similar to a variable-interval one can be introduced.
4. *Variable-ratio schedules.* Variable-ratio schedules are highly efficient, hard to extinguish, and produce high rates of responses. Under this

schedule we may reinforce every second response at one time, and every eightieth response at another time. The student has no way of anticipating when a response will be rewarded and therefore takes no chances.

Note that intervals refer to time whereas ratios are used to designate number. Certain behaviors are more easily responded to on a time basis; other lend themselves to use with frequency of occurrence.

Most teachers are interested in improving behavior in their classrooms. One way to do this—perhaps the best way—is to observe the classroom behaviors of your students directly and to evaluate relevant classroom conditions.

Consider these six conditions:

- *Demographics*. The group's composition.
- *Physical environment*. The use of the room and its furnishings.
- *Time*. The amount of time available in the class and the teacher's and students' use of it.
- *Student encouragement*. The use of positive reinforcement.
- *Provisions for interacting*. Students among themselves and with teachers.
- *Differentiating instruction*. The extent to which and how the instruction is individualized.

These six categories form the basis for assessing classroom behaviors—the first step for improving them. Underlying each category are questions to be answered. Answers will suggest the necessary changes for improving classroom management.

Demographics. How many pupils are in the class? What is the chronological age range? What is the range of IQ or other aptitude scores? The range of achievement test scores? What is the grade level and what type of class is it (regular, special, other)? Which exceptionalities and how many of each are represented in the class? How many teachers, aides, and volunteers work in the class? At the same time or at different times?

Physical Environment. What is the approximate size of the room? The types and numbers of the furnishings? Does the students' furniture fit them? How are the furnishings used—flexibly to increase the probability of achieving the objectives for each activity? What about the room's condition? Is it sanitary?

Time. What is the total amount of class time for all students? For mainstreamed students? What is the occurrence of on-task and off-task behavior? How do students signal the adult workers for assistance? How do the adults gain students' attention?

Student Encouragement. How and with what frequency are students informed of the results of their efforts? Does social reinforcement occur? How and with what frequency? Is contingency contracting used? How is it used? What types of rewards are used (privileges, activities, extra credit, objects)? Is there goal setting by teachers *with* students for behavior and performance?

Provisions for Interactions. Are students involved in planning? Do constructive interactions among students take place? How frequently? Are students encouraged to participate and to ask questions?

Differentiating Instruction. Are instructional plans written and followed? Is planning differentiated for individual or small groups? Are short term instructional objectives a part of the planning? Are the instructional objectives related to the planning? Is adult assistance provided regularly to help individual students?

Answers—How to Get Them. Answers to these questions are only useful if they are valid. There are two ways to increase the accuracy of the answers—use direct observations and collect data. Some questions can be answered by simply counting (e.g., number of students, the amount of time on and off task of specific students). Others will require readings of students records (e.g., ages, exceptionalities). Still others must have functional definitions (e.g., define the "fit of students' furniture"; "flexible use of furnishings and space"; "on and off task").

Answers—What They Mean. First, an overall pattern must be detected. Consider this pattern from a regular sixth grade class:

An Example

Demographics
There are 26 students; 5 are mainstreamed; aptitude range is from 80 to 142 IQ; there is one adult—the teacher.

Physical Environment
The room is standard; nine students sit at desks and/or in chairs that don't fit; students are seated in rows; during small group work, students sit with the teacher at a round table; furnishings and the room are neat and clean.

Time
The school day is from 9 A.M. to 3 P.M. with total in-class time of

240 minutes; the average time in class for the five mainstreamed students is 180 minutes each day; three randomly selected students were on-task on an average of 28 minutes during a 60 minute observation of each student; hand raising is the sole method for students to signal the teacher; the teacher calls students by their names as the primary signal for gaining their attention; "boys and girls" is used to get class attention.

Student Encouragement

Students get immediate feedback to oral answers; with written work feedback is delayed by one or two days; the average rate of verbal reinforcement is 12 every 60 minutes; written statements from the teacher are placed on all high scoring papers; no other types of rewards are used; no contingency contracting is used; teacher's goals are set without involving students.

Provisions for Interactions

Students are not involved in planning; they are discouraged from talking to each other in class; most interactions between teacher and students are teacher initiated (about 80 percent).

Differentiating Instruction

There are three subgroups in reading; arithmetic is individualized through a commercial program of seat work; daily lesson plans are general; short-term objectives for the mainstreamed students are used by their resource-room teacher but not by this fifth grade teacher; the teacher responds to students' requests for help during seat-work assignments but those requests are infrequent (about four per 60 minutes).

This teacher can improve the class performance by encouraging student discussion (rearrange furniture, increase verbal praise, payoff for responses); by differentiating instruction further; by relating plans to instructional objectives; by developing alternative signaling systems for students to ask for help; by increasing on-task time; and by developing student directed activities.

Appendix E contains a *Classroom Management Assessment Guide* that uses the six areas considered in this section.

SUMMARY

- The physical environment in classrooms should be arranged to facilitate instructional objectives.
- Use the classroom time to increase learning opportunities.
- Organize students to achieve instructional objectives.
- Provide opportunity for students to interact with each other and with the teacher.
- Evaluate classroom conditions to determine where changes should be made.

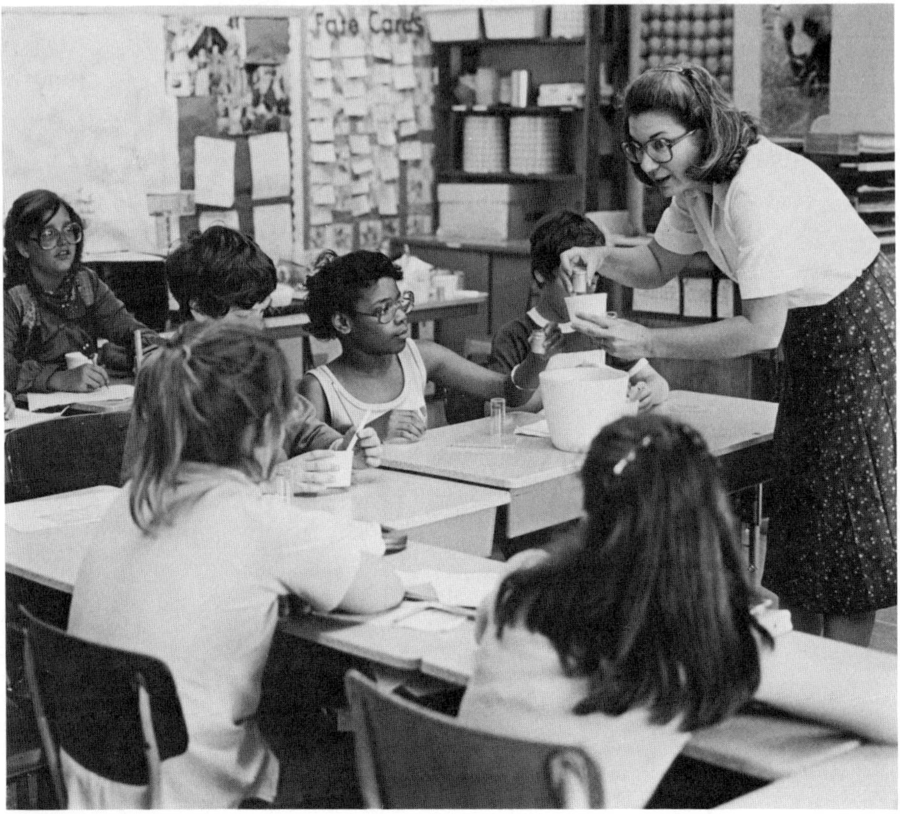

SEVEN

Teacher Competencies For Mainstreaming

- What attitudes are needed for mainstreaming to be effective?
- Who are the professionals involved with mainstreaming efforts? What are their responsibilities?
- What competencies do regular classroom teachers need to effectively teach mainstreamed students?
- How can the mainstreaming competencies be used to guide the professional development activities of teachers?
- What concerns do teachers have about mainstreaming?

As the provision of P.L. 94-142 for educating students in the least restrictive environment began to be implemented in the public schools, a major concern was voiced by teachers, school administrators, and teacher educators. This concern centered around whether regular classroom teachers had the education or experience to successfully integrate handicapped students into their classes. Indeed, it was not uncommon to hear teachers voice the concern, "I'm not competent to mainstream handicapped kids into my classroom."

In an attempt to counter this problem, several efforts in teacher education were mounted. Many school districts initiated in-service training programs that dealt with mainstreaming. A number of states also revised their teacher certification guidelines to require that all students who were to become elementary or secondary teachers take course work in the education of handicapped children. In addition, the federal government funded a number of projects, called "Deans' Grants," that were designed to integrate additional special education content into the general curriculum of colleges of education throughout the country. As the name implies, the deans of the colleges of education were the project directors.

As a part of many of these efforts, an obvious question was raised, What are the competencies that regular classroom teachers need in order to effectively mainstream handicapped students? Once an answer could be obtained for this question, it would then be possible to design appropriate preservice and in-service training programs for teachers.

This chapter deals with the topic of teacher competencies for mainstreaming. It is divided into several sections. The first section describes attitudes that are necessary if mainstreaming is to be effective. The next section emphasizes that the regular classroom teacher does not have sole responsibility for mainstreamed students. Following this, general and specific competencies for successful mainstreaming are described. The next section illustrates a way that mainstreaming competencies can be used by teachers and students who are preparing to be teachers to develop and improve their effectiveness in mainstreaming. Finally, information about concerns that teachers have about mainstreaming is presented. As you read this chapter you should gain a rather detailed view of the roles played by various professionals and the specific teaching skills, concepts, knowledge, and attitudes that are necessary for us to be successful in our mainstreaming efforts.

ATTITUDES NEEDED FOR EFFECTIVE MAINSTREAMING

To be very blunt about it, mainstreaming will *not* be effective if teachers are opposed to the concept and believe that it will not work. Obviously, attitudes are a very personal thing and do not change simply because people are told that they need to develop a particular attitude. Nevertheless, we think that it is important to describe attitudes that seem to be important in order for mainstreaming to be effective.

It has already been mentioned that it is important to view mainstreamed students as students first and that any problems that they may exhibit are secondary to that fact. Several other attitudes are also important. One of the leading authorities of mainstreaming, Dr. Jack Birch, studied a number of school systems in which mainstreaming was being implemented successfully. Through interviews with teachers and administrators, he identified the following six attitudes that appeared to be most conducive to success for mainstreaming:

1. Belief in the right to education for all children.
2. Readiness of special education and regular class teachers to cooperate with each other.
3. Willingness to share competencies as a team in behalf of pupils.
4. Openness to include parents as well as other professional colleagues in planning for and working with children.
5. Flexibility with respect to class size and teaching assignments.
6. Recognition that social and personal development can be taught, and that they are equally as important as academic achievement. (Birch, 1974, p. 94)

If teachers and administrators held such attitudes, it would seem reasonable to believe that mainstreaming would be readily accepted in schools and would have considerable likelihood for success.

SHARING THE RESPONSIBILITIES

Of the six attitudes that influence the effectiveness of mainstreaming, it is interesting to note that three (2, 3, and 4) deal with sharing and/or cooperating with others. This is particularly significant in view of the fact that many teachers who are critical of mainstreaming practices claim that they do not get the type of cooperation and support that they believe is necessary for mainstreaming to work properly. Unfortunately, much of this criticism is justified. Many school districts have established policies that encourage mainstreaming; but they do not provide the type of resources necessary to support its implementation. The result is frequently a group of disgruntled teachers, parents, and other support personnel.

A major point that needs to be emphasized is that the regular classroom teacher cannot successfully operate a mainstreamed class alone. To even attempt to do so is virtually impossible from a logistic standpoint. It is also professionally irresponsible on the part of school officials to attempt to conduct a mainstreamed program without appropriate resources. The regular classroom teacher should be viewed as a member of a team of people who are responsible for the delivery of appropriate educational services to the students who may be mainstreamed. The remainder of this section describes some of the members of this team and the roles that they play in supporting the regular classroom teacher's mainstreaming effort. Not every member of the team will be involved with every student, of course. Team members are selected and involved as necessary.

RESOURCE TEACHERS

Most special educators who are employed in public schools now serve as resource teachers. These professionals provide education on a part-time specialized basis to mainstreamed students. For example, if students need assistance in developing specific skills such as reading or mathematics, they may go to the resource teacher for instruction on those subjects for one or two hours each day. The resource teacher may work with the students individually or in small groups in the resource room. The students then return to their regular classes for the remainder of their lessons.

CONSULTING TEACHERS

Some mainstreamed students receive virtually all of their education in regular classes. Consulting teachers provide advice about ways to modify classroom procedures to meet the needs of mainstreamed students. They are not involved in direct instruction of these students; but they do help to locate instructional materials and equipment for them. Some resource teachers also provide consultation services to regular classroom teachers.

SPECIAL CLASS TEACHERS

Some students need full-time special education services, particularly those who have problems related to behavioral adjustment in school. Special class teachers will work with such students until they exhibit the type of behavior that will enable them to function in the regular class. When this occurs, the students will be placed in the regular class for short periods of time that are gradually extended. Eventually, many of these students are transferred from the special class teacher to the resource teacher for special education services.

SPEECH-LANGUAGE PATHOLOGISTS

These professionals identify, evaluate, and treat students with communication problems. Most often, speech-language pathologists serve more than one school on an itinerant basis. They work with students who have speech or language problems on a one-to-one or small group basis. They also provide suggestions to regular class teachers on ways that speech and language can be improved within the context of the regular class.

AUDIOLOGISTS

Hearing problems are evaluated by audiologists. Not only do they evaluate hearing through the administration of audiometric examinations, they also determine how the students can make best use of their remaining hearing. Audiologists determine whether a student can benefit from the use of a hearing aid, and can assist in selecting an appropriate aid. They also provide advice on the ways that classroom teachers can effectively work with students who have hearing problems.

SCHOOL PSYCHOLOGISTS

Students who are referred for learning or behavior problems are evaluated by school psychologists. These professionals evaluate intellectual ability, personality characteristics, and educational achievement. They also provide valuable advice about ways that classroom teachers can accommodate to individual differences in learning and behavior that occur. Some school districts also employ educational diagnosticians. These people observe students in the context of their classrooms and administer educational diagnostic tests. They are not qualified to administer the psychological tests that are used by school psychologists.

PHYSICAL THERAPISTS

Specialized, individual attention to physical problems is provided by physical therapists. These individuals focus on the development of muscular strength and the extension of range of motion of muscles that are not functioning properly. Most students with cerebral palsy receive physical therapy.

OCCUPATIONAL THERAPISTS

Students who need assistance with activities needed for successful functioning in everyday life will receive services from occupational therapists. They will provide individual instruction in areas such as eating, dressing, bathing, toileting, and other tasks associated with independence and productive functioning.

SOCIAL WORKERS

Interactions between schools and the families of their students can be facilitated by social workers. These people also provide liaisons between schools and other social agencies. Teachers who have concerns about the home life of their students and its effects on school performance should consult with the school social worker for assistance in problem solving in this area.

GUIDANCE COUNSELORS

Counselors assist students in solving personal problems. They help students develop appropriate self-concepts, set realistic goals for themselves, and learn skills to improve interpersonal relations. Older students also receive counseling related to employment and postschool adjustment. Counseling services are frequently made available to the parents of students who are enrolled in special programs.

MEDICAL PERSONNEL

Students with physical problems receive services from various types of medical personnel who perform their traditional roles. These may include school nurses; physicians; orthopedic surgeons; ophthalmologists; pediatricians; psychiatrists; neurologists; ear, nose, and throat specialists; and others.

PRINCIPALS

It may surprise you to see principals included in this listing. In our experience, however, the principal is the key to successful mainstreaming. If the principal is committed to the concept of mainstreaming, other staff members will work to make it successful. Committed principals will also work diligently to make needed instructional materials, equipment, and supportive services available to support mainstreaming efforts. Indeed, the principal is the most important single resource to the teacher who is mainstreaming.

From the above descriptions, it should be apparent that there is a host of professionals available to support mainstreaming efforts. It is important for you to realize that you are not alone in your efforts; and when you encounter specific needs or problems, you should actively seek out the appropriate personnel to provide assistance to you. Mainstreaming is, and should be, a team effort. Additional information about the roles and responsibilities of various support personnel is provided by Schifani, Anderson, and Odle (1980).

GENERAL COMPETENCY AREAS

Several people associated with the Deans' Grants generated a list of 10 general clusters of competence that were necessary for successful mainstreaming. These clusters of competence were subsequently published under the title, *A Common Body of Practice for Teachers: The Challenge of PL 94-142 to Teacher Education* by the American Association of Colleges for Teacher Education (1980) along with several reviews and critiques by educational authorities. The 10 clusters are described in this section.

It was the general consensus of the people who reviewed them that the clusters are not intended to be complete or mutually exclusive. There is obvious overlap among several of them. They should be viewed as a general description of the domains of professional competence that appear to be important for all teachers who are involved in individualized instruction.

CURRICULUM

Teachers should have knowledge and first-hand experience with curriculum development, curriculum guides, principles of curriculum design and adaptation, and ways to modify the curriculum to adapt to the needs of handicapped learners in the regular classroom. Study of this topic should include all areas of curriculum. Although teachers would not be expected to have an in-depth knowledge of all areas, they should have at least a general understanding so that responsible planning can be done with assurances that no essential elements are overlooked.

Although it may be obvious that a knowledge of curriculum is important, what may be less obvious is the emphasis that should be placed upon knowledge of the entire curriculum. The reason for this is that teachers have been working over the past few decades to make their classes more homogeneous. Consequently, many have developed a rather limited perspective on curriculum (i.e., only what they teach in their classrooms). The presence of mainstreamed students within a classroom represents a population that is much more heterogeneous than teachers may have been used to. Consequently, a broader perspective on curriculum is required.

TEACHING BASIC SKILLS

This cluster of skills represents a real departure from traditional teacher competencies—particularly at the secondary level. The general concept that most people have is that a teacher specializes either in a given subject matter, such as mathematics, English, or science, or at a given grade level, such as kindergarten or sixth grade. Consequently, one would naturally assume that the teachers should concentrate on being highly competent in the respective area of their interest.

What this cluster calls for, however, is that all teachers develop competence in teaching basic skills *in addition* to their subject matter or grade level areas. By basic skills, we mean literacy, life maintenance, and personal development. Literacy skills include reading, arithmetic, writing, spelling, study skills, and speaking. Life maintenance skills include health, safety, consumerism, and law as it relates to human rights, the judicial system, and personal liability. Personal development skills are those that relate to personal growth and include the study of such factors as philosophy, moral behavior, ethics, and basic life issues.

The reason for this cluster is that teachers are going to encounter students with a wide array of abilities and disabilities in their classrooms. They should, for example, be able to assist in the teaching of reading to a child who may be integrated into the regular class for a social studies lesson. Also implied in this cluster is the ability to co-teach and collaborate with specialists who may be called upon to provide the type of intensive instruction in basic skill areas that may be required for some students.

CLASS MANAGEMENT

Teachers who are mainstreaming students should be proficient in the application of class management techniques. Such techniques are quite useful to ensure a high level of positive responses from both individual and groups of students. Specific areas of competence included in this cluster are applied behavioral analysis, group alerting, guiding transitions, materials arrangement, crisis intervention techniques, and group approaches to creating a positive affective atmosphere in the classroom. Many of these topics were dealt with in greater detail earlier in this book.

PROFESSIONAL CONSULTATION AND COMMUNICATION

The advent of mainstreaming has resulted in professionals assuming many new roles in public schools. As described earlier, we now have people who serve as resource teachers, who take children out of the regular class for short periods of intensive instruction; consulting teachers, who provide technical assistance and support to the regular classroom teacher; educational diagnosticians, who specialize in developing assessments; and many others, such as physical therapists, mobility specialists for the visually impaired, speech pathologists, and audiologists.

It is imperative that regular classroom teachers develop competence in ways to consult and communicate with these professionals. They need to be able to know how to collect and report the type of information that will be most useful to these specialists and they must be able to apply the information that the specialists provide. (It goes without saying that this is a two-way street. The specialists need to be good consultants and communicators, too.)

TEACHER-PARENT-STUDENT RELATIONSHIPS

Teachers should be able to interact successfully with the parents and siblings of handicapped children who may be in their classes. Included here would also be the development of a sensitivity for multicultural differences. Since the following chapter deals in greater depth with the topic of working with parents, no additional comments will be made on that topic here.

STUDENT-STUDENT RELATIONSHIPS

The ways in which handicapped children are received and treated by other children in the classroom are critical to the success of mainstreaming. Teachers need to be skilled in developing situations that facilitate the most positive types of interaction among the students. Heterogeneous groupings of children, and cross-age or peer tutoring can be particularly beneficial. Counseling and guidance skills are also quite useful in dealing with problems that may occur.

EXCEPTIONAL CONDITIONS

Obviously, if teachers are to be successful with mainstreaming, they should know about the educationally relevant characteristics of exceptional children. A general knowledge can readily be obtained from the study of texts that deal with this topic (e.g., Blackhurst and Berdine, 1981). Teachers who have specifically diagnosed children in their classes, however, should strive for a more in-depth knowledge of the particular educational characteristics of these children. This can be obtained by speaking with specialists in a particular area who can recommend more specific materials for study.

REFERRAL

In most cases, as was pointed out in an earlier chapter, the person who first suspects that a child may have a specific learning or behavior problem is often the regular classroom teacher. Consequently, it is imperative that teachers know what to look for in the children in their classes, how to collect the most useful type of data for diagnostic specialists, and how to refer the child for additional evaluation. Inherent in this cluster is the knowledge of what referral sources are available in the school and community.

INDIVIDUALIZED TEACHING

Teachers need to be adept at assessing a student's individual needs and in designing instruction to meet those needs. Note that this does not mean that each child must be taught on a one-to-one basis, nor does it mean that the teacher must attend to all children in the class with the same amount of time and effort. It does mean, however, that each child should be considered individually in order to accomodate to his or her needs. Homogeneous grouping is one example of how this might be done. Permitting a child to pursue a preferred learning mode such as listening to a tape recording rather than reading, would be another example of individualization.

PROFESSIONAL VALUES

It goes without saying that adherence to moral and ethical codes of behavior should be an integral part of teachers' behaviors. Adherence to the standards of the profession should be of paramount importance. This also includes adherence to the state and federal laws and regulations, and the policies and procedures of the local school board.

SPECIFIC TEACHING FUNCTIONS AND COMPETENCIES

If you closely examine the 10 general competency areas that were described in the previous section, you will probably conclude that proficiency in each would benefit *all* children—not just those with handicaps. While focusing attention upon general areas that should be emphasized, however, the above listing does not provide direction for acquiring the specific skills and competencies that regular classroom teachers should develop for effectively mainstreaming students. That is the purpose of this section—to describe some very specific functions and the competencies that are associated with each function.

In one effort to define the specific competencies that are necessary for mainstreaming, Goldhammer, Rader, and Reuschlein (1977) surveyed 14 of the Deans' Grants projects for lists of competencies that were thought to be important. When these lists were combined and redundancies eliminated, some 464 competencies were identified and clustered into the following 13 areas:

Nature of mainstreaming	Learning styles
Nature of the handicapped	Classroom management
Attitudes	Curriculum
Resources	Communication
Teaching techniques	Assessing student needs
Learning environment	Evaluating student progress
	Administration

The list of competencies provided one of the first comprehensive views of what might be important in mainstreaming students. For example, under the topic of the "nature of mainstreaming," Goldhammer, Rader, and

Reuschlein (1977) claimed that the regular classroom teacher should be able to do the following:

- discuss the 'normalization' principle as it applies to the handicapped.
- have general knowledge of federal legislation concerning education of exceptional children.
- have a basic grasp of the history and philosophy of mainstreaming.
- have a basic knowledge of various mainstreaming models; e.g., consulting teacher, diagnostic prescriptive teacher, itinerant teachers, resource rooms, special education classes, etc.
- have an understanding of the importance of parents and the community at large in a mainstreaming program.
- be able to define what mainstreaming is and what it is not.
- be able to state the rationale for mainstreaming in regard to the following issues: efficacy studies of the academic progress of mildly handicapped students in special vs. regular classes, labeling, minority status, and legislation.
- be able to discuss the state laws and State Department of Education guidelines for programs for exceptional children.
- be able to demonstrate knowledge of how a teacher should respond to legal rights of children and parents.
- be able to discuss the research basis for mainstreaming of the 'special' student. (p. 2)

It is obvious that the above list of competencies is quite useful in providing direction for preservice training programs, in-service programs, or simply for the teacher who may be planning to mainstream children and who is interested in pinpointing some of the areas of knowledge that would be appropriate to master. What becomes less clear, however, is that further on in this list of nearly 500 competencies are statements that are generic to all areas of teaching. For example, "The teacher will have the ability to interpret group achievement tests" or "The teacher will be able to provide frequent success experiences for each learner" do not necessarily appear to be specific to the mainstreaming process. Consequently, statements such as these become less useful for determining effective mainstreaming competencies.

Shores, Cegelka, and Nelson (1973) provide additional criticism of such long lists of competency statements. These autorities, in addressing the topic of competency-based teacher education, were highly critical of statements generated by groups of experts. While acknowledging that professional judgment may have some usefulness, they argue that competency lists should be developed in which the competencies are based upon research that has verified that the statements have some validity. If this is done, then we can have greater faith that we are really focusing in on the skills and competencies that will make a difference in successful teaching.

The problem with the position taken by Shores and his colleagues is that research of the type that they are calling for is very difficult, time consuming, and expensive. They propose that studies be developed in which direct observation is done in various classrooms and data are collected to verify whether there is any validity to a particular competency. They claim, and rightly so, that competencies identified through such studies would be far more preferable to competency lists generated simply out of logic or personal opinion.

Unfortunately, there has not been any research of this nature done on the topic of mainstreaming competencies. However, there has been some research that has been an approximation to direct observation, in which a research procedure known as the Critical Incident Technique (Flanagan, 1962) was used to identify competencies that regular elementary teachers need in order to effectively mainstream students. The competencies that will be described here were reported originally by Redden and Blackhurst (1978), as identified through the doctoral research that Redden conducted in 1976. These competencies were identified by surveying 184 elementary teachers who were involved in mainstreaming. These teachers were asked to identify three specific incidents in which they used successful mainstreaming practices and three incidents in which they were ineffective. For each incident, the teachers had to describe: (1) the antecedents leading up to the incident; (2) the teacher behavior that occurred; and (3) the consequences of the behavior that led them to conclude that their behavior was either effective or ineffective.

As a result of this research, 828 critical incidents were reported by the teachers. After eliminating redundancies, 271 specific tasks related to mainstreaming were identified. These tasks were then clustered into 21 competency statements which were subsequently grouped into the 6 functional areas that are described below. The complete list of all 271 tasks is available in Redden's (1976) doctoral dissertation, and most of the tasks are reflected in the discussions that accompany each of the following competency statements.

The important thing to remember in reviewing the competencies described in this section is that they are based on actual reports of the behavior of teachers who were involved in mainstreaming. As such, they are probably more valid than similar lists of competencies that were generated as a result of peoples' best guesses as to the competencies that would be desirable for facilitating mainstreaming.

By the same token, as Redden (1976) correctly points out, the competencies described here are *not* the *only* competencies for teachers in mainstreaming settings. As with any landmark research, this should only be viewed as an initial list that should be revised as we gain more experience and evidence about teachers who are effectively mainstreaming handicapped students.

The remainder of this section of the chapter will list each of six mainstreaming functions that were identified and provide a discussion concerning the 31 competencies that are subsumed by these functions.

DEVELOPING ORIENTATION STRATEGIES FOR MAINSTREAM ENTRY

Perhaps the biggest complaint from regular class teachers who are mainstreaming is that they had not had sufficient notice, training, or opportunity to prepare for the students who were being placed in their classes. Contrary to what you might think, the role of the regular classroom teacher is not one of only becoming personally prepared through additional training to receive the mainstreamed child. Actually, the regular classroom teacher must be an active participant in the process, if it is to be successful. Naturally, personal reeducation and preparation are necessary; however, these are insufficient, as will be illustrated by the six competencies that are associated with this function.

Teachers Should Be Able to Participate in School-Wide Planning for Mainstreaming Activities. As noted in several places in this text, one of the major keys to successful mainstreaming is the attitude and commitment of the school principal. The principal who concludes the staff orientation at the beginning of the school year with the statement (which was actually made in one situation known to the authors), "Oh, by the way, we are going to mainstream all of the special education students this year," has almost guaranteed failure of the mainstreaming process. We hope that you will not find yourself in this type of educational atmosphere as a teacher.

The principal, the regular classroom teacher, the special education teacher, and other school personnel must all be *actively* involved in the necessary planning and orientation for mainstreaming. Policies and procedures need to be developed to deal with all sorts of administrative arrangements such as coordination of student schedules, arrangement of planning and consultation time among school staff, record keeping, placement of students, and the orientation of both the regular and special education students who will be involved. It may be obvious, but it deserves emphasizing, that the greater the involvement of all school staff and the greater attention to detailed planning and anticipating problems, the greater will be the probabilities of successful mainstreaming.

Teachers Should Set up a Personal Training Program That Will Provide Instruction in Areas Necessary to Teach Effectively in a Mainstreamed Setting. A good school system will have an ongoing program of in-service training in which you should be able to participate. However, in all likelihood, topics in which given teachers feel

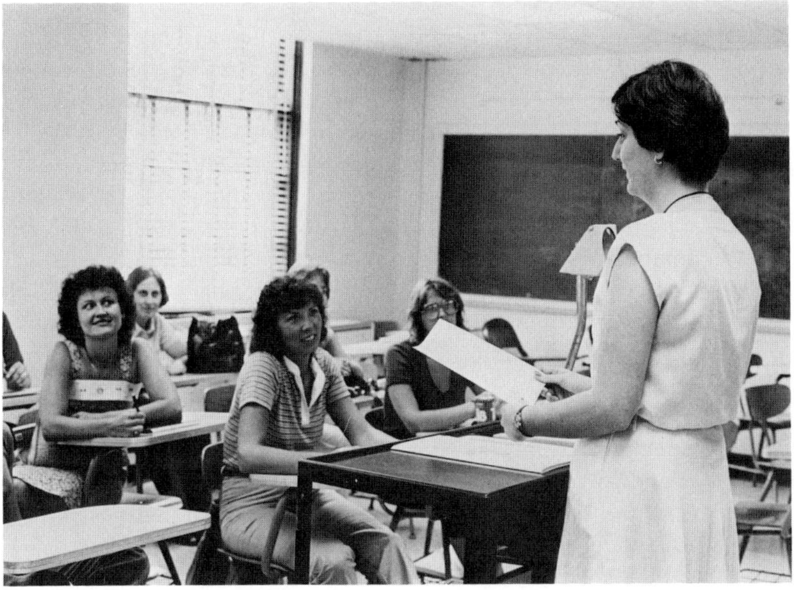

Teachers should attend in-service training programs and participate in the activities of their professional organizations to upgrade their teaching skills.

the need for additional training will have been presented at earlier in-service training programs or will be presented at a time when the training may not be most beneficial. Consequently, the responsibility for upgrading professional skills will fall directly upon the individual teachers.

In designing a personal professional development program, teachers need to objectively assess their strengths and weaknesses to establish priority for training needs. You will undoubtedly want to interact with other teachers to share training ideas and resources and perhaps to encourage school officials to develop training programs to meet your needs. Attendance at in-service training programs and active involvement in professional organizations should be a major part of the professional life of teachers. Because the topic of personal professional development is so important, an entire section has been devoted to it at the end of this chapter.

Teachers Should Be Able to Participate in Parent and Community Orientation Programs on Mainstreaming. After having some five or six years of experience with mainstreaming, people in education find it interesting to see the reactions of some parents to this practice. From information presented earlier, it should be evident that many parents have looked forward to changing practices in the public schools that related to the education of their handicapped children, as mandated by law. However, there has been a rather interesting cross-section of attitudes among various sectors of the community related to mainstreaming practices.

In some cases, we are seeing "backlash" against mainstreaming. We frequently hear comments from teachers such as, "I don't have the time to devote to the mainstreamed kids because I have 25 other kids in my class to worry about." Some parents have said, "I like the individual attention that my child gets from the special education teacher. She doesn't get this in the regular class." Other people have commented, "How come handicapped kids get these IEPs and all sorts of individual attention? Why can't I demand the same sort of treatment for my 'normal' kid?"

Of course, some of these concerns may be well founded. However, many people do not understand the purposes of mainstreaming and what appropriate procedures for implementing this practice are. They need to become involved in the development of parent and community education programs. The regular classroom teacher can play an extremely valuable role in such endeavors by helping to inform people of the value and importance of mainstreaming and to educate the public about how the process actually works. This is not to imply that one should gloss over the problems and weaknesses that may be encountered. Rather, an objective representation of the strengths and the weaknesses of the process should be made public and the assistance of the public should be solicited in helping to overcome the problems that may be encountered.

Note here, that we are talking about parents of both handicapped and nonhandicapped children. Keep in mind that positive support from the parents of the nonhandicapped children in a classroom will help to facilitate positive attitudes in their children. The parent who tells his child, "Why don't you offer to read Ada's homework assignment to her, since she has difficulty seeing," will obviously have a greater positive impact than one who says, "Why don't you just stay away from Harry, because he's crazy and I don't know why they have him in the class, anyway." The implications for parent and community education should be obvious.

Teachers Should Be Able to Seek out Consultative Relationships with Specialists on the School Staff. Teachers should remember that they are not alone in their school efforts (although it may feel like it at times). Unless they are members of a very small school system, it is likely that they will have the services of many specialists available. Regardless of what one may hear about the heaviness of their various workloads, you will find that the overwhelming majority of these specialists are interested and will try to provide assistance if requested.

School psychologists are a useful source of information about how to work with a child's problem behavior. Speech-language pathologists can provide advice about how to react to a child who stutters or how to develop a language development program for the classroom. Educational diagnosticians can help by either testing children or suggesting tests for use in assessing ability levels. They can also help to interpret test data that may be in the child's cumulative records. Guidance counselors can help with problem children as well as provide valuable suggestions for setting up career education programs. School social workers can assist with parent interactions, and school nurses can provide advice relative to health concerns. Many schools have the services of physical therapists available. Generally, these are not on a full-time basis; however, if one has a child with a physical disability in class, chances are that a physical therapist has been involved in the diagnosis and IEP process. This person will be a valuable source of information about the nature of particular physical disabilities or considerations related to modification of the classroom environment that might be helpful to the child. Similarly, specialists outside the school, such as physicians, neurologists, ophthalmologists, and others can frequently be called upon as necessary.

Finally, the special education staff members will play an important part in the education of any mainstreamed children. If the child has a visual impairment, it will be necessary for the vision specialist to provide assistance in obtaining low-vision aids, large-type books, braille materials, audio tapes, etc. The resource teacher may be able to assist in obtaining high-interest, level-low vocabulary materials for children with reading difficulties, in addition to taking the child for short periods of specific instruction during the school day. The teacher of the physically handicapped may be able to help you obtain various assistive and adaptive equipment for physically handicapped children in class. The teacher of the hearing impaired may be able to provide tips about how to work with the child who is wearing a hearing aid.

As a teacher you must seek out and become acquainted with the specialists in your school to develop consultative relationships with them. You will also need to determine the policies and procedures for initiating and using consultative services. Teachers usually discover that there is more help available than they expected. Finally, if assistance is needed that is not available, you should not hestitate to request it from the principal.

Teachers Should Be Able to Develop Programs to Prepare Special Students for Entry into the Regular Class. Frequently, insufficient attention is paid to this activity. Too often, mainstreamed students are simply placed in the regular class with very little orientation or preparation. Ideally, there should be a schoolwide program or policy related to this. You might want to confer with the special students individually and in groups to inform them about their new class and what to expect. Such meetings can be supplemented by visits for the special student to the regular class.

Once the child has been moved into the mainstreamed class, every effort should be made to develop a trust relationship with the child and to allow sufficient time for such a relationship to develop. It is helpful if plans can be made so that the child is gradually placed for longer periods of time, rather than being subjected to the "culture shock" of immediate extended placement. Obviously, it is very important in the early phases of placement to ensure that the child has success experiences.

Teachers Should Be Able to Prepare Members of the Regular Class for the Entry of Special Students into the Class. One of the trickiest parts of mainstreaming is to deal with the reactions and interactions of the regular classroom members and the mainstreamed student. It is quite difficult to predict how much attention will be drawn to the special students by explaining their problems to the rest of the class. Some teachers have used simulations very effectively in orienting their regular classroom members to the problems encountered by children with sensory or physical problems. Others have used specific instructional units focused on topics related to hearing, vision, and different physical disabilities. Appendix D includes a list of books about disabilities that are appropriate for use with regular class students.

It has been our experience that most students with a visual impairment or who wear a hearing aid can participate quite freely in discussions about the nature of their disability. When these children appear to be ready for such an activity, actual instructional units can be developed around these disabilities. We have found that hearing students have been intrigued with hearing aids when they can listen to sounds through an aid when the earmold is held up to a stethoscope. Likewise, a blind student was sent into hysterical laughter when he was asked by a seeing student if he could read braille with his elbow. Such interchanges are potentially beneficial to both the handicapped students and their nonhandicapped classmates.

A word of caution is in order, however. Teachers must be very sensitive to the situations involved in open discussions about student disabilities. For example, it would be inappropriate to call attention to the fact that Patty has a learning disability or that Fred is mentally retarded. The use of such labels and calling attention to the subtle problems that various students might have will serve to stigmatize them. This also has the potential of detracting from the intent of the mainstreamed classroom. Remember that the goal of the mainstreamed classroom is to maximize interaction with nonhandicapped students. By calling attention to problems we may run the danger of exaggerating the differences instead of pointing out the similarities of children. Thus, a mainstreamed student may be physically integrated into the class but may be socially segregated as a result of stereotyping.

Teachers can help to negate problems by fostering an attitude in the classroom that respects the individuality of every student. The special students' areas of particular strength should be subtly brought to the attention of the class. Cooperation of the class in helping each other with problems is also a way to facilitate adjustment of the students.

Wherever possible, the class should be informed in advance about particular problems that a student may encounter. This is particularly the case with students who may have epileptic seizures or who may experience some form of physical problem. This will enable the students to be prepared for any situation that might arise that may have the potential for being traumatic to them.

Finally, if you accustom your entire class to individualized activities, the mainstreamed student who may be working at his or her own pace will become less conspicuous. With students moving in and out of classrooms more frequently these days for various subjects such as band, chorus, remedial reading, speech therapy, it is less conspicuous for those children who may be attending resource rooms for portions of their instruction. Consequently, there is less chance of becoming stigmatized for being in the special education program.

ASSESSING NEEDS AND SETTING GOALS

Most school systems have developed curriculum guidelines that specify the goals and objectives that are expected to be accomplished by the students at various grade levels. Teachers who are concerned with individual differences, however, realize that many children have specific needs that should be taken into consideration while setting goals and designing instruction to meet these goals. The five competencies associated with the function of needs assessment and goal setting illustrate the major considerations in this area.

Teachers Should Be Able to Gather Information to Determine the Educational Needs of Each Student. The most obvious source of information about the students is the cumulative record file that is maintained for each. In examining such records, however, teachers should be careful not to be biased by unsubstantiated statements. For example, students who have been branded as "trouble makers" often have cumulative records that contain such statements as, "Lee is a discipline problem," or "Anita isn't motivated to do school work." Often, statements like these, which do not provide the context or the specific incident that prompted previous teachers to make the remark, stay with the student throughout the school career. Unfortunately, such statements have a tendency to set up negative expectations among those who read them and the child becomes a victim of a "self-fulfilling prophecy."

Fortunately, parents now have the right to examine their children's school records and can ask that unsubstantiated information be purged from the files. However, teachers should view any broad generalization about students cautiously, putting greater faith in very specific information that appears to have a basis in direct, observational data. Although teachers who have had the student in the past may be a valuable source of information, you should attempt to verify their comments and recommendations before adopting them as your own.

Another obvious source of information is the student's parents. If teachers have a mainstreamed student in their classroom, they may have had an opportunity to meet the student's parents earlier when the IEP was developed. If it was not appropriate to do so at that time arrangements should be made to meet with the parents to discuss any unique needs or problems that their child might have. Also, an attempt should be made to find out what has "worked" for the student in the past. Such information can be invaluable in helping to structure instructional activities that will be of interest to the child.

Teachers Should Be Able to Evaluate Each Student's Present Level of Functioning. With the advent of P.L. 94-142 most school districts have developed very specific policies and procedures related to the diagnosis and assessment of children. This is one of the major benefits that has accrued to our educational system. In years past, psychological and educational assessment had most frequently been done only in the most severe cases and in a very unorganized fashion. Assessment was frequently delayed for long periods of time because of the unavailability of trained personnel to perform such tasks.

At the present time, if a child has been identified as being in need of special education services, in all likelihood teachers will have access to a rather detailed assessment of that student's educational level and specific learning, behavioral, or physical characteristics that should be taken into account when designing instruction and teaching the student. Assessment reports will probably have been prepared by psychologists, educational diagnosticians, medical personnel, and others.

As a teacher, however, it is not enough to rely upon the diagnostic skills and reports of others for information that will be needed in order to be effective in the classroom. For example, an educational assessment may have indicated that a student is two years behind grade level in reading. It will still rest with the teacher to determine such things as the student's readiness to begin new reading tasks, what the reading level should be for instructional purposes (where the student can read without frustration), and how to group the student with others for instruction. All of these things require that teachers have skills in the use of both formal assessment tests and informal tests based upon direct observation of the student.

You will also need to collect specific data concerning the child's performance for your records and for interacting with the professional diagnostic specialists in the schools. These people can be of immense assistance in helping plan educational procedures based upon assessment information. Earlier chapters in this text illustrated how such assessment programs could be implemented.

Teachers Should Be Able to Determine Goals for Each Student That Are Appropriate, Realistic, and Measurable. The requirements of the IEP specify that long-range goals and short-term objectives must be specified for each special education student. Most frequently, these goals and objectives are developed in consultation with the teachers, specialists, and parents of the children. Although P.L. 94-142 also specified that the child should be consulted with respect to these, this is seldom done in practice—at least in the IEP meeting.

Surprisingly, however, Redden (1976) found that involvement of the children in goal setting was very important for successful mainstreaming. She found that teachers who reported effective mainstreaming practices involved the students in setting day-to-day goals for learning and behavior that were in line with long-range goals. Students were also involved in the periodic assessment of their progress in meeting these goals and in revising them based upon such assessment. The teachers reported that they believed they were helping to develop a sense of responsibility for their behavior in the students who were involved in goal setting.

Teachers Should Be Able to Determine Group Goals for the Class as a Whole and for Subsets within the Class. Just as individual goal setting is important, so is goal setting for the entire class and the various groups within it. Again, successful mainstreaming teachers involve the children actively in this process. Teachers should negotiate behavioral goals with the entire group and reach consensus on alternatives that are available to class members who fail to meet these goals. Procedures should be developed with the class concerning ways to monitor goal attainment and evaluate its success.

Teachers Should Be Able to Involve Parents in Setting Goals for Their Children. Obviously, this is a specific requirement of the law. However, teachers have found that their effectiveness can be enhanced when both the school personnel and the parents are quite clear about the goals for the children. Clarity of goals enhances consistency in efforts for activities that can be carried on in both the school and the home. More will be said about the topic of parent involvement in the next chapter.

PLANNING TEACHING STRATEGIES

It goes without saying that mainstreaming is hard work. Not only does it take skill in the actual teaching process, but considerable time is required for planning. In fact one could almost say that the key to successful mainstreaming *is* specific and detailed planning. Without careful planning, efforts to mainstream will be met with frustration, difficulty, and ultimate dissatisfaction with the process. The six competencies related to planning should serve to focus attention on the variables that are critical to the planning effort.

Teachers Should Be Able to Design Teaching Procedures That Provide for Individual Differences in Students. Earlier in this chapter, individualized instruction was addressed as one of the general clusters of competence required for mainstreaming. Successful mainstreaming teachers pay particular attention to the design of individualized learning tasks that help control frustration on the part of students by enhancing their probabilities for success. Knowledge of a student's particular background, outside interests, and specific skill deficiencies enhances successful planning.

Teachers Should Be Able to Prepare a Variety of Activities that Will Involve the Entire Class in Grouping Patterns That Are Varied and Flexible. It is important that teachers try to structure learning groups so that stigma are minimized. For example, if Claire is always assigned to the "buzzards" group for all academic programming, she will begin to be known as someone who is less capable than those assigned to the "eagles." The key here is to try to provide activities that allow for a variety of grouping patterns. If a student has academic difficulties, assignment to social groups that include more capable students is beneficial.

It is also desirable to permit students to select their choice of groups, when possible. This helps to provide an opportunity for greater integration of the children. When this does occur, and students of varying ability levels appear in the same group, teachers must be sure to provide materials that accomodate to the level, pace, and style of the learners within that group. Tasks should also be planned to encourage interdependency among the children. Peer tutoring is very successful in such situations.

Teachers Should Be Able to Design a Variety of Alternative Teaching Strategies. Commonly used strategies (e.g., those that involve reading) may create difficulties for some mainstreamed students. Teachers must be resourceful enough to plan for alternative strategies to accomodate their differences. Plans in this area may include devising different levels of activity around a curriculum theme, providing choices of tasks to accomplish goals, planning drill exercises, and having a number of parallel activities that can be used to counter the boredom that frequently comes with repetition. Alternative modes of expression such as writing, speaking, pantomime, singing, dancing, recording, typing, etc., can also be planned for effective use.

Teachers Should Be Able to Develop Plans for Using Human and Material Resources. Teachers who are mainstreaming will find that participation in schoolwide planning for the use of school resources is very beneficial. Included in such planning would be the use of the existing school support staff, parents, volunteers, and cross-age tutors. Assistance is available within the class. For example, you could survey class members to determine experiences and skills of each and their respective families that can be shared with the class.

Teachers must plan for the selection, adaptation, construction, and use of instructional materials and games. Many school systems now have good instructional media centers that supply excellent assistance in this area. Field trips are beneficial and provide opportunities for first-hand experiences that all children can benefit from without regard to their academic abilities.

A special note needs to be made about planning with the school medical staff for some children. For example, if it is known that a child in the class has a health problem such as epilepsy, diabetes, hypoglycemia, heart disease, or some other physical problem, it is extremely important to develop contingency plans in the event that the child has a health-related episode in the classroom. First-aid procedures need to be well-understood as well as direction for the use of medication and notification of parents and other appropriate health personnel.

Teachers Should Be Able to Develop a Flexible Time Schedule that Provides for the Learning, Physical, and Social Needs of Each Student. Effective mainstreaming teachers have had success in allowing the entire class to participate in arranging time schedules. In so doing, however, it is important that time constraints are made clear to the students so that they do not get carried away with this activity. Schedules that are planned should also be reassessed at appropriate intervals, and flexibility should be built in to accommodate temporary or acute time-consuming activities. Allow extra time for movement of students who might have mobility problems. Permit some time for free choice of classroom activities or instructional materials on the part of students, if at all possible. Obviously, sufficient time must be scheduled to permit the completion of assignments, with consideration being given to providing various time intervals to accommodate different attention spans.

The schedule should not be planned so as to preclude spontaneous social interaction, since this is very important to mainstreamed children (and all children, for that matter). Coordinate schedules of students who must leave the room for short periods of instruction in the resource classroom or by other educational specialists. This part of scheduling can be difficult and requires flexibility and "give-and-take" on the part of all professionals involved.

Teachers Should Be Able to Plan Appropriate Arrangements and Adaptations of the Classroom Physical Environment. Common sense dictates that teachers should attend to factors such as lighting, noise level, temperature, and ventilation to ensure that extreme deviations in these variables do not interfere with the learning of all students. In addition, it is necessary to do additional planning of the physical environment if children with visual, hearing, or physical disabilities are to be included in the class.

Classrooms should be free of architectural barriers. Movable desks and chairs are more desirable than stationary desks and permit much more flexible use of classroom space. A free-standing chalkboard on legs that permits a wheelchair to be pushed under it will facilitate the board work of children confined to wheel chairs. Similarly, tables of a height that can accommodate wheelchairs are also helpful.

Space should also be planned for interest centers at which special aids such as magnifiers, tape recorders, braille typewriters, or other special equipment can be stored and made easily accessible to students. Resource teachers and other specialists can be very helpful in assisting in classroom planning and selecting any equipment and tangible aids that will be useful in educating mainstreamed students.

IMPLEMENTING TEACHING STRATEGIES

Six competencies are associated with this teaching function. However, since they deal with the implementation of the plans that were made for teaching mainstreamed students an extended discussion of them would be somewhat redundant. Therefore they will simply be listed here without further elaboration. Teachers should be able to:

- Select and use a variety of individualized teaching methods to instruct all students within their levels of capability
- Maintain a variety of grouping patterns that provide opportunities for students to reach social and academic goals
- Utilize special education resource staff
- Acquire, adapt, and develop instructional materials necessary to achieve learning goals
- Utilize the assistance of volunteers to supplement classroom activities
- Utilize the talents of parents in supporting the activities of the school

FACILITATING LEARNING

In her research, Redden (1976) identified an entire cluster of competencies that teachers reported to significantly affect their success in mainstreaming. Although related to the previous function of implementing teaching strategies, Redden chose to cluster these competencies and skills together into a separate area to highlight their importance. She called this area *facilitation of learning*. Five competencies and numerous tasks were associated with this teaching function. Most dealt with the topic of classroom management, as will become apparent from the following descriptions.

Teachers Should Be Able to Use Various Techniques to Manage Individual and Group Behavior. Effective mainstreaming teachers have identified a variety of ways to reinforce the behavior that they desire in their students. They are effective in identifying when to reinforce the children and when to ignore undesirable behaviors. They are skilled in using successive approximation strategies to accomplish desired behavioral goals; and they involve their students in planning the behavioral management programs they establish.

Teachers also have alternative procedures to substitute when change is necessary. They are able to record the behaviors of their students and use these records to make decisions about which techniques are most effective and which are not working.

Some of the specific procedures that are particularly effective include the following:

- Rewarding students for self-directed behavior by allowing choices of activities
- Teaching students how to respond to disruptive behavior of their classmates
- Using peer role models to advance goals
- Providing students with acceptable ways to relieve aggression and disappointment
- Assigning tasks to active students to give them an excuse for being out of their seats when necessary
- Allowing students "time out" to collect themselves after behavioral breakdowns or violation of established rules
- Arbitration of disputes in an open fashion
- Dealing with the students' feelings about explosive situations as well as the specific behaviors that were exhibited

Even though every effort should be made to maintain the students in the classroom, on occasion, it is necessary for even the most effective teachers to remove a student from the classroom environment. This should only be done when behavior is damaging to other students or deprives them of the opportunity to learn, and where there appears to be no other more constructive ways to deal with the problem in the context of the classroom group.

Teachers Should Be Able to Acknowledge Appropriate Behaviors in Order to Stimulate Continued Effort. Mainstreaming teachers find that positive reinforcement is one of the most powerful tools at their disposal to develop and maintain desired performance in their students. They give recognition to the student within the hearing and sight of other classmates. They encourage behavior by emphasizing the performance of peer models and praising the behavior of peers.

Activities are also structured so that the mainstreamed students can perform in front of the group in areas where they are successful, and opportunity is provided for recognition of students who put in extra effort. Particular attention is given to structuring activities so that even small degrees of improvement in serious problem areas are given special recognition.

Teachers Should Be Able to Conduct Class Activities in Ways to Encourage Student Interaction. Social interaction among students does not occur automatically. Since one of the explicit goals of mainstreaming is to facilitate the interaction of handicapped and nonhandicapped children, the teacher must be particularly attentive to structuring the classroom environment in such a fashion as to foster such interaction among students. Teachers have an opportunity to be creative in ways to help the "special" students become a part of the class group. It is important to build a climate of acceptance for the mainstreamed students by including them in all class activities—including participation in leadership activities and areas of responsibility in which the other students are involved.

Nonhandicapped children can be given the responsibility of serving as "buddies" or tutors for handicapped children. Similarly, less handicapped children can be assigned the responsibility of helping those who are more handicapped. Competitive activities must be organized carefully to avoid hurting those who will not be chosen or who have no chance of winning.

Teachers Should Be Able to Provide Instruction in the Development of Coping Strategies. Although we would all like to believe that mainstreaming will proceed smoothly with few problems, the fact is that the mainstreamed students will encounter some difficulties with their nonhandicapped peers. At times, children can be absolute beasts in their treatment of others who may show even the slightest deviation from the perceived norms of the class or age group. How often have we heard expressions such as "four-eyes," "fatso," "retard," and other more-or-less vicious taunts? Such practices will not be diminished with mainstreaming, and, in fact, may be heightened (although one of the goals of mainstreaming is to help develop a greater tolerance for individual differences among the nonhandicapped population). Consequently, it is incumbent upon the teacher to become aware of such problems and to help the mainstreamed students to develop coping strategies that will enable them to become less conspicuously different from the norm and to deal with interpersonal problems as they arise.

Successful mainstreaming teachers provide opportunities for students who are having difficulty to explain their problems and to propose solutions for them. Ways to "escape" from untenable situations and opportunities for students to ask for assistance that might be needed to complete assignments or solve problems are provided.

Try to identify special talents of all students and provide opportunities for the students to use these to their advantage. Encourage them to pursue new areas of interest to help them find ways in which they can express themselves in a positive manner to their peers. Alternative methods of expression can overcome weaknesses and students should be taught about the teaching strategies that work for them and how to ask that they be used when the students are encountering difficulty in learning.

Accentuating positive characteristics of mainstreamed students can influence nonhandicapped peers to develop a greater appreciation for their classmates. For example, higher respect was gained by a blind student when he participated in exercises with his seeing peers in which the children were not allowed to use paper to take notes or to assist in arithmetic computation. This same student excelled at locating a ball that emitted an audio beep. When his classmates were blindfolded, they found that they could not match this child's ability to locate the ball on the playground. His stature improved considerably as a result of these activities.

Teachers Should be Able to Plan with the Students for Systematic Appraisal and Improvement of the Psychological Climate of the Class. Teachers who are successful at mainstreaming provide a classroom atmosphere that is calming, supportive, and consistent. They avoid embarrassing students in front of their peers and relate to each student on a personal level.

Effective teachers structure success experiences for each student and accept genuine effort and build upon it rather than pointing out weaknesses of the students. They use curriculum materials that avoid embarrassing students by disguising the grade level for those who are working below the level of others in the class. They show warmth and genuine acceptance of special students while avoiding situations where their disabilities might be "spotlighted." They also conduct group discussions dealing with subjective feelings and interpersonal relations.

EVALUATING LEARNING

Although the evaluation of learning was dealt with in more detail in an earlier chapter, the three competencies that were identified as being critical for effective mainstreaming by Redden (1976) will be briefly highlighted here.

Teachers Should Be Able to Collect and Record Data to Evaluate Student Progress. Successful teachers design data collection systems that are clear to the students and their parents as well as to the teacher. Such systems are designed to allow the students to participate in their own record keeping. Procedures are developed so that students are permitted to evaluate and correct their own errors.

Teachers should have a variety of evaluation methods at their disposal so that an appropriate one can be selected for a given student at a given time. Much use is made of criterion-referenced tests by which achievement can readily be measured as it relates to the individual goals of the student—as opposed to only comparing performance with class norms or test norms. Standardized testing materials are also adapted to accommodate specific handicapping conditions; although there is some danger in interpreting test results under such circumstances because validity is threatened due to violation of the standardized procedures.

Teachers Should Be Able to Develop a Feedback System That Will Furnish Continuous Data to Students, Teachers, and Parents. Successful teachers develop feedback systems that become a real part of their mainstreamed students' learning experiences. Immediate feedback helps students take charge of their own learning. It is frequent, yet adequate time is allowed for correction of errors. Anxiety over grading is relieved (partially) by giving positive feedback, as well. There are numerous methods, including charts, check marks, verbal praise or correction, pats on the back, stars, tokens, and other visual, auditory, and kinesthetic procedures.

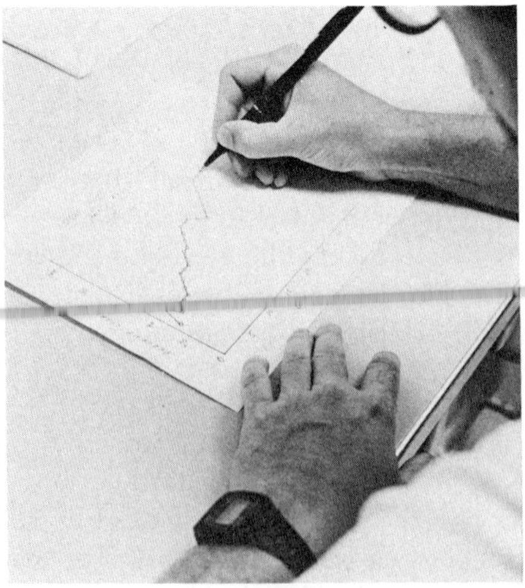

Graphs of student progress are helpful in evaluating the effectiveness of instruction.

Feedback is also important to the parents of the mainstreamed students—particularly in cases where less frequent feedback had been made available. Such procedures help to improve the relationship parents have with the school. Positive feedback helps parents develop a more positive image of their children.

Teachers Should Be Able to Use Evaluation Data to Assess the Attainment of Goals and to Set New Goals. It is important to reassess placement and services to mainstreamed children often. The law requires that an evaluation be done at least annually; however, many people think that this is insufficient for many students. If teachers employ continuous measurement systems, evaluations are greatly facilitated and decisions can be made about program modifications in a timely fashion.

USING THE MAINSTREAMING COMPETENCIES

Now that we have presented the general competency areas and many of the specific competencies that are necessary for teachers to be successful in their mainstreaming efforts, the problem becomes one of knowing how best to use this knowledge. You may recall from the previous section that one of the first competencies identified through Redden's research was that the teacher must be able to "set up a personal training program that will provide instruction in areas necessary to teach effectively in a mainstream setting." This is often more easily said than done.

Most teachers pursue the topic of their own professional development in a rather haphazard fashion. They may take courses as part of an advanced degree program or to renew their teaching certificates. They may also attend in-service training programs offered by their school districts and most will read the journals published by their professional organizations. Seldom, however, do they engage in a process of systematically planning and implementing a professional development program for themselves.

In addressing the topic of the development of a program to expand one's professional competence, Blackhurst (1981) described a model to facilitate this process. It is a seven-step process that a teacher can use to design a personal training program. Each of these steps will briefly be described in the remainder of this chapter, with an illustration of how they might be used in developing mainstreaming competencies.

STEP ONE: DEVELOP A PHILOSOPHY OF MAINSTREAMING

One's philosophy serves as the conceptual underpinning of all professional activities. If you do not have a well articulated philosophy of mainstreaming, you will find that your mainstreaming efforts will not be well grounded.

Quite likely, they will vacillate and appear somewhat confused—as if you were engaged in trial and error behavior. The most successful teachers are those who have well developed philosophies of education and can articulate them. They are also the most self-confident teachers.

Consequently, the first order of business is to concentrate on the development of a philosophy on mainstreaming that you are personally comfortable with and that can serve as a guideline for your actual mainstreaming practices. It is our hope that this text will serve to provide you with the rudiments of such a philosophy. Upon completion of the text, you should be able to critically analyze what you have read and determine which of the concepts that are presented are consistent with your beliefs and value system and which you want to incorporate into your personal philosophy of education. With that as a basis, you can then move confidently ahead.

As part of the development of a philosophy of mainstreaming, you will need to address the following questions, as a minimum:

- Do I believe in mainstreaming and think that it should be implemented?
- How do I define mainstreaming?
- What are my responsibilities as a professional teacher who is attempting to mainstream handicapped children?
- What are my goals for children who are mainstreamed into my classroom?
- What stance do I want to take in dealing with people who affect mainstreamed students (e.g., their peers, parents, school administrators)?
- What skills do I have as a teacher that can facilitate mainstreaming and what ones do I need to develop in order to become more effective?

There are undoubtedly many other factors that should be considered in developing one's philosophy of mainstreaming; however, this list should serve as a starter for those who have not given much thought to the topic. Once you are satisfied that you have a viable philosophy, you can then proceed to the next step.

STEP TWO: DEFINE MAINSTREAMING TEACHING FUNCTIONS

We have already defined mainstreaming teaching functions for you in the previous section of this chapter. We have said that the teacher who is mainstreaming handicapped children should be able to perform the following general mainstreaming functions:

- Developing orientation strategies for mainstream entry.
- Assessing needs and setting goals.
- Planning teaching strategies.

- Implementing teaching strategies.
- Facilitating learning.
- Evaluating learning.

Although we are convinced that a teacher who can perform these functions will be an effective mainstreaming teacher, it should be reemphasized that this is just an *initial* list of functions. By the time you finish reading this text, there may be additional research studies that point to other functions that have not yet been identified. Furthermore, it should be emphasized that different school systems might have different policies about mainstreaming. Consequently, the teacher who is involved in mainstreaming efforts needs to develop a list of teaching functions that are consistent with his or her personal philosophy and that of the school system in which the mainstreaming is to take place.

STEP THREE: IDENTIFY NEEDED MAINSTREAMING COMPETENCIES

We have identified the competencies that are associated with each mainstreaming function. You may want to examine these carefully, as you do with the teaching functions above, and decide which are important for your own personal situation. Once you have decided upon your list of competencies, you must then conduct a critical appraisal of your ability to perform each. Those competencies for which you believe you need additional training then become the basis for your individual professional development program. The checklist shown in Figure 7.1 should be helpful in performing a self-evaluation.

STEP FOUR: DEFINE AND PRIORITIZE OBJECTIVES

Each of the competencies that you identify as appropriate for additional training can be subdivided into a list of much more specific tasks. For example, the competency related to acquiring, adapting, and developing materials necessary to achieve learning goals could have the following subcomponents (in part):

- Select appropriate materials that are developed for individualized instruction.
- Develop new materials when available materials are not appropriate to meet goals.
- Use special materials that allow students to compensate for handicaps without "watering down" the curriculum.
- Use games to develop concepts.
- Combine audiovisual materials with other learning aids to supply input from more than one source.

Xerox

PART 1: MAINSTREAMING TEACHER COMPETENCY CHECKLIST

Check the column at the right that best indicates the appraisal of your needs for additonal information about mainstreaming or the development of skills related to that objective. Check the columns according to the following key:

1. Not relevant for my situation
2. Already competent in this area
3. Need to develop additional awareness
4. Need to develop skills for application

COMPETENCY	EVALUATION			
	1	2	3	4
A. Developing Orientation Skills for Mainstream Entry	X	X	X	X
1. Participate in school wide planning for mainstreaming				
2. Develop a personal training program about mainstreaming				
3. Participate in parent and community orientation programs about mainstreaming				
4. Seek out consultative relationships with schools specialists				
5. Prepare special students for entry into the regular class				
6. Prepare members of the regular class for entry of special students into the class				
B. Assessing Needs and Setting Goals	X	X	X	X
1. Gather information to determine the educational needs of students				
2. Evaluate the present level of functioning of students				
3. Determine goals for students that are appropriate, realistic, and measurable				
4. Determine group goals and goals for subgroups within the class				
5. Involve parents in setting goals for their children				
C. Planning and Implementing Teaching Strategies	X	X	X	X
1. Planning and teaching in response to individual differences				
2. Operate grouping patterns that are flexible and varied				

3. Utilize special education resource staff				
4. Acquire, adapt, and/or develop instructional materials				
5. Use volunteers and parents to supplement classroom activities				
6. Develop flexible time schedules				
7. Plan adaptations of the classroom physical environment				
D. Facilitating Learning	X	X	X	X
1. Use techniques to manage individual and group behavior				
2. Conduct class activities to encourage interaction				
3. Provide instruction in coping strategies				
4. Plan for appraisal and improvement of the psychological climate of the class				
E. Evaluating Learning	X	X	X	X
1. Collect and record data for evaluating student progress				
2. Develop a feedback system to furnish data to students, teachers and parents				
3. Use evaluation data to assess goal attainment				

PART 2: MAINSTREAMING KNOWLEDGE CHECKLIST

In the following items, check off those items for which you believe you have sufficient knowledge.

____1. The least restrictive environment principle as it applies to mainstreaming
____2. Federal legislation concerning education of the handicapped
____3. Understanding of the history and philosophy of mainstreaming
____4. Basic knowledge of various mainstreaming models (e.g., consulting teacher, resource room, special class)
____5. Understanding of the role of parents in the mainstreaming process
____6. Ability to define what mainstreaming is and is not
____7. Knowledge of state laws and guidelines for the education of mainstreamed students
____8. Knowledge of legal rights of students
____9. Knowledge of the research basis for mainstreaming

Figure 7.1 Teacher competencies for mainstreaming self-evaluation checklist.

By task analyzing each competency that you have selected for your professional development program, you will begin to get a more specific idea about your own strengths and weaknesses. By prioritizing these, you can then give direction for the next step in the sequence. For example, you may decide that you already know about commercially available materials; however, you may have never really developed a good instructional material, nor are you comfortable in using games for instructional purposes. You might then decide that you will take a course in the development of instructional materials and obtain a text on the use of games that you can read in your leisure time.

STEP FIVE: IDENTIFY CONTENT AND RESOURCES

With your prioritized objectives in hand, you can embark upon a search for appropriate materials, resources, people, and information that can be used to implement your professional development program. Obvious sources are college courses, in-service training workshops, professional texts, journals, and professional organizations. Do not overlook your professional colleagues as sources for assistance. It can be quite profitable to sit in on a colleague's class to observe how that person interacts with children.

A relatively new source is the *ERIC* System. Because it is relatively new, we believe that we should provide a brief explanation of how to use this important resource. *ERIC* stands for *Educational Resources Information Center*. The *ERIC* system was developed in the late 1960s to serve as a clearinghouse for information about various branches of education. In the area of special education, the clearinghouse for information is operated by the Council for Exceptional Children (CEC) in Reston, Virginia. This clearinghouse is called the CEC Information Center. The CEC Information Center monitors the great majority of special education literature published throughout the world.

Periodically, CEC submits abstracts of articles that have been identified to *ERIC* Central, which publishes a periodical abstract journal *Resources in Education* (*RIE*). Because there are several clearinghouses, all of which submit abstracts to *RIE*, there is insufficient space in that journal to publish all of the abstracts that have been written. Consequently, the various clearinghouses publish their own abstracts. The journal in special education is called *Exceptional Child Education Resources* (ECER). (This journal was originally called *Exceptional Child Education Abstracts*.)

Vast amounts of material are abstracted in *ECER*, but its most useful feature is the system used to search for information about a particular topic. Once a topic has been selected, the searcher selects a series of descriptors that are used to conduct the search. Each descriptor has a list of abstract numbers associated with it. When the abstract numbers match up for each descriptor, the searcher has located a "hit." The abstract that has been identified will relate specifically to the topic. The searcher can then go to the abstract, read this, and then decide whether time would be well spent to examine the article in its entirety. An example should serve to illustrate the utility of this system.

Let us suppose that a vocational education teacher has been informed that several mildly handicapped students will be placed in his class during the coming school year. Never having dealt with such students before, he is anxious to locate information that might be of assistance to him. He visits the library of his local university and locates the *Exceptional Child Education Resources* materials in the reference room. First he defines the problem: "I need to find information related to the mainstreaming of handicapped children in vocational education programs." Satisfied that he has defined the problem, he then selects appropriate descriptors with which to conduct his search. These are *mainstreaming, handicapped children*, and *vocational education*.

Turning to the latest issue of *ECER* at his disposal, he looks up each of the descriptors and finds the following entries with lists of numbers after them:

Mainstreaming

Handicapped Children

108, 117, 119, 156, 165, 168, 315, (323), (324), 328, (362), (363), 381, (407), 420, 466, 510, (511), (585), (586), (591), (592), 691, 753, 756, 758, 836, 865, 904, 908, 915, 922, 968, 1017, 1052, 1087

Vocational Education

Handicapped Children

(323), (324), (362), (363), 364, 365, 366, 267, 268, (407), (511), 579, 581, (585), (586), (591), (592), 717, 862, 1048

Each of the numbers corresponds to an abstract of a journal article, text, microfilm, or other document related to the topic of each descriptor.

Our teacher then goes back to both lists and identifies the numbers that are common to each. These have been circled above. These numbers represent "hits." That is, each hit indicates that the article that was identified is related to the topic of "mainstreaming handicapped children in vocational education."

Pleased that he has identified 10 hits, he then turns to the section of *ECER* that has the abstracts in it. He scans all 10 abstracts and finds that several relate to technical research reports that are of little interest to him. Another is an interview with two authorities that does not seem to have much practical relevance. Still another article appears to be written for administrators, and others deal with planning and attitude change. Out of the ten hits, he finds that one refers to a special feature issue of the journal, *School Shop*, published in April 1978, which was devoted entirely to mainstreaming. Another of the hits is an autoinstructional module about mainstreaming that was developed for vocational educators under a federal grant. The abstract indicated that the module provides a general understanding of mainstreaming in vocational education programs, components of appropriate programs, laws, regulations, and information about handicapping conditions. This module was available on microfiche or a copy could be purchased from the *ERIC* Document Reproduction Service.

Our teacher was elated. He was able to identify essentially all of the relevant literature to his topic that was published during a three-month period of time covered by that issue of *ECER*. Had he wanted additional information, he could have gone to other issues of *ECER*. What amazed him even more was that he had conducted his search in a little less than 20 minutes. Previously, he would have had to sort through issues of *Education Index* and other reference sources and would have only had the title of the articles identified. The abstracts helped considerably in winnowing the information that he located.

STEP SIX: IMPLEMENTING THE PROFESSIONAL DEVELOPMENT PROGRAM

Obviously, procedures followed during this step will be specifically tailored to the objectives and content identified. This could involve independent study, attendance at a conference, taking a short workshop or a course at a university, or visiting other programs to observe them and meet with the personnel who are involved. In most cases, the barriers that need to be overcome during this step are time and financial resources.

STEP SEVEN: EVALUATE, REVISE, AND REFINE

You should not get the impression that the previous six steps represent a rigid, lockstep sequence. On the contrary, at every step of the way, you should be questioning, evaluating, and analyzing the information that is obtained. As a result, modifications are generally made in previous steps. For example, while locating the content about a particular topic, you will probably unearth information that will influence your philosophy. Similarly, while implementing the program, you may discover things that will cause you to revise your perceived teaching role or competencies. Thus, your professional development program should be something that is dynamic and constantly changing.

TEACHER CONCERNS

The idea of mainstreaming is very appealing from both a logical and an emotional standpoint. It makes sense to educate all children who can profit from regular class instruction together. All children are entitled to a free and appropriate education in our democratic system. Not only is it good for the mainstreamed students, but a strong case can be made for the notion that mainstreaming is good for other students, as well. Mainstreaming will help to improve attitudes toward people with handicaps and will help to stimulate a greater tolerance for individual differences in our society.

Unfortunately, however, there are many potential problems between the conceptualization of mainstreaming and its implementation. Many teachers, administrators, and parents have voiced concerns that mainstreaming might fail because it is not properly implemented. Indeed, the authors are aware of a number of school systems that have had significant problems with mainstreaming because there was insufficient planning for its implementation and insufficient policies, resources, and support services for its implementation.

The National Education Association (NEA) addressed some of the issues and concerns of teachers in their NEA Resolution 77-33 (Ryor, 1977). NEA members supported the concept of mainstreaming while acknowledging many of their concerns about its implementation. In taking a positive approach toward the topic, the NEA Resolution spelled out a number of things that teachers and school officials should keep in mind when developing a favorable learning experience for both handicapped and nonhandicapped students. Some of these bear repeating because they can serve as guidelines that school personnel can strive to follow in order to maximize the probability of being successful in mainstreaming efforts.

- *Regular and special education teachers, administrators, and parents must share in planning and implementation of education for children with disabilities.* Note that the key here is *sharing*. The authors know of one school district that attempted to "implement" mainstreaming by announcing to the teachers at the end of the preschool in-service training session that "all special education students would be mainstreamed this year." That was the extent of the planning and discussion. Needless to say, mainstreaming was a dismal failure in that school system.

- *All staff must be adequately prepared for their roles through in-service training and retraining.* It is insufficient to simply have an "expert" on mainstreaming speak at an in-service meeting or series of in-service meetings. Teachers need to know more than just characteristics of children who may be mainstreamed. They need to learn about specific alternatives for teaching them within the context of their classrooms. (We hope that the chapters in this text will provide *some* of this information.)

- *All students must be adequately prepared for the program.* To "dump" students with problems into the regular class is unfair both to the regular classroom students and the mainstreamed students. Both groups must be oriented to this new type of educational arrangement.
- *The appropriateness of educational methods, materials, and supportive services must be determined in cooperation with regular classroom teachers.* This again underscores the importance of viewing education for mainstreamed students as a joint effort. Specialists should not attempt to require a particular instructional material or method without discussing this with the teacher and setting up procedures to monitor its effectiveness, with the idea in mind of making changes as they are needed.
- *An appeal procedure regarding the implementation of the program, especially in terms of student placement, must be made available.* As much as we might not like to admit it, there are cases in which a particular student cannot be accommodated in a particular classroom. There are several reasons for this, ranging from personality conflict between teacher and student to problems with interpersonal relationships among students, to inability to structure an educational environment that is conducive to the learning of that particular student. We need to acknowledge the possibility of such occurrences and to provide a mechanism that permits alternative placement to facilitate the learning and mental health of all involved.
- *Modification must be made in class size, scheduling, and curriculum design to accommodate program demands.* Modification in class size is perhaps one of the most difficult of the NEA guidelines to implement because of the obvious implication that this has for finances. Schedule and curriculum modifications are more amenable to change. Perhaps the enrollment decreases that are projected for the coming years will permit some reduction in class size in order to provide the extra time and effort needed for greater individualization of instruction.
- *There must be a systematic evaluation and reporting of program developments using a plan that recognizes individual differences.* Note that the emphasis here is on program evaluation, not child evaluation. Program evaluation is frequently not done systematically or not done at all. It is through this type of evaluation that data are collected that can be used for making decisions about needed program modifications. Such evaluations should be done on a regular basis.
- *Adequate funding must be provided and then used exclusively for this program.* Federal funds are made available to support the excess costs of operating special education programs through P.L. 94-142. Although considerable amounts of monies are made available to local school districts, the funding appropriation from Congress does not yet approach the amount that was authorized in the original legislation. There is a need for us to continue to educate our legislative represent-

atives about the importance of this program and the need for full funding of the legislation.

- *Classroom teachers must have a major role in determining individual educational programs and should become members of school assessment teams*. As was pointed out in a previous chapter, classroom teachers do have the responsibility of collecting data and making appropriate referrals. They should also participate in the IEP meetings that relate to children they are referring or might receive as a result of mainstreaming placement. This relates back to the concept of the teacher as part of the educational team.
- *Adequate released time must be made available for teachers so that they can carry out the increased demands upon them*. Like the issue of reduced class size, this is difficult to carry out for financial reasons. However, involvement in IEP conferences, assessment, in-service training, parent conferences, and planning for mainstreaming activities all require time. If released time is not made available for these activities, problems will undoubtedly be encountered.
- *Staff must not be reduced*. Some school officials have looked upon mainstreaming as a way to reduce staff. They have attempted to do this by eliminating some of the special education teachers by placing their students in regular class programs. Fortunately, such practices, which are based on uninformed decision making, are rare. Mainstreaming should never be looked upon as a vehicle for reducing the school staff. Just because a student is removed from a special class and placed in the mainstream does not mean that fewer special education teachers are needed. The role of the special education teacher merely changes from that of a self-contained class teacher to one of a resource or consulting teacher.
- *All teachers must be made aware of their right of dissent concerning the appropriate program for a student, including the right to have the dissenting opinion recorded*. Frequently, there are differences of opinion about the most appropriate placement for a child. Sometimes parents disagree with the placement decisions; at other times there are differences of opinion among the educational staff members. Decisions need to be made based upon the best data available at that particular point in time. Teachers do not have to sit docilely and have these educational decisions made for them. They have the right (and the responsibility) to speak up and let their opinions be heard about such matters. They should have their opinions recorded in the event of appeals and possible litigation.
- *Individual educational programs should provide appropriate services for the handicapped students and not be used as criteria for the evaluation of the teacher*. This guideline is particularly important. Teachers have expressed concern that they would be evaluated negatively if the goals and objectives specified in a child's IEP were not met. While teachers

are accountable for instruction, there are numerous variables that could lead to situations in which a child does not meet the items specified in the IEP. Teachers should do everything that they can to live up to the letter and intent of the IEP. If they do and the child still does not learn, the teachers should not be punished for this. Instead, efforts should be made to determine why the child has not learned and modifications should be made accordingly. If it is determined that faulty learning has occurred as a result of inappropriate teaching, then efforts shoud be made to retrain the teacher to use more appropriate procedures.

Teachers should be aware of the NEA guidelines as they go about the business of implementing mainstreaming programs. Implicit in the guidelines is that classroom teachers become actively involved in their implementation. For example, if a particular school does not provide appropriate in-service education, then the teachers should actively negotiate with administrators for better training programs. Efforts should also be expanded to develop policy statements that would incorporate those of the above guidelines that are deemed appropriate for a particular school system. Mainstreaming is something that will not automatically happen. It requires the efforts of all people who are involved with the educational enterprise. It also represents a departure from a number of practices that have been part of educational tradition. Although mandated by law, we should remember that we, as teachers, have certain rights as well. These should also be respected in the implementation of mainstreaming practices.

SUMMARY

- Mainstreaming is more likely to be effective when teachers favor the concept and believe that it will work.
- Regular classroom teachers do not have sole responsibility for mainstreaming. Instead, mainstreaming should be viewed as a team effort with shared responsibilities.
- Many specialists are available to help support mainstreaming efforts in the schools.
- A national study identified 10 clusters of competences that relate to mainstreaming. These include curriculum, teaching basic skills, class management, professional consultation and communication, teacher-parent-student relationships, student-student relationships, exceptional conditions, referral, individualized teaching, professional values.
- Some 31 competencies have been defined as a result of studying effective and ineffective mainstreaming strategies. These competencies are clustered around the following six teaching functions: developing orientation strategies for mainstream entry, assessing needs and setting goals,

planning teaching strategies, implementing teaching strategies, facilitating learning, and evaluating learning.

- Mainstreaming teachers have the responsibility for designing a personal program of professional development.
- The National Education Association has identified a number of concerns that teachers have about implementing mainstreaming. These concerns should be taken into consideration as school personnel design and implement mainstreaming programs.

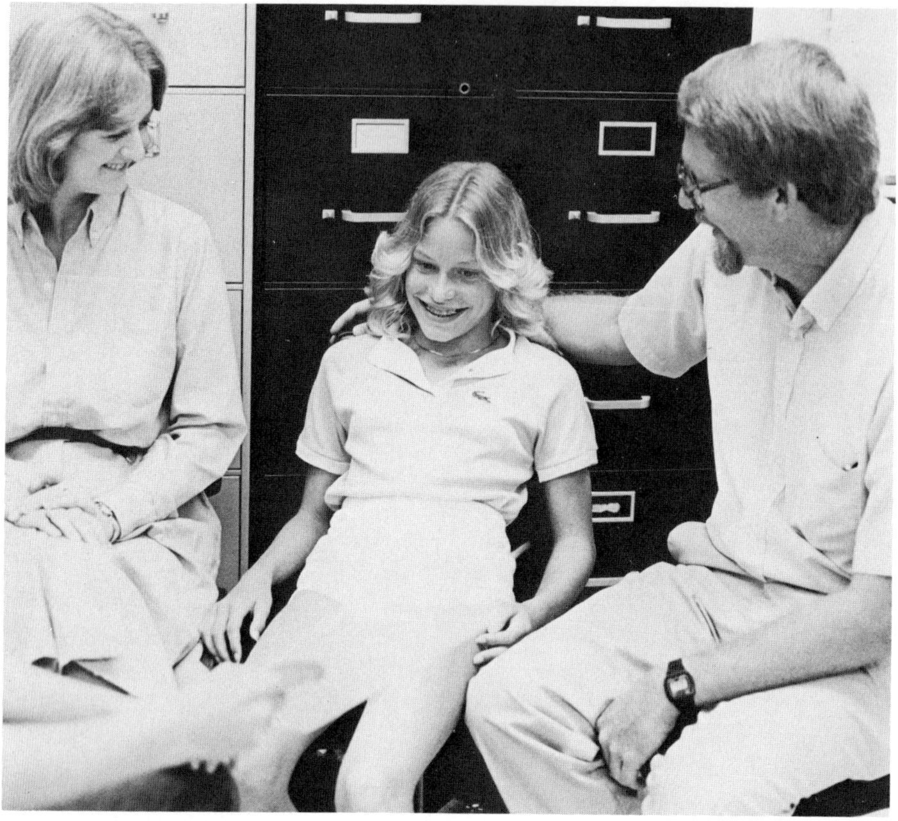

EIGHT

Working with Parents of Mainstreamed Students

- What rights do parents have with respect to the education of their children?
- What attitudes and reactions do parents have when they learn that they have a handicapped child?
- What needs for information do parents of mainstreamed students have?
- How can parents be involved in the education of their mainstreamed children?
- How can effective parent conferences be conducted?
- What principles should be followed in communicating with parents?

There are several reasons why parents should be involved in the education of their children who are mainstreamed, other than the natural concern for their welfare. For example, parents have vital information that teachers can use in their children's educational programs. Also, because parents have considerable influence on learning, they need to be in close contact with the school in order to support the teachers' efforts when children are at home. Consistency between home and school practices can have a strong facilitating effect on mainstreaming efforts.

In considering the scope of parent involvement in educational programs, Lillie (1976) describes four major dimensions that appear to be most important. The first of these relates to social and emotional support. Parents of mainstreamed students often need help in reducing anxieties and feelings of inadequacy. They can be assisted in developing positive attitudes about their child, their family as a unit, and themselves as parents.

A second dimension related to parent involvement is the exchange of information. Parents have needs for information that school personnel can meet. Conversely, teachers need information that only parents can provide. An open and on-going flow of information can be most beneficial in support of mainstreaming efforts.

Active participation is a third important element of parent programs. Active involvement (e.g., serving as a volunteer aide) will help parents to increase their understanding of children, in general. It will also provide them with additional strategies to use in interactions with their own children. As consumers, parents can also provide valuable recommendations for consideration in developing their child's IEP, and they can participate actively in the decision-making process related to the overall mainstreaming program.

Finally, good programs can assist parents in improving the interactions with their children and their general child rearing practices. As they develop better parenting skills, they become better equipped to facilitate the social and intellectual growth of their children.

The rights of parents in regard to the education of their children are described in this chapter. Following this is a discussion of attitudes and reactions that are common among parents who discover that their children may be in need of special education services. Then the information needs of parents are presented, followed by a description of some of the ways that parents can be directly involved in educational programs for their mainstreamed children. Procedures for establishing and maintaining communication with parents are presented and suggestions are made for resources that parents might find useful. The chapter concludes with a description of the specific roles that teachers should assume in order to maximize success in working with parents of mainstreamed students.

PARENT RIGHTS

In recent years, parents have become more active in pursuing litigation to resolve real and imagined grievances with school policies and practices. In addition, new laws and regulations are continually being developed that affect the schools. Because of these factors, it is becoming increasingly difficult for teachers to remain familiar with their legal responsibilities and the rights of students and their parents. The following table summarizes a number of parent rights that relate to all children in school. It is obviously incumbent upon teachers to be familiar with these rights and the policies of their local school board.

Twenty-One Parent Rights

Rights	States Where Applicable
Student Discipline	
• To take legal action against a school official if your child has been disciplined with "excessive or unreasonable" physical force.	All
• To appeal the suspension of your child.	All
• To appeal an administrator's decision to place your child in a class for students labeled "disruptive" or "troublemakers."	All, except CA, DC, GA, KY, MO, ND, and WA
Student and Other Records	
• To look at *all* your child's school records. You may challenge any record you believe is untrue or unfair. School officials must respond to your challenge within a "reasonable time." If still dissatisfied you may request a hearing.	All

• To look at all official school policies.	All, except IL
• To look at other official school records, such as research and planning reports (but not personnel records).	AL, AK, AR, CO, CT, DC, FL, HI, ID, IN, KS, LA, ME, MD, MN, MO, MT, NB, NM, NV, NH, NY, ND, OR, SC, TX, UT, WI

Student Instruction

• To see instructional materials used in research programs funded by the U.S. Department of Education and National Science Foundation.	All
• To have your handicapped child placed in an "appropriate" public school program. Parents also must be consulted about the evaluation and placement of their handicapped child.	All
• To appeal an administrator's decision prohibiting your daughter from trying out for and playing in male-dominated sports.	All, except CA, IA, IL, IN, KS, KY, MN, NB, ND, NM, WY
• To visit your child's classroom(s) at any time during the day, providing you first notify the school office.	AL, AK, AZ, CO, DE, DC, FL, IN, IA, LA, MD, MI, MS, MT, NB, NV, NH, NY, ND, OH, OK, SC, SD, TN, TX, UT, VA
• To attend a minimum number of conferences with your child's teacher(s).	AL, AK, AZ, CT, DC, DE, FL, LA, MD, MI, NB, NV, NH, NC, OH, OK, TN
• To educate your child at home, providing you meet conditions and standards set by your state.	AL, AK, AZ, CA, CO, CT, DC, FL, GA, HI, IL, IA, ME, MD, MA, MN, MS, MO, MT, NV, NH, NJ, NM, NY, NC, OK, RI, SD, TX, UT, WV
• To request that your child be excused from studying subjects you object to on religious, moral, or other *reasonable* grounds.	AK, AZ, CO, DE, DC, FL, ID, IL, IN, IA, LA, MD, MI, NV, NH, NY, NC, OH, PA, VT, WV, WI

Twenty-One Parent Rights (continued)

Rights	States Where Applicable
• To request that your child be excused from reading assigned books you object to on religious, moral, or other *reasonable* grounds.	AL, AK, AZ, CO, DC, FL, ID, IL, IN, LA, MD, MI, MS, NV, NH, NY, NC, OH, PA, RI, VT, VA, WV
• To request that your child be excused from school activities you object to on religious, moral, or other *reasonable* grounds.	AL, AK, AZ, CO, DE, FL, ID, IL, IN, IA, KS, LA, MD, MI, MS, NV, NH, NY, ND, NC, OH, OK, PA, RI, VT, VA, WA, WV, WI
Other Rights	
• To appeal a school policy or decision that prevents your child from expressing controversial views, so long as they are not obscene, slanderous, or libelous, and do not cause serious disruption.	All
• To speak at all public meetings of the local school board.	AL, AK, AR, CO, CT, DC, FL, GA, HI, ID, IN, KY, LA, ME, MD, MI, MN, MS, NB, NM, NV, NH, NC, ND, OH, OK, SD, TX, UT, VT, WS, WY
• To appeal some local board decisions to a higher state authority (other than a court).	AL, AZ, CO, CT, DE, FL, GA, IL, IN, IA, LA, MD, MA, MN, MS, MT, NB, NV, NH, NJ, OH, OK, OR, ST, TX, UT, VT, WV, WI
• To appeal a policy or decision that prevents your child from joining a club or activity that is controversial but otherwise lawful.	AL, AR, CO, DE, DC, FL, GA, IN, IA, LA, MD, MI, MS, MO, MT, ND, NV, NH, NJ, NY, NC, OH, OK, OR, RI, SC, SD, TX, WA, WY, WV
• To appeal a policy or decision that allows school employees to search your	AL, AR, CO, CT, DC, FL, GA, IA, LA, MD,

child or his property without a legal warrant or your permission.	MS, MO, MT, NB, NH, NJ, NY, NC, OH, OK, OR, PA, RI, SC, SD, TX, UT, WA, WV
• To be a member of any parent/citizen group and have your group recognized and heard by school officials.	AL, AK, AZ, AR, CO, DC, FL, HI, ID, IL, IN, LA, ME, MI, MS, MT, NB, NM, NV, NH, NY, NC, OH, VT, VA, WV

Source: The rights listed were granted by federal or state laws, regulations, and court decisions as of November 1, 1977. It is possible that a right may not apply throughout a particular state but may still be granted by local school board policy. Permission to reprint this information was granted by the National Committee for Citizens in Education, 410 Wilde Lake Village Green, Columbia, MD 21044.

It may be recalled from the first chapter that there were a number of rights that relate specifically to the parents of students who have been referred for special education services. Because teachers are often the first to refer students for such services, parents may first ask them what their rights are. Although the wise policy is to refer such inquiries to the appropriate school administrator, teachers should be aware of the general nature of these rights. Consequently, we will summarize them for you here (Ballard, 1977):

- *Notice*. Before a student is tested or placed in a special education program, parents have the right to be notified of what the school plans to do.
- *Consent*. Parents must give their consent before special tests are conducted and before their child is placed in a special education program.
- *Evaluation*. Parents have the right to obtain a full evaluation of their child's educational needs.
- *Records*. Parents have a right to know what records are kept on their children and they have a right to inspect these.
- *Individualized Education Program (IEP)*. Parents have the right to participate in the design of an educational plan for their child, which is appropriate for the specific needs of that child. Parents must give written approval prior to the time that the IEP is implemented. They also must be given the opportunity to review the IEP and their child's progress on at least an annual basis.
- *Confidentiality of information*. With the exception of certain individuals, such as school officials and teachers with legitimate educational interests, no one may see a child's records unless parents grant specific written permission.

- *Least Restrictive Environment.* Parents have the right to have a child with a disability educated with nondisabled children to the maximum extent that is possible.
- *Hearings.* If parents disagree with the decisions made about their child's educational placement or procedures used in educating their child, they may request a hearing by an impartial hearing officer. Results of hearings can further be appealed to the State Department of Education, and, ultimately, to Federal Court.

All school districts should now have specific policies and procedures related to the implementation of the above mentioned rights. Consequently, teachers should obtain copies of these policies so that they can be an informed source if parents request information about their rights within the context of that school system.

PARENT ATTITUDES AND REACTIONS

Parents of mainstreamed students will exhibit a whole range of attitudes toward their children, the educational program that they are in, and the teachers who are involved in implementing the IEP. It is important to be aware of these different attitudes and reactions in order to understand some of the statements that parents might make. This knowledge will also help in maintaining the most positive communication with parents.

It is important to realize that the regular class teacher may be the first one to draw the parents' attention to the fact that their child may be having difficulties that are severe enough to warrant referral to a special education program. Information of this type, when first conveyed to parents, will precipitate different reactions from different parents. After referrals have been made and mainstreamed students are placed, in all likelihood other attitudes will be apparent.

McLoughlin (1981) summarized the research and opinions of many professionals concerning the reactions that parents have to their children with disabilities. Some authorities believe that parents go through a rather specific series of stages as they learn to cope with the difficulties in rearing such children. Others believe that there is no set series of stages, and that some parents will exhibit some reactions and others will not. We will describe the range of reactions that might be exhibited by different parents at different times as reported by McLoughlin, and some of the implications for dealing with these. Several of the recommendations have been drawn from the work of Leydorf (1978). We will provide a series of "clues" to illustrate each of the stages. The clues are typical of statements that are made by parents who are exhibiting a particular attitude and might be useful in helping to understand the reactions that a particular parent may be having.

SHOCK

The initial reaction that most parents have to the information that their child might have a disability is shock. Even though the parents may have suspected that there is a problem, its confirmation still comes as a shock. Confusion frequently accompanies this stage, particularly when professionals have not completed their diagnosis.

Clues: I can't believe it!

I knew that he was having problems, but I didn't think they were this serious.

What are we going to do? (often accompanied by tears)

As the first one to confront a parent with the possibility of a severe problem, the teacher may be the first to feel the impact of this stage. While attempting to be as sympathetic as possible, you should convey the image to the parents of being a person who is concerned with the welfare of their child. In dealing with parents during this initial stage, it is important to assist them in understanding that it is necessary to get a thorough diagnosis in order to either confirm the suspicions or to find the source of their child's difficulty. Parents report that speed is of the essence, here. They want to know what the problem is and what they can do about it. If it is not possible to have an immediate diagnosis, a full explanation for the delay should be given. Refer the parents to the appropriate school official who is in charge of working with special education referrals and explain to the parents that this person will be the one to provide direct assistance to them.

DENIAL

After being presented with a diagnosis confirming a disability, many parents will deny its existence. They may attribute the diagnosis to errors on the part of the person making it. They may engage in a search for a more favorable diagnosis by seeking the advice and evaluation of other specialists. Attention is often focused on things that the child can do satisfactorily as evidence that a problem does not exist. Although denial is a temporary stage for some parents, others may remain at this stage for years. In the latter case, evidence that parents deny the existence of a problem frequently takes the form of unrealistic planning for the child.

Clues: How can that doctor claim that my daughter has problems? He has never seen her before, and was only with her for about an hour.

I've heard that the University has a new specialist in learning disabilities on their special education staff. I think I'll take my son to him for another evaluation. [Although second opinions are valuable, denial creates problems when parents are engaged in a constant search for a 'second opinion.']

Aunt Harriet's boy had exactly the same problem when he was my son's age and he turned out OK.

Patty can't be retarded. She spells her name and knows her address.

Our plans are to have Lee follow in his Dad's footsteps and enroll in the business administration program at Ohio State.

Parents who remain at this stage may create additional problems for their children. By denying the existence of a problem, they often delay the delivery of appropriate remedial services; thus, a problem can get worse. In working with parents who exhibit denial reactions, it is important to ensure that a thorough assessment has been done and that all variables have been examined. Parents must be assured that the evaluations have been done by highly qualified specialists. It also helps to have both parents present when reports of the diagnostic evaluation are given. All questions that they have should be answered fully. Long-term implications of the disability should also be explained in order to help the parents develop realistic expectations for their child.

ANGER/GUILT

Although these two reactions may seem to be different, they are related. Anger is sometimes directed outward toward the school and other factors, with the result that a parent may then feel guilty about being angry. Similarly, the parent may direct anger inwardly, which will also contribute to guilt feelings. Parents may blame themselves, schools, circumstances, other people, or deity. Spouses are particularly vulnerable targets, as are obstetricians and teachers.

Clues: That damn first grade teacher never did teach my kid to read!

Anita was delivered by that young partner of Dr. Welby. I knew we should have insisted on a more experienced doctor.

Why is God punishing me this way?

I told my wife to stop smoking during her pregnancy. Now look what's happened.

What did I do wrong while I was carrying Mike?

You're the teacher! You're supposed to teach her!

An angry parent is obviously very difficult to deal with. Keep in mind that the parent's anger is often the result of a sense of frustration and that it might be beneficial to the parent to have an opportunity to vent some of this frustration in an angry outburst. On occasion, it might just be best to be quiet and let the parent be angry. Of course, continual anger over several sessions is counterproductive.

Anger and guilt can best be dealt with by helping the parents to see the realities of the situation. More often than not, the parents did not do something that contributed to the condition. Explanations of the etiology (cause) of the particular problem help to reduce the guilt and the anger. Specialists can help in these explanations. In some cases, particularly with problems in learning, we do not know the causes of a particular problem and it is usually sufficient to acknowledge this fact and then move on to discuss ways in which the home and school can work together to remediate the difficulty.

UNREALISTIC HOPE

Some parents may express excessive hope for a miracle cure. They may engage in "shopping sprees" which involve going from one specialist to another and insisting that school personnel follow the advice that they have received. Parents in this stage frequently latch onto fads that are described in the popular press. These might include things such as vitamin therapy, special diets without food additives, complicated exercise regimens, and the application of various types of tutorial programs and instructional materials. In most cases, parents will try various approaches and discard them when they do not seem to be effective. Sometimes, they do not give promising practices sufficient time to show results.

Clues: I'm taking Edna to Eureka Clinic three times each week for perceptual-motor training.

We've restricted Dave's sugar intake and he is not allowed to eat foods with artificial additives. Please see that he doesn't cheat on his diet at school.

We have a series of appointments with the best specialists who will be designing a special tutorial program for Marie.

I've just spoken to Fred's pediatrician and he has assured me that Fred will outgrow his problem by the time he goes through puberty.

You should realize that parents who are in this stage are particularly vulnerable to quackery and should be protected. When alternatives are mentioned, teachers should do everything possible to provide parents with information relative to the validity of claims for "miracle cures" or they should direct the parents to those who may have evidence about such practices. Evidence about programs that have not worked should be shared with the parents. There are cases on record in which families have spent all of their financial resources in the search for nonexistent cures for their children with disabilities.

DEPRESSION

Some parents develop a resigned attitude to the fact that they have a child with a disability. This attitude is an unhealthy one and can result in a range of reactions from listlessness, to intense sorrow, to severe withdrawal. Some parents may even go so far as to try to hide their child from others. Overprotectiveness is also common among parents who are in this stage.

Clues: No, I can't come to the parent meeting. I don't even want to talk about it.

I'm just sick about Ada's problem, and won't take her anywhere.

Jim is such a frail child, don't let him roughhouse with the other boys on the playground.

Everytime I think about Marge's future, I burst into tears.

For parents who are depressed, it is very important to try to get them into a parent education and support program. Other parents of mainstreamed students who have healthier attitudes can be very helpful in these efforts. Membership in parent groups and parent counseling should be suggested to such parents. Depression can be quite debilitating and can permeate all aspects of a parent's life—thus negatively affecting other family members.

REJECTION

Unfortunately, some parents reject their children with disabilities. Rejection can be of two types: overt and disguised. Overt rejection is illustrated by open resentment of the child. Professionals or society, in general, may be scapegoats for the child's difficulty. Disguised rejection is often difficult to detect; however, it may be illustrated by an over-solicitous attitude toward the child. People who subtly view their disabled child as a disgrace are guilty of disguised rejection.

Clues: What kind of child is this? He only brings you trouble.

My life has just been ruined because of Ed. I'll probably have to spend my retirement years looking after him.

I don't like to have Clyde around when boys come over to pick up his sister for dates. They will probably think he's weird and won't date her anymore.

Do what you want with her. I'm not interested in what you do, just don't bother me with problems.

Rejecting parents place low expectations for performance on their disabled child which, in turn, does damage to the child's feelings of worth and ultimately on the level of achievement. Consequently, it is important for teachers to do everything possible to see that a child is achieving to the greatest extent possible. Parents who reject their children are quite difficult to work with. In many cases, psychiatric care is warranted to change this type of attitude. Teachers can help by being positive in their dealings with children of such parents and report positive things about their children, highlighting gains that are made. This type of approach by teachers helps parents to realize that their children are worthy and do have potential.

ACCEPTANCE AND UNDERSTANDING

When parents reach the realization that they do have a child with a disability, and they feel no guilt about it, and do not blame others or society, then they have reached the stage of understanding and acceptance. Unfortunately, not all parents reach this stage; however, this is the stage that we should help parents strive for. Parents who accept and understand their child will work diligently for the best possible program for the child. They will insist on the availability of comprehensive services and will serve as willing members of the team of people needed to provide the best services for their child.

Clues: I understand the nature of Lottie's problem, although I'm not quite sure what caused it. The important thing is for us to work together to be sure that she learns.

I would like to volunteer to help in the classroom. That's the least I can do to assist in your efforts with my son.

Tell me what additional services you think would benefit Bess and I'll see what I can do to make them available.

Please call me immediately if Joe creates any kind of problem that you believe I can help with.

Parents at this stage of development usually can establish a good parent-child relationship. They will accept their children for what they are and view them as children first—and children with problems second. Parents will usually feel better about themselves and about their interactions with other family members. Not only can parents at this stage help themselves, they can also help each other. These parents are prime targets for involvement in parent-teacher organizations and as sources of support for other parents who may not yet be at this stage of development.

Before leaving this topic, it should again be emphasized that not all parents will exhibit attitudes that are reflected in all of the above stages. Some will go through all stages, others will not. Some will move rapidly through the stages, others will proceed at a snail's pace. Just as with our students, parents exhibit individual differences in the development of attitudes and reactions to their children with disabilities. It is important to keep in mind some of the attitudes that were reflected in this section; it may lead to better understanding of the parents of mainstreamed students.

INFORMATION NEEDS OF PARENTS

Parents of mainstreamed students have a number of information needs. Naturally, regular classroom teachers would not be expected to have answers for all of these needs since they are not specialists in working with exceptional children. However, you should be aware of the needs and prepare yourself to refer parents to appropriate sources. The information needs can be clustered around the following questions that are frequently asked by parents of mainstreamed students.

- *What is the nature of the problem*? Parents want a detailed and precise explanation of the problem that their child is experiencing. General definitions of the diagnostic category to which the child has been assigned are important; however, parents want more than this. They want to know the history of the child's performance that has led school personnel to suspect that a problem exists. They want to know how students with similar problems have been treated and what has been the result of such treatment. They are interested in the educational options that are available for their child and what the prognosis is for improvement.
- *What caused the problem*? The etiology of the problem is of particular interest to parents. They want to know if they were responsible in any way for their child's problem and are particularly interested in whether heredity played a part in the etiology or whether it was some accident or factor during pregnancy or delivery that precipitated it. They are curious about effects environmental factors have had on the problem and the extent to which schooling or inappropriate teaching contributed to it. If they have younger children, they want to know whether they will be similarly affected or whether there is a danger that their future children might also have the problem. Unfortunately, these questions are extremely difficult to answer. In fact, there may not be easily identifiable answers to these concerns. Diagnostic specialists should be involved in providing whatever information is available about etiology.
- *What diagnostic services are available*? Because it is so difficult (and sometimes impossible) to provide well-defined answers to many of the parents' questions related to etiology and prognosis, parents seek information about specialists who may be able to provide these answers and may ask for referrals to appropriate agencies and people who do diagnostic evaluations. They will want to know about types of procedures these people use, the reputation of the speicalists, and information about costs.
- *What can I expect from my child*? Parents are naturally concerned about the present welfare of their children and what the future holds for them. With young children, they will particularly be concerned about such areas as motor development, conceptual development, communication skills, social and emotional skills, self-help skills, and perceptual devel-

opment. Academic achievement will be of particular concern and great care should be taken to help them develop realistic expectations in this area. As children grow older, their parents will be concerned with factors related to vocational training and adjustment, career prospects, and employability. Social adjustment will be of concern, particularly with respect to relationships with the opposite sex.

- *What is the best educational program for my child?* Parents want to know what type of educational and treatment programs will be provided for their child and they want to be assured that it is the best program. They are interested in how the various subject matter areas will be taught and who will teach them. They want to know what types of special materials or equipment will be of particular benefit, and, if such are required, where they can be obtained and what they will cost.

  They will have questions about what alternatives are appropriate. Such things as the advisability of obtaining tutors and placement in private schools will be discussed. The pros and cons of special class placement and regular class placement with resource-room supplementary services will be discussed. Other treatment options such as use of drugs, dietary control, vitamin therapy, and other medical treatments are also of interest. As teachers, we are in the best position to speak about issues related to the actual instruction of the children. Inquiries about issues not related to the educational process are best referred to specialists in those areas.
- *How can we help at home?* Those parents who are truly concerned about the welfare of their children will inquire about things that they can do at home that will aid their child and complement the activities that

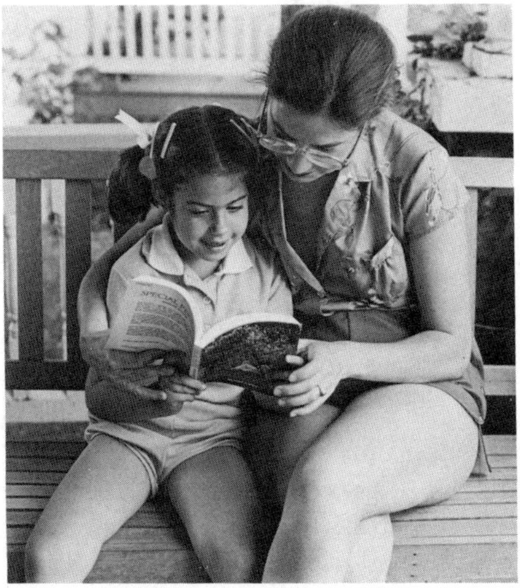

Parents of mainstreamed students can help by working with their children at home.

are conducted in school. Topics of interest include approaches to managing the child's behavior, instructional techniques that can be applied by the parents, how to handle discipline, scheduling techniques, modifications in the physical environment and family routines, projected problems related to sexual behavior and dating, and other issues related to child management. Although teachers can frequently help by providing suggestions relative to the educational program and some aspects of discipline and management, psychologists and counselors can frequently provide better assistance in some of the other areas of concern.

- *What effect will this problem have on interpersonal relationships?* Although closely related to the previous category, concerns that parents have here are specifically related to the relationships that they have with the child who has the problem, with other family members, and with themselves. For example, they want to know how to behave toward the child and whether they should do anything different than they have been doing or if they should treat the child differently from their other children. They want to know how to deal with their own feelings, which may vary from guilt, shame, anger, frustration, and so forth. The place of the child in relation to other children is of particular interest. They want to know if special considerations need to be given, and, if so, how this can be done without having a negative effect on the other siblings. They are also interested in how to explain their child's problems to siblings, other family members, and neighbors and friends. Problems related to finding playmates and recreational activities are also critical. Again, although teachers may be of some assistance here, social workers, psychologists, and other specialists may be able to provide more cogent advice. Particularly good help is often available from other supportive parents, either on an individual basis or as part of parent groups that are frequently formed by parents who have children with similar problems.

- *What other services are available for help?* Schools cannot provide all of the services and resources that are needed to support the education and development of a child with disabilities. Obviously, if the child's problem is mostly educational, the school will deliver most services. As we have seen earlier, however, many students have physical or sensory problems that are best dealt with by other specialists. To further complicate matters, services to parents and their children are often quite expensive and beyond the means of many families.

  Consequently, parents are interested in the availability of financial support and assistance, accessibility of medical services, names of government agencies that provide different services, availability of parent training programs, transportation for children who have special travel needs, information about special tax allowances, and so forth.

Although school personnel may be of some assistance in providing information of this type, parent organizations are frequently better sources of information. Governmental agencies such as state departments of education and local mental health centers are also convenient sources.

ROLES OF PARENTS IN THE EDUCATIONAL PROGRAM

It would be nice if we could say that the interaction between school personnel and parents of students with disabilities has always been positive, with both groups working in concert to provide the best possible education for the students. Unfortunately, this has often not been the case. Although parents have been strong advocates for their children, they have frequently been excluded from the educational programs of their children. It has not been uncommon to hear professionals characterize parents as "uncaring," "over-protective," "unable to understand the educational process," or "meddlers." However, many parents have viewed school personnel as "uncaring," "incompetent," "insecure," or "not interested in my child." Attitudes such as these have frequently placed school personnel and parents in adversarial positions—often to the detriment of all involved.

Fortunately, the situation is beginning to change. One reason for this is P.L. 94-142, which now mandates greater parental involvement in the design of a child's IEP and the evaluation of its effectiveness. Although some school personnel may still view this mandate as placing the schools and the parents in an adversarial relationship (which it may well do in cases where agreement cannot be reached on an appropriate program), most professionals view this requirement for greater parent interaction as positive. Schools are now viewing greater parental involvement as an opportunity to move forward together on a cooperative basis in the development and delivery of improved services for children with disabilities.

Actually, parents can provide an excellent resource for the implementation of mainstreaming programs. Through cooperative planning, parents can become involved in many aspects of the educational program—certainly more so than has been done in the past. McLoughlin, Edge, and Strenecky (1978) address this issue and describe a number of functions that could be performed by parents. These include parents helping to identify children who need special education services, assisting in the collection of data that can be used to assess the nature of the child's problem, helping with the implementation of the program, and evaluating program effectiveness. These authorities also indicate several ways that professionals can facilitate parent activities in each of these areas. The remainder of this section will describe various ways that parents can be involved in the educational program for their children.

PARENTS AS AIDES

Parents can play a valuable role as aides in the classroom. Given the typical number of students in any given class, plus the individual attention that is often necessary with some children, the services of a teacher aide can be invaluable. Before initiating any discussions with parents relative to this activity, however, teachers should check with the building principal in order to determine local school system policies about such arrangements.

Aides can free teachers from many of the routine duties that require little training but large amounts of time. They may be able to assume responsibility for such things as operating audiovisual equipment, taking attendance and maintaining records, preparing instructional materials, duplicating, providing drill to students, monitoring group activities, and numerous other routine daily tasks.

The way that teachers utilize aides is primarily a function of their own personality and how comfortable they feel with the presence of other people in the classroom. Some teachers use aides primarily as helpers; others use them in a quasi-teaching role. As Smith and Neisworth (1975) point out, however, it is very important that a firm set of expectations be established for aides and the limits of their authority be defined. At all times teachers should strive for consistency in the ways that the aides and they deal with students. Otherwise, the students will learn to play them off against one another. Initially, aides should be assigned relatively simple and routine tasks until they learn the classroom routines and get to know the children. As they appear ready, more complex tasks can be assigned. Remember to provide feedback to the aide in order to reinforce appropriate behavior and as a means of correcting any problems that may arise. The key to the successful use of aides, however, is good planning and making expectations clearly understood. Given this orientation, parents may make excellent classroom aides.

PARENTS AS DIAGNOSTICIANS

At first glance, professionals might be opposed to the concept of the parent as a diagnostician. However, we are not speaking here about using parents to administer diagnostic instruments for which they lack appropriate training or to usurp the role of other diagnostic specialists in the school system. Rather, we are speaking about the use of parents in helping to collect certain types of information that are helpful in the assessment and diagnostic process.

Specifically, parents can be asked to maintain logs about the times and sequences when their children reach certain developmental milestones. They can participate in responses to requests for information that relate to the social development or adaptive behavior of their children. They can collect data on the performance of their children on tasks that can be only observed in the home, but that have relevance for educational practices.

Finally, they can participate in diagnostic staffings as a member of the team that is attempting to specify the nature of the child's problem and designing an IEP in response to it.

When used in the capacity of diagnostician, it is obviously incumbent upon the teacher to be highly specific in terms of procedures to be followed. Parents will need to be trained to collect the types of data that are being requested and checks will need to be made to verify the accuracy of the data collected by parents. This is particularly true in the case when subjective judgments are made (as opposed to counting and recording specific observable behaviors). Keep in mind that many parents find it difficult to be objective about their children—particularly if the child has been identified as having a problem related to the area in which observations are being performed.

PARENTS AS TEACHERS

We often overlook the contributions that parents can make in the direct instruction of their mainstreamed students. Although we may ask parents to assist in providing drill in the learning of spelling words or arithmetic facts, or listen to their children read, we do not often ask them to provide direct instruction to their children. By following such a course of action, we are overlooking a valuable source of assistance.

Some people may think that parents should not be involved in the direct instruction of their children, this being the province of the schools. However, it has been shown that parents can be quite effective in the specific instruction of their children with disabilities. This has been most dramatically shown at the preschool level, where parents at literally hundreds of locations throughout the country have been taught to teach their handicapped children. Examples of some of these projects have been included in the interesting and informative text, *Teaching Parents to Teach* by David Lillie and Pascal Trohanis (1976).

Perhaps the most famous of the projects involved in teaching parents to teach their young children with disabilities is the project at Portage, Wisconsin (Shearer, 1976). An illustration from the Portage Project is included here to show how parents can serve as teachers.

An Example

A young girl, named Jill, was having difficulty with differentiating between the concepts of big and little. The child's mother was taught to provide direct instruction related to these concepts. The instructions that were given to Jill's mother are illustrated in Figure 8.1 and the graph that she maintained illustrates that she provided at least five minutes of direct instruction on this task each day.

PORTAGE PROJECT

Child's Name *Jill*

Home Teacher's Name *Susan*

Week of *September 18th*

BEHAVIOR:

Mom will tell Jill which of 2 like objects is big and which is little (5 minutes/day)

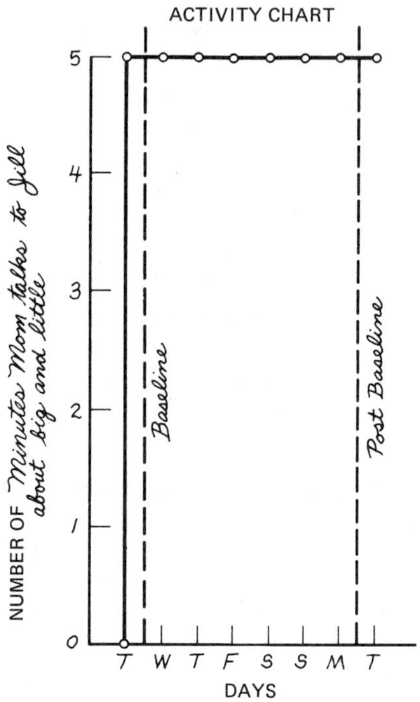

DIRECTIONS:

1. *Use paired objects or pictures that are the same - except for size.*
2. *Talk with Jill pointing to and naming the objects that are big and little, and encourage Jill to repeat the size word in imitation of you.*
3. *Praise her each time she imitates.*
4. *Use as many different examples of like pictures and objects as possible.*
5. *Record the number of minutes you spend naming big and little each day.*

Figure 8.1 Portage project parent activity sheet. (From M. S. Shearer, A home-based parent training model. In D. Lillie and P. Trohanis (Eds.), *Teaching Parents to Teach*. New York: Walker and Co., 1976, page 138. Reproduced with permission of the publisher.

After being involved in the instruction of parents as teachers for a number of years, Shearer (1976, pp. 143–145) formulated six principles that should be followed in the implementation of such a program:

1. *Set weekly curriculum goals*. At the beginning of the program, goals should be set that can be quickly and easily accomplished. This is so the parents can be shown that they can be successful in their teaching activities. In the beginning of the program, the choice of goals should be based almost as much on the chance for success as on the importance of the skill.

2. *Show the parent what to do and how to do it.* The parents in Shearer's program learned better when they were shown what to do than when they were just told what to do. By having the teacher explore what works with the child, the probabilities of success will also be enhanced. After a decision is made about a workable teaching technique, the specific steps are recorded for reference by the parent.
3. *Have the parents practice teaching the skill.* After having the parent see the teacher have success, the parent must also experience that success to convince themselves that they are able to implement the program and that it is not successful just because the teacher was able to do it. The teacher can also spot potential errors on the part of parents during this process.
4. *Reinforce the parents.* Just as a child is more likely to repeat actions that are reinforced, so are parents. Do not expect instant success. After all, some parents may be asked to do things (e.g., ignore inappropriate behavior) that are counter to past practices. Remember that it takes time, practice, and reinforcement to change old behavior patterns.
5. *Individualize for parents.* Be prepared to modify the approach, based upon the reactions and preferences of parents. Remember that parents are individuals, too.
6. *Involve the parents in planning.* If parents participate in planning the goals and activities, they will be more committed to the implementation of the teaching program. As parents become used to the technique they will become more active and will initiate activities. Gradually, the teacher will require less and less time for instruction of the parent and the parents will assume greater responsibility for the program.

PARENTS AS ADVOCATES

Parents of students with disabilities have been particularly active as advocates for their rights and the rights of their children since 1950, when the National Association for Retarded Children (now the National Association for Retarded Citizens) was established. It was through the efforts of parents that much of the litigation and legislation mentioned in earlier chapters came to pass.

The advocacy role of parents can be both a source of support to teachers and a source of dismay. On the one hand, parents may work diligently and effectively to secure needed services for their children. On the other hand, in seeking support, they may perceive that the schools are not doing their job satisfactorily, which results in school personnel sometimes being on the receiving end of the advocacy efforts.

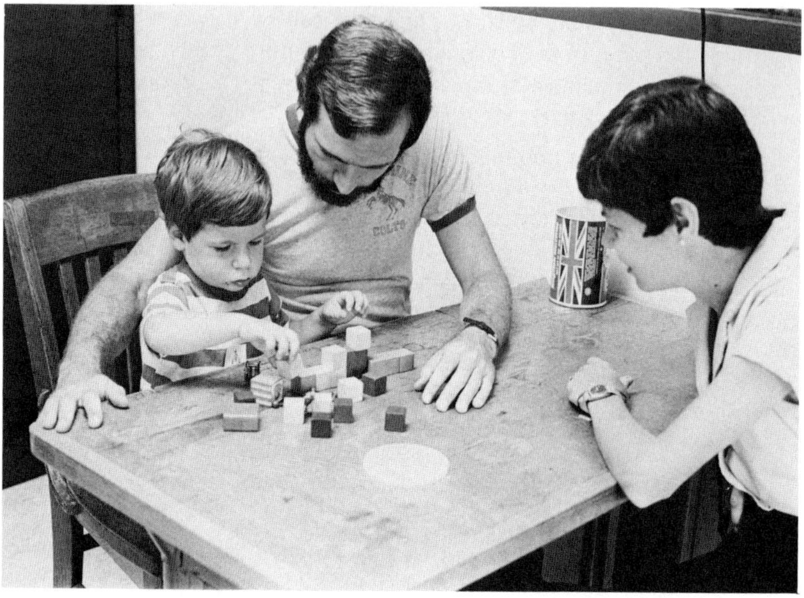

Parents who want to teach their child at home should be encouraged to practice under the direction of the teacher who can spot potential errors and provide useful advice.

Because parents have been so successful in securing their rights, they have become more active in pursuing them and feel more confident that they can "change the system." Unfortunately, some parents will jump immediately to the "I'm dissatisfied, and I want a hearing" stage instead of negotiating with appropriate officials for resolution of the problem that they perceive. Hearings are generally uncomfortable experiences for all parties involved because they are usually conducted in an air of confrontation. (They are also terribly expensive.) It is almost always better to attempt to resolve problems before they go to the hearing stage.

Although the unpleasantness of confrontation does exist in some cases, parents can create some very positive changes as a result of their advocacy efforts. Their effectiveness in petitioning school board members for additional services and resources and their efforts to obtain community support such as the reduction of architectural barriers or the provision of transportation is well known. Many teachers who have been ineffective in obtaining such services have secretly smiled at the success that parent-advocates have been able to achieve in obtaining better educational services in the schools.

The most productive approach to the role of the parent as an advocate is one in which the parents and the school personnel engage in dialogue about the needs of the mainstreamed students and then establish goals that both groups can work toward in a complementary fashion. This type of approach is much more productive than one of confrontation.

PARENT CONFERENCING

As a teacher of mainstreamed students, you may have to attend parent conferences as required under P.L. 94-142. Different school systems have different policies about who will be in attendance at such meetings. If you are involved in a meeting to design an IEP for a mainstreamed student, your role as a regular classroom teacher will probably be that of the "receiving" teacher. That is, you will be asked for recommendations and reactions to the placement of a mainstreamed student in your classroom and your specific role in teaching the child. We will not dwell in detail about the possible involvement in such a conference because local school policies will generally dictate this role and the building principal will undoubtedly discuss potential contributions prior to the meeting. If you are interested in further reading on this topic, however, the work of Michaelis (1980) provides considerable detail about formal IEP conferences and options for activities that might occur during such a conference.

Undoubtedly, teachers will be involved much more frequently in small conferences with parents concerning the progress of their mainstreamed children and any potential problems that they might be encountering. Occasionally, these conferences might be on an individual basis. Often, they will be with the parents and the resource teacher or other personnel who are supporting the educational program of the mainstreamed student. In this section of the chapter are some suggestions you will find useful when preparing for and conducting parent conferences. Also included are some tips for communicating with parents that are based upon actual recommendations that have been received from parents concerning their interactions with teachers.

PREPARING FOR THE CONFERENCE

One of the most traumatic experiences for new teachers is their first parent conference at which they must deal with a problem that one of their students is experiencing. Most frequently, these teachers have had little direct experience with situations that are emotionally charged although they may have read about techniques that are recommended for such situations. Fortunately, their effectiveness improves with experience; however, each interaction is still a cause for some concern.

It has been our experience that the key to successful parent conferences is *preparation*. If you focus attention on only four factors prior to the actual conference, the probability of having a successful conference will be quite high. We can not guarantee that you will not run into some difficulties during the conference; however, any problems that do arise will not be due to the fact that you are unprepared. Following is a brief discussion of the four factors that are critical in preparing for parent conferences.

1. *Establish objectives for the conference.* If you are initiating the conference, develop a specific statement about what you want to accomplish by it. It helps to be as specific as possible. You might start by establishing a goal such as, "to inform the parents about their child's progress." Under that goal, you might then develop specific objectives related to reading comprehension, reading rate, mathematics computation, etc. If you want to solicit the parents' cooperation in developing a home instruction program, specify this. Be sure to write down the goals and objectives. Do not just try to commit them to memory. If the conference is being called at the parents' request, be sure to ask them what they want to talk about at the conference. If a student brings a note from home that simply asks for a conference, call the parents and ask what they want to speak about so that you can adequately prepare for the meeting.
2. *Review the student's cumulative records.* Make sure that you review the records in light of the objectives that you have established for the meeting. In this way you will have the necessary background information for support. For example, if the child has been making steady progress in an academic area, this should be pointed out to the parents. Similarly, if you have a documented history of a particular problem that you want to discuss, it will make it easier for you to build a case for the necessity of developing solutions to that problem. If you show parents that you know a lot about their child and can discuss factors that may be unrelated to the specific objectives of the conference, you convey the impression that you are really interested in the child and the parents will realize that you are concerned and have their child's best interests in mind. This will help them to decide positively to cooperate with you.
3. *Prepare specific data for inspection by parents.* The importance of this step cannot be overemphasized. If you are presenting data relative to the student's performance on achievement tests, prepare the information in a graphic format. For example, if you give weekly spelling tests, present a graph of the percentage of correct words spelled during the past five weeks. Such a graph might look like the one presented in Figure 8.2.

   It should be apparent that this type of presentation dramatically documents the fact that Terwiliger's performance on spelling tests is declining. Parents could readily see that a problem exists in this area. This type of presentation is much more effective than the statement, "Terwiliger is not doing well in spelling." Not only does it offer proof of such a statement, parents will be less likely to argue the point and will move quickly to the position of, "What can we do to try to help Terwiliger improve his spelling grades?"

   Keep in mind that we do not want to use this type of approach only to convey bad news to the parents. Remember that they are also interested in good news, and want to know the effectiveness of the program

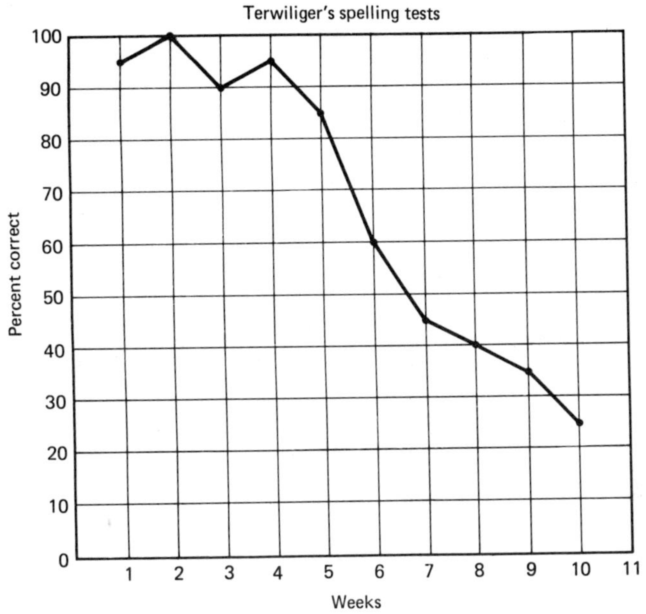

Figure 8.2 An example of a graph of student performance.

in which their child is enrolled. A graph can also be used to report this type of information so that parents can see their child's progress prior to and during placement in the mainstream (Figure 8.3).

Prunella's parents could readily see from the graph in Figure 8.3 that Prunella could not correctly "do" her times tables prior to the time that she was mainstreamed. They can see that she is making good progress, being able to recall correctly her multiplication facts through the six tables. The graph also shows that she still has a way to go, however, in working on her seven, eight, nine, and ten tables.

Note that the preparation of graphs such as these is not difficult and does not consume a great deal of time. In fact, many teachers have their students keep their own records and construct their own performance graphs. It has been found that this practice can serve as a powerful incentive for improvement and gives the students a sense of accomplishment when they are able to record good scores.

4. *Prepare an agenda for the meeting.* After deciding upon the objectives, reviewing the child's records, and preparing visual displays of the child's performance, you should jot down a series of notes to yourself about how you want to sequence the parent conference. This would include some thoughts about how you might want to greet the parents and open the conference, the points that you want to make with the

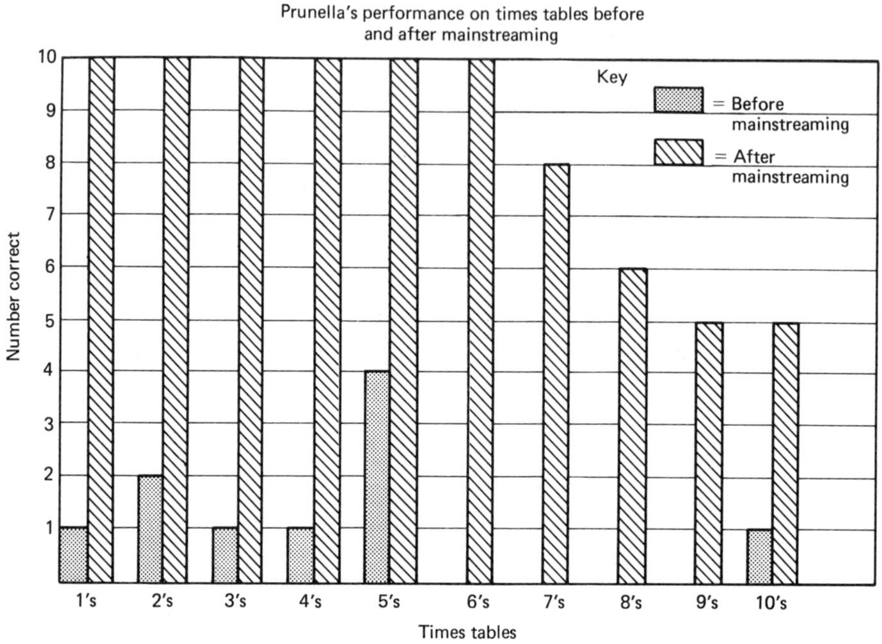

Figure 8.3 An example of a student performance graph showing the effects of treatment.

parents, the desired outcomes, and how you want to end the conference. It is always best to try to end the conference on a positive note in order for the parents to remember the last interaction that they had with you as a positive one. By thinking through the conference in this way, you will be "rehearsing" what you will say and thus preclude uncomfortable lapses in conversation, false starts, and the appearance that you are unsure of yourself.

CONDUCTING THE CONFERENCE

Assuming that you have prepared adequately for the conference, the actual meeting with the parents can be facilitated by a number of other considerations. For example, physical arrangements are more important than many people think. The best place to hold the conference is in your classroom. Bennett and Henson (1977) claim that the classroom is the best place for four reasons. First, it will make you feel comfortable because you are in familiar surroundings. Second, you will generally have immediate access to your files, if you need something that was unanticipated in your preparation or if you want to show examples of instructional materials or student work. Third, the classroom will serve as a reminder of things that the child has done or said. Fourth, because there are desks, student materials, and other teaching-related items in the classroom, it will serve as a stimulus for both parents and teacher that the purpose of the meeting is to deal with issues that are oriented toward improving the student's education.

In further considering the physical environment, do not position yourself behind your desk with the parents in front of it. This will set up an artificial barrier between you and the parents and will make it more difficult for them to interact with you in a natural fashion. Similarly, do not seat yourself in your desk chair and have the parents wrestle with the undersized chairs of the students. Place the seats so that you can all easily face each other. If you are at your desk, place the parents to one side. If there are no adult-sized chairs in the classroom, then all of you sit in the student's chairs.

Although you are prepared for talking in the conference, remember that communication is a two-way street. Consequently, you must be prepared to *listen* as well. In talking with parents, you should make every effort to not speak over the parents' heads, avoid an authoritarian manner, and be honest and direct. In listening, you should give every indication that you are attending to what is being said. You can do this by "active listening" which is a reflection to the parents of what they are saying in order to convey the fact that you are understanding them.

Stephens and Wolf (1980) recommend that teachers follow four steps when conducting parent conferences. These steps in order are:

1. Rapport building
2. Obtaining information
3. Providing helpful information
4. Summarizing and recommending

Importance of Rapport.[1] A relationship based upon mutual trust facilitates effective instruction. When parents and teachers have the best interests of students in mind and believe this to be true of each other, a comfortable relationship can develop. Communicating the educational needs of students is enhanced by rapport.

Some of the issues of rapport building include how teachers can develop rapport with the parents, how to assist students when rapport with their parents is not feasible, how to relate to single parents and to parents who are quarrelsome and/or divided in their approaches.

Obtaining Information. It is risky for teachers to assume that they are fully knowledgeable about their students. The true experts are parents. They know their child in ways that teachers cannot. Conversely, teachers

[1]Thomas M. Stephens and Joan S. Wolf, *Effective Skills in Parent/Teacher Conferencing*, Columbus, Oh.: NCEMMH/OSU, Copright 1980. Reproduced with permission of the publisher.

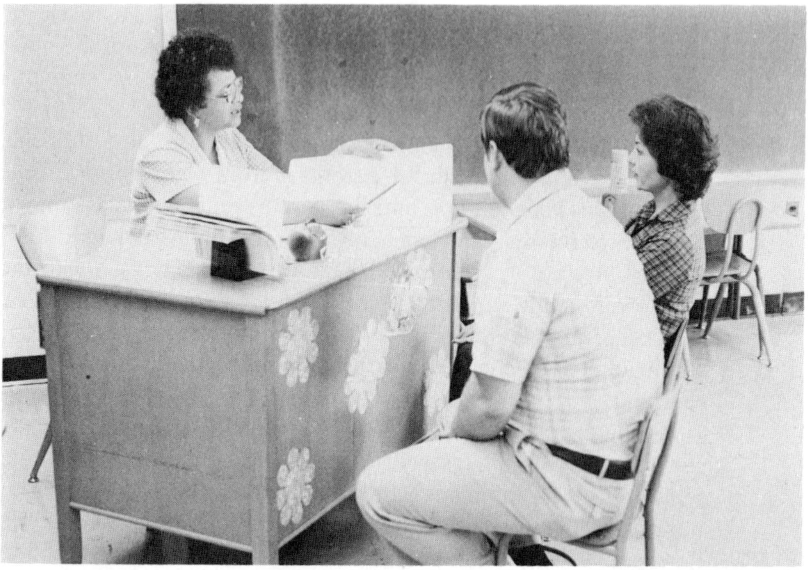

Barriers are set up when parents are forced to sit across the desk from the teacher in undersized chairs as in the top photo. Communication with parents is enhanced when they are seated comfortably alongside the teacher.

may know aspects of students that are new to parents. Together parents and teachers can do more to assist students to achieve success in school than either can alone.

It is sometimes helpful when conferencing with parents, to convey the concept that home and school lives of students represent separate performances. With this notion firmly established, we can consider the parent-teacher conference as a meeting of interested persons for discussing and planning ways to improve students' performances.

Information must first be obtained from the parents about the youngster's current performances in the home and the community. Procedures and tactics can then be considered for improving these behaviors. Among issues to be considered when eliciting information from parents are what information to consider, parameters to use when seeking information, and tactics to use for obtaining information and discussing it.

Providing Information. It is important to inform parents and to involve them in creating their children's educational programs. Accurate information, when presented sensitively, can clarify roles and responsibilities and serve as a solid basis for developing a working, helping relationship with parents. Most parents are well intentioned. They want to help their children. Sometimes, they need to be assured that they are not to blame for their children's problems. Often, teachers must give parents the same understanding they give to their students.

Parent-teacher conferences must not be limited to or allowed to become cathartic experiences for parents or teachers. Time is a limiting factor and teachers are trained as educators of children, not as therapists. Throughout, teachers should strive to focus on the students' needs, not on their faults or failures. Thus, information regarding students' school performances and behaviors should be presented in a descriptive and objective manner. Students' progress should be related to those objectives contained in their IEPs, but not necessarily limited to these objectives.

Summarizing and Recommending Final stages of the conference consist of summarizing what has been discussed, identifying (where necessary) new objectives, and making recommendations. Teachers' behaviors, at this point, require skillful integration of bits of information that are important to formulating additional instructional objectives. As the teacher, you may find it necessary to recommend actions for the parents without having an opportunity to consult with other school personnel. For example, parents may seek particular types of advice from you that are beyond your role and competencies. You should never assume therapeutic roles with parents or provide advice that exceeds your knowledge and training. It is important to know the school's policies concerning referrals for assistance within the organization and to other agencies. Obviously, you must be knowledgeable about available resources in the schools and within the community. If you are unable to give parents the information sought, admit your uncertainty and indicate that you will obtain the necessary information and contact the parents.

Numerous issues pervade this part of the conference. Included are such items as skills needed by teachers, sources of community and school information, parameters for identifying additional objectives and for making recommendations (Stephens and Wolf, 1980, pp. 4-5).

For additional information about communicating with parents of mainstreamed students, review the work of Chinn, Winn, and Walters (1978), Kroth and Simpson (1977), and Nedler, and McAfee (1979).

TIPS FROM PARENTS

It is also instructive to look at the communication process from the perspective of the parents. The list below notes the important points to keep in mind. Letha Patterson (1956) is the parent of an exceptional child. After having a number of very exasperating experiences with physicians, psychologists, and teachers, she wrote an article that provides pointers that professionals should consider in their dealings with parents. We have paraphrased these pointers and have written them from the perspective of the parent:

- *Tell us the nature of the problem as soon as possible*. We realize that it is difficult to be the bearer of unpeasant news. If you suspect a problem, bring it to our attention. Don't withhold information from us. Regardless of what you might think, we have the best interest of our child at heart and want to get about the business of solving whatever problems the child might have. Above all, be honest. Even though it may be uncomfortable for you (and it certainly will be uncomfortable for us), don't try to hedge or sugarcoat the problem by telling us that the child will grow out of it if your experience tells you that children don't grow out of it. Avoid making statements that may give unrealistic hope; but don't deny hope for improvement.
- *Always see both parents*. We know that this is probably an impossibility; but please try to see both of us—at least in the early stages of our relationship. You must remember that we are individuals and have different perceptions of what we hear. Because we are often somewhat upset in hearing about problems that our child might be having, we may not fully understand what you tell us. In addition, we may not be able to transmit the exact meaning of our conversation to our mates if they are not present. If you can see us both at the same time it will help in our understanding of the problem and we will be better able to deal with the situation.
- *Watch your language*. Rmember, you are the professional. We don't have the educational background that you have, so keep your use of jargon to a minimum. Don't tell us that our child "has a developmental lag caused by minimal cerebral dysfunction that has resulted in specific developmental dyslexia" when the problem is that the child is not reading at the level that should be appropriate for his age. If there are jargon words or initials that we will hear and will be sure to encounter in our future dealings with the schools [such as IEP], take the time to ex-

plain these to us. In our next meeting, don't take it for granted that we have learned what those words or initials mean. Ask us if we understand.

- *Help us see that this is our problem*. This does not mean that you are to place the blame for the problem on us. Rather, it means that we, as parents, must make the ultimate decisions about what is best for our child. Too often, it is easy for us to say, "You are the professionals, whatever you think is best is OK with us." It is important for us to maintain our responsibility for our child. If the schools take over the decision-making process, our effectiveness as parents will be reduced.
- *Help us to understand our problem*. Remember that you didn't learn all about our child's problem in half an hour or 45 minutes, so don't expect that we will be able to either. It may take repeated visits before we are able to grasp the nature and extent of the problem. Give us some literature to read about it that is understandable.
- *Know your resources*. We will have many questions about places to go for additional information about our child's problem. We will need things to read and we will probably want to talk with other professional people such as psychologists or diagnosticians who may be able to help us to better understand the nature of our child's problem and whether there are things that we can do to help that the schools cannot provide. We would also benefit from talking with parents of other children who might have the same problems in order to see how they have handled the situation. If you can't provide the information immediately, either refer us to someone who can or find the information for us and get it to us as soon after our meeting as possible.
- *Never put us on the defensive*. We know that we are going to make mistakes in our child rearing practices. Don't blame us for our child's problems (even if you think we are to blame). Deal with us in a positive manner. If we tell you that we have done something with our child that you think is inappropriate, don't tell us that we've made a mistake. Rather, tell us to consider some other alternative in dealing with that situation, should it reoccur, and then help us to develop the skills to follow your advice. Remember, we feel bad enough about our child's problem; and having you call attention to our mistakes only makes us feel worse. Be positive.
- *Remember that parents of mainstreamed students are just people*. We have the same aspirations, problems, joys, and disasters as other parents. Because we may have a child with learning problems does not mean that we are ogres, are illiterate, are less caring, or are different than other parents. We are parents first and then parents of a child with problems, second. Please treat us as such.
- *Remember that we are parents and you are professionals*. We are more emotionally involved with the situation and, therefore, cannot be as ob-

jective in the dealings with our child as you can. We look to you as the source of help for our child. Please provide it in a professional manner. Don't do things that undermine your credibility as a professional, such as talking about other parents or criticizing your professional colleagues.

- *Remember the importance of your attitude toward us.* Have empathy for us and try to look at the problem from our perspective. If we are convinced that you understand our problem and are truly interested in our child, we can work wonders in our mutual efforts to teach our child.

If teachers keep these suggestions in mind, they should be able to develop a very positive relationship with the parents of their mainstreamed students. They will find that the parents will learn to respect them and will come to trust their professional judgement. When this point has been reached, it will be found that working with parents will be easier than expected and will be a rich and rewarding experience for both teachers and parents of mainstreamed students.

RESOURCES FOR PARENTS

Several times in this chapter we have indicated that it is important for teachers to know their resources so that they can be prepared to respond to any questions that might be raised by parents. We realize, of course, that regular classroom teachers are not specialists in the delivery of services to children with special needs; consequently, it may frequently be necessary for them to refer parents to other sources for information.

AGENCIES

Many agencies have been established to provide supportive services to parents and professionals and to serve as advocates for specific groups of people with disabilities. These agencies frequently have descriptive literature that is useful for explaining important concepts related to the problems that they represent. Some (e.g., National Association for Retarded Citizens) maintain state and local organizations that provide a host of direct services, such as parent education, fund raising, direct services to children. A list of agencies that provide useful information and other resources is provided in Appendix A. The name of the agency generally reflects the area of specialty. If you are interested, you might want to contact the agencies that are relevant to your purposes and ask for information about the types of services that they have that would be of interest to parents. Maintenance of a file of this information could be quite useful in helping parents with their search for information and other services.

READINGS

Often, parents of children with disabilities inquire about materials that they can read that will assist them in in understanding the nature of their child's problem and provide helpful suggestions for things that the parents can do to help. Many of the agencies that were mentioned in the previous section have literature that is available at no cost. In addition, most have available reading lists that relate to the specific area covered by that agency. We have provided a list of readings that may be of interest to adults in Appendix C. Kroth (1975) also provides an annotated bibliography of readings organized according to various disabilities, that is appropriate for parents. Following are several suggestions for books that may be of interest to parents, regardless of the disability of their child:

Gordon, T. *Parent Effectiveness Training*. New York: Wyden, 1970.

Heisler, V. *A Handicapped Child in the Family: A Guide for Parents*. New York: Grune and Stratton, 1972.

McDonald, E. *Understand Those Feelings*. Pittsburgh: Stanwix House, 1962.

Parents might also consider subscribing to *The Exceptional Parent*. This magazine has many timely features about exceptional children and practical tips for child rearing practices. It also provides a means for parents to share some of their experiences and to describe some of the problems that they have encountered and ways that they have dealt with them. Articles of this nature can be very reassuring to parents, as well as providing them with ideas that could be used with their own children. Subscriptions can be obtained by writing to: *The Exceptional Parent*, P.O. Box 4944, Manchester, New Hampshire, 03108.

TRAINING PACKAGES

There are several very good multimedia training packages that are available for use in parent training workshops. In the event that school districts become involved in the systematic training of parents, they might want to consider these for use in parent training sessions. All of them are relatively systematic in the way that information is presented, and they have been field tested with groups of parents.

Even Love is Not Enough: Children with Handicaps and *Children with Handicaps: Parents Who Care*. Both of these kits contain several sound/filmstrips that are designed to familiarize parents with the special problems that are encountered by exceptional children. They can be obtained from *Parent Magazine* Films, 52 Vanderbilt Avenue, New York, New York 10017.

STEP (Systematic Training for Effective Parenting) is designed for use in weekly sessions of small groups of parents. The kit contains cassette tapes, posters, charts, and discussion cards. It's goal is to assist parents in raising responsible children and feeling satisfied as a parent. The kit is published by American Guidance Service, Inc., Publisher's Building, Circle Pines, Minnesota 55014.

We've Been There . . . Can We Help? Includes a small manual, filmstrip, and audio tape. It provides sufficient information for use in six sessions with parents and is designed to be used with parents who have just learned that their child might have a developmental disability. It can be purchased from the Ontario Pomona Association for Retarded Citizens, 9160 Monte Vista Avenue, Montclair, California 91763.

Preparing for the IEP Meeting: A Workshop for Parents is a two-hour package that includes a sound/filmstrip, parent checklists, and other resource materials that are designed to prepare parents for participation in the meeting at which their child's individualized educational program is designed. The vendor for this package is the Council for Exceptional Children, 1920 Association Drive, Reston, VA 22091.

If any of these packages are to be used (or any other for that matter) remember to always preview them thoroughly prior to their actual use. This will help to determine whether they are relevant for your particular purposes. It will also prevent being caught off guard about any aspect of the presentation.

THE ROLE OF TEACHERS

Parents can play an invaluable role in the education of mainstreamed students. In fact, they can make the difference between successful mainstreaming and unsuccessful mainstreaming, depending upon the type and quality of the relationship that exists between them and the teacher. Simmons-Martin (1976) identified eight roles that teachers often need to assume in their interaction with parents.

1. *Listener*. Remember that many parents have no one else they can talk to about their children and the problems that they are encountering. Simply by being an active and sympathetic listener, you can gain the parent's confidence and support.
2. *Enabler*. You can support parents both in their efforts to assist in the implementation of their child's educational program and in the improvement of their parenting skills.
3. *Model*. By being effective in your interpersonal relationships with their children and by being an effective teacher, you can serve as a role model for parents to emulate in these areas. They do not have the educational background and experience that you have; consequently, the

availability of an effective model is quite useful in helping them to develop an appropriate style for dealing with their child.

4. *Reality tester*. Parents often need someone outside the family to help them to test the reality of various situations. On some occasions, they may think that they are engaged in an appropriate course of action, when, in reality, they are not. On other occasions, they may be unsure of a course of action to take. By providing feedback to the parents, you can serve as a valuable resource as they evolve procedures to deal with their special child. It is likewise important to provide positive feedback when parents are engaged in appropriate actions in order to reinforce and strengthen those behaviors.
5. *Integrator*. Parents of mainstreamed students are faced with a virtual avalanche of information and concepts from different sources and on different topics, many of which have been addressed in this chapter. This is particularly the case in the early stages, when the parents have initially been informed that their child may have a problem. Teachers can be of invaluable assistance to the parents in helping to pull the bits and pieces together into a meaningful whole.
6. *Interpreter*. Unfortunately, educators have a tendency to use a lot of jargon that gradually creeps into conversations with those who may not be privy to its meaning. You can help immensely by translating jargon that may be used into language that is understandable to parents.
7. *Resource person*. You will be viewed by the parents as the expert concerning the education of their child. They will turn to you for information about services and will view you as the primary resource person that they can contact when questions arise.
8. *Teacher*. If you keep these roles in mind, along with the suggestions that were made earlier in this chapter relative to specific practices, you should be able to develop a strong, positive relationship with the parents of your mainstreamed students.

SUMMARY

- Parents have numerous rights with respect to the education of their mainstreamed children. Chief among these are the right to due process and the right to participate in the development of the IEP.
- Parents may exhibit a wide array of attitudes and reactions toward their mainstreamed children. These may include shock, denial, anger, guilt, unrealistic hope, depression, rejection, acceptance and understanding.
- Parents have need for a wide array of information about their mainstreamed students, ranging from the need to understand the nature of the problem to how they can help at home.

- Parents can play a number of roles in the education of their mainstreamed students including teacher aide, diagnostician, home teacher, and advocate.
- Proper advance planning is critical if parent conferences are to be effective.
- Numerous agencies are available that can provide useful information and resources to parents of mainstreamed students.

NINE

A Mainstreaming Simulator

- What is the process used by school personnel regarding educational and instructional services?
- What are the processes used for referral? Parental involvement? Multifactored evaluation? IEP development?
- How well can you—the reader, perform in these various activities?

The case study method presents opportunities to examine the mainstreaming process in detail. When presented with a particular student with certain types of problems, what process does a school staff embark upon to arrive at decisions relating to services and instruction? One may know the requirements of how this process is to occur, but a better understanding is achieved by being involved with the process.

In this chapter we examine a slice of mainstreaming in action for discussion and study. Through this book and perhaps through small group simulation as a part of course activities the essence of the process can be known. However, you may initially benefit from this case study by completing the exercises in this chapter.

This case study is about Sam Rinaldi, a nine year old student who is learning disabled. He is fictitious as a person but does represent a composite student with problems diagnosed with increasing incidence these days, the specific learning disabled student. Although there has been a great deal of discussion of just what a specific learning disability (SLD) is, the official definition is contained within the *Rules and Regulations* of P.L. 94-142. In individual cases there is a considerable amount of difference between one SLD student and another. There appears to be a growing number of professionals who prefer using the term *mildly handicapped* rather than *mentally retarded* or *learning disabled*. In many ways, it makes little difference how one classifies a student. That person remains the same student irrespective of the classification; the purposes and procedures of instruction are also little affected. In the classification process however, considerable care must be taken before placing any label on a student; it may have long-term repercussions for everyone involved.

Within the following case study, the processes of referral (as one type of child identification activity), parental involvement, multifactored evaluation, and the IEP development are described. Introductory information is provided about each process followed by a set of directions. Within each section, there are exercises to be completed by the individual reader. In the final section we encourage readers, if you are reading this as part of a college class or workshop, to organize into small groups with assigned roles from the case study. Directions in this section with exercises will lead the group through the basic elements of developing an IEP. However, it should be understood that the various differences of IEPs really reflect the specific characteristics of the groups developing the IEP. There is also room for considerable improvisation for a group developing an IEP in the last section since further role definitions may be developed by inference on the part of the player or course instructor.

The reports, forms, and exercises in this chapter are listed below by areas:

Area	*Report*	*Form*	*Exercise*
Referral	1. Diagnostive & Prescriptive Observation	A. Request for Consultation B. Cumulative record summary	1. Referral
Parental involvement	2. Interview Protocol	C. Parents as Partners	
Multifactored evaluation	3. Multi-disciplinary Team Report	D. Multidis-ciplinary Team Report	2. Present Levels of Educational Performance
IEP development			3. Stating Annual Goals 4. Stating Objectives 5. Placement

CASE DESCRIPTION

Sam Rinaldi is a nine-year-three-month-old boy. He is now entering third grade. He participated in a local Montessori Preschool Program when he was four, but this lasted only two months. The Montessori staff members indicated to the parents that Sam was too "immature" to participate in the program.

Sam entered first grade at age six. His first teacher had just graduated from an undergraduate program at the nearby university; she was not very effective with Sam in this important first year. He floundered in learning his basic skills and soon several of the children in the class had begun to tease Sam for his awkwardness on the playground and his responses in class when the teacher called upon him. The first year had been a disaster for Sam and increased the anxieties of his parents. In an end-of-the-year meeting, it had been recommended by the school staff that he repeat first grade. At that meeting, the school staff indicated to Mr. and Mrs. Rinaldi that Sam was developmentally immature.

Would repetition of the first year do any good? Mr. and Mrs. Rinaldi were assured that many children benefit from such repetition to gain time to catch up developmentally with other children. They remembered that Sam was late about other things according to Sam's pediatrician: he learned to walk when he was three and only began to say one-word responses when he was about four. Perhaps, they thought, another year in first grade might be what Sam needs. In addition, he'd be getting a more experienced teacher.

Sam's second year in first grade did not seem to make a lot of difference except Sam was showing increased signs of frustration. The more experienced teacher was of some help since she structured her classroom well; every student was taught a routine of classroom activities and was required to stay on task.

This was less confusing for Sam. However, this teacher believed in teaching all the children as a group with no exceptions. Sam's evaluation reports were always low, and Sam received little encouragement from this teacher in any consistent way. The social ridicule for Sam had reached higher levels. He was left out of the other children's games during recess. The teacher's attitude toward Sam seemed to be imitated by the children. She tolerated him but provided little acceptance for him.

Sam Rinaldi's second-grade teacher at Jefferson Elementary was alarmed when Sam started the year. He was far behind most of the children in the class. His reading skills were particularly weak. She worked with Sam on an individual basis when she could, but did not seem to have enough time for him on any consistent basis. She noticed he was hesitating to try new tasks and constantly seeking her attention. He turned in his written work only after much prompting and explanation of the directions. She referred him to the remedial reading specialist. The remedial reading teacher tested him for achievement and he scored quite low. She also said that Sam appeared to be "retarded" and probably should be in special education rather than remedial reading but there was little supportive help for Sam so she did what she could. The parents worked with Sam at home on work she provided and she worked with him individually when she could. Sam did not seem to be making much progress with any of the many methods tried.

By the end of his third year, Mr. and Mrs. Rinaldi were getting desperate. No one seemed to know what to do. The principal suggested to them that perhaps Sam should be considered for special education. The principal also indicated this would mean Sam would be sent to a special program in a school facility across the city. The principal had set up an appointment for the Rinaldis with one of the school psychologists in the central offices. The school psychologist described the special class to Mr. and Mrs. Rinaldi and invited them to visit it. From his descriptions, the Rinaldis rejected it out of hand. The special classes were located in an old building which had been vacated by a regular elementary school and set up entirely with special classes and its own principal. The school psychologist explained that the Rinaldis would need to sign a permission form for testing, but the whole process would not have to take long. Sam could be attending the special school next fall. No one expressed the idea that Sam should stay at the regular elementary school. As the principal had said proudly, "Our school is one to two grade levels above the national average and if a child is to be in the regular classroom, he must meet the standards like every other child."

Mrs. Rinaldi heard of a pilot program called the Continuum of Educational Services for children with special needs at Palomar Elementary School. One of her friends who lived in that school's area heard about this innovative program at one of the PTA meetings. From the report it sounded like the kind of program that was based on each child's educational needs and provided a lot of help to the children with special needs.

The Rinaldis visited Palomar Elementary School and were impressed. Children seemed to be individuals here and there was respect for individual differences apparent everywhere. They noticed a homemade flag attractively colored, which bore the name of the School and their welcoming slogan: The School of Friends. The principal, Mr. Dudley, took time to explain the program in detail particularly emphasizing the philosophy of the school. Mr. Filippo, the assistant principal, took the Rinaldis through the large open areas, called pods, where 3 to 4 teachers were working with groups or individual children. Mr. Filippo pointed out the rooms of different sizes along the perimeter of the pod areas where teachers, aides, or tutors could work with varying numbers of children on an individual or small-group basis.

The Rinaldis were impressed with the relaxed attitude of the children who were busy and involved with their learning tasks. Although Mr. Dudley had indicated there were special children in this school, no visible identifying signs could be found.

Sam Rinaldi was enrolled in the Palomar Elementary School for the coming September. This meant that Mrs. Rinaldi would have to transport Sam from their home to the Palomar School every day. The Rinaldis realized they could have placed pressure on the staff at Jefferson Elementary to develop more appropriate options for Sam besides a segregated class or a segregated school, but it seemed a long, drawn-out process. Sam needed the kind of help that Palomar Elementary School could provide immediately. So Mrs. Rinaldi resigned herself to transporting Sam every day to and from school. Mr. Dudley, the principal at Palomar, had indicated transportation would be provided as a "related service" if Sam was found eligible for special education.

After Mr. and Mrs. Rinaldi discussed Sam's problems at Jefferson Elementary, Mr. and Mrs. Rinaldi and Mr. Dudley decided that Sam should be given an opportunity to participate in the regular third grade class at Palomar during the Fall. If there were problems, something could be done quickly.

REFERRAL

The referral is the first step in many school districts for a student to be considered for special education services. It may be made by various professionals, but it is usually initiated by the teacher with primary teaching responsibilities for the student. Parents may initiate the process by contacting a teacher or the principal requesting a conference about a problem or concern. Referrals are generally directed to the principal with copies to other professionals (e.g., special education director, school psychologist). A form is usually available in most schools for this purpose.

The use of a referral form is recommended for several reasons. First, it prevents referrals of children on a spontaneous basis; teachers and children have "bad" days and the use of a referral form discourages referrals based on momentary problems. Second, it requires the person making the referral to review its basis. Third, it notifies all persons involved in special education placement of an upcoming case that may require their attention.

Following receipt of the initial referral (Form A: *Request for Consultation*) Mr. Dudley arranged for a meeting between Ms. Gina Howard, the third-grade teacher and Ms. Wanita Smith, the Diagnostic and Prescriptive (D & P) teacher. At this meeting, the group discussed Ms. Howard's referral. Mr. Dudley has asked Ms. Smith to gather together information from Sam Rinaldi's cumulative record folder for presentation to the group (Form B: Cumulative Record Summary). Since Ms. Smith had spent several hours on two separate days observing Sam in Ms. Howard's class, Mr. Dudley asked her to provide a brief summary of her observations at the meeting (Report 1: D & P Observation).

Directions. Study the information on the Request for Consultation (Form A) and the Cumulative Record Summary (Form B). Reconsider this information with reference to the Case Description provided on Sam Rinaldi. Include the observation report (Report 1) prepared by Ms. Smith as part of the referral information.

Through this first meeting, Mr. Dudley was able to determine the major problems Sam Rinaldi was having, to determine that an alternative learning situation or change in present classroom procedures would not remedy the problem, by itself, and to decide to continue the process of referral for special education services. It was decided at this conference that multifactored evaluation would provide the additional information necessary for the next steps.

In Exercise 1, answer the questions with regard to this referral.

FORM A

PALOMAR ELEMENTARY SCHOOL: REQUEST FOR CONSULTATION

TO: Mr. Gary Dudley
FROM: Ms. Gina Howard
DATE: October 15, 1980
Student: Sam Rinaldi Parent/Guardian: Mr. & Mrs. James Rinaldi
Home Address: 1000 King Boulevard
Age: 9 Sex: Male Grade: 3 Home Room Teacher: Gina Howard

Reason for Referral: Sam seems slow. His academic progress for the past several weeks has been very limited. He cannot yet produce all the letters of the alphabet. He's received extensive practice with an alphabet learning station in the classroom but is unable to retain learning correctly over several days.

He only follows directions correctly when there is close individual supervision. Following written directions or instructional materials has not occurred. He gives up quickly on written assignments or turns in assignments that are extremely messy.

He does seem to try hard. When he recognizes how poorly he is doing compared to what is expected of him, he becomes withdrawn and irritable. He is very conscious of his inadequacies.

Although he receives individual assignments each day, his level and rate of progress are significantly different from other children in this group of third graders.

Parental Contact(s): I have met Mr. and Mrs. Rinaldi briefly when they visited in September. I have sent Sam's work home every night. In addition, I sent home a note each Friday of the next week's assignments.

I have not received a call or note from them since our meeting in September.

Additional Comments: I am not sure what Sam's problem is. He just does not seem to be making consistent progress in his program. Other children are noticing his difficulties and giving him a few "looks."

Signature ______________________________

FORM B
CUMULATIVE RECORD SUMMARY

Student: Sam Rinaldi
Birth Date: June 1, 1971
Age as of September 1, 1980: 9 years, 3 months

Educational History:

The Cumulative Record Folder for Sam Rinaldi was received from his former school, Jefferson Elementary School. The records were forwarded to us from Jefferson Elementary at the request of Mr. and Mrs. Rinaldi. We received them early in October. The information summarized below is based on reading this folder since efforts to gain information by telephone were fruitless.

Records indicate Sam had no preschool experience of any length. He entered first grade at the age of six years, three months. He failed the first grade and repeated. There were no comments from either first grade teacher.

The second-grade teacher did include some anecdotal information within the folder. From her comments, she seemed quite concerned about Sam's problems, academic and with peers. She noted that Sam had poor work and study habits and was quite inconsistent in his work. She also indicated that Sam, in her opinion, would be a candidate for special education services, but school district policy discouraged referrals in the first two grades. She thought Sam had not mastered second grade level work but recommended promoting him to third grade because of his size in comparison to other second graders and his eligibility for referral for special education assistance.

She noted a tendency on Sam's part to be progressively more frustrated and moody as the school year unfolded.

She indicated she did refer Sam to the remedial reading teacher. The remedial reading teacher gave Sam the Wide Range Achievement Test (WRAT). The scores are below (administration date—11/8/79):

Reading—1.6
Arithmetic—2.4
Spelling—1.2

However, no evidence of Sam receiving remedial reading services was noted. No other testing or services were noted or requested.

There were several comments from the principal that I have excluded since I believe they are irrelevant and pejorative regarding parental cooperation.

It's my recommendation that these comments be deleted from our cumulative records of Sam Rinaldi.

Summary: There is little of substance in the forwarded Cumulative Folder from Sam Rinaldi's previous school. Overall, it does indicate a record of school failure and inadequate social skills.

Health History:

Hearing—Tested in first grade (12/1/77)
Right ear: normal   Left ear: normal

Vision—Tested in second grade (11/4/79)
Right eye: 20/20   Left eye: 20/20

The parents had been asked by the school personnel at Jefferson Elementary to take Sam to the J. F. Kennedy Clinic for assessment, as noted in the principal's comments. The parents did so at their own expense. The records sent to the School from the clinic are summarized below:

Bender Visual Motor Gestalt Test—Results indicated that Sam had poor visual motor functioning for an eight-year-old child. There were indications of perseveration, poor planning, and difficulty in organizing materials. There were indications that Sam's human-figure drawings were immature and incomplete. The testor indicates the drawings were crowded into one corner of the paper and he was slow in working on the drawings. The psychologist recommended a neurological examination be performed.

Neurological Examination—A pediatric neurologist notes good muscle tone. Deep tendon reflexes +2 and equal. Cranial nerves intact. Ocular movements complete. No abnormal movements noted. An EEG (Electroencephalogram) showed no spikes or abnormal patterns.

Pediatric Examination—The family pediatrician notes that Sam is physically, neurologically, and nutritionally healthy.

Summary: There do not appear to be any physiological problems noted. However, there is some indication of neurological difficulties which may directly influence his school performance.

Family History:

There were no relevant family history facts included in the folder.

Ms. Wanita Smith, D & P Teacher

REPORT 1
D & P OBSERVATION

TO: Mr. Gary Dudley
Ms. Gina Howard
FROM: Ms. Wanita Smith
DATE: October 28, 1980
RE: Referral of Sam Rinaldi—D&P Report

On two separate days, I observed Sam Rinaldi in four situations: twice in the classroom and twice in nonclassroom situations (cafeteria and playground).

My first goal was to see what adjustments we could make immediately in the regular classroom that will assist Sam Rinaldi by teaching through his strengths and/or changing classroom practices that are a problem for the student. My second goal was to determine if more extensive evaluation should be pursued.

October 1: During my first observation I examined Sam's recent papers in arithmetic, spelling, handwriting, and reading assignments. I observed Sam during reading and arithmetic activities in his classroom. I was particularly interested in his work and study skills, language behaviors, learning approach to materials, interaction with materials, motivation, and social behaviors with other students. My summary of these observations is below:

Work and Study Skills: Sam's work habits are inconsistent. He will only complete parts of his assignments when doing independent seat activities. He is not following or reading any directions correctly. However, when given specific oral directions, he does proceed accordingly. Without some immediate feedback on his efforts, he tends to repeat errors and learn some incorrect responses. He is quite slow and plodding in his work. His response time is rather laborious. He does attempt to complete each task accurately before moving on to the next task, but his time on task is usually so long that he fails to complete assignments.

Language Behaviors: From listening to Sam speak with his teacher and other students, I note obvious difficulties here. Sam's vocabulary seems quite limited. There seem to be specific expressive problems; he is having problems expressing his thoughts.

Learning Approach: Sam seems to do well when he has both visual and auditory cues in his learning materials. His synthesis of information seems limited to two or three segments of information at best. He loses track of the central ideas or purpose after that.

Motivation: He is well motivated. He tries to work up to expectations. He responds well to praise.

Social Behaviors: He's having difficulties relating to other students his own age mainly because of conversational inadequacies. His interests and his expression of these interests are developmentally below many of the children in the classroom. He is nonassertive and shy in many situations. He does try to interact positively with others, always ready with a smile.

After I shared these initial observations with Ms. Howard, I recommended several approaches to take with Sam Rinaldi. We set up a peer tutoring situation which we felt would provide some individual help for Sam during math time and perhaps promote some positive social interactions.

We set up a "check-off" system whereby Sam would bring his papers to Ms. Howard at 15 minute intervals, or sooner if he was having problems.

We arranged for some individual learning stations in areas for which Ms. Howard identified Sam's working levels in reading activities.

October 10: I checked on Sam's reactions to Ms. Howard's modifications. Sam was still displaying a great deal of inconsistent and inaccurate work. The learning station activities do not really seem to be giving Sam the kind of repetition he needs.

There is a need for extensive assessment, particularly in reading and arithmetic. Sam's responses and progress are slow and tedious even with peer tutoring.

He does seem to be responding to his peer tutor well though.

Cafeteria and Playground Observations: On October 1 and 10, I observed Sam in these two situations. He is left out of most social interaction with other children during these times. He is rather withdrawn from many interactions. However, he is developing friendships with two other students, albeit rather superficial at this point.

Recommendations: I believe we need a multifactored evaluation of Sam Rinaldi. He has problems in many of the basic skill areas. His skills are far below those of other children in the room at this point.

Ms. Wanita Smith

Ms. Wanita Smith

Exercise 1: Referral

1. In evaluating the referral process at Palomar and at Jefferson, summarize what you believe are appropriate and inappropriate actions by the school staff.

2. What are the major problems that Sam Rinaldi exhibits that indicate a possible need for special education services? Why does it indicate a need?

3. Which policies and procedures at Palomar and Jefferson elementary schools are in compliance and which are in noncompliance of provisions of P.L. 94-142?

4. What other types of information would you have requested if you had been in Mr. Dudley's position?

5. What role did Ms. Smith, the D & P teacher, play during this initial meeting?

PARENTAL INVOLVEMENT

Parental involvement in the educational process of their child with a learning disability is not only required in specific ways under P.L. 94-142, but members of the educational staff at Palomar think it is a good idea. It helps them perform their jobs more effectively and fosters community acceptance and support for their programs. The philosophy of Palomar encourages parents of all their students to become involved. The staff hopes parents of the disabled learners will be more extensively involved but they understand that parents will participate in different degrees and some parents will leave all the decision making up to school personnel.

There are four major areas that need active parental involvement. Some are required by P.L. 94-142; others are indicated because they assist the school and the student.

1. Parents should contribute to the referral and evaluation process.
2. Parents must give their informed consent for evaluation and must participate in the IEP process.
3. Parents must be informed of their rights and the rights of their disabled child during the entire process from identification to programming.
4. Parents should aid the school personnel in finding any factors in the home environment that indicate a possible need for alternative assessment instruments or procedures aside from the usual assessment activities.

The earlier parents are informed about any suspected learning problems of their child, usually the easier and more effective the process of parental involvement is. Parents have considerable information which may not be available to school personnel; some of this information can only be revealed in a face-to-face discussion. Factors that are important to the assessment process include the native language spoken in the home or the parents' mode of communication. For example, if the parents are non-English speaking or use sign language or braille to communicate, the school district must respond to these differences when informing the parents of their rights and when discussing students' problems. Such information is critical to the assessment process and in the selection of procedures or instruments.

Directions: Mr. Dudley involves Mr. Luis Perez, school psychologist, in the parent involvement process. In line with the usual policy of Palomar Elementary, the parents are asked to attend an interview to discuss the referral. In this manner several important areas may be covered.

Mr. Perez has been involved with the development of the Continuum of Educational Services at Palomar since its inception. He has demonstrated considerable skills in interviewing. These skills have been useful in airing parent concerns, gathering information, informing parents of their rights, and bringing the school staff and parents to consensus on the nature of the student's problems and goals to be set to help resove these problems.

Along with a general understanding of the student's problems, it becomes very important to map out the strategy for multifactored evaluation during these interviews. The purposes of evaluation (eligibility for special education services and information for instructional planning) and the types of information and procedures must be clear to everyone. Read the Interview Protocol and examine the pamphlet "Parents as Partners."

REPORT 2
INTERVIEW PROTOCOL

Participants

Mr. Perez (Mr. P.)
School Psychologist

Ms. Howard (Ms. H.)
Third Grade Teacher

Mrs. Smith (Ms. S.)
D & P Teacher

Mr. Rinaldi (Mr. R.)
Parent

Mrs. Rinaldi (Mrs. R.)
Parent

Following some initial introductions, Mr. Perez opened the discussion:

Mr. P: The reason we've called this meeting today is to follow up on a referral made by Mrs. Howard, Sam's third grade teacher, for consultation on a learning problem Sam may have. We'd like to have your view as Sam's parents, on any learning problems you've noticed and we'll share ours with you.

Mr. R: Well, I'm sometimes not sure whether Sam has the problem or its the school he's going to. . .

Mr. P: Um-hm. What specifically disturbs you here at Palomar?

Mrs. R: I think Jim is saying we've had some real concerns about the way the teachers at Sam's last school, Jefferson Elementary, responded to his problems. We never had much confidence in their explanations of what should be done.

Mr. P: Ms. Smith, our D & P teacher did summarize the information from Jefferson Elementary School for us. We appreciate your request for them to send it early. Now that Sam is here at Palomar, let's ask Ms. Howard to explain what type of problem and assistance is needed.

Ms. Howard summarized the information in her Request for Consultation. Mr. and Mrs. Rinaldi were encouraged to interrupt if there was something not clear to them.

Mr. R: Is Sam causing any problems in your class?

Ms. H: If you mean behavior problems Mr. Rinaldi, no, he does not disrupt the classroom. He is getting frustrated with some of the work that's expected though.

Mr. P: Mr. and Mrs. Rinaldi, have there been reactions at home or other places where Sam gets upset with himself for not doing something quite right?

Mrs. R: Not very often, I'd say. He takes things in stride most of the time.

Mr. P: When he does get upset with himself, what prompts this?

Mrs. R: I've noticed that when Jim and Sam are playing catch in the backyard, Sam has some real problems judging the ball. This happens in a lot of physical activities. I'd say you could call it clumsy but it's more than this.

Mr. P: Mr. Rinaldi, what do you say about that?

Mr. R: He'll never be an athlete that's for sure.

Mr. P: Well I think there's something else here that goes beyond athletics. Sam is exhibiting a number of gross and fine motor problems that are affecting his work. We'll ask Wanita Smith to explain her observations of Sam's strengths and weaknesses and our efforts at modifying Sam's program.

Ms. Smith presented her D & P Report to the Rinaldis and encouraged comments or suggestions.

Mr. P: From Ms. Howard's and Ms. Smith's directions, Sam needs assessment to determine his exact needs and eligibility for the special educational services here at Palomar that you're acquainted with, and once this is completed an Individualized Education Program developed to meet his needs can be designed. With the information we've given, is there anything which you'd like to ask or add to your viewpoint?

Mr. R: Well, Sam's been having problems for a while and I'm glad someone's finally taking a look at it.

Mrs. R: Are there some things we can do at home with Sam that will help him?

Ms. S: We have developed a packet of materials explaining our suggestions for working together with our teachers. I'd like to set up a time with you at the end of the meeting to review these materials.

Mr. P: We have a pamphlet called *Parents as Partners* I'd like to give you. Its important for you to understand the assessment process we'll use with Sam and the kind of information we hope to get from our assessment. First, we'll need assessment information to determine if Sam is eligible for special education as indicated by our State standards. Second, we want information we can use for determining the goals and instructional objectives that will be a part of his IEP.

Mr. Perez reviewed *Parents as Partners* with Mr. and Mrs. Rinaldi. He was particularly careful in explaining the rights of the child and the parents under P.L. 94-142. See Form C for this review.

FORM C
PALOMAR ELEMENTARY SCHOOL: PARENTS AS PARTNERS

When Your Child Has a Learning Problem. . .

Children learn in different ways. That is why Palomar Elementary School emphasizes individualized teaching methods.

Some children have very special learning needs. We have adopted the Continuum of Education Services to provide this special assistance. Both special teachers and regular teachers work together so that your child can receive the special educational assistance he or she needs with as much time in the regular classroom as possible.

You are a member of this Continuum Team. Your input is valuable. Our teaching staff has developed special materials for use at home to further support the assistance your child is receiving at school. Let us work together as partners to give your child the best program possible.

Under a new federal law, PL 94-142, you and your child have certain rights. This pamphlet provides information about them. In addition, there is specific information you should know about the evaluation and placement process.

Your Child's Rights

Right to a free appropriate public education.

All the rights of the parent shall pass to the child upon reaching the age of majority except in cases where the child is legally determined under State statute to be incompetent.

Parents Rights

Right to deny permission for any proposed evaluation activities.

Right to review and inspect all records upon which educational decisions are made, to obtain a copy of such records at actual cost of copying, and to request amendments be made to the data.

Right to obtain an independent evaluation of the child at your own expense and introduce such information into the child's record.

Right to present complaints with respect to the evaluation or educational placement of the child, or the provision of special education, to the superintendent of the school district in which the child resides.

Right to a due process hearing conducted by an impartial hearing officer including:

1. The right to be accompanied and advised by counsel and by individuals with special knowledge or training with respect to the problems of handicapped children.

2. The right to present evidence and confront, cross-examine, and compel the attendance of witnesses.
3. The right to written or electronic verbatim record of such hearing.
4. The right to written findings of facts and decisions.

Right to be fully informed, in writing and oral form of all proposed evaluation, placement, and periodic review, activities, and decisions, in the native language of the home.
Right to obtain a description of the kinds and number of facilities, program options, services, and personnel provided to handicapped children by the school district or other education.
Right to have a conference (or communicate in other ways) with any person participating in educational decisions during the evaluation placement, and/or periodic review process.

What's Next . . .

We need to gather important information through assessment. Our assessment team will use classroom observations, interviews, academic aptitude tests, achievement tests, and other special tests as needed. We shall review our methods with you and begin the process by asking you for certain information. We shall not proceed until you have given us your signed approval.

Please call Mr. Gary Dudley, Principal of Palomar School, if you have further questions.

MULTIFACTORED EVALUATION

Students must be evaluated for the purposes of making decisions about placement and instruction. To some degree, the various types of evaluation are exclusive of each other since their purposes are divergent. There has been a movement to reconcile the differences (e.g., interpretation of intelligence tests for instructionally relevant information). This reconciliation has not been very successful, probably because of the manner in which standardized tests such as intelligence tests and achievement tests are constructed. The issue of the relevancy of norm-referenced tests was discussed in Chapter 4.

There are many controversies surrounding the use of standardized tests. Many such tests have been demonstrated to be discriminatory if given inappropriately. Biases toward groups of children can be built into a test by its designers through the selection of the items in the test and by normalization of the test using mainstream samples of white, Anglo-Saxon-type children. When such biases exist, children with cultural, language, cognitive, or physiological differences appear to perform in a subnormal manner and their true potential is not revealed. Thus, the evaluation team must be on guard that the assessment process be nondiscriminatory in nature and provide instructionally relevant information as much as possible.

The staff involved in the evaluation process must be multidisciplinary. The number and type of professionals will be dictated by the type of situational factors the student presents to the evaluation process. This varies for the type of disability. For the student suspected of a specific learning disability, the multidisciplinary team must develop a written report specifying the following information:

1. Whether the student has a specific learning disability as defined in state standards for handicapping conditions
2. The basis for making this decision
3. The relevant behaviors observed during the evaluation process
4. The relationship of the behaviors to the student's academic functioning.
5. The relevant medical findings
6. The identification of a severe discrepancy between achievement and ability that may not be correctable without special education and related services
7. The determination by the team of environmental, cultural, economic, or other types of conditions on the student's perfomance which may be the discrepancy factor between achievement and ability.

Other factors must be considered in performing multifactored evaluation. No single test score may be used for making decisions (e.g., intelligence test). Any standardized tests used must be carefully selected. They must reflect the variables the test purportedly measures rather than reflecting the presence of a sensory impairment or other handicap in a depressed score. The tests must also be in the native language of the home when appropriate or in the child's mode of communication. Assessors are not permitted to utilize testing procedures that unfairly penalize the student's performance or to use only one test or procedure for deciding the appropriateness of placement.

The assessment information is gathered in a number of areas depending upon the specific case. For example, evaluating a student with an articulation problem requires far less information than evaluating one with a suspected specific learning disability. In our case, Sam Rinaldi is a student who might have a learning disability. The multidisciplinary team must make selections of areas for assessment that are based on the state standards for classifying a student as *specific learning disabled* and that will provide the type of assessment data that will be helpful in developing an Individualized Education Program for the student. The areas from which they may select include:

- Educational and developmental history
- Medical evaluation
- Social/emotional functioning
- Academic functioning
- Cognitive functioning
- Vocational/occupational needs
- Communication skills
- Fine/gross motor skills
- Adaptive behaviors
- Social/cultural background
- Physical development

The multifactored evaluation may be done through observation of the student, standardized instruments, criterion-referenced tests in various academic areas, interviews, informal checklists, or other teacher-made measures.

Directions. Mr. Perez has been placed in charge of the multidisciplinary team evaluation. He provides a summary of the data in the Multidisciplinary Team Report (Report 3)

Read the report and use this information to complete Exercise 2. Your data in Exercise 2 will be used to complete the area of present level of educational performance in the IEP simulation.

FORM D

PALOMAR ELEMENTARY SCHOOL: MULTIDISCIPLINARY TEAM REPORT

Name Samuel Rinaldi M-Team Referral Date October 15, 1980
Parents Mr. and Mrs. James Rinaldi Staffing Date Oct. 17, 1980
Address 100 King Boulevard
Phone 555-1214
Grade 3 Age 9
Date of Parental Consent Oct. 15, 1980

Team members:

Name	Title	Signature
Mr. Luis Perez	School Psychologist	Luis Perez
Ms. Gina Howard	Third Grade Teacher	Gina Howard
Ms. Wanita Smith	D & P Teacher	Wanita Smith

Mr. Tim Hallahan	Speech/Language Therapist	Tim Hallahan
Mr. Gary Dudley	Principal	Gary Dudley

Parent Involvement in Multidisciplinary Staffing:

(Check one or both)

__X__ The Multidisciplinary Team Staffing was attended by:

Mrs. James Rinaldi
Name(s) of parent or guardian in attendance

__X__ The Parent Conference was conducted by Perez 10/17/80
Name Date

Mrs. James Rinaldi
Signature of Parent or Guardian

Multidisciplinary Team Recommendations:

The Multidisciplinary Team believes that Samuel Rinaldi (Student's name) has

__X__ General Educational Needs
_____ Special Program Needs
__X__ Continuum of Education Services Needs
_____ Refer for Further Study

Referrals Are Being Made to the Following Services:

Follow-up Date 1/5/81

Multidisciplinary Team Coordinator Mr. Luis Perez

REPORT 3
MULTIDISCIPLINARY TEAM REPORT

Name Sam Rinaldi

Reason for Referral:

Sam Rinaldi has not been making adequate progress in his third-grade class. This follows problems of failure in previous grades prompting retention in first grade. Although he has received individualized assignments and assistance in adjusting to Palomar Elementary, he still is having great problems learning his materials with consistency and accuracy. Adjustments made in the classroom, suggested by the D & P teacher, have not remedied the problems Sam is having. There are significant concerns of the third-grade teacher involving learning, language development, and social skills development that may require special education.

Assistance Techniques or Instruments Used:

Assessment Instrument or Procedure:

Wechsler Intelligence Scale for Children-R	Perez	11/6/80
Informal Behavior Observation	Perez	Summary
Keymath Diagnostic Arithmetic Test	Smith	11/9/80
Durrell Analysis of Reading Difficulty	Smith	11/10/80
Speech and Language Assessment	Hallahan	11/13/80
Social Studies and Science	Howard	Summary

Report of Psychological Evaluation:

On the Wechsler, Sam made a verbal score, performance score, and a full-scale score that places his general intellectual functioning approximately one standard deviation below normal. This places him within the acceptable range for ability as defined in state standards for learning disabilities particularly in regard to his disparity of performance in several areas.

He made the following Scales Scores on the Wechsler subtests. Average performance would be reflected by a scaled score of 10 on each subtest.

Verbal	***Scaled Score***	***Performance***	***Scaled Score***
Information	8	Picture Completion	11
Similarities	11	Picture Arrangement	6
Arithmetic	5	Block Design	7
Vocabulary	6	Object Assembly	—
Comprehension	3	Coding	6
Digit Span	10	Mazes	—

There was significantly low scoring on several of the subtests. The tests usually involved integration skills or physical abilities. His attention seemed to wax and wane most noticeably during the final part of the test.

Sam has noticeable weakness in tasks directly related to school areas: vocabulary and arithmetic. His performance in tasks related to short-term memory are quite variable. Sam does show strength in his ability to reason abstractly and general acquisition of information from home and the school environment. However, his inconsistencies in performance have been noted as attentional deficits in the testing situation.

Luis Perez

Luis Perez, School Psychologist

Report of Behavioral Observation:

Because of Sam's variable performance on the WISC-R, I arranged with Mrs. Howard to observe Sam in a number of reading and math sessions. I set up an observation post in the classroom that was not distracting to Sam. My observational target was Sam's on-task behaviors during these sessions. Although I did the observations by myself (a reliability check by another observer was not possible), I do believe they represent a fairly accurate measurement of Sam's attending skills.

Sam's attention to printed matter is quite variable. On observation samples during silent reading, he was attending the page only about 35 percent of the time. His attention to teacher discussion and directions were higher, at 65 percent of the time sampled.

In combination with his performance on the intelligence test, it seems quite fair to say that Sam is exhibiting a significant attentional deficit that must be considered by teachers in working with him.

Luis Perez

Luis Perez, School Psychologist

Report of Arithmetic Skills:

Sam was very cooperative in his performance on the Keymath Diagnostic Arithmetic Test. His third-grade teacher reported significant problems in Sam's arithmetic performance. Overall, however, what we see is that Sam is having great difficulties with some areas of arithmetic but is at or above his current grade placement.

Keymath—total grade level score: 2.8

A. Numeration (2.0)
   1. Sam can recognize number sequence and state what numbers are missing in sequence through 100.
   2. He has no concepts of roman numerals.

B. Fractions (3.4)
   1. Sam understands the concept of 1/2.
   2. He can read the written fraction 2/3 but not 3/8.
   3. He cannot identify 1/4 of a circle.

C. Geometry and Symbols (3.1)
   1. Identifies circle, square, triangle
   2. Confuses tallest and largest
   3. Knows basic math symbols

D. Addition (2.5)
   1. Adds simple problems with carrying
   2. Difficulties with higher addition facts (7 + 9)
   3. Difficulties adding large numbers (86 + 29)
   4. Once added horizontally instead of vertically

E. Subtraction (3.4)
   1. Subtracts two-digit numbers with no borrowing
   2. Confused on borrowing concept

F. Multiplication (3.9)
   1. Knows lower multiplication facts
   2. Cannot multiply two-digit numbers

G. Division (2.4)
   1. Performs simple story problems like "Have 4 oranges and 2 bowls—how many oranges in each bowl?"
   2. Does not consistently know basic division facts

H. Mental computation (2.9)
   1. Given problems orally, adds two single-digit numbers (3 + 1)
   2. Given problems orally, does not add three one-digit numbers

I. Numerical reasoning (2.7)
   1. Does the following problems: 1 + ____ = 2, ____ + 6 = 9
   2. Does not perform following types of problems correctly:
      5 − ____ = 2, 9 − ____ = 6, therefore 3 + ____ = ____

J. Word problems (1.2)
   Only successful involving word problems of adding two one-digit numbers

K. Missing elements (0)
   This part of the test involved telling what information you needed to have before you could work a problem. Sam could not perform the initial information sorting to begin problem.

L. Money (2.9)
   1. Can name and give value of coins
   2. Can add coins
   3. Cannot add bills and coins

4. Cannot make change
5. Does not know how to read a check

M. Measurement (2.6)
1. Recognizes and reads a ruler to half inches
2. Knows a pair equals two
3. Cannot compare inches, feet, yards, miles
4. Does not know one dozen = 12 or 12 inches are in a foot

N. Time (3.7)
1. Tells time correctly
2. Knows the seasons
3. Reads a calendar accurately
4. Has difficulty grouping months by seasons

Report on Reading Skills:

Sam's reading skills are quite disparate. He does grade level work in certain areas (e.g., word recognition) but is far below grade level performance in other areas. I believe his skill development is quite spotty; he seems to have missed whole areas of reading skill development. Overall, his memory is quite good for specific words but reading the words in sentences and comprehending the meaning provides a great deal of difficulty for him.

Durrell Analysis of Reading Difficulty

A. Oral Reading—below grade 2
B. Silent Reading Comprehension—below grade 2
C. Listening Comprehension—3.6 grade level
D. Word Recognition—3.4 grade level
E. Word Analysis—below grade 1
F. Auditory Discrimination—2.6 grade level
G. Visual Memory—3.4 grade level

Grade placement on basis of subtest scores:

Some of Sam's skills are at the preprimer stage. Specific skills in oral reading and comprehension will need to be taught on an individual basis. He should work well in a small group slightly below third-grade level of difficulty in word recognition exercises and sight words.

Behavioral Observations during Assessment:

Sam does not display any overt problems. He does tend to be shy and dependent upon teacher direction. He does interact readily and will ask questions when he is not sure he has his directions straight. His motivation seems adequate and he is responsive to praise and comments about his work. He was not defensive in an earlier assessment situation when certain errors were pointed out.

Wanita Smith

Wanita Smith, D & P Teacher

Report of Speech and Language Assessment:

I assessed Sam in the speech and language area by using direct observation and the Peabody Picture Vocabulary Test (Form B), Goldman Fristoe Test of Articulation, Test of Language Development, and several informal language assessment techniques. I have summarized the results below:

1. Uses appropriate sentences while speaking—he interacts well	**1.** Distorts b, s, v
2. Follows linguistic rules of syntax on most oral output	**2.** Vocabulary usage is quite limited
3. No outstanding articulation problems requiring therapy	**3.** Use of categories, labels, specific names developmentally inadequate
	4. Response to questions are not well organized

From the language assessment, I believe Sam Rinaldi has several indications of a language delay in his vocabulary usage and general integration of information and expression when interacting. There are no specific behavioral indications that he is aware that his communication skills are inadequate. I believe his social use of language in conversations with peers is also developmentally below that of other children of his age.

Tim Hallahan

Tim Hallahan, Speech and Language Therapist

Social Studies and Science Report:

Sam participates in oral work during social studies and science on his own initiative. He has a great deal of interest in science materials although his questions and responses during these classes are not always clear or cogent.

When we use small group projects, Sam does participate with the other students. However, lately they have tended to ignore his participation without some specific intervention upon my part.

I believe he understands the concepts in science, for example, the relationship between force and mass, the elements that plants need for growth, but he has a great deal of difficulty verbalizing these concepts.

He seems to do better with audio-filmstrip work than with printed matter. With reading materials he either loses interest quickly or seems to struggle with the materials and then give up.

Gina Howard

Gina Howard, Third Grade Teacher

Summary and Recommendations:

It appears that Sam Rinaldi's intellectual aptitude is within the normal range for his age. He has shown some abilities of memory and reasoning abilities that reinforce this finding.

His academic performance is quite inadequate for his age-grade level. His skills are splintered in reading and math. He is able to use some skills adequately whereas he has difficulty with other skills.

He has a great deal of difficulty with written materials and written responses that are required of him.

His work-study skills are inadequate and he appears to be disorganized in his approach to assignments and confused in following instructions.

He does seem motivated and eager to participate.

At this point he has a problem in the expressive area and word usage language capabilities.

The Multidisciplinary Team recommends consideration in a Specific Learning Disabilities class (resource-room setting), direct assistance to the regular third-grade teacher through the D & P Teacher in social studies and science, and a biweekly session with the Speech and Language Therapist.

There does not appear to be any special equipment required. However, some special individualized materials in certain subjects, additional manipulative materials for arithmetic, and the use of audio tapes in certain areas would be appropriate.

Further evaluation is not indicated at the present time. A nine-week review of Sam Rinaldi's progress should be scheduled following development of the IEP to monitor progress and make adjustments.

Luis Perez

Luis Perez, School Psychologist

INDIVIDUALIZED EDUCATION PROGRAM (IEP)

The Individualized Education Program (IEP) is the foundation upon which rests all of the activities of identification, evaluation, and program and instructional decision making. It requires that individual consideration be given to instruction and service delivery to the eligible disabled student. The IEP provides the format for ensuring that all eligible children receive a free appropriate public education.

The minimal requirements in terms of parent involvement are specifically stated in P.L. 94-142. Parents must give signed consent for multifactored evaluation; they must be informed of their rights to disagree and seek redress through impartial hearings; and they should participate through their input in a multifactored evaluation and the IEP. The parents of the

Exercise 2: Present Levels of Educational Performance

Directions: Through studying the case materials, much of the assessment information is included in the IEP in a required section Present Levels of Educational Performance. It is important to understand that not all assessment information should be included in this section. Some performance levels may have to be inferred from tests or observations; however, the most useful statements will be based on factual data. In the following exercise, synthesize the assessment information.

Area	Present Levels of Educational Performance
Academic achievement	
Reading	
Arithmetic	
Written-oral language	
Spelling	
Subject areas	
Other	
Social Skills	
Self-help skills	
Speech-language	
Prevocational skills	
Fine-Gross Motor skills	

student must sign the IEP in order for the IEP to be the operational plan. School districts find it very useful to go beyond these minimal requirements. Parental cooperation with school programs, carried over to the home, makes everyone's efforts more effective.

In essence the IEP can be a relatively simple document. The required content includes the following items:

- Statements of present levels of educational performance
- Annual goals
- Short-term objectives
- Special education services to be provided (initiation and duration dates)
- Percentage of time in regular education
- Provisions for monitoring and review of IEP

School districts usually develop an IEP that contains these elements but also includes other useful information. In the following simulation of the basic contents of the IEP from the case material of Sam Rinaldi, we wish to emphasize the process of IEP development. That is, as you study this simulation you will begin to have a better understanding of the IEP process once you understand the relationship of evaluation data to program and instructional decision making. There is no doubt that the IEPs developed for our student, Sam Rinaldi, would noticeably vary depending upon the professionals involved or the school.

One important factor should be reiterated here. Palomar Elementary School has undergone a multiyear plan for developing its Continuum of Educational Services. The principal, Mr. Dudley, supports the concepts underlying the normalization of experiences for disabled students. The teachers have been in-serviced throughly in instructional techniques and materials for the disabled; special and regular educators have been trained to work cooperatively. Very importantly, a continuum of services for the student is available. For mainstreaming to work effectively, there must be strong leadership, a continuous and effective in-service program, and a number of alternative services available to the student in either special settings or in the regular classroom. For mainstreaming to work, there can be no substitutes for organizational development, expertise, and resources.

The continuum of services available at Palomar Elementary School involves one or more of the following placement options:

- Regular classroom with consultative services
- Regular classroom with consultation and materials from special educators
- Regular classroom with tutoring by an SLD specialist
- Regular classroom with itinerant services
- Regular classroom with resource room services
- Regular classroom and/or special class
- Special class in the regular school building

Directions. The simulations of the IEP development should most appropriately be done as small group sessions. In these sessions, of one to two hours in length, members of the group would assume the following roles:

Principal (Mr. Dudley)

Parents (Mr. and Mrs. Rinaldi)

School psychologist (Mr. Perez)

Diagnostic and prescriptive teacher (Ms. Smith)

Speech/Language therapist (Mr. Hallahan)

Third-grade teacher (Ms. Howard)

The roles and information for playing these roles can be inferred from this chapter. The principal would assume the role of the chairperson of this IEP meeting. The chairperson's responsibilities are to invite parents to the meeting and encourage their involvement, facilitate the flow of communication, keep the group on task, and ensure that the elements of the IEP are completed appropriately.

Through Exercises 3 to 5 the basic elements of the IEP would be in place. If the simulation occurs as a small group, the chairperson can use the exercises as guides to the collection and exchange of information. The other members would not refer directly to these exercises. If the simulation is to be done individually, the exercises would be completed in sequence.

In small group simulations of the IEP development, once the process has been completed the members should make notes for further discussion on the following points: (1) group process; (2) quality and use of data; and (3) interaction with parents and other professional staff.

Exercise 3: Stating Annual Goals

Directions: In the following chart, state the current levels of educational performance on the left and the translation of this assessment information into annual goals on the right. The annual goals are derived from a noted discrepancy in student's level of performance and desired level of performance. The numbering of four levels is arbitrary: There may be more or less.

Level	Current Educational Performance Levels	Annual Goals
1.0		
2.0		
3.0		
4.0		

Exercise 4: Stating Objectives

Directions: The short-term objectives are the intermediate steps in accomplishing the annual goal and should be in sequential order (i.e., the student must accomplish the first objective before attempting the second). The numbering follows this procedure: goal 1.0; objectives 1.1, 1.2, etc.; goal 2.0; objectives 2.1, 2.2, etc.

Since the objectives are the subject of review on some periodic basis there must be an indication of the criteria for evaluating (on what basis do you decide mastery of the objective has been achieved?), procedure for evaluation (how will mastery be measured?), and the person responsible for the evaluation.

Complete the following charts. More charts may be needed and attached.

Annual Goal 1.0:			
Objectives	Criteria	Evaluation	Person Responsible
1.1			
1.2			

Annual Goal 2.0:			
Objectives	Criteria	Evaluation	Person Responsible
2.1			
2.2			
+			

Exercise 5: Placement

Directions: In this exercise, the placement function occurs. The delivery of services to the student must be specified by initiation date and duration of service. The initiation date relates to the IEP timeline (service might start the day following the IEP meeting) and the duration date may be stated in terms of each school year if appropriate.

The percentage of estimated time in the regular classroom should be stated where appropriate. This time will be different from one student to another depending upon need.

Finally, a specific note must be made of special materials or equipment that will be supplied by special educators.

Specific Continuum Service	Initiation Date/ Duration	Special Material/ Equipment

SUMMARY

- A case study of nine year old Sam Rinaldi was presented.
- This case study was applied to the processes used for referral, parental involvement, multifactored evaluation, and IEP development.

APPENDIX A

Agencies Serving Exceptional Children

Alexander Graham Bell Association for the Deaf
3417 Volta Place, N.W.
Washington, D.C. 20007

Allergy Foundation of America
801 Second Avenue
New York, N.Y. 10017

American Academy for Cerebral Palsy
1255 New Hampshire Avenue, N.W.
Washington, D.C. 20036

American Association for the Advancement of Behavior Therapy (AABT)
305 E. Forty-fifth Street
New York, N.Y. 10017

American Association of Elementary—Kindergarten—Nursery Educators
1202 Sixteenth Street, N.W.
Washington, D.C. 20036

American Association for Gifted Children
45 Gramercy Park
New York, N.Y. 10003

American Association for Health, Physical Education, and Recreation
1201 Sixteenth Street, N.W.
Washington, D.C. 20036

American Association on Mental Deficiency
5101 Wisconsin Avenue, N.W.
Washington, D.C. 20016

American Association of Psychiatric Clinics for Children
250 W. Fifty-seventh Street
New York, N.Y. 10019

American Association of Psychiatric Services for Children
1701 Eighteenth Street, N.W.
Washington, D.C. 20009

American Association of School Administrators
1801 North Moore Street
Arlington, Va. 22209

American Association of Workers for the Blind
1511 K Street, N.W.
Washington, D.C. 20005

American Coalition of Citizens with Disabilities
1346 Connecticut Avenue, N.W., No. 817
Washington, D.C. 20036

American Council for the Blind
1211 Connecticut Avenue, N.W.
Washington, D.C. 20006

American Educational Research Association
1126 Sixteenth Street, N.W.
Washington, D.C. 20006

American Heart Association
44 East Twenty-third Street
New York, N.Y. 10010

American Humane Association
Children's Division
P.O. Box 1266
Denver, Colo. 80201

American Library Association
110 Maryland Avenue, N.E., Box 54
Washington, D.C. 20002

American Optometric Association
7000 Chippewa Street
St. Louis, Mo. 20852

American Personnel and Guidance Association
1607 New Hampshire Ave, N.W.
Washington, D.C. 20009

American Physical Therapy Association
1156 Fifteenth Street, N.W., Suite 500
Washington, D.C. 20005

American Printing House for the Blind
1839 Frankfort Avenue
Louisville, Ky. 40206

American Psychiatric Association
1700 Eighteenth Street, N.W.
Washington, D.C. 20009

American School Health Association
1521 Water Street
Kent, Ohio 44240

American Society for Public Administration
1225 Connecticut Avenue, N.W.
Washington, D.C. 20036

American Speech, Language, and Hearing Association
10801 Rockville Pike
Rockville, Md. 20852

American Vocational Association
2020 North Fourteenth Street
Arlington, Va. 22201

Architectural Barriers Committee
National Association of the Physically Handicapped
6473 Grandville Avenue
Detroit, Mich. 48228

Arthritis Foundation
1212 Avenue of the Americas
New York, N.Y. 10036

Association for Childhood Education International
3615 Wisconsin Avenue, N.W.
Washington, D.C. 20016

Association for Children with Learning Disabilities
4156 Library Road
Pittsburgh, Pa. 15234

Association for Education of the Visually Handicapped
919 Walnut Street
San Francisco, Calif. 94121

Association for the Severely Handicapped
1600 West Armory Way
Seattle, Wash. 98119

Association for Supervision and Curriculum Development
1701 K Street, N.W.
Washington, D.C. 20006

Black Child Development Institute
Suite 514
1028 Connecticut Avenue, N.W.
Washington, D.C. 20036

Center for Independent Living, Inc.
2539 Telegraph Avenue
Berkeley, Calif. 94704

Center for Innovation in Teaching the Handicapped
Indiana University
2805 East Tenth Street
Bloomington, Ind. 47401

Child Study Association of America
9 East Eighty-ninth Street
New York, N.Y. 10028

Child Welfare League of America
67 Irving Place
New York, N.Y. 10003

Children's Defense Fund
1520 New Hampshire Avenue, N.W.
Washington, D.C. 20036

Children's Foundation
1026 Seventeenth Street, N.W.
Washington, D.C. 20036

Closer Look—National Information Center for Handicapped
Box 1492
Washington, D.C. 20013

Conference of Executives of American Schools for the Deaf
5034 Wisconsin Avenue, N.W.
Washington, D.C. 20016

Convention of American Instructors of the Deaf, Inc.
5034 Wisconsin Avenue, N.W., Suite 11
Washington, D.C. 20016

Co-Ordinating Council for Handicapped Children
407 South Dearborn, Room 400
Chicago, Ill. 60605

Council of Administrators of Special Education
1920 Association Drive
Reston, Va. 22091

Council for Educational Development and Research
1518 K Street, N.W., No. 206
Washington, D.C. 20005

Council for Exceptional Children
1920 Association Drive
Reston, Va. 22091

Council of State Administrators of Vocational Rehabilitation
1522 K Street, N.W., No. 610
Washington, D.C. 20005

Creative Education Foundation
State University College at Buffalo
218 Chase Hall
1300 Elmwood Avenue
Buffalo, N.Y. 14222

Cystic Fibrosis Foundation
3379 Peachtree Road, N.E., Suite 950
Atlanta, Ga. 30326

Day Care and Child Development Council of America
1401 K Street, N.W.
Washington, D.C. 20005

Dental Guidance Council for Cerebral Palsy
122 East Twenty-third Street
New York, N.Y. 10010

Down's Syndrome Congress
1802 Johnson Drive
Normal, Ill. 61761

Education Commission of the States
Suite 321
444 North Capitol Street, N.W.
Washington, D.C. 20001

Educational Development Center
55 Chapel Street
Cambridge, Mass. 02138

Educational Facilities Laboratories
477 Madison Avenue
New York, N.Y. 10022

Epilepsy Foundation of America
1828 L Street, N.W.
Washington, D.C. 20036

Family Services Association of America
44 East Twenty-third Street
New York, N.Y. 10010

International League of Societies for the Mentally Retarded
12 Rue Forestiere
Brussels 5, Belgium

International Reading Association
800 Barksdale Road
P.O. Box 8139
Newark, Del. 19711

Joint Commission on Mental Health of Children
5454 Wisconsin Avenue
Chevy Chase, Md. 20015

Juvenile Diabetes Foundation
23 East Twenty-third Street
New York, N.Y. 10010

League Against Child Abuse
21 East State Street
Columbus, Ohio 43215

Library of Congress Division for the Blind and Physically Handicapped
1291 Taylor Street, N.W.
Washington, D.C. 20542

Little People of America
Box 126
Owatonna, Minn. 55060

March of Dimes/Birth Defects Foundation
1275 Mamaroneck Avenue
White Plains, N.Y. 10605

Mental Health Materials Center—Human Relations Aide
419 Park Avenue South
New York, N.Y. 10016

Merrill-Palmer Institute
51 East Ferry Avenue
Detroit, Mich. 48202

Muscular Dystrophy Associations
810 Seventh Avenue
New York, N.Y. 10019

National Association of Administrators of State and Federal Education Programs
1902 Lundwood Avenue
Ann Arbor, Mich. 40103

National Association of the Deaf
814 Thayer Avenue
Silver Spring, Md. 20910

National Association of the Deaf-Blind
2703 Forest Oak Circle
Norman, Okla. 73071

National Association for the Education of Young Children
1834 Connecticut Avenue, N.W.
Washington, D.C. 20009

National Association of Elementary School Principals
1801 North Moore Street
Arlington, Va. 22209

National Association of ESEA Title I Coordinators
Iowa Office of Public Instruction
Grimes Office Building
Des Moines, Iowa 50319

National Association of Hearing and Speech Action
814 Thayer Avenue
Silver Spring, Md. 20910

National Association for Mental Health
10 Columbus Circle
New York, N.Y. 10019

National Association of the Physically Handicapped
76 Elm Street
London, Ohio 43140

National Association of Private Residential Facilities for the Mentally Retarded
6269 Leesburg Pike
Falls Church, Va. 22044

National Association of Private Schools for Exceptional Children
7700 Miller Road
Miami, Fla. 33155

National Association for Retarded Citizens
2709 Avenue E East
P.O. Box 6109
Arlington, Tex. 76011

National Association of School Psychologists
1246 Maryland Avenue, N.E.
Washington, D.C. 20002

National Association of Secondary School Principals
1904 Association Drive
Reston, Va. 22091

National Association of State Boards of Education
Suite 526
444 North Capital Street, N.W.
Washington, D.C. 20001

National Association of State Directors of Special Education
1510 H Street, N.W., Suite 301C
Washington, D.C. 20005

National Association for the Visually Handicapped
3201 Balboa Street
San Francisco, Calif. 94121

National Audio Visual Association
3150 Spring Street
Fairfax, Va. 22031

National Center for the Prevention and Treatment of Child Abuse and Neglect
1205 Oneida Street
Denver, Colo. 80220

National Committee for Citizens in Education
Suite 410
Wild Lake Village Green
Columbia, Md. 21044

National Congress of Parents and Teachers
1201 16th Street, N.W.
Washington, D.C. 20036

National Consortium for Child Mental Health Services
1424 Sixteenth Street, N.W., Suite 201A
Washington, D.C. 20036

National Cystic Fibrosis Research Foundation
521 Fifth Avenue
New York, N.Y. 10017

National Easter Seal Society for Crippled Children and Adults
2023 W. Ogden Avenue
Chicago, Ill. 60612

National Education Association
1201 Sixteenth Street, N.W.
Washington, D.C. 20036

National Epilepsy League, Inc.
6 North Michigan Avenue
Chicago, Ill. 60602

National Federation for the Blind
Suite 212, Dupont Circle Building
1346 Connecticut Avenue, N.W.
Washington, D.C. 20036

National Foundation of Dentistry for the Handicapped
1121 Broadway, Suite 5
Boulder, Col. 80302

National Foundation, The March of Dimes
School Relations and Health Education
Box 2000
White Plains, N.Y. 10602

National Headquarters for Mental Health Association
1800 North Kent Street
Rosslyn, Va. 22209

National Hemophilia Foundation
25 W. 39th Street
New York, N.Y. 10018

National Institute of Child Health and Human Development
National Institute of Health
Building 31, Room 2A34
Bethesda, Md. 20014

National Institute of Mental Health
5454 Wisconsin Avenue
Chevy Chase, Md. 20015

National Center on Educational Media and Materials for the Handicapped
The Ohio State University
356 Arps Hall
1945 North High Street
Columbus, Ohio 43210

National Kindergarten Association
8 West Fortieth Street
New York, N.Y. 10018

National Paraplegia Foundation
333 North Michigan Avenue
Chicago, Ill. 60601

National Quadriplegia Foundation
333 North Michigan Avenue
Chicago, Ill. 60601

National Rehabilitation Association
1522 K Street, N.W., Suite 1120
Washington, D.C. 20005

National School Supply and Equipment Association
1500 Wilson Boulevard, Suite 609
Arlington, Va. 22209

National Society for Autistic Children
169 Tampa Avenue
Albany, N.Y. 12208

National Society for Crippled Children and Adults (Easter Seal Society)
2023 West Ogden Avenue
Chicago, Ill. 60612

National Society to Prevent Blindness, Inc.
79 Madison Avenue
New York, N.Y. 10016

National Tay/Sach's Foundation and Allied Diseases Association
122 East Seventh Street
Austin, Tex. 78701

National Technical Institute for the Deaf
One Lomb Memorial Drive
Rochester, N.Y. 14623

National Therapeutic Recreation Society
c/o National Recreation and Park Association
1601 North Kent Street
Arlington, Va. 22209

National Urban League
425 Thirteenth Street, N.W.
Washington, D.C. 20004

Orton Society
8415 Bellona Lane, Suite 113
Towson, Md. 21204

Parenting Materials Information Center
Southwest Educational Development Laboratory
211 East Seventh Street
Austin, Tex. 78701

President's Committee on Employment of the Handicapped
1111 Twentieth Street, N.W., Suite 600
Washington, D.C. 20036

Research for Better Schools
1700 Market Street
Philadelphia, Pa. 19103

Society for Research in Child Development
University of Chicago
5801 Ellis Avenue
Chicago, Ill. 60637

Society for Visual Education
1345 Diversey Parkway
Chicago, Ill. 60614

Spina Bifida Association of America
343 South Dearborn Street, Room 319
Chicago, Ill. 60604

State Higher Education Executive Officers
One American Place, Suite 1530
Baton Rouge, La. 70825

United Cerebral Palsy Association
66 East Thirty-fourth Street
New York, N.Y. 10016

Vision Conservation Institute, Inc.
P.O. Box 2591
Sacramento, Calif, 95821

APPENDIX B

References for Teaching Mainstreamed Students by Selected Content Areas

PART I: READING AND LANGUAGE ARTS

Adams, D., Crandall, A., Eckhoff, B., and Woods-Elliot, C. *Sparks for learning: Ideas for teaching reading and language arts*. Watertown, Mass.: ESN Press, 1980.

Aulls, M. W. *Development and remedial reading in the middle grades*. Boston: Allyn and Bacon, 1978, 366.

Blumenfeld, S. L. *How to tutor*. New Rochelle, N.Y.: Arlington House, 1973, 29-137.

Bond, G. L., Maker, M. A., and Wasson, B. B. *Reading difficulties: Their diagnosis and correction* (4th ed.). Englewood Cliffs, N.J.: Prentice-Hall, 1979, 466.

Burmeister, L. E. *Reading strategies for middle and secondary school teachers* (2nd ed.). Reading, Mass.: Addison-Wesley, 1978.

Carney, J. Content-integrated reading instruction. In H. Herber and R. Vacca (Eds.), *Research in reading in the content areas—Third report*. Syracuse: Syracuse University Reading and Language Arts Center, 1977.

Carnine, D., and Silbert, J. *Direction instruction reading*. Columbus, Oh: Charles E. Merrill, 1979.

Cartwright, C. A., Cartwright, G. P., Ward, M., and Willoughby, H. S. *Activities, guidelines and resources for teachers of special learners*. Belmont, Calif.: Wadsworth, 1981, 250.

Cook, J. E., and Earlley, E. C. *Remediating reading disabilities: Simple things that work*. Germantown, Md: Aspen Systems Corporation, 1979.

Dale, E., O'Rouke, J., and Bamman, H. A. *Techniques of teaching vocabulary*. Palo Alto: Field Education Publications, 1976, 376.

Davis, A. L., Doughtrey, E. L., Brinson, V. L., and Hall, K. D. *A study of the effectiveness of teaching reading in the content areas of English, math, science, and social studies*. Unpublished research report, Norfolk City Schools, 1971.

Deno, E. Special education as developmental capital. *Exceptional Children*, 1970, *37* (3) 229-237.

Dechant, E. V., and Smith, H. P. *Psychology in teaching reading* (2nd ed.). Englewood Cliffs, N.J.: Prentice-Hall, 1977, 436.

Dillner, M. H., and Olson, J. P. *Personalizing reading instruction in middle, junior and senior high schools—Utilizing a competency-based instructional system*. New York: Macmillan, 1977.

Estes, T. J., and Vaughn, J. *Reading and learning in the content classroom*. Boston: Allyn and Bacon, 1978.

Forgan, H. W., and Mangrum, C. T. *Teaching content area reading skills—A modular preservice and inservice program*. Columbus, Oh.: Charles E. Merrill, 1976.

Hafner, L. E. *Improving reading in middle and secondary schools: Selected readings* (2nd ed.). New York: Macmillan, 1974.

Hafner, L. E. *Teaching of reading in the middle and secondary school*. New York: Macmillan, 1977.

Harris, A. J., and Sipay, E. R. *How to increase reading ability: A guide to developmental and remedial methods* (7th ed.). New York: Longman, 1980, 763.

Harris, L. A., and Smith, C. B. *Individualizing reading instruction: A reader*. New York: Holt, Rinehart and Winston, 1972, 361.

Harris, L. A., and Smith C. B. Assessing student progress and needs. Chapter 6 In *Reading instruction: Diagnostic teaching in the classroom* (2nd ed.). New York: Holt, Rinehart and Winston, 1976, 98-129.

Heasley, B. E., and Grosklos, J. R. *Programmed lessons for young language-disabled children: A handbook for therapists, educators, and parents*. Springfield, Ill.: Charles C. Thomas, 1976.

Herber, H. L. An experiment in teaching reading through social studies content. In J. A. Figural (Ed.), *Changing concepts of reading instruction, International Reading Association conference proceedings*, 1961, *6*, 122-24.

Herber, H. L. Teaching reading and physics simultaneously, in J. A. Figural (Ed.), *Improvement in reading through classroom practice*. International Reading Association, 1964, *9*, 84-85.

Herber, H. L. Reading in the social studies: Implications for teaching and research. In J. L. Laffey (Ed.), *Reading in the content areas*. Newark, Del.: International Reading Association, 1972.

Herber, H., L. *Teaching reading in the content areas* (2nd ed.). Englewood Cliffs, N. J.: Prentice-Hall, 1978.

Herber, H. L, and Riley, J. D. *Research in reading in the content areas—Fourth report*. Syracuse: Syracuse University Reading and Language Arts Center, 1979.

Herber, H. L., and Vacca, R. *Research in reading in the content areas—Second report*. Syracuse: Syracuse University Reading and Language Arts Center, 1973.

Herber, H. L., and Vacca, R. *Research in reading in the content areas—Third report*. Syracuse: Syracuse University Reading and Language Arts Center, 1977.

Karlin, R. *Teaching reading in high school* (2nd ed.). Indianapolis: Bobbs-Merrill, 1977.

Karnes, M. B. *Helping young children develop language skills: A book of activities*. Reston, Va.: Council for Exceptional Children, 1973.

Kennedy, E. C. *Methods in teaching developmental reading*. Itasca, Ill.: Peacock, 1974, 402.

Kent, L. R. *Language acquisition program for the retarded or multiply impaired*. Champaign, Ill.: Research Press, 1974a.

Kent, L. R. *Language acquisition programs for the severely retarded*. Champaign, Ill.: Research Press, 1974b.

Kirk, S. A., Kleibhan, J. M., and Learner, J. W. *Teaching reading to slow and disabled learners*. Boston: Houghton Mifflin, 1978.

McIntyre, V. *Reading strategies and enrichment activities for grades 4-9*. Columbus, OH.: Charles E. Merrill, 1977.

Olson, A. V., and Ames, W. S. *Teaching reading skills in secondary schools*. Scranton: Intext, 1972

Piercey, D. *Reading activities in content areas*. Boston: Allyn and Bacon, 1976, 369.

Robinson, H. A. *Teaching reading and study strategies: The content areas.* Boston: Allyn and Bacon, 1975.

Roe, B. D., Stoodt, B. D., and Burns, P. C. *Reading instruction in the secondary school.* Chicago: Rand McNally, 1978.

Sanders, P. L. *An investigation of the effects of instruction in the interpretation of literature on the responses of adolescents to selected short stories.* Unpublished doctoral dissertation, Syracuse University, 1970.

Schiefelbusch, R. *Language intervention strategies.* Baltimore: University Park Press, 1978.

Shepard, D. L. *Comprehensive high school reading methods.* Columbus, Oh.: Charles E. Merrill, 1973.

Stephens, T. M., Hartman, A. C., and Lucas, V. H. *Teaching children basic skills: A curriculum handbook.* Columbus, Oh.: Charles E. Merrill, 1978, 21-232.

Tansley, A. E., and Gulliford, R. *The education of slow learning children.* London: Routledge and Kegan Paul, 1965, 118-148.

Throgmorton, L. R. (Ed.). *Reading further: A supplementary reading list of recommended books for young people.* Berkeley: (SAVI) Regents of the University of California, 1979. (Compiled by S. Jagoda and P. Watson.)

Tinker, M. A., and McCullough, C. M. *Teaching elementary reading* (3rd ed.). New York: Appleton-Century-Crofts, 1968, 671.

Vacca, Richard T. An investigation of a functional reading strategy in seventh grade social studies. In H. Herber and R. Vacca (Eds.), *Research in reading in the content areas—Third report.* Syracuse: Syracuse University Reading and Language Arts Center, 1977.

Van Allen, R. *Language experience activities.* Boston: Houghton Mifflin, 1976.

Zintz, M. V. *Corrective reading,* (2nd ed.). Dubuque, Iowa: William C. Brown, 1972, 449.

PART II: SOCIAL STUDIES

Adams, A. H., Coble, C. R., and Hounshell, P. B. *Mainstreaming language arts and social studies: Special ideas and activities for the whole class.* Santa Monica, Calif.: Goodyear Publishing, 1977.

Baker, R. L., The use of informational organizers in ninth grade social studies. Unpublished doctoral dissertation, Syracuse University, 1971. *Catalog of large type publication—Supplement No. 1.* American Printing House for the Blind, Inc., January, 1981.

Horne, R. E., and Cleaves, A. (Eds.). *The guide to simulations/games for educating and training* (4th ed.). Beverly Hills: Sage Publications, 1980, 556.

Rockler, M. J. *Social studies games and simulations: An evaluation.* In R. E. Horne and A. Cleaves (Eds.), *The guide to simulations/games for educating and training* (4th ed.). Beverly Hills: Sage Publications, 1980, 469.

Shaver, J. P., and Curtis, C. K. *Handicapism and equal opportunity: Teaching about the disabled in social studies.* Reston, Va: The Foundation for Exceptional Children, 1981.

PART III: MATHEMATICS

Blumenfeld, S. L. *How to tutor*. New Rochelle, N. Y.: Arlington House, 1973, 179-298.

Fletcher, R. C. (Ed.). *The teaching of science and mathematics to the blind (with section on raised diagrams): Report to the Viscount Nuffield Auxiliary Fund*. London: Royal National Institute for the Blind, 1973, 172.

Holmes, E. E. What do pre-first-grade children know about number? In W. Barbe, M. Milone, V. Lucan, and J. Humphrey (Eds.), *Basic Skills in kindergarten*. Columbus, Oh.: Zaner-Bloser 1980, 188.

Horne, R. E. and Cleaves, A. (Eds.): *The guide to simulations/games for educating and training* (4th ed.). Beverly Hills: Sage Publications, 1980, 464.

Kurtz, V. R. Kindergarten mathematics: A survey. In W. Barbe, M. Milone, V. Lucas, and J. Humphrey, (Eds.), *Basic skills in kindergarten*. Columbus: Zaner-Bloser, 1980.

Riedesel, C. A. *Teaching elementary school mathematics* (3rd. ed.). Englewood Cliffs, N.J.: Prentice-Hall, 1980.

Schwartz, A. N. Assessment of mathematical concepts of five-year-old children. In W. Barbe, M. Milone, V. Lucas, and J. Humphrey, (Eds.), *Basic Skills in kindergarten*. Columbus, Oh.: Zaner-Bloser, 1980, 203.

Stephens, T. M., Hartman, A. C. and Lucas, V. H. *Teaching children basic skills: A curriculum handbook*. Columbus, Oh.: Charles E. Merrill, 1978, 240-389.

Williams, A. H. Mathematical concepts, skills and abilities of kindergarten entrants. In W. Barbe, M. Milone, V. Lucan, and J. Humphrey, (Eds.) *Basic skills in kindergarten*. Columbus, Oh.: Zaner-Bloser, 1980, 194.

Williams, R. Testing for number readiness: Application of the Piagetian theory of the child's development of the concept of number. In W. Barbe, M. Milone, V. Lucas, and J. Humphrey (Eds.), *Basic skills in kindergarten*. Columbus, Oh.: Zaner-Bloser, 1980.

PART IV: SCIENCE

American Association of Instructors of the Blind. *General Science: A one year course of study adapted for use in schools for the blind*. New York: American Foundation for the Blind, 1933, 27.

American Federation for the Blind. *Products for people with vision problems: Twenty-fifth anniversary edition*. New York: American Federation for the Blind, Fall 1979, 162.

Benham, T. A., et al. *Recording science texts for the blind*. New York: American Federation for the Blind, July 1957, 40.

Bluhm, D. L. *Teaching the retarded visually handicapped: Indeed they are children*. Philadelphia: Saunders, October, 1978, 127. (ED 026 773).

Fletcher, R. D. (Ed.). *The teaching of science and mathematics to the blind (with section on raised diagrams): Report to the Viscount Nuffield Auxiliary Fund*. London: Royal National Institute for the Blind, 1973, 172.

Glass, R. D. *An annotated bibliography on science education and the visually handicapped*. American Printing House for the Blind, Louisville: December, 1979.

Hadary, D. E. Laboratory science and art for blind and deaf children. In H. Hofman and K. Ricker, (Eds.), *Science Education and the Physically Handicapped: Sourcebook*. Washington, D.C.: National Science Teachers Association, 1979, 87-93.

Hadary, D. E., and Cohen, S. H. *Laboratory science and art for the blind, deaf and emotionally disturbed children: A mainstreaming approach*. Baltimore: University Park Press, 1978.

Introducing SAVI: Science activities for the visually impaired. Berkeley: Regents of the University of California, 1979.

Tombaugh, D. *Biology for the blind*. Disseminated by: Ohio Resource Center for Low Incidence and Severely Handicapped, Columbus, Oh. Printed by Euclid Public Schools, Euclid, Oh., 1973.

APPENDIX C

Books for Adults, Parents, and Teachers to Develop Understanding

PART I: ADULTS

Aiello, B. (Ed.). *Places and spaces: Facilities planning for handicapped children.* Reston, Va.: Council for Exceptional Children, 1976.

Anderson, E. M. *The disabled schoolchild: A study of integration in primary schools.* New York: Barnes and Noble, 1973.

Axline, V. M. *Dibs: In search of self.* New York: Ballantine Books, 1964.

Birch, J. W. *Mainstreaming: Educable mentally retarded children in regular classes.* Reston, Va.: Council for Exceptional Children, 1974.

Blatt, B., and Kaplan, F. *Christmas in purgatory: A photographic essay on mental retardation.* Boston: Allyn and Bacon, 1966.

Boston, B. O. *The sorcerer's apprentice: A case study in the role of a mentor.* Reston, Va.: Council for Exceptional Children, 1976.

Bourgeon, R. *In darkness.* New York: William Morrow, 1969.

Braithwaite, E. R. *To sir, with love.* Englewood Cliffs, N. J.: Prentice-Hall, 1959.

Bristow, R. O. *Laughter in darkness.* New York: Crown, 1974.

Buck, P. *The child who never grew.* New York: John Day, 1950.

Caldwell, E. *Tobacco road.* New York: Grosset Dunlap, 1948.

Cartwright, C., and Forsberg, S. *Exceptional previews: A self evaluation handbook for special education students.* Belmont, Calif.: Wadsworth, 1979.

Chevigny, H. *My eyes have a cold nose.* New Haven: Yale University Press, 1946.

Christopher, D. A. *Manual communication: A basic text and workbook with practical exercises.* Baltimore: University Press, 1976.

Christopher, M. *Long shot for Paul.* New York: Archway, 1974.

Clark, R. W. *Einstein: The life and times.* New York: World Publishing, 1971.

Cleaver, V., and Cleaver B. *Me too.* New York: New American Library, 1975.

Cohen, S. *Special people.* Englewood Cliffs, N.J.: Prentice-Hall, 1977.

Duncan, I. *My life.* New York: Liveright, 1955. (Isadora).

Faulkner, W. *The sound and the fury.* New York: Vintage Books, 1954.

Fields, R. *And now tomorrow.* New York: Macmillan, 1955.

Fukurai, S. *How can I make what I cannot see?* New York: Van Nostrand Reinhold, 1974.

Goertzel, V. H., and Goertzel, M. G. *Cradles of eminence.* Boston: Little, Brown, and Co. 1962.

Green, H. *I never promised you a rose garden.* New York: Holt, Rinehart and Winston, 1964.

Grost, A. *Genius in residence.* Englewood Cliffs, N. J.: Prentice-Hall, 1970.

Guilford, J. P. *Way beyond the IQ.* Buffalo, New York: Creative Education Foundation, 1977.

Hersey, J. *The child buyer.* New York: Alfred A. Knopf, 1960.

Hunt, N. *The world of Nigel Hunt.* New York: Garrett Publications, 1967.

Hunter, E. *Child of the silent night.* Boston: Houghton Mifflin, 1969.

Husing, E. B. *My eyes are in my heart.* New York: Random House, 1959.

Huxley, A. *Eyeless in Gaza.* New York: Harper and Brothers, 1936.

Israelson, O. W. *Forty years of sound and forty years of silence: An autobiography.* Salt Lake City: Utah Print Company, 1968.

Itard, J., and Gaspard, G. *The wild boy of Aveyron*. New York: Appleton-Century-Crofts, 1962.

Johnson, W. *Because I stutter*. New York: Appleton, 1930.

Kazin, A. *A walker in the city*. New York: Grove, 1958.

Kesey, K. *One flew over the cuckoo's nest*. New York: Viking Press, 1962.

Keyes, D. *Flowers for Algernon*. New York: Harcourt Brace Jovanovich, 1966.

Klein, G. *The blue rose*. Westport, Conn.: Lawrence Hill and Company, 1974.

Kliment, S. A. *Into the mainstream: A syllabus for a barrier-free environment*. Washington, D.C.: U. S. Government Printing Office, 1976.

Kugelmass, A. J. *Louis Braille: Windows for the blind*. New York: Julian Nessner, 1951.

Landau, E. D., Epstein, S. L., and Stone, A. P. *The exceptional child through literature*. Englewood Cliffs, N.J.: Prentice-Hall, 1979.

Long, K. *Johnny's such a bright boy, what a shame he's retarded*. Boston: Houghton Mifflin, 1978.

Lowman, E. W. and Klinger, J. L. *Aids to Independent living: Self-help for the handicapped*. New York: McGraw-Hill, 1969.

Mace, R., and Iaslett, B. *An illustrated handbook of the handicapped section of the North Carolina state building code*. Raleigh: The North Carolina State Building Code Council and the North Carolina Department of Insurance, 1977.

McCullers, C. *The heart is a lonely hunter*. New York: Bantam Books, 1970.

Mullins, J., and Wolfe, S. (Eds.). *Special people behind the 8-ball: An annotated bibliography of literature classified by handicapping conditions*. Johnstown, Pa.: Mafex Associates, 1975.

Nazarro, J. *Exceptional timetables: Historical events affecting the handicapped and gifted*. Reston, Va.: Council for Exceptional Children, 1977.

Nichols, P. *Joe Egg*. New York: Grove Press, 1968.

Payne, J. S., Kauffman, J. M., Patton, J. R., Rown, G. B., and DeMott, R. M. *Exceptional children in focus: Incidents, concepts, and issues in special education* (2nd. ed.). Columbus, Oh.: Charles E. Merrill, 1979.

Renzulli, J. S., and Stoddard, E. P. *Under one cover: Gifted and talented education in perspective*. Reston, Va.: Council for Exceptional Children, 1980.

Reynolds, M. C. (Ed.). *Futures of education for exceptional students: Emerging structures*. Reston, Va.: Council for Exceptional Children, 1978.

Roberts, N. *David*. Atlanta, Ga.: John Knox Press, 1974.

Rogers, D. *Angel unaware*. New York: Pillar Books, 1975.

Russell, R. *To catch an angel*. New York: Vanguard Press, 1962.

Seagoe, M. *Yesterday was Tuesday, all day and all night*. Boston: Allyn and Bacon, 1964.

Segal, E. *Love story*. New York: G. H. Doran, 1975.

Sharp, M. *The innocents*. New York: Barnes and Noble, 1972.

Spencer, E. *The light in the piazza*. New York: McGraw-Hill, 1960.

Stein, S. B. *About handicaps*. New York: Walder & Company, 1974.

Stone, A. A., and Stone S. S. (Eds.). *The abnormal personality through literature*. Englewood Cliffs, N.J.: Prentice-Hall, 1966.

Sullivan, T. *If you could see what I hear*. Toronto: Peter Martin Association Limited, 1974.

Tucker, C. *Betty Lee*. New York: Macmillan, 1954.

Vonegut, K. Harrison Bergeron. In K. Vonnegut, *Welcome to the monkey house*. New York: Dell, 1968.

Vonnegut, K. *Slapstick*. New York: Delacorte Press, 1976.

Walker, P. *Twyla*. Englewood Cliffs, N.J.: Prentice-Hall, 1973.

Wallace, G., and McLoughlin J. *Learning disabilities: Concepts and characteristics*. Columbus, Oh.: Charles E. Merrill, 1975.

Whitehill, J. *Able Baker and others*. Boston: Little, Brown, and Co. 1957.

Wiggins, J. *No sound*. New York: Silent Press, 1970.

Wright, D. *Deafness*. New York: Stein and Day, 1970.

PART II: PARENTS

Abraham, W. *Barbara, a prologue*. New York: Rinehart, 1958.

Angus, J. *Watch my words: An open letter to parents of young deaf children*. Cincinnati, Oh.: Forward Movement Publishing, 1974.

Axline, V. *Dibs: In search of self*. New York: Ballantine Books, 1964.

Baldwin, V. L., Fredericks, H., and Brodsky, G. *Isn't it time he outgrew this? Or, a training program for parents of retarded children*. Springfield, Ill.: Charles C. Thomas, 1976.

Bannatyne, A., and Bannatyne, M. *How your children can learn to live a rewarding life: Behavioral modification for parents and teachers*. Springfield, Ill.: Charles C. Thomas, 1973.

Bateman, B. *So you're going to hearing*. Northbrook, Ill.: Hubbard, 1979.

Becker, W. C. *Parents are teachers: A child management program*. Champaign, Ill.: Research Press, 1971.

Belton, S., and Terbough, C. *Sparks: Activities to help children learn at home*. New York: Human Sciences Press, no date.

Brehm, S. S. *Help for your child: A parent's guide to mental health services*. Englewood Cliffs, N.J.: Prentice-Hall, 1978.

Breisky, W. *I think I can*. Garden City, N. J.: Doubleday, 1974.

Brown, D. L. *Developmental handicaps in babies and young children: A guide for parents*. Springfield, Ill.: Charles C. Thomas, 1972.

Brutten, M., Richardson, S. D., and Mangel, C. *Something's wrong with my child: A parents' book about children with learning disabilities*. New York: Harcourt Brace Jovanovich, 1973.

Chalfant, J. C. and Van Dusen Pysh, M. *The compliance manual: A guide to the rules and regulations of P.L. 94-142*. New Rochelle, N.Y.: Pathescope Educational Media, 1980.

Chinn, P. C., Winn, J., and Walter, R. H. *Two-way talking with parents of special children*. St. Louis, Mo.: C. V. Mosby, 1978.

Croft, D. *Parents and teachers: A resource book for home, school and community relations*. Belmont, Calif.: Wadsworth, 1979.

Dorward, B. *Teaching aids and toys for handicapped children*. Reston, Va.: Council for Exceptional Children, 1960.

Evans, J. *How to fill your toyshelves without emptying your pocketbook: 70 inexpensive things to do or make*. Reston, Va.: Council for Exceptional Children, 1976a.

Evans, J. *Working with parents of handicapped children*. Reston, Va.: Council for Exceptional Children, 1976b.

Fennie, N. R. *Handling the young cerebral palsied child at home*. New York: E. P. Dutton, 1975.

Freeman, S. *Does your child have a learning disability?* Springfield, Ill.: Charles C. Thomas, 1974.

Gardner, R. A. *MBD: The family book about minimal brain dysfunction. Part 1: For parents; Part 2: For boys and girls*. New York: Jason Aronson, 1973.

Gordon, S., and Wollin, M. McD. *Parenting: A guide for young people*. New York: Oxford University Press, 1975.

Gosciewski, F. W. *Effective child rearing: The behaviorally aware parent*. New York: Human Sciences Press, 1976.

Hanson, M. *Teaching your Down's Syndrome infant*. Baltimore: University Park Press, 1978.

Heisler, V. *A handicapped child in the family: A guide for parents*. New York: Grune & Stratton, 1972.

Help for parents of handicapped children. King of Prussia, Pa.: Eastern Pennsylvania Regional Resource Center for Special Education and Pennsylvania Resources and Information Center for Special Education, no date.

Helping the handicapped through parent/professional partnerships. Niles, Ill.: Developmental Learning Materials, no date.

Henderson, L. T. *Open doors: My child's first eight years without sight*. New York: John Day, 1954.

Hersey, P., and Blanchard, K. H. *The family game: A situational approach to effective parenting*. Reading, Mass.: Addison-Wesley, 1978.

Hewett, S., and Newson, J. *The family and the handicapped*. Chicago: Aldine Press, 1970.

Isaacs, S. *Troubles of children and parents*. New York: Schocken Books, 1973.

Jenkins, J. K., and MacDonald, P. *Growing up equal: Activities and resources for parents and teachers of young children*. Englewood Cliffs, N.J.: Prentice-Hall, 1979.

Karnes, M. B. *Learning language at home*. Reston, Va.: Council for Exceptional Children, 1977.

Katz, L., and others. *The deaf child in the public schools—A handbook for parents of deaf children*. Danville, Ill.: Interstate Printers and Publishers, 1974.

Kaufman, F. *Your gifted child and you*. Reston, Va.: Council for Exceptional Children, 1977.

Kozloff, M. A. *Reaching the autistic child: A parent training program*. Champaign, Ill.: Research Press, 1973.

Kozloff, M. A. *A program for families of children with learning and behavior problems*. New York: Wiley, 1979.

Kroth, R. *Communicating with parents of exceptional children: Improving parent teacher relationships*. Denver, Colo.: Love Publishing, 1975.

Leitch, S. M. *A child learns to speak: A guide for parents and teachers of preschool children*. Springfield, Ill.: Charles C. Thomas, 1977.

Linde, T. F., and Kopp, T. *Training retarded babies and preschoolers*. Springfield, Ill.: Charles C. Thomas, 1974.

Love, H. D. *The emotionally disturbed child: A parents' guide for parents who have problem children*. Springfield, Ill.: Charles C. Thomas, 1970a.

Love, H. D. *Parental attitudes toward exceptional children*. Springfield, Ill.: Charles C. Thomas, 1970b.

Madsen, C. K., and Madsen, Jr., C. H. *Parents and children love and discipline: A positive approach to behavior modification*. Arlington Heights, Ill.: AHM, 1975.

McDonald, E. *Understand those feelings*. Pittsburgh: Stanwix House, 1962.

Millman, J., and Behrmann, P. *Parents as playmates: A games approach to the preschool years*. New York: Human Sciences Press, 1979.

Mopsik, S. I., and Agard, J. A. *An education handbook for parents of handicapped children*. Cambridge, Mass.: Abt Associates, 1979.

Newman, S. *Guidelines to parent-teacher cooperation in early childhood education*. New York: Book-Lab, 1972.

Parent's home activity guides. Saturday schools: A school and home learning program for four-year-olds. Ferguson, Mont.: Ferguson-Florissant School District, 1974. (ERIC NO. ED101835).

Perske, R., and Perske, M. *New directions for parents of persons who are retarded*. Nashville, Tenn.: Abingdon Press, 1973.

Pope, L. *Learning disabilities glossary*. New York: Book-Lab, 1976.

Riley, M. T. *LATON: The parent book*. Atlanta, Ga.: Humanics, 1978.

Ross, A. O. *The exceptional child in the family*. New York: Grune & Stratton, 1964.

Schachter, F. F. *Everyday mother talk to toddlers: Early intervention*. New York: Academic, 1979.

Sparling, J., and Lewis, I. *Learning games for the first three years: A guide to parent-child play*. New York: Walker & Company, 1979.

Toys for early development of the young blind child: A guide for parents. Washington, D.C.: U.S. Department of Health, Education, and Welfare, Office of Education, 1971. (ERIC No. ED 065-201)

Turnbull, A., and Turnbull, H. R. *Parents speak out: Views from the other side of the two-way mirror*. Columbus, Oh.: Charles E. Merrill, 1978.

Wender, P. H. *The hyperactive child—A handbook for parents*. New York: Crown, 1973.

Wentworth, E. H. *Listen to your heart: A message to parents of handicapped children*. Boston: Houghton Mifflin, 1974.

West, P. *Words for a deaf daughter*. New York: New American Library, 1974.

Wiegerink, R., Posante, R., Bristol, M., and Hocutt, A. *Parent involvement in early education for handicapped children: A review*. Chapel Hill, N.C.: UNC Carolina Institute for Research on Early Education of the Handicapped, 1978.

Wing, L. *Autistic children: A guide for parents*. New York: Brunner/Mazel, 1972.

Wolfensberger, W., and Zauha, H. *Citizen advocacy and protective services for the impaired and handicapped*. Toronto: National Institute on Mental Retardation, 1973.

PART III: TEACHERS

Abeson, A. R., Bolick, N., and Hass, J. *A primer on due process—Education decisions for handicapped children*. Reston, Va.: Council for Exceptional Children, 1975.

Abidin, R. R. *Parenting skills: Trainer's manual and workbook*. New York: Human Sciences Press, 1976.

Achievement unlimited: Enhancing self-concept through improvement of academic, motor and social skills. Gainsville: Florida University, College of Education, 1973.

Adams, A. H. *Research data concerning school referral for services from the special education center, Oxford, Mississippi*. Oxford, Miss.: Special Education Services Center, 1969.

Adams, C. D., and others. *The student with impaired hearing*. Shorewood, Wis.: Shorewood Public Schools, 1963.

Adamson, G. *Final report of the educational modulation center*. Olathe, Kans.: Olathe Public Schools, 1970.

Adapting materials for educating blind children with sighted children. Albany: University of the State of New York, 1978.

Adelman, H. *Facilitating change and preparing educational change agents*. Riverside, Calif.: University of California, 1973.

Adkins, P. G. *A priceless playground for exceptional children*. El Paso, Tex.: Early Learning Center for Exceptional Children, 1973.

Ainscow, M., and Tweddle, D. A. *Preventing classroom failure: An objective approach*. New York: Wiley, 1979.

Alley, G. A., and Deshler, D. D. *Teaching the learning disabled adolescent: Strategies and methods*. Denver, Colo.: Love Publishing, 1979.

Almy, M., and Genishi, C. *Ways of studying children: An observational manual for early childhood teachers*. New York: Teachers College Press, 1979.

Altman, R., Chandler, M. R., Connoly, A. J., and Meyen, E. L. *Interim report: Competency research phase. Prototype training program for the preparation of curriculum consultants for exceptional children*. Columbia, Mo.: University of Missouri, 1971.

Anderson, R. *Individualizing educational materials for special children in the mainstream*. Baltimore: University Park Press, 1978.

Auerback, S. A. *Creative homes and centers*. New York: Human Sciences Press, 1978.

Auerback, S. A. *Special needs and services*. New York: Human Sciences Press, 1979.

Axelrod, S. *Behavior modification for the classroom teacher*. New York: McGraw-Hill, 1977.

Banas, N., and Wills, I. H. *Identifying early learning gaps: A guide to the assessment of academic readiness*. Atlanta, Ga.: Humanics, 1975.

Barnes, E., and others. *Teach and reach: An alternate guide to resources for the classroom*. Syracuse, N.Y.: Human Policy Press, 1974.

Baskin, B. H., and Harris, K. H. *Notes from a different drummer: A guide to juvenile fiction portraying the handicapped*. New York: Bowker, 1977.

Baskin, B. H., and Harris, K. H. *Books for the gifted child*. New York: Bowker, 1979.

Bateman, B. *So you're going to hearing*. Northbrook, Ill.: Hubbard, 1979.

Behavior management strategies for the classroom. Philadelphia: Research for Better Schools, 1979.

Bender, M. and Bender, R. K. *Disadvantaged preschool children: A source book for teachers*. Baltimore: Paul H. Brooks, 1979.

Bender, M. and Valletutti, P. J. *Teaching the moderately and severely handicapped—Volume 1: Behavior, self-care, and motor skills; Volume 2: Communication, socialization, safety, and leisure skills; Volume 3: Functional academics for the mildly and moderately handicapped*. Baltimore: University Park Press, 1976.

Berry, K. E. *Models for mainstreaming*. Sioux Falls, S. Dak.: Adapt Press, 1972.

Beter, T. R., and Cragin, W. E. *The mentally retarded child and his motor behavior: Practical diagnosis and movement experiences*. Springfield, Ill.: Charles C. Thomas, 1972.

Birch, J. W. *Mainstreaming: Educable mentally retarded children in regular classes*. Reston, Va.: Council for Exceptional Children, 1974.

Birch, J. W. *Hearing impaired children in the mainstream*. Reston, Va.: Council for Exceptional Children, 1975.

Birch, J. W., and Stevens, G. D. *Reaching the mentally retarded*. Indianapolis, Ind.: Bobbs-Merrill, 1955.

Blackwell, R. B., and Joynt, R. R. (Eds.). *Learning disabilities handbook for teachers*. Springfield, Ill.: Charles C. Thomas, 1976.

Blatt, B. (Ed.). *Selected media reviews: Exceptional children, 1970-1973*. Reston, Va.: Council for Exceptional Children, 1973.

Blumenfeld, J. *Help them grow!* Nashville, Tenn.: Abingdon Press, 1971.

Boland, S. K. Integration: Parent alliance. In *In-Service Consultor*, 1974, *1*, (1).

Bowden, M. G., and Otto, H. J., (Eds.). *The education of the exceptional child in Casis School*. Austin: Casis Elementary School, 1964.

Bremer, C. *Utilizing the resource room concept*. Austin: Austin Winters Group 1972, P.O. Box 12642, Capital Station, Austin, Texas 78711.

Brolin, D. E. (Ed.). *Life centered career education—A competency based approach*. Reston, Va.: Council for Exceptional Children, 1978.

Brown, D. *Behavior modification in child, school, and family mental health*. Champaign, Ill.: Research Press, 1972.

Brown, J. W. *A humanistic approach to special education. Resource monograph 8*. Gainesville: University of Florida, P. K. Yonge Lab. School, 1973 (ERIC NO. ED102742).

Burgdorf, Jr. R. L., (Ed.). *The legal rights of handicapped persons—Cases, materials and text*. Baltimore: Paul H. Brooks, 1979.

Caldwell, B. M., and Stedman, D. J., (Eds.). *Infant education: A guide for helping handicapped children in the first three years*. New York: Walker Company, 1977.

Calhoun, M. *Teaching and learning strategies for physically handicapped students*. Baltimore: University Park Press, 1979.

California State Department of Health. *Leisure time activities for deaf-blind children*. Northridge, Calif.: Joyce Media, no date.

Callahan, C. M. *Developing creativity in the gifted and talented*. Reston, Va.: Council for Exceptional Children, 1978.

Carlson, B. W. and Ginglend, D. *Play activities for the retarded child*. Nashville, Tenn.: Abingdon Press, 1971.

Carter, R. D. *Help! These kids are driving me crazy*. Champaign, Ill.: Research Press, 1972.

Cartwright, C. A., and Cartwright, G. P. *Developing observation skills*. New York: McGraw-Hill, 1974.

Cartwright, C. A., and Forsberg, S. *Exceptional previews: A self-evaluation handbook for special education students*. Belmont, Calif.: Wadsworth, 1979.

Chaffin, J., and Geer, F. *The Pinchney project: An innovative approach to mainstreaming exceptional children*. Lawrence, Kan.: Kansas State University, 1975.

Cicenia, E. F., and others. *The challenge of educating the blind child in the regular classroom. Albany: New York State University, 1957.*

Clarification of P.L. 94-142 for the classroom teacher. Philadelphia: Research for Better Schools, 1979.

Clark, G. M. *Career education for the handicapped child in the elementary classroom*. Denver, Colo.: Love Publishing, 1979.

Cohen, M. A., and Gross, P. J. *The developmental resource: Behavioral sequences for assessment and program planning: Volumes 1 and 2*. New York: Grune & Stratton, 1979.

Coletta, A. J. *Working together: A guide to parent involvement*. Atlanta, Ga.: Humanics, 1976.

Communications Carousel. Chatsworth, Calif.: Opportunities for Learning, 1977.

Conner, F. P., Williamson, G. G., and Siepp, J. M. *Program guide for infants and toddlers with neuromotor and other developmental disabilities*. New York: Teachers College Press, Columbia University, 1978.

Corrigan, D. C., and Howey, K. R. *Special education in transition: Concepts to guide the education of experienced teachers, with implications for P.L. 94-142*. Reston, Va.: Council for Exceptional Children, 1980.

Council for Exceptional Children. *Career education: Teaching exceptional children*. Reston, Va.: Council for Exceptional Children, 1973.

Council for Exceptional Children. *Guidelines for personnel in the education of exceptional children*. Reston, Va.: Council for Exceptional Children, 1976.

Council for Exceptional Children. *Teacher idea exchange: A potpourri of helpful hints*. Reston, Va.: Council for Exceptional Children, no date.

Cratty, B. J. *Developmental games for physically handicapped children*. Palo Alto: Calif. Peek Publications, 1969.

Cratty, B. J. *Adapted physical education for handicapped children and youth*. Denver, Colo.: Love Publishing, 1980.

Cratty, B. J., and Breen, J. *Educational games for physically handicapped children*. Denver, Colo.: Love Publishing, 1972.

Cross, L., and Goin, K. (Eds.). *Identifying handicapped children: A guide to casefinding, screening, diagnosis, assessment, and evaluation*. New York: Walker & Company, 1977.

Davis, H. S. *Instructional materials center, an annotated bibliography*. Cleveland: Educational Research Council of Greater Cleveland, 1967, 39. (ERIC NO. ED 022257.)

Dayan, M., Harper, B., Malloy, J. S., and Witt, B. T. *Communcation for the severely and profoundly handicapped*. Denver, Colo.: Love Publishing, 1975.

Dean, M. (Comp.). *Teacher-pupil package: Visually handicapped handbook*. Lansing: Michigan State Department of Education, 1972. (ERIC NO. ED 089512).

Dehaan, R. F., and Havighurst, R. J. *Educating gifted children*. Chicago: University of Chicago Press, 1961.

Demers, L. A. Effective mainstreaming for the learning disabled student with behavior problems. *Journal of Learning Disabilities*, 1981, *14* (4): 179-188.

Deno, E. (Ed.). *Instructional alternatives for exceptional children*. Reston, Va.: Council for Exceptional Children, 1973.

Dibner, S. S., and Dibner, A. S. *Integration or segregation for the physically handicapped child*. Baltimore: Paul H. Brooks, 1979.

Directory of services for handicapping conditions. Washington, D.C.: Information Center for Handicapped Children, 1980.

Dorward, B. *Teaching aids and toys for handicapped children*. Reston, Va.: Council for Exceptional Children, 1960.

Dreyer, S. S. *The book finder*. Circle Pines, Minn.: American Guidance Service, 1977.

Dupont, H., (Ed.). *Educating emotionally disturbed children: Readings* (2nd. ed.). Clifton, N.J.: Holt, Rinehart and Winston, 1975.

ECE: A workbook for administrators, parents and volunteers in the classroom: A handbook for teachers. Saratoga, Calif.: R. E. Research Association, no date.

Edgington, D. *The physically handicapped child in your classroom: A handbook for teachers*. Springfield, Ill.: Charles C. Thomas, 1976.

Eissler, R. S., Freud, A., Kris, M., and Solnit, A. J., (Eds.). *Physical illness and handicap in childhood*. New Haven: Yale University Press, 1977.

Evans, T. *Working with parents of handicapped children*. Reston, Va.: Council for Exceptional Children, 1976.

Faas, L. A. *Learning disabilities: A competency-based approach*. Boston: Houghton Mifflin, 1976.

Faas, L. A. *Children with learning problems: A handbook for teachers*. Boston: Houghton Mifflin, 1980.

Feingold, B. A., and Bank, C. L. *Developmental disabilities of early childhood*. Springfield, Ill.: Charles C. Thomas, 1977.

Filter, M. D. *Communication disorders: A handbook for educators*. Springfield, Ill.: Charles C. Thomas, 1977.

Fink, A. H. *International perspective on future special education*. Reston, Va.: Council for Exceptional Children, 1979.

Fraser, B. *Gross Motor Management. Volume 2: A gross motor curriculum for severely and multiply impaired students*. Baltimore: University Park Press, 1979.

French, A. *Disturbed children and their families: Innovations in evaluation and treatment*. New York: Human Sciences Press, 1977.

Friedlander, B. Z. *Exceptional infant. Volume 3: Assessment and intervention*. New York: Brunner/Mazel, 1975.

Fusfeld, I. (Ed.). *A handbook of readings in education for the deaf and postschool implications*. Springfield, Ill.: Charles C. Thomas, 1967. (ED34351).

Gadow, K. D. *Children on medication: A primer for school personnel*. Reston, Va.: Council for Exceptional Children, 1979.

Gallagher, J. J. Organizational needs for quality special education. In *Futures of education for exceptional children: Emerging structures*, Reynolds, Maynard (Ed.), pp. 133-150.

Gallagher, P. A. *Positive classroom performance: Techniques for changing behavior*. Denver, Colo.: Love Publishing, 1971.

Gallagher, P. A. *Education games for visually handicapped children*. Denver, Colo.: Love Publishing, 1977.

Gallagher, P. A. *Teaching students with behavior disorders*. Denver, Colo.: Love Publishing, 1979.

Gallender, D. *Teaching eating and toileting skills to the multi-handicapped in the school setting*. Springfield, Ill.: Charles C. Thomas, 1979.

Garrison, M., and Hammill, D. *Who are the retarded: Multiple criteria applied to children in educable classes?* Philadelphia: Temple University, College of Education, 1970. (ED047485)

Garwood, S. G. *Educating young handicapped children: A developmental approach*. Germantown, Md.: Aspen Systems Corporation, 1979.

Gearhart, B. R., and Willenberg, E. P. *Application of pupil assessment information*. (3rd. ed.). Denver, Colo.: Love Publishing, 1979.

Glavin, J. P. (Ed.). *Ferment in special education*. New York: MSS Information Corporation, 1974.

Goldberg, M. L., and others. *The effects of ability grouping*. New York: Teachers College Press, Columbia University, 1966.

Gordon, I. J., and Breivogel, W. F. (Eds.). *Building effective home/school relationships*. Boston: Allyn and Bacon, 1978.

Gorelick, M. C., and Brown, P. A. (Comps.). *Preschools willing to integrate children with handicaps*. Directory 1974. Northridge, Calif.: California State University/Northridge, Preschool Lab., 1974.

Graubard, P., and Rosenberg, H. *Classrooms that work: Prescriptions for change*. New York: E. P. Dutton, 1974.

Green, A. C. (Ed.), *Educational facilities with new media*. Final report. Published by National Education Association, Washington, D.C., 1966.

Green, P. (Ed.). *One of ten: School planning for the handicapped*. New York: Educational Facilities Labs, 1974.

Gregg, E., and Boston Children's Medical Center Staff. *What to do when there's nothing to do*. New York: Dell, 1970.

Griffiths, C. (Ed.). *Proceedings of the international conference on auditory techniques*. Springfield, Ill.: Charles C. Thomas, 1974.

Griswold, V. T., and Starke, T. *Multi-cultural art projects*. Denver, Colo.: Love Publishing, 1980.

Grzynkowicz, W. *Basic education for children with learning disabilities*. Springfield, Ill.: Charles C. Thomas, 1979.

Grzynkowicz, W., and others. *Meeting the needs of learning disabled children in the regular class*. Springfield, Ill.: Charles C. Thomas, 1974.

Guidelines for program planning for emotionally disturbed children. Richmond: State Department of Education, 1966.

Guralnick, M. J. (Ed.). *Early intervention and the integration of handicapped and non-handicapped children*. Baltimore: University Park Press, 1978.

Hackett, L. *Movement exploration and games for the mentally retarded*. Palo Alto, Calif.: Peek Publications, 1970.

Hammill, D. D., and Wilderholt, J. L. *The resource room: rationale and implementation*. Philadelphia: Journal of Special Education Press, 1972.

Handbook for learning centers. 1972. (ERIC NO. ED 098779.)

Handicapped children in the regular classroom. Ventura, Calif.: Fountain Valley School District, 1972. (ED073592).

Handicapped children in the regular classroom: Project 1232, 1972-1973. (end of budget period report) Title III, ESEA. Ventura, Calif.: Fountain Valley School District, 1973. (ERIC NO. ED097784.) see also ED096805 and ED096806)

Hanninen, K. A. *Teaching the visually handicapped*. Columbus, Oh.: Charles E. Merrill, 1975.

Harford-Cecil supplementary education: A handbook of activities. Harford-Cecil Supplementary Education Center, 1969. (ED036942).

Haring, N. G. *Special education for the severely handicapped: The state of the art in 1975*. Reston, Va.: Council for Exceptional Children, 1976a.

Haring, N. G., and Schiefelbusch, R. L. (Eds.). *Teaching special children*. New York: McGraw-Hill, 1976b.

Harshman, H. W. (Ed.). *Educating the emotionally disturbed: A book of readings*. New York: Thomas Y. Crowell, 1960. (ED031020.)

Hart, V. *Beginning with the handicapped*. Springfield, Ill.: Charles C. Thomas, 1974.

Havill, S. J., and Mitchell, D. R. *Classes in New Zealand special education*. Auckland 1, New Zealand: Hodder and Stoughton Limited, 1972 (52 Cook Street).

Hawkins, R. P. *The public classroom as a behavioral laboratory*. Kalamazoo: Western Michigan University, 1967.

Hayes, G. M., and Griffing, B. L. *A guide to the education of the deaf in the public schools of California*. Sacramento: California State Department of Education, Bureau for Physically Exceptional Children, 1967. (ED022292.)

Hayes, R. P., and Stevenson, M. G. *Teaching the emotionally disturbed/learning disabled child: A practical guide. Volume 1: Developing behavior, instruction and affective programs; Volume 2: Assessment for instruction; Volume 3: Teacher made ready-to-use learning activities and games; Volume 4: Public law 94-142: A practical guide for teachers, administrators, and parents*. Washington, D.C.: Acropolis Books, 1979.

Hebeler, J. R., and Reynolds, M. C. *Guidelines for personnel in the education of exceptional children*. Reston, Va.: Council for Exceptional Children, 1976.

Helping the handicapped through parent/professional partnerships. Niles, Ill.: Developmental Learning Materials, 1979

Hennon, M. L. *Identifying handicapped children for child development programs: A recruitment and selection manual*. Atlanta: Ga.: Humanics, 1974.

Heward, W., Dardig, J., and Rossett, A. *Working with parents of handicapped children*. Columbus, Oh.: Charles E. Merrill, 1979.

Hirst, C. C., and Michaels, E. *Developmental activities for children in special education*. Springfield, Ill.: Charles C. Thomas, 1972.

Honig, A. S. *Parent involvement in early childhood education* (rev. ed.). Washington, D. C.: NAEYC, 1979.

Hopkins, C. D., and Antes, R. L. *Classroom testing: Administration, scoring, and score interpretation*. Itasca, Ill.: Peacock, 1979.

Irwin, D. M. and Bushnell, M. M. *Observational strategies for child study*. New York: Holt, Rinehart and Winston, 1980.

Jenkins, J. R., and Mayhall, W. F. *Dimensions and attitudes of resource teacher systems serving handicapped learners*. Las Cruces: New Mexico State University, Southwest Regional Resource Center, 1973.

Johnson, N., Jens, K. G., Anderson, J. D. Cognition and affect in infancy: Implication for the handicapped. *New Directions for Exceptional Children: Young Exceptional Children*, 1980, *3*, pp 21-36.

Johnson, S. B., and Radius, M. *Teacher in-service*. Castro Valley, Calif.: Castro Valley Unified School District, 1974. (ERIC NO. ED 109856.)

Jones, M. V. *Special education programs within the United States*. Springfield, Ill. Charles C. Thomas, 1968.

Jones, R. L. (Ed.). *Mainstreaming and the minority child*. Reston, Va.: Council for Exceptional Children, 1976.

Jordan, J. B. *Teacher please don't close the door—The exceptional child in the mainstream*. Reston, Va.: Council for Exceptional Children, 1976.

Jordan, J. B. *Exceptional child education at the bicentennial: A parade of progress*. Reston, Va.: Council for Exceptional Children, 1976-1977.

Jordan, J. B., Hayden, A. H., and Wood, M. (Eds.). *Early childhood education for exceptional children: A handbook of ideas and exemplary practices*. Reston, Va.: Council for Exceptional Children, 1972.

Jordan, J. B., and Robbins, L. S. (Eds.). *Let's try doing something else kind of thing—Behavioral principles and the exceptional child*. Reston, Va.: Council for Exceptional Children, 1972.

Kaplan, P., Kohfeldt, T., and Sturla, K. *It's positively fun: Techniques for managing learning environments*. Denver, Colo.: Love Publishing, 1974.

Kaplan, S. *Providing programs for the gifted and talented—A handbook*. Reston, Va.: Council for Exceptional Children, 1975.

Karnes, M. B. *Early childhood*. Reston, Va.: Council for Exceptional Children, 1978.

Karnes, M. B. *Creative art for learning*. Reston, Va.: Council for Exceptional Children, 1979.

Kelly, L. J. *A dictionary of exceptional children*. New York: MSS Educational Publishing Company, 1972.

Kirk, S. A., and Lord, F. E. (Eds.). *Exceptional children: Educational resources and perspectives*. Boston: Houghton Mifflin, 1974.

Kliment, S. A. *Into the mainstream: A syllabus for a barrier-free environment*. Washington, D.C.: U. S. Government Printing Office, 1976.

Kline, T. *Children move to learn*. Tucson, Ariz.: Communication Skill Builders, 1977.

Koocher, G. P. (Ed.). *Children's rights and the mental health professions*. New York: Wiley, 1976.

Korn, M. (Comp.). *Bibliography: Precision teaching*. Toronto, Canada: National Institute on Mental Retardation, 1974. (ERIC NO. ED096807.)

Kozloff, M. A. *Reaching the autistic child: A parent training program*. Champaign, Ill.: Research Press, 1973.

Kratoville, B. L. *And miles to go*. San Rafael, Calif.: Academic Therapy Publications, 1971. (a case study)

Krone, A. *Art instruction for handicapped children*. Denver, Colo.: Love Publishing, 1978.

Kroth, R. L. *Communicating with parents of exceptional children—Improving parent-teacher relationships*. Denver, Colo.: Love Publishing, 1977.

Kroth, R. L., and Scholl, G. T. *Getting schools involved with parents*. Reston, Va.: Council for Exceptional Children, 1978.

Kroth, R. L., and Simpson, R. L. *Parent conferences as a teaching strategy*. Denver, Colo.: Love Publishing, 1977.

Krumboltz, J., and Krumboltz, H. *Changing children's behavior*. Englewood Cliffs, N.J.: Prentice-Hall, 1972.

Larrivee, B. *Behavior management strategies for classroom application: An in-service training manual for use with classroom teachers*. Philadelphia: Research for Better Schools, 1979.

Larsen, S. C., and Poplin, M. S. *Methods for educating the handicapped: An individualized education program aproach*. Boston: Allyn and Bacon, 1980.

Laslett, R. *Educating maladjusted children*. Denver, Colo.: Love Publishing, 1978.

Leitch, L. J. *Learning disabilities: Review of the literature and selected annotated bibliography. Reports in Education No. 3*. Montreal (Quebec), Canada: Department of Educational Administration and Department of Educational Psychology and Sociology, McGill University, 1973.

Lerner, J. W., Dawson, D. K., and Horvath, L. T. *Cases in learning and behavior problems: A guide to individualized education programs*. Boston: Houghton Mifflin, 1979.

Lillie, D. L. *Teaching parents to teach: Education for the handicapped*. New York: Walker & Company, 1976.

Linde, T. F., and Kopp, T. *Training retarded babies and preschoolers*. Springfield, Ill.: Charles C. Thomas, 1974.

Lindsay, Z. *Art and the handicapped child*. New York: Van Nostrand Reinhold, 1972.

Long, K. *Johnny's such a bright boy, what a shame he's retarded*. Boston: Houghton Mifflin, 1977.

Long, N. J., Morse, W. C., and Newman, R. G. *Conflict in the classroom: The education of emotionally disturbed children*. (4th. ed.). Belmont, Calif.: Wadsworth, 1980.

Love, H. D. *Educating exceptional children in a changing society*. Springfield, Ill.: Charles C. Thomas, 1974.

Love, H. D., Mainord, J. C., and Naylor, D. *Language development of exceptional children*. Springfield, Ill.: Charles C. Thomas, 1977.

Lovitt, T. C. *Managing inappropriate behaviors in the classroom*. Reston, Va.: Council for Exceptional Children, 1978.

Lowell, E. L. *Play is by ear*. Los Angeles: John Tracy Clinic, 1963.

Lukeoff, I. F., and Whiteman, M. *The social sources of adjustment to blindness*. Research Series No. 21. New York: American Foundation for the Blind, Inc., 1969.

Lustman, S. L. (Ed.), *Mental health of children: Services, research, and manpower*. New York: Harper & Row, 1973.

Mager, R. *Preparing instructional objectives*. Palo Alto, Calif.: Fearon, 1962.

Magrab, P. R., and Elder, J. O. *Planning for services to handicapped persons: Community, education, health*. Baltimore: Paul H. Brooks, 1979.

Mann, L., Goodman, L., and Wiederholt, J. L. *Teaching the learning disabled adolescent*. Boston: Houghton Mifflin, 1977.

Mann, P. H., and Suiter, P. *Handbook in diagostic teaching: A learning disabilities approach*. Boston: Allyn and Bacon, 1974.

A manual for the classroom teacher of a blind student. Chicago: Vision Hearing Services, 1969. (Catholic Charities, 126 North Des Plaines Street)

Marcy, C., and others. *Implementing an individualized data-based model of education to keep a nine-year-old boy in his regular, public school classroom*. Briston, Vt.: Addison Supervisory Union, 1973.

Markel, G., and Greenbaum, J. L. *Parents are to be seen and heard: Assertiveness in educational planning for handicapped children*. San Luis Obispo, Calif.: Impact Publishers, 1979.

Martin, G. J., and Hoben, M. (Eds.). *Supporting visually impaired students in the mainstream: The state of the art*. Reston, Va.: Council for Exceptional Children, 1977.

Martin, H. P. (Ed.). *The abused child: A multidisciplinary approach to developmental issues and treatment*. Cambridge, Mass.: Ballinger, 1976.

Mather, J. *Learning can be child's play: How parents can help slower-than-average preschool children learn and develop through play experiences*. Nashville: Abingdon Press, 1976.

Mazyck, A. *Suggested equipment and supplies for infant-toddler centers*. Greensboro: North Carolina University, 1969.

McCollum, A. T. *Coping with prolonged health impairment in your child*. Boston: Little, Brown and Co., 1975.

McElderry, T., and Escobedo, L. *Tools for learning—Activities for young children with special needs*. Denver: Love Publishing, 1980.

McLean, J., and Yoder, D. E. (Eds.). *Language intervention with the retarded*. Baltimore: University Park Press, 1972.

McMurrain, T. T. (Ed.). *Orientation to preschool assessment*. Atlanta, Ga.: Humanics, 1979.

Meierhenry, W. C. *Planning for the evaluation of special educational programs: A resource guide*. Lincoln: Nebraska University, 1969. (ED040555).

Meisels, S. J. *Developmental screening in early childhood: A guide*. Washington, D. C.: National Association for the Education of Young Children, 1978.

Merkin, P., and Deno, D. (Eds.). *Data based program modification*. Reston, Va.. Council for Exceptional Children, 1977.

Metz, A. S. *Statistics on education of the handicapped in local public schools, spring 1970*. Washington, D.C.: National Center for Educational Statistics 1970, (DHEW/OE).

Metz, A. S., and Cramer, H. L. *Professional staff for handicapped in local public schools, spring 1970*. Washington, D.C.: National Center for Educational Statistics 1974, (DHEW/OE).

Meyen, E. L., Vergason, G. A., and Whelan, R. J. *Alternatives for teaching exceptional children*. Denver, Colo.: Love Publishing, 1977.

A model program of comprehensive educational services for students with learning problems. Union, N.J.: Union Township Board of Education, 1973.

Moffett, J., and Wagner, B. J. *Student-centered language arts and reading. K-13: A handbook for teachers* (2nd. ed.). Boston: Houghton Mifflin, 1976.

Moor, P. M. *A blind child, too, can go to nursery school.* New York: American Foundation for the Blind, 1962.

Moran, M. R. *Assessment of the exceptional learner in the regular classroom.* Denver, Colo.: Love Publishing, 1979.

Mullins, J. B. *A teacher's guide to management of physically handicapped students.* Springfield, Ill.: Charles C. Thomas, 1979.

Murphy, P. *A special way for the special child in the regular classroom.* San Raphael, Calif.: Academic Therapy Publications, 1971.

National Association of State Directors of Special Education. *Maximizing staff potential: An individualized approach to personnel development.* Washington, D. C.: National Association of State Directors of Special Education, 1978.

Neisworth, J. T., and Smith, R. M. *Modifying retarded behavior.* Boston: Houghton Mifflin, 1973.

Neisworth, J. T., Willoughby-Herb, S., Bagnato, S., Cartwright, C., and Laub, K. *Individualized education for preschool exceptional children.* Germantown, Md.: Aspen Systems Corporation, 1980.

Nelson, M. *Crisis intervention: Behavior management of mildly handicapped children in a "mainstream" setting.* Lexington: University of Kentucky, 1981.

Noland, R. L. *Counseling parents of the mentally retarded: A sourcebook.* Springfield, Ill.: Charles C. Thomas, 1978.

The Ohio State University Research Foundation. *Toilet training: Help for the delayed learner.* New York: McGraw-Hill, 1977.

Open the door in '74: Chapter 766. Boston, Mass.: Massachusetts Teacher Association, 1974.

O'Quinn, Jr., G., *Developmental gymnastics: Building physical skills for children.* Austin, Tex.: University of Texas, 1979.

Orem, R. C. (Ed.). *Montessori and the special child.* New York: Paragon, 1970.

Otto, W., and Smith, R. J. *Corrective and remedial teaching.* Boston: Houghton Mifflin, 1973.

Owsley, P. J. *Readings in the education of hearing impaired children.* Mt. Airy, Pennsylvania School for the Deaf, 1965.

Paolucci, P. W., Knight, M. F., and McKenzie, H. S. *The 1969-1970 yearly report of the consulting teacher program: South Burlington School district.* Burlington, Vt.: Special Education Program, College of Education, University of Vermont, 1971.

The parent-professional partnership. *Exceptional Children*, May 1975, *41* (8) (available in college libraries or from the Council for Exceptional Children, 1920 Association Dr., Reston, Va. 22091.)

Parker, C. A., (Ed.). *Psychological consultation: Helping teachers meet special needs.* Reston, Va.: Council for Exceptional Children, 1975.

Patterson, G. R. *Living with children: New methods for parents and teachers.* Champaign, Ill.: Research Press, 1976.

Peck, J. *Young children's behavior: Implementing your goals.* Atlanta: Humanics, 1978.

Pelone, A. J. *Helping the visually handicapped child in a regular class.* New York: Teachers College Press, Columbia University, 1957.

People you'd like to know. Chicago: Encyclopaedia Britannica Educational Corporation, 1979.

Peter, L. J. *Prescriptive teaching*. New York: McGraw-Hill, 1965.

Piazzo, R., and Rothman, R. *Preschool education for the handicapped*. Guilford, Conn.: Special Learning Corporation, 1979.

Precision teaching: Teaching exceptional children (vol. 3). Reston, Va.: Council for Exceptional Children, 1971.

Progress by partners in step, special issue on IEP: Teaching exceptional children (vol. 10). Reston, Va.: Council for Exceptional Children, 1978.

Propp, G. E., (Ed.). *Media, methods, and materials for special educators*. Lansing: Michigan State Department of Education, Division of Special Education, 1972. (ED081161.)

Pupil and teacher materials for exceptional children. Curriculum Research Report. New York: New York City Board of Education, 1963.

Puzzled about 766? Evaluation and planning. Boston: Massachusetts Teacher Association, 1974.

Puzzled about 766? Mainstreaming. Boston: Massachusetts Teacher Association, 1974.

Quigley, S. P., and Thomure, F. E. *Some effects of hearing impairment upon school performance*. Urbana: Institute for Research on Exceptional Children, Illinois University, 1969.

Reichard, C. L., and Blackburn, D. B. *Music based instruction for the exceptional child*. Denver, Colo.: Love Publishing, 1973.

Reynolds, M. C. *Futures of education for exceptional students: Emerging structures*. Reston, Va.: Council for Exceptional Children, 1978.

Reynolds, M. C., and Davis, M. D. (Eds.). *Exceptional children in regular classrooms*. Minneapolis, Minn.: Leadership Training Institute/Special Education, 1971.

Richman, V. *Mental health services program, 1967 report*. ESEA (Elementary and Secondary Education Act) Title I Project. Pittsburgh, Pa.: Pittsburgh Public Schools, 1967. (ED028554)

Roger, R. *Preschool programming of children with disabilities*. Springfield, Ill.: Charles C. Thomas, 1974.

Ross, A. O. *The exceptional child in the family—Helping parents of exceptional children*. New York: Grune & Stratton, 1964.

Rubin, E. J., and others. *Emotionally handicapped children and the elementary school*. Detroit: Wayne State University, 1968.

Rumanoff, L. A. *Curriculum model for individuals with severe learning and behavior disorders*. Baltimore: University Park Press, 1979.

Safford, P. L., and Arbitman, D. C. *Developmental intervention with young physically handicapped children*. Springfield, Ill.: Charles C. Thomas, 1975.

Salvia, J., and Ysseldyke J. *Assessment in special and remedial education*. Boston: Houghton Mifflin, 1978.

Schattner, R. *Early childhood curriculum for multiply handicapped children*. New York: Crowell, 1971.

Schenck, S. J. An analysis of IEP's for learning disabled youngsters. *Journal of Learning Disabilities*, 1981, *14*, (4): 221-223.

Schiefelbusch, R. *Language perspectives—Acquisition, retardation, and intervention*. Baltimore: University Park Press, 1974.

Schifani, J. *Implementing learning in the least restrictive environment*. Baltimore: University Park Press, 1980.

Scholl, G. T. *The principal works with the visually impaired*. Washington, D.C.: Council for Exceptional Children, 1968. (ED025058).

Schopler, E. *Teaching strategies for parents and professionals*. Baltimore: University Park Press, 1979.

Schwartz, L. and Oseroff, A. *Clinical teacher competencies for special education: An individualized performance-based teacher-education curriculum*. Tallahassee, Fla.: Florida State University, 1972.

Schwartz, L., and Oseroff, A. *The clinical teacher for special education*. Final report (vol. 1, 2). Tallahassee, Fla.: Florida State University, 1975.

Seaver, J. W., Cartwright, C. A., and Ward, C. B., and Heasley, C. A. *Careers with young children: Making your decision*. Washington, D.C.: National Association for the Education of Young Children, 1979.

Segal, S. S. *No child is ineducable: Special education—provision and trends*. Elmsord, N.Y.: Pergamon, 1974.

Sehler, A. *Institute for the study of Michigan experimental programs for the educationally handicapped institute report*. Lansing: Michigan State Department of Education, 1972.

Seligman, M. *Strategies for helping parents of exceptional children: A guide for teachers*. Riverside, N.J.: Free Press, 1979.

Semb, G. (Ed.), and others. *Behavior analysis and education—1972*. Lawrence, Kan.: University of Kansas, 1972.

Siegel, E. *Special education in the regular classroom*. New York: John Day, 1969.

Smith, J. *Secondary school educable mentally handicapped*. (Program guidelines.) Lincoln, Neb.: Lincoln Public Schools, 1965.

Smith, S. L. *No easy answers—Teaching the learning disabled child*. Cambridge, Mass.: Winthrop, 1979.

Special education curriculum guides. Memphis, Tenn.: Shelby County Schools, 1968.

Sponseller, D. (Ed.). *Play as a learning medium*. Washington, D.C.: National Association for the Education of Young Children, 1974.

Stabenow, T., and Cratty, B. L. *Speech and language problems in children: A guide for parents and teachers*. Denver, Colo.: Love Publishing, 1978.

Stanley, J. C. (Ed.). *Preschool programs for the disadvantaged: Five experimental approaches to early childhood education*. Baltimore: John Hopkins University Press, 1972.

Stanton, J. E., and Cassidy, V. M. *A study of differences between children in residential school classes and special and regular classes in Ohio*. Columbus, Oh.: College of Education, Ohio State University, 1961.

Stearns, J., and Vasa, S. F. *A primer of diagnostic-prescriptive teaching and programming*. Laramie: Center for Research, Service and Publication, College of Education, University of Wyoming, 1973.

Stephens, T. M. *Instructional games: DTIMS reading and math*. Columbus: The Ohio State University Press, 1973.

Stephens, T. M. *Social skills in the classroom*. Columbus, Oh.: Cedars Press, 1978.

Stephens, T. M. *Teaching skills to children with learning and behavior disorders*. Columbus, Oh.: Charles E. Merrill, 1977.

Stephens, T. M. Teachers as managers. *The Directive Teacher*, 1980, *2*, (5): 4, 25.

Stone, J. G. *A guide to discipline*. Washington, D.C.: National Association for the Education of Young Children, 1978.

Stoppleworth, L. J. (Ed.). *Everything is fine now that Leonard isn't here*. New York: MSS Information Corporation, 1973.

Stott, D. H. *The hard-to-teach child: A diagnostic—remedial approach*. Baltimore: University Park Press, 1977.

Stovall, B. J., and Tongue, C. *Handbook for resource teachers of gifted children*. Raleigh: North Carolina State Department of Public Instruction, Division of Exceptional Children, 1971. (ERIC NO. ED055399.)

Suarez, T. M., and Vandivier, P. *Planning for evaluation—A resource book for programs for preschool handicapped children: Documentation*. Chapel Hill, N.C.: Technical Assistance Development System, 1978.

Suliver, M. E. *Assisting the hearing impaired in the classroom*. Madison: Wisconsin State Department of Public Instruction, Bureau for Handicapped Children, 1968.

Sullivan, M. G. *Understanding children who are partially seeing: A classroom teaching guide*. Seattle: Wash. Special Child Publications, Bernie Straub, 1974.

Swick, K. T., and Duff, E. *Building a successful parent/teacher partnership*. Atlanta, Ga.: Humanics, 1980.

Teaching children with learning disabilities. Doylestown, Pa.: Bucks County Public Schools, 1964.

Thiagarajan, S. (Ed.). *Instructional development for training teachers of exceptional children: A source book*. Reston, Va.: Council for Exceptional Children, 1974.

Thomas, M. A. (Ed.). *Very special children series: Developing skills in severely and profoundly handicapped children*. Reston, Va.: Council for Exceptional Children, 1977.

Thomas, M. S. (Ed.). *Hey, don't forget about me! Education's investment in the severely, profoundly, and multiply handicapped*. Reston, Va.: Council for Exceptional Children, 1976.

Thorum, A. R., *Instructional materials for the handicapped: Birth through early childhood*. Salt Lake City: Olympus Publishing, 1976.

Treblas, P. V., McCormick, S. H., and Cooper, J. O. Problems in mainstreaming at the grassroots. *The Directive Teacher*, in press, 1981.

Trevana, T. H. *The role of the resource teacher in mobility instruction*. Hayward, Calif. 1971.

Turnbull, A. P. Parent-professional interactions. in M. E. Snell (Ed.), *Systematic instruction for the moderately and severely handicapped*. Columbus, Oh.: Charles E. Merrill, 1978.

Turnbull, A. P., and Schulz, J. B. *Mainstreaming handicapped students: A guide to classroom teachers*. Boston: Allyn and Bacon, 1978.

Turnbull, A. P., Strickland, B. B., and Brantley, J. C. *Developing and implementing individualized education programs*. Columbus, Oh.: Charles E. Merrill, 1978.

Turnbull, H. R., and Turnbull, A. P. *Free appropriate public education: Law and implementation*. Denver, Color.: Love Publishing, 1979.

Valett, R. E. *Effective teaching: A guide to diagnostic-prescriptive task analysis*. Belmont, Calif.: Fearon, 1970.

Van Etten, C. *Directory of selected instructional materials*. Reston, Va.: Council for Exceptional Children, 1974.

Vaughn, G. R. *Education of deaf and hard of hearing adults in established facilities for the normally hearing*. Final report. Pocatello: Idaho State University, 1967.

Wabash Center for the Mentally Retarded. *Guide for early developmental training*. Boston: Allyn and Bacon, 1977.

Walden, S. B., and others. *Special services personnel: A source of help for the teacher*. Iowa City: Special Education Curriculum Development Center, Iowa University, 1971. (ERIC NO. ED05455.)

Walker, H. M. *The acting-out child: Dealing with classroom disruption*. Boston: Allyn and Bacon, 1979.

Walker 3rd. S. *Help for the hyperactive child*. Boston: Houghton Mifflin, 1978.

Wallace, G., and Larsen, S. C. *Educational assessment of learning problems: Testing for teaching*. Boston: Allyn and Bacon, 1978.

Watson, Jr. L. S. *Child behavior modification: A manual for teachers, nurses, and parents*. Elmsford, N.Y.: British Book Center, 1973.

Webster, E. J. *Professional approaches with parents of handicapped children*. Springfield, Ill.: Charles C. Thomas, 1976.

Wedeneyer, A., and Cejyka, T. *Learning games for exceptional children*. Denver, Colo.: Love Publishing, 1971.

Wedeneyer, A., and Cejyka, T. *Creative ideas for teaching exceptional children*. Denver, Colo.: Love Publishing, 1975.

Wehman, P. *Recreation programming for developmentally disabled persons*. Baltimore: University Park Press, 1978.

Wehman, P. *Vocational curriculum for developmentally disabled persons*. Baltimore: University Park Press, 1979.

Weinberg, R. A., and Wood, F. H. (Eds.). *Observation of pupils and teachers in mainstream and special education settings: Alternative strategies*. Reston, Va.: Council for Exceptional Children, 1975.

Weintraub, F. J., Abeson, A. R., Ballard, J., and Lavor, M. L. (Eds.). *Public policy and the education of exceptional children*. Reston, Va.: Council for Exceptional Children, 1976.

Welch, D. C. *Prescriptive materials laboratory development, EPDA special education final report*. Olathe, Kans.: Olathe Public Schools, 1972.

Westman, J. C. *Child advocacy*. Riverside, N.J.: Free Press, 1979.

What teachers should know about children with heart disease. New York: American Heart Association, Inc., 1964.

White, A. H. *National Center on Educational Media and Materials for the Handicapped report on needs in special education*. Columbus, Oh.: Information Services, The Ohio State University, n.d. (ERIC NO. ED 010523.)

Wiederholt, J. L., and Hammill, D. D. *The resource teacher: A guide to effective practices*. Boston: Allyn and Bacon, 1978.

Wiegerink, R., Pelosi, J. Educational Planning in planning for services to handicapped persons: Community, education, health. Baltimore: Paul H. Brooks, 1979.

Wilson, G. B. *Parents and teachers: Humanistic educational technique to facilitate communication between parent and staff of child development centers*. Atlanta, Ga.: Humanics, 1974.

APPENDIX D

Books for Children to Develop Understanding

PART I: PRESCHOOL AND PRIMARY GRADES

Aimar, C. *Waymond the whale*. Illustrated by M. L. Heath. Englewood Cliffs, N.J.: Prentice-Hall, 1975.

Arthur, C. *My sister's silent world*. Pictures by N. T. Chicago: Children's Press, 1979.

Blue, R. *Me and Einstein: Break through the reading barrier*. Illustrated by P. Luks. New York: Human Science Press, 1979.

Charlip, R. *Handtalk*. New York: Four Winds Press, 1974.

Christopher, M. F. *Glue fingers*. Illustrated by J. Venable. Boston: Little, Brown and Co., 1975.

Clifton, L. *My friend Jacob*. Illustrated by T. DiGrazia. New York: E. P. Dutton, 1980.

Fassler, J. *One little girl*. Illustrated by M. J. Smith. New York: Human Science Press, 1969.

Fassler, J. *Boy with a problem*. Illustrated by S. Kranz. New York: Human Science Press, 1971.

Fassler, J. *Howie helps himself*. Illustrated by J. Lasker. Chicago: A. Whitman, 1975.

Goldfeder, C., and Goldfeder, J. *The girl who wouldn't talk*. Illustrated by C. Goldfeder. Silver Spring, Md.: National Association of the Deaf, 1974.

Heide, F. *Sound of sunshine, sound of rain*. New York: Parents' Magazine Press, 1970.

Hodges, E. J. *Free as a frog*. Illustrated by P. Giovanopoulos. Reading, Mass.: Addison-Wesley, 1969.

Hunter, E. F. *Child of the silent night*. New York: Dell, 1963.

Krasilovsky, P. *The shy little girl*. Illustrated by T. S. Hyman. Boston: Houghton Mifflin, 1972.

Kraus, R. *Leo the late bloomer*. Illustrated by J. Aruego. New York: E. P. Dutton, 1973.

Lee, M. *The skating rink*. New York: Dell, 1970.

Levine, E. S. *Lisa and her soundless world*. Illustrated by G. Kamen. New York: Human Sciences Press, 1974.

Litchfield, A. B. *A button in her ear*. Pictures by E. Mill. Chicago: A. Whitman, 1976.

Litchfield, A. B. *A cane in her hand*. Illustrations by E. Mill. Chicago: Whitman, 1977.

Mack, N. *Tracy*. Photographs by H. Kluetmeier. Milwaukee: Raintree, 1976.

Madsen, J., and Bockoras, D. *Please don't tease me. . . .* Illustrated by K. T. Brinko. Valley Forge, Pa.: Judson Press, 1980.

Peter, D. *Claire and Emma*. Photographs by J. Finlay. New York: John Day, 1977.

Peterson, J. W. *I have a sister, my sister is deaf*. Illustrated by D. Ray. New York: Harper Row, 1977.

Peterson, P. *Sally can't see*. New York: John Dav, 1974.

Rogers, F. *Josephine, the short-neck giraffe*. Northbrook, Ill.: Hubbard, 1979b.
Rogers, F. *A piece of red paper*. Northbrook, Ill.: Hubbard, 1979c.
Rogers, F. *Speedy delivery*. Northbrook, Ill.: Hubbard, 1979d.
Rogers, F. *Who am I?* Northbrook, Ill.: Hubbard, 1979.
Ronnei, E. C., and Porter, J. *Tim and his hearing aid* (rev. ed.). Alexander Graham Bell Association, 1965.

Sesame Street. *Sign language fun*. New York: Random House, 1980.
Showers, P. *How you talk*. New York: Crowell, 1966.
Simon, N. *I was so mad!* Pictures by D. Leder. Chicago: A. Whitman, 1974.
Simon, N. *Why am I so different?* Illustrations by D. Leder. Edison, N.J.: Gryphon House, 1979.
Sobol, H. L. *My brother Steven is retarded*. Photographs by P. Ayre. New York: Macmillan, 1977.
Stein, S. B. *About handicaps: An open family book for parents and children together*. Photographs by D. Frank. New York: Walker & Co., 1974.

Wolf, B. *Don't feel sorry for Paul*. Philadelphia: Lippincott, 1974.
Wosmek, F. *A bowl of sun*. Chicago: Children's Press, 1976.

Yashima, T. *Crow boy*. New York: Viking Press, 1955.

PART II: MIDDLE GRADES

Albert, L. *But I'm ready to go*. New York: Bradbury Press, 1976.

Baker, M. J. *The sand bird*. Illustrated by F. Garet. Nashville, Tenn.: Nelson, 1973.
Baldwin, A. N. *A little time*. New York: Viking Press, 1978.
Beckwith, L. *The spuddy*. New York: Delacorte Press, 1974.
Brancato, R. *Winning*. New York: Alfred A. Knopf, 1977.
Branfield, J. *Why Me?* New York: Harper Row, 1973.
Bunting, E. *One more flight*. Illustrated by D. de Groat. New York: Warne, 1976.
Byars, B. *The summer of the swans*. Avon, 1974.
Carpelan, B. *Bow island*. Delacorte Press, 1971. (Translated from the Swedish by S. La Farge.)
Carper, L. D. *A cry in the wind*. Independence, Mo.: Herald, 1973.
Christopher, M. *Stranded*. Illustrated by G. Owens. Boston: Little, Brown and Co. 1974.
Cleaver, V. and Cleaver, B. *Me too*. New American Library, 1975.
Corcoran, B. *A dance to still music*. New York: Atheneum, 1974.
Corcoran, B. *Ax-time/sword-time*. New York: Atheneum, 1976.
Courlander, H. *The son of the leopard*. Illustrated by R. Negri. New York: Crown, 1974.
Cunningham, J. *Burnish me bright*. Drawings by D. Freeman. New York: Pantheon, 1970.

de Angeli, M. *Door in the wall: Story of medieval London*. New York: Doubleday, 1949.

First, J. *Flat on my face*. New York: Avon, 1975.
Forbes, E. *Johnny Tremain*. Illustrated by L. Ward. Boston: Houghton Mifflin, 1943.

Gill, D. L. *Tom Sullivan's adventures in darkness*. New York: McKay, 1976.
Gold, P. *Please don't say hello*. Photographs by C. Baker. New York: Human Sciences Press, 1975.

Heide, F. P. *Secret dreamer, secret dreams*. New York: Lippincott, 1978.
Hickok, L. A. *The story of Helen Keller*. Scholastic Book Services, 1958.

Killilea, M. *Wren*. New York: Dell, 1968.

Little, J. *Mine for keeps*. Little, Brown and Co., 1962.
Little, J. *Take wing*. Boston: Little, Brown and Co., 1968.
Little, J. *From Anna*. Harper & Row, 1972.
Little, J. *Listen for the singing*. New York: E. P. Dutton, 1977.
Leggett, L., and Andrews, L. *The rose-colored glasses*. Illustrated by L. Hartman. New York: Human Sciences Press, 1979.

MacIntyre, E. *The purple mouse*. Nashville, Tenn.: Nelson, 1975.

Parker, R. *He is your brother*. Brockhampton Press, 1974. (Available from Musson Book Compny, 30 Lesmill Road, Don Mills, Ontario, Canada, M3B 2T6.)

Reynolds, P. *A different kind of sister*. Lothrop, Lee and Shepard, 1968.
Rich, L. D. *Three of a kind*. Illustrated by W. M. Hutchinson. New York: Franklin Watts, 1970.
Rinkoff, B. *The watchers*. New York: Alfred A. Knopf, 1972.
Rook, D. *Run wild, run free*. Scholastic Book Services, 1967. (Original title: *The white colt.)*
Rubin, T. I. *Jordi/Lisa and David*. Ballantine, 1962. (two stories in one volume)

Savitz, H. M. *Fly, wheels, fly*. John Day, 1970.
Shyer, M. F. *Welcome home, Jellybean*. New York: Scribner's, 1978.
Smith, D. B. *Kelly's creek*. Illustrated by A. Tiegreen. New York: Crowell, 1975.
Southall, I. *Let the balloon go*. St. Martin's Press, 1968.

Tate, J. *Ben and Annie*. Illustrated by J. G. Brown. Garden City, N.Y.: Doubleday, 1974.
Taylor, T. *Teetoncey*. Illustrated by R. Cuffari. Garden City, N.Y.: Doubleday, 1974.
Terris, S. *The drowning boy*. New York: Doubleday, 1972.

White, E. B. *The trumpet of the swan*. Harper & Row, 1970.
Wilkinson, B. *Ludell*. New York: Harper & Row, 1975.
Wolf, B. *Connie's new eyes*. Philadelphia: Lippincott, 1976.
Wrightson, P. *A racecourse for Andy*. Harcourt, Brace, and World, 1968.

Yolen, J. *The transfigured heart*. Illustrated by D. Diamond. New York: Crowell, 1975.

PART III: YOUNG ADULTS

Allan, M. E. *Ship of danger*. New York: Abelard-Schuman, 1974.

Blume, J. *Deenie*. Scarsdale, N. Y.: Bradbury, 1973.
Brown, F. G. *You're somebody special on a horse*. Chicago: A. Whitman, 1977.

Brown, R. *The white sparrow*. New York: Seabury, 1975.
Butler, B. *Gift of gold*. New York: Dodd, 1973.

Cavanna, B. *Joyride*. New York: Morrow, 1974.
Cleaver, V., and Cleaver, B. *Me too*. Philadelphia: Lippincott, 1973.
Corcoran, B. *A dance to still music*. Illustrated by C. Robinson. New York: Atheneum, 1974.

Davies, P. *Fly away Paul*. New York: Crown, 1974.

Griffiths, H. *The mysterious appearance of Agnes*. Illustrated by V. Ambrus. New York: Holiday House, 1975.

Harnishfeger, L. *Prisoner of the mound builders*. Illustrated by G. Overlie. Minneapolis, Minn.: Lerner, 1973.
Hunter, M. *The stronghold*. New York: Harper & Row, 1974.

Lawrence, M. *The touchmark*. Illustrated by D. Hollinger. New York: Harcourt Brace Jovanovich, 1975.
Levine, E. S. *Lisa and her soundless world*. Illustrated by G. Kamen. New York: Human Sciences Press, 1974.

Mathis, S. B. *Listen for the fig tree*. New York: Viking Press, 1974.
McCracken, M. *Lovey: A very special child*. Philadelphia: Lippincott, 1976.

Oppenheimer, J. *On the outside looking in*. Chicago: Scholastic, 1973.

Richard, A. *Wings*. Boston: Little, Brown, and Co., 1974.
Rinaldo, D. L. *Dark dreams*. New York: Harper & Row, 1974.
Rodowski, C. F. *What about me?* New York: Watts, 1976.

Savitz, H. M. *The lionhearted*. New York: John Day, 1975.
Smith, G. *The hayburners*. Illustrated by T. Lewin. New York: Delacorte, 1974.
Swarthout, G., and Swarthout, K. *Whales to see*. Illustrated by P. Bacon. Garden City, N.Y.: Doubleday, 1975.

Terris, S. *Plague of frogs*. Garden City, N.Y.: Doubleday, 1973.

Watson, S. *The partisan*. New York: Macmillan, 1975.

APPENDIX E

Classroom Management Assessment Guide

This inventory is designed to assess six categories for classroom management.[1]

1.0 Demographics
2.0 Physical Environment
3.0 Time
4.0 Student Encouragement
5.0 Provisions for Interactions
6.0 Differentiating Instruction

CATEGORIES FOR CLASSROOM MANAGEMENT

1.0 DEMOGRAPHICS

1.1 Number of pupils

1.2 Age range of students

1.3 IQ range of students

1.4 School grade

1.5 Type of class

1.6 Types of exceptionalities

1.7 Adult supervision

2.0 PHYSICAL ENVIRONMENT

2.1 Room size

2.2 Furnishings
- 2.21 Types
- 2.22 Fit
- 2.23 Use

2.3 Sanitation

3.0 TIME

3.1 Student time in class

3.2 On task

3.3 Signaling systems
- 3.31 Students
- 3.32 Adults

[1]Copyright © 1979 by Thomas M. Stephens. All Rights Reserved. Reprinted with author's permission.

4.0 STUDENT ENCOURAGEMENT

4.1 Knowledge of results

4.2 Social reinforcement

4.3 Contracting

4.4 Types of rewards

4.5 Goal setting

5.0 PROVISIONS FOR INTERACTIONS

5.1 Involvement of students in planning

5.2 Constructive pupil-pupil interactions

5.3 Opportunities for pupil questions

6.0 DIFFERENTIATING INSTRUCTION

6.1 Written instructional plans

6.2 Short-term objectives

6.3 Instructional procedures

6.4 Adult assistance to individual pupils

INSTRUCTIONS FOR COMPLETING CLASSROOM MANAGEMENT ASSESSMENT GUIDE

1.0 DEMOGRAPHICS

1.1 Number of pupils
Indicate number of pupils assigned to the class

1.2 Age range
Show the ages in years and months for the youngest and oldest pupil served in the class (e.g., 6-5 to 9-3).

1.3 IQ range of students
Show the most recent scores, indicate test, lowest to highest (e.g., 70 to 88).

1.4 School grade
Indicate grade level or, where appropriate, indicate *ungraded* and show range of grades (e.g., 4–6).

1.5 Type of class
Check the appropriate type.

1.6 Types of exceptionalities
Check type and specify number of students for each (diagnosed) exceptionality. Note: *Diagnosed* here means as defined by the state.

1.7 Adult supervision

Show number of certified teachers, aides, and volunteers. If adult aide is not paid, show as volunteer.

2.0 PHYSICAL ENVIRONMENT

2.1 Room size

Show approximate dimensions in *feet.*

2.2 Furnishings

2.21 Types and numbers

Show numbers for each. Show number of *shelves* for each book case. Show number and type of *instructional equipment.*

2.22 Fit

Fit means that height of chairs permit students to place feet flat on floor with their knees even with seat of the chair. Desks and tables have been adjusted so that students can comfortably write on the surfaces. When arm chairs are used, fit includes the same requirements *plus* left and *right* arm rests correctly assigned to students.

2.23 Use

Rate the use of the furnishings. Note any equipment in disrepair.

2.3 Sanitation

Rate the condition of room and furnishings. Be stringent when assigning an *A* rating.

3.0 TIME

3.1 Student time in class

Record the number of students present, the amount of minutes in the school day, and the range of time students are in *this* class. Show range from shortest to longest.

3.2 On task

Select students to observe at random. In classes with few students present, select three students. With larger size classes, select five students. In this instance, add D and E to student line. Each block represents 10 seconds—observe one student at a time for 10 seconds, then proceed to the next for a maximum of five minutes. Use sweeping second hand for timing (hand watch or wall clock). Show check (✓) for on task during interval and X for off task during interval. If it is important to know which students were observed, indicate under Notes names for each letter. Show time of day observation occurred under Notes.

3.3 Signaling systems

3.31 Students

After observing students working independently for *at least* 15 minutes, check the item that *best* applies. *Signaling* in this context means acceptable ways in which students call to adults' (teachers, aides, volunteers) attention their need for assistance. These signals may include (but are not limited to) hand raising, going to adults, placing markers on their desks, and other means that are not disruptive to other classroom members. *System* in this context means that the adults *respond* to the signals. In other words, by their behaviors, both students and adults recognize the signals' purposes.

3.32 Adults

After observing adults for *at least* 30 minutes, check the item that *best* applies. In this context *consistent* means *every time*, and *appropriate* means in ways that are not disruptive to other students and that are supportive (not punitive).

4.0 STUDENT ENCOURAGEMENT

4.1 Knowledge of results

Select students to observe at random. In classes with few students present, select three students. With larger size classes, select five students. In this instance add D and E to student line. Each block represents 10 seconds—observe one student at a time for 10 seconds, then proceed to the next for a maximum of five minutes. Use sweeping second hand for timing (hand watch or wall clock).

If it is important to know which students were observed, indicate under Notes names for each letter. Show time of day observation occurred under Notes. Show check (✓) for any time during time interval that an adult (teacher, aide, volunteer) provided the student being observed with immediate knowledge of the accuracy of their response. Show an X for non-occurrence and P for punishment. Note such feedback may be provided verbally (e.g. "that is right"; "no, the answer shoud be ______.") Or, it may be given in written form with the student present. Correcting a number of written responses *without* the student present does *not* meet the requirements of immediate feedback.

4.2 Social reinforcement

Select students to observe at random. In classes with few students present, select three students. With larger size classes, select five students. In this instance, add *D* and *E* to student line. Each block represents 10 seconds—observe one student at a time for 10 seconds, then proceed to the next for a maximum of five minutes. Use sweeping second hand for timing (hand watch or wall clock).

If it is important to know which students were observed, indicate under Notes names for each letter. Show time of day observation occurred under Notes. Show check (✓) for any time during time interval that an adult (teacher, aide, volunteer) provided this student with immediate social reinforcement for desirable behavior and/or academic performance. Show an X if no reinforcement occurred. Show P if punishment occurred during this interval. In this context *social reinforcement* means *praise* (e.g. "nice try," "keep up the good work"), use of symbols (e.g. happy faces, stars). It does not include privileges, activities, extra credit, or objects.

4.3 Contracting

In this context, contracting means a verbal or written agreement indicating what behavior-performance is required for a specific reward.

4.4 Types of rewards

In this context, *privileges* means *special rights* earned as a result of desirable behavior-performance. *Activities* refers to rewards that involve permission for students to participate in certain events such as table games, jobs, extra recess. *Extra credit* towards a better grade meets the definition of item C. *Object* rewards include edibles, toys, books, and other items that students may consume and/or keep.

4.5 *Goal setting*

Goal setting, in this context, means establishing behaviors and/or levels of achievement to be attained with or without rewards. These goals must be explicit in written or oral forms.

5.0 PROVISIONS FOR INTERACTIONS

5.1 Involvement of Students in planning

Evidence of students' involvement in planning should be seen in discussions, setting of goals, and establishing rules for classroom conduct with adult guidance.

5.2 Constructive pupil-pupil interactions

Evidence is seen with pupils interacting in performing tasks, assisting each other, talking about relevant matters. To meet the requirements of *A*, interactions must occur *without* disrupting or distracting other students.

5.3 Opportunities for pupil questions

Requirements for *A* are met only when adults *encourage* questions and are *responsive* to them.

6.0 DIFFERENTIATING INSTRUCTION

6.1 Written instructional plans

A is met when a written instructional plan is readily available and appears to be followed. There is a plan for each student enrolled and the plans are individualized to show specific objectives for each student across the *entire* instructional day.

B is met when written plans are readily available and appear to be followed. There is a plan for subgroups of students and the combined subgroups encompass all students enrolled. The plan must be across the entire instructional day.

C is checked when a single instructional plan is written for the entire class of students across the entire instructional day.

D should be used when written instructional plans are available for selected students or for part of the instructional day. Note the bases for selecting these students and/or instructional times.

E indicates that no written plans are available for any student at any time.

6.2 Short-term objectives

The objectives must be in writing and in terms of outcome behaviors (what the student will do).

A is met when there are objectives for each student for all instructional activities.

B is met when there are objectives for the entire class for all instructional activities.

C is met when there are objectives for *selected* students and/or selected instructional activities. Note the bases for using C.

D is used when there are no objectives used or available.

6.3 Instructional procedures

The procedures must be in writing and contain tactics to be used for achieving those instructional objectives rated in 6.2.

A is met when there are procedures for each objective.

B is used when there are some procedures for each objective.

C is used when there are no procedures in writing.

6.4 Adult assistance to individual pupils

A is met when adults seem to anticipate students' need for help and make themselves available.

B is used when help is provided *only* when requested by students.

C is used when adults ignore requests for student help or when no help is requested by students. If *C* is used, observers should be assured that during the times of observations the activities would typically occasion requests for help.

CLASSROOM MANAGEMENT ASSESSMENT GUIDE

Teacher ______________ School ______________

Address ______________ Room no. ______

Observation completed by ______________ Title ______

Date(s) of observations ______________

1.0 DEMOGRAPHICS

1.1 Number of pupils (total): ______

1.2 Age range: From ______ to ______

1.3 IQ range: Test(s) ______ From ______ to ______

1.4 School grade (check one):

- ______ Elementary
- ______ Middle school (Junior high)
- ______ Secondary school
- ______ Ungraded: (From ______ to ______
- ______ Other (specify) ______________

1.5 Type of class:

- ______ Regular
- ______ Special (specify) ______________
- ______ Other (specify) ______________

1.6 Exceptionalities served:

	Type	Number
______	Gifted	______
______	Educable mentally retarded	______
______	Learning disabled	______
______	Emotionally disturbed	______
______	Trainable mentally retarded	______
______	Physically handicapped	______
______	Hearing handicapped	______
______	Visually handicapped	______

_____ Multiexceptional _____
_____ None _____
_____ Other (specify) _____

1.7 Adult supervision
Teacher(s) _____ Aide(s) _____ Volunteer(s) _____

2.0 PHYSICAL ENVIRONMENT

2.1 Room size: Approximately _____ feet × _____ feet.

2.2 Furnishings

2.21 Types and numbers

_____ Student-size chairs
_____ Student-size desks
_____ Student-size tables
_____ Adult desk(s) and chair(s)
_____ Book shelves
_____ Chalkboards: check ___ permanent ___ portable
_____ Bulletin boards
_____ Instructional equipment (specify): (e.g. cassette recorders) _____
_____
_____ Other _____

2.22 Fit (✓ for yes; X for no; N/A for not applicable)

_____ Student's chairs fit
_____ Student's desks fit
_____ Student's tables fit
_____ Student's arm chairs fit

Notes: _____

2.23 Use: (check one)

[ ] A. Furnishings are flexibly used to increase the probability of achieving the outcomes for each activity (e.g., chairs and desks are arranged to increase or decrease student interactions as required).

[ ] B. Some furnishings are flexibly used for achieving outcomes.
Notes: _____
_____

[ ] C. Use of furnishings appear unrelated to outcomes.
Notes: _____
_____

2.3 Sanitation (check one):

[ ] A. Room and furnishings are very clean, for example, chalkboards and display areas are clean; room is not dusty, floor is free of litter; chairs, desks, and tables

are clean and maintained in good condition; student work area is not cluttered.

[ ] B. Room and furnishings are generally clean but some aspects need improving (specify): ________________

____

[ ] C. Room and furnishings are in poor condition (specify): ________________________________

____

3.0 TIME

3.1 Student time in class:

Number of students in class when observed: ________

Length of school day (in minutes): ________

Range of time spent by students in class each day (from shortest to longest): ________ to ________

3.2 On Task

Each time block represents *10* seconds.

Student	A	B	C	D
✓ Occurrence X Nonoccurrence				

Student	A	B	C	D
✓ Occurrence X Nonoccurrence				

Student	A	B	C	D
✓ Occurrence X Nonoccurrence				

Student	A	B	C	D
✓ Occurrence X Nonoccurrence				

Student	A	B	C	D
✓ Occurrence X Nonoccurrence				

Notes: ____

____

3.3 Signaling systems

3.31 Students (check the *one* that best applies):

[ ] A. There is a clear pattern of signaling from students to adults for assistance or attention with minimal disruption to others.

[ ] B. There is a pattern of signaling but it is not followed by all students—some students disrupt others when asking for assistance.
Notes:______________________________

[ ] C. There is no clear pattern for signaling adults by students.
Notes:______________________________

3.32 Adults (check the *one* that best applies):

[ ] A. Adults consistently use appropriate means to gain students' attentions—individually and as a group.

[ ] B. Adults use appropriate means to gain students' attentions but they are inconsistent in their use.
Notes:______________________________

[ ] C. Adults use inappropriate means to gain students' attention.
Notes:______________________________

4.0 STUDENT ENCOURAGEMENT

4.1 Knowledge of results
Each time block represents *10* seconds.

Student	A	B	C	D
✓ Occurrence X Nonoccurrence P Punishment				

Student	A	B	C	D
✓ Occurrence X Nonoccurrence P Punishment				

Student	A	B	C	D
✓ Occurrence X Nonoccurrence P Punishment				

Student	A	B	C	D
✓ Occurrence X Nonoccurrence P Punishment				

Student	A	B	C	D
✓ Occurrence X Nonoccurrence P Punishment				

Notes:______________________________

4.2 Social Reinforcement
Each time block represents *10* seconds.

Student	A	B	C	D
✓ Occurrence X Nonoccurrence P Punishment				

Student	A	B	C	D
✓ Occurrence X Nonoccurrence P Punishment				

Student	A	B	C	D
✓ Occurrence X Nonoccurrence P Punishment				

Student	A	B	C	D
✓ Occurrence X Nonoccurrence P Punishment				

Student	A	B	C	D
✓ Occurrence X Nonoccurrence P Punishment				

Notes:______________________________

4.3 Contracting (check the *one* that best applies):

[ ] A. There is evidence of contingency contracting in which students are involved in establishing the behaviors (performances) *and* rewards.

[ ] B. There is evidence of contingency contracting but students are *not* involved in establishing the behaviors (performances) *and* rewards.

[ ] C. There is *no* evidence of contingency contracting.
Notes:____________________________________
____

4.4 Types of rewards (check items that apply):

[ ] A. Privileges [ ] C. Extra credit

[ ] B. Activities [ ] D. Objects

4.5 Goal setting (check the *one* that best applies):

[ ] A. Teachers *and* students establish goals for individual behavior and performance.

[ ] B. Teachers establish goals for individual students.

[ ] C. There is no evidence of goal setting for students.

5.0 PROVISIONS FOR INTERACTIONS

5.1 Involvement of students in planning (check the *one* item that best applies)

[ ] A. Pupil planning is an essential part of procedures.

[ ] B. A few pupils make suggestions but adults dominate activities.

[ ] C. Pupils do not make suggestions. Adults dictate and dominate all activities.
Notes:____________________________________
____

5.2 Constructive pupil-pupil interactions (check the *one* item that best applies):

[ ] A. Relevant pupil-pupil exchanges occur freely without class disruptions.

[ ] B. Relevant pupil-pupil exchanges occur freely but with class disruptions.

[ ] C. Pupils do *not* interact in any constructive manner.
Notes:____________________________________
____

5.3 Opportunities for pupils' questions (check the *one* that best applies):

[ ] A. Pupils' questions invited and answered by adults.

[ ] B. Pupils ask questions but are not answered by adults.

[ ] C. Pupils do not ask questions and are not encouraged to do so.

Notes:____

6.0 DIFFERENTIATING INSTRUCTION

6.1 Written instructional plans (check the *one* that best applies):

[ ] A. Written instructional plans for *each* student are available.

[ ] B. Written instructional plans for only *small groups* of students are available.

[ ] C. Written instructional plans for only *entire class* instruction are available.

[ ] D. Written instructional plans for some but *not all* students are available.

Notes:____

[ ] E. No written instructional plans are available.

Notes:____

6.2 Short-term objectives (check the *one* that best applies):

[ ] A. Short-term instructional objectives are established for each pupil.

[ ] B. Short-term instructional objectives are established on a group basis.

[ ] C. Short-term instructional objectives are established for selected students or for selected activities.

Notes:____

[ ] D. No short-term instructional objectives are established.

Notes:____

6.3 Instructional procedures (check the *one* that best applies):

[ ] A. Instructional procedures are related to all objectives.

[ ] B. Instructional procedures are related to some objectives but not for all objectives.

[ ] C. No instructional procedures are available.

6.4 Adult assistance to individual pupils (check the *one* that best applies):
- [ ] A. Adults regularly make efforts to provide individual assistance.
- [ ] B. Help provided only when requested.
- [ ] C. No individual help provided.

Additional notes:

____
____
____
____
____
____

APPENDIX F

Easy to Read, High-Interest Content Area Material[1]

[1]Compiled by Dr. Sandra McCormick, College of Education, The Ohio State University. Copyright © 1981 by Sandra McCormick. All rights reserved. Reproduced with permission of the author.

This appendix lists content area materials that are easy to read and was compiled to assist content area teachers who have mainstreamed students in their classes. Students who are not reading at grade level frequently perform poorly in content area subjects because they have difficulty reading materials assigned in these classes. With secondary level mainstreamed students the responsibility of the special education teacher goes beyond assistance given in the special class. Although it is important to help students develop appropriate reading strategies, it is also necessary for the older student to plan adaptations in instructional programs that depend heavily on reading to convey information.

To assist underachievers, special teachers should provide information to content teachers about the availability of materials that address the same topics as assigned to the class in general, but that are easier to read. Listed below are easy-to-read, high interest materials which can be used in English, history, math, science, health, vocational awareness, geography, and literature courses. A suggested interest level (I.L.) is given for each book as well as its approximate reading level (R.L.). Addresses for the publishers from whom these materials may be obtained are also provided.

English

Title	Publisher	I. L.	R . L.
Get It Down in Writing	X	7-12	2.5-4.5
The Learning Language Skills Series: Language Arts	W	7-Adult	1.5
Learning our Language Books One and Two	F	7-Adult	5
Guidebook to Better English	E	7-Adult	4.7
Getting Help (skill area: language arts)	X	9-12	3.5-4.5
Write for the Job	X	9-12	3.5-4.5
Read It Right (using reference materials)	X	7-12	2.5-4.5
Language Workshop: A Guide to Better English	GL	7-12	4-5
The World of Vocabulary Series	GL	8-12	2-7
Everyday English	GL	7-12	3-4
Writing Sense	GL	7-12	5-6
Writing a Research Paper	GL	7-12	5-6
Writing Power	GL	7-12	5-6
Open-Ended Stories	GL	7-12	4-5
Open-Ended Plays	GL	7-12	3-4

English (cont.)

Title	Publisher	I. L.	R. L.
Spell It Out: Reading/Spelling Workshop	GL	7-12	3-6
Essential Grammar Competency Lab	H	7-12	2.5-4.5
Mechanics and Usage Perfomance Packs	H	7-12	2.5-3.5
Parts of Speech Performance Pack	H	7-12	2.5-3.5
Parts of Speech Workshop	H	7-12	4.0-5.0
Using Spelling, Capitalization, and Punctuation Performance Packs	H	7-12	2.5-3.5
The Business of Basic English	H	7-12	4.5-5.5
English for Everyday Living	H	7-12	3.0-4.0
Language Drills, Book 1-52 Duplicating Masters	H	7-12	3.0-4.0
Language Drills, Book 2-50 Duplicating Masters	H	7-12	3.5-4.5
Big Time Comics—Complete Collection (written expression: paragraphs and sentences)	H	7-12	2.0-6.0
Letter Writing Learning Lab	H	7-12	3.0-4.0
Writing Skills for Everyday Life—A Multimedia Program	H	8-12	5.0-7.0
Spotlight on Writing (reproducible activities)	H	7-12	2.0-4.0
Letter Writing Skills (reproducible activities)	H	7-12	3.5-4.5
Writing to Others Program	H	8-12	3.0-4.0
English for Employment	H	8-12	4.0-5.0
English for Everyday	H	7-12	3.0-4.0
How Do I Fill Out a Form? Duplicating Masters	H	9-12	3.5-4.5
Basic Writing Skills: The Freddy Klinker Skill Box Series	H	7-12	3.0-5.5
Improve Your Writing for Job Success (handwriting kit)	H	7-12	3.0-4.0
Handwriting Legibility Kit	H	7-12	2.5-3.5
Webster's Alphabetical Thesaurus	H	7-12	5.5-6.5

Title	Publisher	I. L.	R . L.
Super Dictionary Activity Unit	H	7-12	4.0-5.0
Using a Dictionary Duplicating Masters	H	7-12	4.5-5.5
Library Strategies Learning Lab	H	7-12	3.0-4.0
Libraries Are for Finding Out: Using the Encyclopedia	H	7-12	3.5-4.5
Libraries Are for Finding Out: Using the Card Catalog	H	7-12	3.5-4.5
Using Reference Skills Performance Pack	H	7-12	3.5-5.0
Language Skills Crossword Puzzles Duplicating Masters	H	7-12	3.0-5.0
Grammar for Adult Living	H	9-12	3.0-4.0
English Exercises Duplicating Masters	H	7-12	2.0-3.0
Spinning Grammar Game Set	H	7-12	3.0-4.0
Spelling Rules and Problem Areas Learning Lab	H	7-12	2.0-3.0
Spell Stumpers Duplicating Masters	H	7-12	2.5-3.5
Basic Writing Game Module	H	7-12	3.0-4.0
Right Your Writing Performance Pack	H	7-12	3.5-4.5
Spotlight on Sentences	H	7-10	2.5-3.5
Sentence Writing Learning Lab	H	7-12	3.0-4.0
Paragraph Writing Learning Lab	H	7-12	3.5-4.5
Descriptive Writing: Using Nouns and Verbs	H	7-12	3.0-4.0
Sentences and Paragraphs Workshop	H	7-12	3.0-4.0
Activities for Writing and Rewriting	H	7-12	3.5-4.5
Outlining Skills Duplicating Masters	H	7-12	4.5-5.5
Flub Stubs (Composition)	H	7-12	2.5-3.5
Everyday Reading and Writing	N	7-12	5-6
From A to Z (handwriting)	SV	7-Adult	1
Using English	SV	10-Adult	3-4
Everyday English	SV	10-Adult	4-5

English (cont.)

Title	Publisher	I. L.	R. L.
Learning Our Language Revised Books One and Two	SV	7-Adult	6-8
English Essentials: A Refresher Course, Revised	SV	11-Adult	8-10
Fundamental English Review	SV	11-Adult	8-12

History

Title	Publisher	I. L.	R. L.
The New Exploring World History	GL	7-12	5-6
Exploring American Citizenship	GL	7-12	5-6
Cultures in Conflict	GL	7-12	5-6
Our Nation of Immigrants	GL	7-12	5-6
Inquiry: Western Civilization	GL	7-12	5-7
Afro-American in the United States History	GL	7-12	5-6
Pollution of the Environment	GL	9-12	8
The New Exploring Our Nation's History	GL	7-12	6-7
United States Government	B	7-12	4-6
The War Between the States	EI	7-12	4
Frontiers West	EI	7-12	4
American History Study Lessons Units 1-9	F	7-12	5
Study Lessons in Our Nation's History	F	7-12	5
World History Study Lessons Units 1-9	F	7-12	5
Study Lessons in Civics	F	7-12	6-9
The New Exploring American History	GL	7-12	5-6
Civilizations of the Past: Peoples and Cultures	GL	7-9	6
The United States: Its People and Leaders	GL	7-9	4
The Story of William Penn	PH	7-12	3
William Penn: Founder of Pennsylvania	WM	7	4-5
Human Cargo: The Story of the Atlantic Slave Trade	G	7	6

Title	Publisher	I. L.	R. L.
North to Liberty: The Story of the Underground Railroad	G	7-9	6
The American Revolution	EI	7-12	4
Our Indian Heritage	X	7-9	4-5
Women in American Life	X	7-9	4-5
Youth Crime and Punishment	X	7-9	4-5
America Moves West	X	7-9	4-5
The Great Depression	X	7-9	4-5
Juveniles and the Law	X	7-9	4-5
The Labor Movement	X	7-9	4-5
Land of Immigrants	X	7-9	4-5
A Nation in Rebellion	X	7-9	4-5
Exploring Civilizations: A Discovery Approach	GL	7-12	5-6
The United States in the Making	GL	7-12	5-6
Our American Minorities	GL	7-12	3-4
(Benjamin) Franklin/(Martin Luther) King	P	7-12	4-6
We Honor Them, Volumes 1, 2, 3 (short biographies of blacks in America)	N	7-12	3-5
Insights about America	I	7-12	4
The Police and Us	N	7-12	3-4
Claiming a Right (biography of 24 Indians)	N	7-12	3-4
Our United States	N	7-12	3-4
Government by the People	N	7-12	4-5
The Peoples' Power	N	7-12	4-5
Blacks in Time	N	7-12	4-5
I Am One of These (real life stories of blacks, whites, Mexican-American, Native American, Cuban, foreign-born citizens)	N	7-12	3-4
Martin Luther King	N	7-12	4-5
The Men Who Won the West	S	7-12	4-7
Lincoln/Roosevelt	P	7-12	4-6

History (cont.)

Title	Publisher	I. L.	R. L.
Washington/Jefferson	P	7-12	4-6
Crockett/Boone	P	7-12	4-6
Lindbergh/Earhart	P	7-12	4-6
Forts in the Wilderness	CP	7-12	4
Explorers in a New World	CP	7-12	4
Men on Iron Horses	CP	7-12	4
Pioneering on the Plains	CP	7-12	4
Settlers on a Strange Shore	CP	7-12	4
The Story of World War II	BT	7-12	3

Math

Title	Publisher	I. L.	R. L.
Daily Math Application Program	H	10-12	4.5-5.5
Real-Life Math Program	H	8-12	4.5-5.5
Using Checks and Charge Cards Learning Lab	H	8-12	3.0-4.0
Survival Math Skills Program	H	9-12	4.0-5.0
Using Money Wisely	X	9-12	3.5-4.5
Math for the Road	X	9-12	3.5-4.5
Checking Account: A Multimedia Kit	H	9-12	5.5-6.5
Lakeshore Math Competency Performance Packs	H	9-12	3.0-4.5
Math in the Marketplace Filmstrip Activity Library	H	8-12	2.5-4.0
Basic Skills in Using Money	H	9-12	4.0-5.0
Money Management Duplicating Masters	H	8-12	4.5-5.5
Job Simulations Using Math	H	9-12	4.0-5.0
Math For Employment 1 Skillbook	H	9-12	4.5-5.5
Math For Employment 2 Skillbook	H	9-12	4.5-5.5
Math for the Worker Skillbook	H	9-12	4.5-5.5
Payroll Deductions Activity Unit	H	9-12	5.5-6.5

Title	Publisher	I. L.	R. L.
Basic Buying Skills Duplicating Masters	H	7-12	2.5-4.0
Using Consumer Math Competency Lab	H	7-12	3.5-4.5
Consumer Math for Self Defense	H	7-12	5.0-6.0
Grocery Bills Skillbook	H	7-12	2.5-3.5
Arithmetic for Grocery Shopping	H	7-12	2.0-3.0
Consumer Math Strategies	H	7-12	4.5-5.5
Newspaper Math Tasks	H	7-10	4.5-5.5
Using Dollars and Sense Activity Book	H	7-12	2.5-3.5
Everyday Math Survival Skills	H	7-12	3.5-4.5
Mathematics and You: A Hands-on Approach	H	7-12	4.5
Your Daily Math Skills Books 1 and 2	H	7-12	4.5-5.5
Math Marathon	H	7-12	2.5-3.5
Math Puzzlers	H	7-12	4.5-5.5
Metric Football	H	7-12	4.0-5.0
Metric Puzzles Duplicating Module	H	7-12	5.0-6.0
Measurement Learning Labs	H	7-12	2.8-3.8
Money Makes Sense Activity Book	H	7-12	2.0-3.0
Multi-Step Math Drill Cassettes	H	7-12	2.5-3.5
Basic Math Facts Competency Lab	H	7-12	2.0-4.0
Number Power Skillbook	H	7-12	2.0-4.0
Back to Basics from Addition to Division	H	7-12	2.5-4.5
Lifeskills Math Activity Book	H	7-12	3.2-4.5
Veri-Tech: A Self-Check Basic Math System	H	7-12	3.0-4.0
Sports Cards Math Kit	H	7-12	3.0-4.0
Making Basic Math Easy	H	7-12	4.2-5.5
Single Topic Math Duplicating Series	H	7-12	4.5-5.5
Fractions Sequential Activity Card Set	H	7-12	3.5-4.5
Lakeshore Learning Lab (fractions and decimals)	H	7-12	3.0-4.5
Decimals Sports Cards	H	7-12	4.5-5.5

Math (cont.)

Title	Publisher	I. L.	R. L.
Figure It Out	X	5-9	2.5-3.5
The Learning Skills Series Arithmetic, 2/e	W	6-Adult	2-3
Understanding Word Problems Multimedia Kit	H	7-12	4.5-5.5
How to Solve Word Problems Practice Cards	H	7-12	3.5-4.5
Solving World Problems Duplicating Masters	H	7-12	4.5-5.5
High Interest Math Duplicating Library	H	7-12	3.0-3.5
Basic Math Operations	H	7-12	2.5-3.5
Whole Number Operations	H	7-12	3.5-4.5
Captain Quotient	H	7-12	3.0-4.0
Mysteries of History (multiplication)	H	7-12	3.0-4.0
Arithmetic Drills Review	H	7-10	2.5-4.5

Science

Title	Publisher	I. L.	R. L.
Spaceship Earth/Life Science	HM	8-12	7
Spaceship Earth/Physical Science	HM	8-12	6-7
Spaceship Earth/Earth Science	HM	9-12	7-3
Edison/Bell	P	7-12	4-6
Curie/Einstein	P	9-12	4-6
Biology Workshop 1: Understanding Living Things	GL	9-12	4-5
Earth Science Workshop 1: Understanding the Earth's Surface	GL	9-12	4-5
Chemistry Workshop 1: Understanding Matter	GL	9-12	4-5
Physics Workshop 1: Understanding Energy	GL	9-12	4-5
Biology Workshop 2: Understanding the Human Body	GL	9-12	4-5
Earth Science Workshop 2: Understanding the Atmosphere and Oceans	GL	9-12	4-5
Chemistry Workshop 2: Understanding Mixtures	GL	9-12	4-5
Physics Workshop 2: Understanding Forces	GL	9-12	4-5

Title	Publisher	I. L.	R. L.
Biology Workshop 3: Understanding Reproduction	GL	9-12	4-5
Earth Science Workshop 3: Understanding Space	GL	9-12	4-5
Chemistry Workshop 3: Understanding the Chemistry of Metals	GL	9-12	4-5
Physics Workshop 3: Understanding Light and Sound	GL	9-12	4-5
What is an Atom?	BP	7-8	4
What is a Cell?	BP	7-8	4
What is Energy?	BP	7-8	4
What is Gravity?	BP	7-8	4
What is Heat?	BP	7-8	4
What is an Insect?	BP	7-8	4
What is a Machine?	BP	7-8	4
What is a Magnet?	BP	7-8	4
What is Matter?	BP	7-8	4
What is a Solar System?	BP	7-8	4
What is Sound?	BP	7-8	4
What is Space?	BP	7-8	4
What is Weather?	BP	7-8	4
What Makes a Light Go on?	L	7-Adult	3
The Bug Club Book: A Handbook for Young Bug Collectors	HH	7	4
A Book of the Milky Way Galaxy	C	7-Adult	3.4
What Colonel Glenn Did All Day	JD	7-Adult	4
The Riddle of Seeds	CM	7-Adult	3
Magic With Chemistry	GD	7-Adult	4
This is Cape Kennedy	M	7-Adult	3
Experiments for Young Scientists	L	7-Adult	3
Psychic Stories Strange but True	BT	7-9	2.4

Health

Title	Publisher	I. L.	R. L.
Keeping Fit!	X	9-12	3.5-4.5
Health and Safety: Keeping Fit Multimedia Kit	H	7-12	5.0-6.0
Human Body Activity Cards	H	7-12	3.5-4.5
Your Life in Your Hands	H	7-12	4.0-5.0
Health Resource Cards	H	7-12	5.0-6.0
First Aid: Newest Techniques Multimedia Program	H	7-12	3.0-4.0
Health Survival Skills Multimedia Kit	H	7-12	3.0-4.0
Sigh of Relief: First Aid Guide for the Classroom	H	7-12	3.0-4.5
Having a Baby Series	N	7-12	4
Be Informed on Drugs	N	7-12	4-5
Contemporary Reading Series (seven books on topics such as drugs, alcohol, V.D., pregnancy)	EA	7-12	4-5
Emergency Medical Care Worktext	H	7-12	5.0-6.5
Health and Nutrition Reference Library	H	8-12	5.0-7.5
Is It Safe to Eat Anything Anymore?	H	7-12	3.0-5.0
The Basics of Nutrition, A Multimedia Program	H	7-12	4.0-5.0
Nutrition Survival Kit	H	7-12	4.5-6.0
Nutrition: Food vs. Health	H	7-12	3.0-4.0
You & Food Additives Activity Unit	H	7-12	5.0-6.0
Label Literacy: How to Read Food Packages	H	7-12	2.0-3.0
Modern Human Sexuality	HM	7-9	4-5
The Body Machine: Parts and Functions	X	7-9	4.0-6.0
The Body Machine: Care and Maintenance	X	7-9	4.0-6.0

Careers

Title	Publisher	I. L.	R. L.
Survival Skills for Work	H	9-12	4.5-5.5
The Very Basics of Work Reading Series	H	9-12	1.5-2.5

Title	Publisher	I. L.	R. L.
The Job Hunt Cassette Activity Program	H	9-12	5.0-6.0
The Job Hunting Game	H	9-12	3.5-4.5
Don't Get Fired Activity Book	H	9-12	2.0-3.0
Job Applications Activity Book	H	8-12	2.5-3.5
Job Interview Worktext	H	8-12	2.5-3.5
You and Others on the Job Reading Series	H	8-12	3.5-4.5
Janus Job Interview Guide	J	7-12	2.5
Janus Job Planner	J	7-12	2.8
People Working Today (10 books about teenage workers)	J	7-12	1.9
Get Hired! 13 Ways to Get Your Job	J	7-12	2.5
Don't Get Fired! 13 Ways to Hold Your Job	J	7-12	2.5
First Jobs Multimedia Program	H	7-12	3.0-4.0
Your First Job Reading Series	H	7-12	2.0-3.0
Career Exploration Resource Library	H	7-12	5.5-6.5
The Info-Job Resource Center	H	7-12	4.5-5.5
Real People at Work Library 1	H	7-12	2.0-4.0
Real People at Work Library 2	H	7-12	4.0-5.0
Getting into Pro Baseball	BT	7-12	7
Getting into Pro Basketball	BT	7-12	8
Getting into Pro Football	BT	7-12	8

Geography

Title	Publisher	I. L.	R. L.
The Earth: Regions and Peoples	GL	7-8	3
Homelands of the World: Resources and Cultures	GL	7	5
Exploring the Western World	GL	7	5
The New Exploring the Non-Western World	GL	7-12	5-6
The New Exploring A Changing World	GL	7-12	5-6
Exploring the Urban World	GL	7-12	5-6

Geography (cont.)

Title	Publisher	I. L.	R. L.
The Congo: River into Central Africa	G	7	5
The Niger: Africa's River of Mystery	G	7	5
The Nile: Lifeline of Egypt	G	7	5
The Ganges: Sacred River of India	G	7	5
The Indus: South Asia's Highway of History	G	7	5
The Yangtze: China's River Highway	G	7	5
The Rhone: River of Contrasts	G	7	5
The Seine: River of Paris	G	7	5
The Shannon: River of Loughs and Legends	G	7	5
The Thames: London's River	G	7	5
The Tiber: The Roman River	G	7	5
The Volga: Russia's River of Five Seas	G	7	5
The Amazon: River Sea of Brazil	G	7	5
The Mississippi: Giant at Work	G	7	5
The St. Lawrence: Seaway of North America	G	7	5
The Jordan: River of the Promised Land	G	7	5
The Colorado: Mover of Mountains	G	7	5
The Rio Grande: Life for the Desert	G	7	5
The Changing Eskimos	BT	7-8	2.7
A World Explorer: Roald Amundsen	G	7	4

Literature

Title	Publisher	I. L.	R. L.
Great American Library—Biography (Junior A + B, Senior A + B)	S	7-12	3-7, 4-8
House of the Seven Gables	GL	8-12	6-7
An O. Henry Reader	GL	9-12	7-8
Short World Biographies	GL	9-12	5-6
Profiles: A Collection of Short Biographies	GL	9-12	5-6

Title	Publisher	I. L.	R. L.
A Tale of Two Cities	GL	9-12	5-6
Moby Dick	GL	9-12	5-6
Jane Eyre	GL	8-12	4-5
An Edgar Allen Poe Reader	GL	8-12	6-7
Turning Point: A Selection of Short Biographies	GL	8-12	3
Lorna Doone	GL	8-12	5-6
Journeys to Fame (a series of short biographies)	GL	7-12	2-3
Modern Short Biographies	GL	7-12	5-6
Tales Worth Retelling (Rudyard Kipling)	GL	7-12	5-6
The Adventures of Sherlock Holmes	GL	8-12	6-7
Tom Sawyer	GL	7-12	3-4
Chitty Chitty Bang Bang	S	7-12	6
Kidnapped	GL	7-12	5-6
The Odyssey	GL	7-12	5-6
Twenty Thousand Leagues under the Sea	GL	7-12	4-5
Treasure Island	GL	7-12	5-6
American Folklore and Legends	GL	7-12	4
Legends for Everyone	GL	7-12	3
Myths and Folk Tales around the World	GL	7-12	4
The Magnificent Myths of Man	GL	7-12	4-5
Scholastic Reluctant Reader Libraries (Junior A + B, Senior A + B)	S	7-12	4-8
Their Eyes on the Stars: Four Black Writers	G	7-9	6
The George Foster Story	BT	7-10	6
Jimmy Young, Heavyweight Challenger	BT	7-9	4
Nancy Lopez	BT	7-8	2
The Picture Life of Muhammed Ali	BT	7-8	2.9
The Picture Life of O. J. Simpson	BT	7-8	2.8

Literature (cont.)

Title	Publisher	I. L.	R. L.
Steve Garvey	BT	7-8	2
Tom Seaver: Portrait of a Pitcher	BT	8-12	7
Winners on the Ice	BT	7-8	2.3
Winners in Gymnastics	BT	7-8	2.5
Winners on the Ski Slopes	BT	7-8	2.8
Winners on the Tennis Courts	BT	7-8	2.3

ADDRESSES OF PUBLISHERS

BP Benefic Press
1900 N. Narrangansett
Chicago, Ill. 60639

BT The Baker and Taylor Company
1515 Broadway
New York, N.Y. 10036

B Bowmar
P.O. Box 5225
Glendale, Calif. 91201

CP Childrens Press
1224 West Van Buren Street
Chicago, Ill. 60607

CM Coward McCann
200 Madison Avenue
New York, N.Y. 10019

C Crowell Publishers
201 Park Avenue South
New York, N.Y. 10019

DC D. C. Heath
125 Spring Street
Lexington, Mass. 02173

E The Economy Company
Drawer A
5811 W. Minnesota
Indianapolis, Ind. 46241

EA Educational Activities
P. O. Box 392
Freeport, N.Y. 11520

EI Educational Insights
School Days
760 Elma Street
Akron, Ohio 44310

F Follett Corporation
1010 W. Washington Boulevard
Chicago, Ill. 60607

G Garrard Publishing Company
Champaign, Ill. 61820

GL Globe Book Company, Inc.
50 West 23rd Street
New York, N.Y. 10010

GD Grosset & Dunlap, Inc.
51 Madison Avenue
New York, N.Y. 10010

H Holcombs Educational Materials Mart
3000 Quigley Road
Cleveland, Ohio 44113

HH Holiday House
18 E. 53rd Street
New York, N.Y. 10022

HM Houghton Mifflin
1900 South Batavia Avenue
Geneva, Illinois 60134

J Janus Book Publishers
3541 Investment Boulevard
Suite 5P
Hayward, Calif. 94545

JD John Day Company, Inc.
257 Park Avenue South
New York, N.Y. 10010

L Little, Brown, & Company
34 Beacon Street
Boston, Mass. 02106

M The Macmillan Company
School Department
539 Turtle Creek South Dr.
Indianapolis, Ind. 46227

N New Reader's Press
Box 131
Syracuse, N.Y. 13210

P Pendulum Press, Inc.
Academic Building
Saw Mill Road
West Haven, Conn. 06516

PH Prentice-Hall, Inc.
Educational Books Division
Englewood Cliffs, N.J. 07632

S Scholastic
906 Sylvan Avenue
Englewood Cliffs, N.J. 07632

SR Science Research Associates, Inc.
259 E. Erie Street
Chicago, Ill. 60611

SF Scott Foresman & Company
1900 E. Lake Avenue
Glenview, Ill. 60025

SV Steck-Vaughn
P. O. Box 2028
Austin, Tex. 78768

W Webster/McGraw-Hill
Manchester Road
Manchester, Mo. 63011

WM William Morrow and Company
425 Park Avenue South
New York, N.Y. 10016

X Xerox Education Publications
1250 Fairwood Avenue
P. O. Box 16618
Columbus, Ohio 43216

Glossary

Ability training: An instructional approach that emphasizes intervening into the individual's cognitive and perceptual processes to remediate problems.

Adaptive behavior: The individual person's skill to adjust to the environment at adequate levels of independence and responsibility through maturation, learning, and social adjustment.

Adaptive physical education: Physical education programs designed to meet the special needs of exceptional persons.

Annual goals: An important element of the Individualized Education Program (IEP) that specifies targets of achievement to reach during the school year.

Baseline data: Performance data measured through direct observation to establish the status of the individual before intervention or the removal of intervention.

Behavior disorder: A functional category of special education that refers to children whose behavior is inappropriate and/or unacceptable in the usual school environment.

Behavior modification: The systematic process of applying consequences or reinforcers to encourage appropriate behaviors and diminish or eliminate inappropriate behaviors of the individual.

Behavioral objective: A statement that specifies desirable, measurable outcomes.

Child find: A required search under P.L. 94-142 whereby each state identifies and locates all handicapped children requiring an appropriate education.

Class action suit: Litigation instituted on behalf of a group of individuals seeking legal relief or assistance.

Communication disorder: A malfunction of the individual during communications.

Consulting (or crisis) teacher: A special educator who provides resource help to other teachers and exceptional students within the regular environment.

Contingency contracting: An agreement (written or oral) between teacher and student(s) that specifies the rewards if certain behaviors are exhibited.

Continuum of special education services: A complete range of special education services to serve the instructional needs of the exceptional student from the regular grades to the special facility.

Council for Exceptional Children (C.E.C.): A national professional organization for personnel working with exceptional students. Based in Reston, Virginia, it also has various sub-divisions for specific exceptionalities.

Criterion-referenced test: Assessment of individual performance on a specific skill in terms of a stated or desired level of performance.

Curriculum: The logical, systematic arrangement of learning objectives for students supplemented by suggested materials and methods.

Directive Teaching: A system of teaching enabling teachers to be effective in academic and social instruction. It consists of assessing students' academic and social performances, planning instruction based upon the assessment information, instructing according to plan, and a direct evaluation of the effects of instruction.

Disability: A specific limitation of functioning due to an impairment.

Due process: Procedural guarantees under P.L. 94-142 that protect exceptional students from deprivation of their rights to equal educational opportunities.

Duration recording: A behavior observation recording procedure that measures the amount of time a student engages in a specific behavior.

Educable mentally retarded: A special education category (variable definition from state to state) for children who exhibit considerably below average performance on intelligence tests (e.g., 50 to 70 IQ) and adaptive behavior assessment.

Efficacy studies: Research designed to determine if specific educational practices achieve their desired effect on student performance or other factors.

Etiology: The study of the underlying causes of a disease or disorder.

Event recording: A behavior observation recording procedure that measures the frequency of a specific behavior over a certain period of time.

Fading: The gradual removal of prompts or cues to allow more independent activity of the learner.

Generalization: The application of a learned behavior from one setting or opportunity to another.

Handicap: A functional limitation or disability that creates barriers to successful achievement in the individual without some type of adjustment or assistance.

Hyperactivity: Behavior characterized by excessive motor activity, implusiveness, and lack of attention.

Hypoactivity: Behavior characterized by lack of activity.

IEP: Individualized Education Program that is used as a management tool for each exceptional childs' individual needs.

Integration: Movement toward the mainstream; from most restrictive to less restrictive, depending on contact with nonhandicapped students.

Interdisciplinary: A cooperative effort of professionals from various disciplines for assessment and services.

Intrinsic reinforcers: Behavior that is rewarding by its performance.

Itinerant teacher: traveling teacher working one to one with students or on a small group basis.

Language: Any system of communication consisting of words, symbols, or gestures and rules for their use.

Learning disability: A disorder in one or more basic psychological processes, manifesting itself in an imperfect ability to listen, think, speak, read, write, spell or do mathematical calculations.

Least restrictive environment: Placement determined by the IEP that considers education program environment, and proximity to non-handicapped students—all as near the norm as the IEP indicates is appropriate.

Mastery: The level at which a child consistently succeeds.

Mental retardation: A handicapping condition characterized by significant subaverage general intellectual function and deficits in adaptive behavior occuring during the developmental period.

Modeling: The acting out of a desired behavior for direct imitation.

Negative reinforcement: Any stimulus which, by its removal, strengthens the behavior it follows.

Norm referenced tests: Formalized assessment of individual performance or specific skills as compared with the performance of a reference group.

Occupational therapy: Upper extremity directed therapy intended to develop skills of daily living.

Paraprofessionals: Educational assistants or aides to a teacher.

Peer tutors: School children who assist other children with specific tasks, as directed by teacher.

Perceptual disorders: Disorders associated with inaccurate visual, auditory, tactual, or kinesthetic processing.

Perseveration: Purposeless repetition.

Physical therapy: Lower extremity directed therapy intended to develop movement for gait, posture and relaxation of lower body muscles.

Positive reinforcement: Any object, event, or activity that follows a behavior that increases the likelihood the behavior will occur again.

Public Law 94-142: The Education of all Handicapped Children Act of 1975 that entitles all exceptional children to a free and appropriate public education.

Referral: A formal process whereby educators or parents indicate a particular student is having difficulty and may need special education services.

Reliability: The degree of consistency of data recordings by two observers.

Resource room: A special education service that is usually provided in a room or area separate from the regular school environment for a portion of the day.

Screening: A process of surveying a general school population at a certain age or grade level to identify potential problems.

Section 504: The specific section of the Rehabilitation Act of 1973 that guarantees the civil rights of the handicapped.

Short-term objectives: A specific part of the Individualized Education Program (IEP) that states the measurable student objectives in reaching the annual goals of the IEP.

Special educator: A teacher with training and state certificate to work with specific types of handicapped children.

Target behavior: A specific behavior to be modified through intervention.

Task analysis: The process of breaking down a task into its components.

Tokens: A concrete, tangible object that is used to signify a positive reinforcement for the student.

Validity: the degree to which a test measures what it says it measures.

Visual acuity: A measured ability to see.

Vocational training: A program for preparing students for employment.

References

Abeson, A., and Zettel, J. The end of the quiet revolution: The Education for All Handicapped Act of 1975. *Exceptional Children*, 1977, *44*(2), 114-127.

Anderson, R. M., Greer, J. G., and Odle, S. J. *Individualizing educational materials for special children in the mainstream*. Baltimore: University Park Press, 1978.

Armstrong, S., Stahlbrand, K., and Pierce, M. The minimum objectives system. *The Directive Teacher*, 1980, *2*(5), 9-11.

Ashlock, R. B. *Error patterns in computation: A semi-programmed approach* (2nd. ed.). Columbus, Oh.: Charles E. Merrill, 1976.

Baldwin, W. D. The social position of the educable mentally retarded in the regular grades in the public schools. *Exceptional Children*, 1958, *25*(3), 106-108.

Ballard, J. *Public Law 94-142 and Section 504—Understanding what they are and are not*. Reston, Va.: Council for Exceptional Children, 1977.

Bandura, A. *Principles of behavior modification*. New York: Holt, Rinehart, and Winston, Inc., 1969.

Bennett, L. M., and Henson, F. O. *Keeping in touch with parents: The teacher's best friend*. Austin: Learning Concepts, 1977.

Berry, K. *Models for mainstreaming*. San Rafael, Calif.: Dimension Publishing Company, 1973.

Birch, J. W. Mainstreaming: Definition, development, and characteristics. In C. Hawkins-Shepard (Ed.), *Making it work: Practical ideas for integrating exceptional children into regular classes*, (rev. ed). Reston, Va.: Council for Exceptional Children, 1978.

Birch, J. W. *Mainstreaming: Educable mentally retarded children in regular classes* Reston, Va.: Council for Exceptional Children, 1974.

Blackhurst, A. E. Continuing professional development. In A. E. Blackhurst and W. H. Berdine (Eds.), *An introduction to special education*. Boston: Little, Brown and Co., 1981.

Blackhurst, A. E., and Berdine, W. H. (Eds.). *An introduction to special education*. Boston: Little, Brown and Co., 1981.

Blatt, B., and Kaplan, F. *Christmas in purgatory*. Boston: Allyn and Bacon, 1966.

Bogden, R., and Biklen, D. Handicapism. *Social Policy*, March-April, 1977.

Borg, W. R. *Learner accountability*. Logan, Utah: Utah Protocal Materials Project, Utah State University, 1977.

Broden, M., Hall R., Dunlap, A., and Clark, R. Effects of teacher attention and a token reinforcement system in a junior high school special education class. *Exceptional Children*, 1970, *36*(5), 341-349.

Bruininks, V. L. Peer status and personality characteristics of learning disabled and nondisabled students. *Journal of Learning Disabilities*, 1978, *11*(8), 484-489.

Bryan, P, and Bryan, J. H. The social-emotional side of learning disabilities. *Behavior Disorders*, May 1977, 141-145.

Bryan, P., Wheeler, R., Felcan, J., and Henek, T. Come on dummy: An observational study of children's communications. *Journal of Learning Disabilities*, 1976, *9*(10), 661-669.

Bush, W. J., and Waugh, K. W. *Diagnosing learning disabilities* (2nd. ed.). Columbus, Oh.: Charles E. Merrill, 1976.

Cassidy, V. M., and Stanton, J. E. *An investigation of factors involved in the educational placement of mentally retarded children*. Columbus: The Ohio State University, 1959.

Chinn, P. C., Winn, J., and Walter, R. H. *Two-way talking with parents of special children: A process of positive communication*. St. Louis, Mo.: C. V. Mosby, 1978.

Cohen, S. *Special people*. Englewood Cliffs, N. J.: Prentice-Hall, 1977.

A common body of practice for teachers: The challenge of P.L. 94-142 to teacher education. Washington, D.C.: American Association of Colleges for Teacher Education, 1980.

Cooper, J. O. *Measurement and analysis of behavioral techniques* (2nd. ed.). Columbus: Charles E. Merrill, 1981.

Council for Exceptional Children Bulletin: Official Actions of the Delegate Assembly at the 54th Annual International Convention. Definition of mainstreaming (April 4-9, 1976), *Exceptional Children*, 1976, *43*(1), 43.

Demers, Lois A. Effective mainstreaming for the learning disabled student with behavior problems. *Journal of Learning Disabilities*, 1981, *14*(4), 179-188.

Deno, E. Special education as developmental capital. *Exceptional Children*, 1970, *37*(3), 229-237.

Dimond, P. The constitutional right to education: The quiet revolution. *The Hastings Law Journal*, 1973, *24*, 1087-1127.

Doll, E. A. The essentials of an inclusive concept of mental deficiency. *American Journal of Mental Deficiency*, 1941-42, Index to Vol. 46, 214-219.

Dreyer, S. S. *The book finder*. Circle Pines, Minn.: American Guidance Service, 1977.

Dunn, L. M. Special education for the mildly retarded—is much of it justifiable? *Exceptional Children*, 1968, *35*(1), 5-24.

Engelmann, S. *Preventing failure in the primary grades*. Chicago: Science Research Associates, 1969.

Engelmann, S., and Bruner, E. C. *DISTAR: An instructional system*. Chicago: Science Research Associates, 1974.

Fernald, G. M. *Remedial techniques in basic school subjects*. New York: McGraw-Hill, 1943.

Flanagan, J. *Measuring human performance*. Pittsburgh, Pa.: American Institutes for Research, 1962.

Friedman, Paul R., and Beck, Ronna Lee. Mental retardation and the law: A report on status of current court cases. Washington, D.C.: Department of Health, Education and Welfare Publication No. (OHD) 76-21012. 1975.

Frostig, M. *Movement education: Theory and practice*. Chicago: Follett, 1970.

Frostig, M., and Horne, D. *The Frostig program for the development of visual perception: Teacher's guide*. Chicago: Follett, 1968.

Frostig, M., and Maslow, P. *Learning problems in the classroom*. New York: Grune & Stratton, 1978.

Gearheart, B. R., and Weishahn, M. E. *The handicapped child in the regular classroom*. St. Louis, Mo.: C. V. Mosby Company, 1976.

Gickling, E., and Theobald, J. Mainstreaming: Affect or effect. *Journal of Special Education*, 1975, *9*(3), 317-328.

Goldhammer, K., Rader, B. T., and Reuschlein, P. *Mainstreaming: Teacher competencies*. East Lansing, Mich.: College of Education, Michigan State University, 1977.

Goodman, H., Gottlieb, J., and Harrison, R. H. Social acceptance of EMR: Integrated into a nongraded elementary school. *American Journal of Mental Deficiency*, 1972, *76*(4), 412-417.

Gottlieb, J., and Budoff, M. Social acceptability of retarded children in nongraded schools differing in architecture. *American Journal of Mental Deficiency*, 1973, *78*(1), 15-19.

Graham, S., Burdg, N., Hudson, F., and Carpenter, D. Educational personnel's perceptions of mainstreaming and resource room effectiveness. *Psychology in the Schools*, 1980, *17*(1), 128-134.

Gresham, F. M. Misguided mainstreaming: The case for social skills training with handicapped children. *Exceptional Children*, (in press, 1981).

Hammill, D. D., and Larsen S. C. The effectiveness of psycholinguistic training. *Exceptional Children*, 1974, *41*(1), 5-14.

Hammill, D. D., and Larsen, S. C. The effectiveness of psycholinguistic training: A reaffirmation of position. *Exceptional Children*, 1978, *44*(6), 402-417.

Hardyck, C., and Haapanen, R. Educating both halves of the brain: Educational breakthrough or neuromythology? *Journal of School Psychology*, 1979, *17*(3), 219-230.

Hofstadter, R. *Social Darwinism in American thought*. Boston: The Beacon Press, 1955.

Hollingsworth, L. S. *Gifted children: Their nature and nurture*. New York: Macmillan, 1926.

Hudson, F., Graham, S., and Warner, M. Mainstreaming: An examination of the attitudes and needs of regular classroom teachers. *Learning Disability Quarterly, 2*(3), 1979, 58-62.

Johnson, G. O. Special education for the mentally handicapped—a paradox. *Exceptional Children*, 1962, *29*(2), 63-69.

Johnson, G. O., and Kirk, S. A. Are mentally handicapped children segregated in the regular grades? *Journal of Exceptional Children*, 1950, *17*, 65-68, 87, 88.

Johnson, D. J., and Myklebust, H. R. *Learning disabilities: Educational principles and practices*. New York: Grune & Stratton, 1967.

Jordan, A. M. Personal-social traits of mentally handicapped children. In T. G. Thurstone (Ed.), *An evaluation of educating mentally handicapped children in special classes and in regular classes*. Chapel Hill: School of Education, University of North Carolina, 1959.

Journal of Learning Disabilities. The teacher's role in P. L. 94-142: A conversation with Attorney Reed Martin. *Journal of Learning Disabilities*, 1978, *11*(6), 331-341.

Kabler, M. D. The teacher connection. *The Directive Teacher*, 1980, *2*(4), p. 13, con't p. 17.

Kaufman, M. J., Semmel, M. I., and Agard, J. A. Project PRIME—An overview. *Education and Training of Mentally Retarded*, 1974, *9*(2), 107-112.

Kazdin, A. E., and Polster, R. Intermittent token reinforcement and response maintenance in extinction. *Behavior Therapy*, 1973, *4*(3), 386-391.

Kennedy, D. The cloze procedure: Use it to develop comprehension skills. *Instructor*, 1974, *84*(3), pp. 82-84.

Keogh, B. K., Kukie, S. J., and Sbordonc, M. W. *Five years of research in special education: A summary report*, (Technical Report, SERP 1975-A-19). Los Angeles: University of California, 1975.

Keogh, B. K., and Levett, M. L. Special education in the mainstream: A confrontation of limitations? *Focus on Exceptional Children*, 1976, *8*(2), 1-11.

Kephart, N. C. Influencing the rate of mental growth in retarded children through environmental stimulation. *Yearbook of the National Society for the Study of Education, Part 2*, 1940, *39*, 223-230.

Kerr, D. H. *Educational policy: Analysis, structure, and justification*. New York: David McKay Company, 1976.

Kidd, J. W. The "adultated" mentally retarded. *Education and Training of the Mentally Retarded*, 1970, *5*(2), 71-72.

Kirk, S. A. Research in education. In H. Stevens and R. Herber (Eds.), *Mental retardation: A review of research*. Chicago: University of Chicago Press, 1964.

Kirk, S. A., and Johnson, G. O. *Educating the retarded child*. Boston: Houghton-Mifflin, 1951.

Kirk, S. A., McCarthy, J. J., and Kirk, W. D. *Examiner's manual, Illinois test of psycholinguistic abilities*. Urbana: University of Illinois Press, 1968.

Kroth, R. L. *Communicating with parents of exceptional children*. Denver: Love Publishing Company, 1975.

Kroth, R. L., and Simpson, R. L. *Parent conference as a teaching strategy*. Denver, Love Publishing Company, 1977.

Kunzelman, H. *Precision teaching: An initial training sequence*. Seattle: Special Child Publications, 1970.

Leitenberg, H. Is time-out from positive reinforcement an aversive event? A review of the experimental evidence. *Psychological Bulletin*, 1965, *64*, 428-441.

Leydorf, M. L. The seven stages. In J. M. Travers, *We've been there . . . Can we help?* Montclair, Calif.: Ontario Pomona Association for Retarded Citizens, 1978, 26-28.

Lillie, D. L. An overview to parent programs. In D. L. Lillie and P. L. Trohanis (Eds.), *Teaching parents to teach*. New York: Walker & Co., 1976.

Lillie, D. L., and Trohanis, P. L. (Eds.). *Teaching parents to teach*. New York; Walker & Co., 1976.

Lovitt, T. C. Applied behavior analysis and learning disabilities, Part 1: Characteristics of ABA, general recommendations and methodological limitations. *Journal of Learning Disabilities*, 1975, *8*(3), 432-443.

Lowman, E. W. and Klinger, J. L. *Aids to independent living: Self-help for the handicapped*. New York: McGraw-Hill, 1969.

Lund, K. A., Foster, G. E., and Perez, F. C. The effectiveness of psycholinguistic training: A reevaluation. *Exceptional Children*, February 1978, 310-321.

MacDonough, T. S., and Forehand, R. L. Response-contingent time out: Important parameters in behavior modification with children. *Journal of Behavior Therapy and Experimental Psychiatry*, 1973, 4(3), 231-236.

Macmillan, D. B., and Becker, L. D. Mainstreaming the mildly handicapped learner. In L. D. Kneedler and S. G. Tarver (Eds.), *Changing perspectives in special education*. Columbus, Oh.: Charles E. Merrill, 1977.

Mager, R. *Preparing instructional objectives*. Palo Alto: Fearon, 1962.

Mann, L. The case against ability assessment and training. *Journal of Special Education*, 1971a, *5*(1), 3-65.

Mann, L. Perceptual training revisited: The training of nothing at all. *Rehabilitation Literature*, 1971a, *32*(11), 322-335.

Mann, L. *On the trail of process training*. New York: Grune & Stratton, 1979.

Mann, L. Diagnostician. *Journal of Special Education*, 1981, *15*(2), 98-99.

Martin, E. Individualism and behaviorism as future trends in educating handicapped children. *Exceptional Children*, 1972, *38*(7), 517-525.

Martin, R. *Legal challenges to behavior modification*. Champaign, Ill.: Research Press, 1975.

McLoughlin, J. A. The role of parents. In A. E. Blackhurst and W. H. Berdine (Eds.), *An introduction to special education*. Boston: Little, Brown and Co., 1981, 534-556.

McLoughlin, J. A., Edge, D., and Strenecky, B. Perspective of parent involvement in the diagnosis and treatment of learning disabled students. *Journal of Learning Disabilities*, 1978, *11*(5), 291-296.

Melichar, J. F. *ISAARE*, Vols. 1 to 7. San Matero, Calif.: Adaptive Systems Corporation, 1977.

Michaelis, C. T. *Home and school partnerships in exceptional education*. Rockville, Md.: Aspen, 1980.

Millburn, J. *Special education and regular class teacher attitudes regarding social behaviors of children: Steps toward the development of a social skills curriculum*. Unpublished doctoral dissertation. The Ohio State University, 1974.

Moran, M. R. *Assessment of the exceptional learner in the regular classroom*. Denver, Colo.: Love Publishing Company, 1978.

Morsink, C. *Mainstreaming: Making it work in your classroom*. Lexington, Ky.: College of Education, University of Kentucky, 1981.

National Society for the Prevention of Blindness. *Vision screening in schools* (Publication No. 257). New York: National Society for the Prevention of Blindness, 1969.

Nedlar, S. E., and McAfee, O. D. *Working with parents: Guidelines for early childhood and elementary teachers*. Belmont, Calif.: Wadsworth, 1979.

Orton, S. *Reading, writing and speech problems in children*. New York: Norton, 1937.

Parkhurst, M. Dalton laboratory plan. In G. M. Whipple, (Ed.), *Adapting the schools to individual differences*. 24th Yearbook of the National Society for the Study of Education, Part 2. Bloomington, Ill.: Public School Publishing Company, 1925, 83-94.

Parmenter, T. R. Critique of White article. *Journal of Learning Disabilities*, 1980, *13*, 115-116.

Patterson, L. L. Some pointers for professionals. *Children*, 1956, *3* (Jan.), 13-17.

Peters, L. J. *Prescriptive teaching*. New York: McGraw-Hill, 1965.

Peterson, N. L., and Haralick, J. G. Integration of handicapped and nonhandicapped preschoolers: An analysis of play behavior and social interaction. *Education and Training of the Mentally Retarded*, 1977, *12*(3), 235-245.

Phares, S. E. *The attitudes of teachers of learning disabled towards language usage skills in elementary schools*. Unpublished doctoral dissertation. The Ohio State University, 1980.

Quay, H. C. Special education: Assumptions, techniques, and evaluative criteria. *Exceptional Children*, 1973, *40*(3), 165-170.

Rawson, M. B. Teaching children with language disabilities in small groups. *Journal of Learning Disabilities*, 971, *4*(1), 22-30.

Redden, M. R. *An investigation of mainstreaming competencies of regular elementary teachers*. Unpublished Ed.D. dissertation. University of Kentucky, 1976.

Redden, M. R., and Blackhurst, A. E. Mainstreaming competency specifications for elementary teachers. *Exceptional Children*, 1978, *44*(8), 615-617.

Reynolds, M., and Rosen, Special education: Past, present, and future. *Educational Forum*, May 1976, 551-562.

Reynolds, M. C., and Birch, J. W. *Teaching exceptional children in all America's Schools*. Reston, Va.: The Council for Exceptional Children, 1977.

Roberts, L. Comments made as a panel member discussing mainstreaming. In S. Salend (Ed.), *I have to believe: A conversation with three mainstreaming experts*. Bethlehem, Penn.: Videotape produced by College of Education, Lehigh University, 1980.

Robinson, F. P. *Effective study* (4th ed.). New York: Harper & Row, 1970.

Robinson, N. M., and Robinson, H. B. *The mentally retarded child* (2nd. ed.). New York: McGraw-Hill, 1976.

Ryor, J. Integrating the handicapped. *Today's Education*, 1977, *66*(3), 24-26.

Salvia, J., and Ysseldyke, J. E. *Assessment in special and remedial education*. Boston: Houghton Mifflin, 1978.

Sarason, S., and Doris, J. Mainstreaming dilemmas, opposition, opportunities. In M. C. Reynolds (Ed.), *Futures of education for exceptional students: Emerging structures*. Minneapolis: National Support Systems Project, 1978.

Schifani, J. W., Anderson, R. M., and Odle, S. J. (Eds.). *Implementing learning in the least restrictive environment: Handicapped children in the mainstream*. Baltimore: University Park Press, 1980.

Schleifer, M. J. Parents and the I. E. P. *The Exceptional Parent*, 1979, *9*(4), E10-E-13.

Schubert, M. A., and Glick, H. M. Least restrictive environment programs: Why are some so successful? *Education Unlimited*, 1981, *3*(2), 11-13.

Scranton, T. R. and Ryckman, D. B. Sociometric status of learning disabled children in an integrative program. *Journal of Learning Disabilities*, 1979, *12*(6), 402-407.

Shearer, M. S. A home-based parent-training model. In D. L. Lillie and P. L. Trohanis (Eds.), *Teaching parents to teach*. New York: Walker and Company, 1976, 131-148.

Shores R., Cegelka, P., and Nelson, C. M. A review of Research on teacher competencies. *Exceptional Children*, 1973, *40*, 192-197.

Simmons-Martin, A. S. Facilitating positive parent-child interactions. In D. L.

Lillie and P. L. Trohanis (Eds.), *Teaching parents to teach*. New York: Walker & Company, 1976, 75-85.

Skeels, H. M. A study of the effects of differential stimulation on mentally retarded children: A follow-up report. *American Journal of Mental Deficiency*. 1941-42, Index to Vol. 46, 340-350.

Skeels, H. M. and Dye H. B. A study of the effects of differential stimulation on mentally retarded children. *Convention Proceeding, American Association on Mental Deficiency*, 1939, *44*, 114-136.

Smith, R. M., and Neisworth, J. T. *The exceptional child: A functional approach*. New York: McGraw-Hill, 1975.

Speens, G. S. The mental development of children of feebleminded and normal mothers. *Yearbook of the National Society for the Study of Education*, Part 2, 1940, 309-314.

Stainback, W., Payne, J., Stainbeck, S., and Payne R. *Establishing a token economy in the classroom*. Columbus: Charles E. Merrill, 1973.

Stephens, T. M. *DTIMS: Classroom management handbook*. Columbus: The Ohio State University Press, 1973a.

Stephens, T. M. *Instructional games: DTIMS reading and math*. Columbus: The Ohio State University Press, 1973b.

Stephens, T. M. *Implementing behavioral approaches in elementary and secondary schools*. Columbus, Oh.: Charles E. Merrill, 1975.

Stephens, T. M. *Directive teaching of children with learning behavioral handicaps* (2nd ed.). Columbus, Oh.: Charles E. Merrill, 1976.

Stephens, T. M. *Teaching skills to children with learning and behavior disorders*. Columbus, Oh. Charles E. Merrill, 1977.

Stephens, T. M. *Social skills in the classroom*. Columbus, Oh.: Cedars Press, 1978.

Stephens, T. M. *The directive teaching language usage curriculum*. Unpublished paper, Faculty for Exceptional Children, The Ohio State University, 1979.

Stephens, T. M. An interview with Dr. Burton Blatt. *The Directive Teacher*, 1980a, *2*(4), 5-8.

Stephens, T. M. Teachers as managers. *The Directive Teacher*, 1980b, *2*(5), 4-25.

Stephens, T. M. *Social behavior assessment* (rev. ed.). Columbus, Oh.: Cedars Press, 1980.

Stephens, T. M., Hartman, A., and Cooper, J. Directive teaching of reading with low-achieving first- and second-year students. *The Journal of Special Education*, 1973, *7*(2), 187-196.

Stephens, T. M., Hartman, A., and Lucas, V. H. *Teaching children with basic skills: A curriculum handbook*. Columbus, Oh.: Charles E. Merrill, 1978.

Stephens, T. M., McCormick, S., Sutherland, H., and Genshaft, J. Huelsman Clinic at The Ohio State University. *Journal of Learning Disabilities*, 1980, *13*(7), 406-409.

Stephens, T. M., and Wolf, J. S. *Effective parent/teacher conferencing*. Columbus, Oh.: NCEMMH/OSU, 1980.

Stephens, T. M., and Wolf, J. S. Instructional models: Sequence for academic skills and concepts. *The Directive Teacher, 4*(1), 1982. (In press)

Strauss, A. R., and Lehtinen, L. E. *Psychopathology and education of the brain injured child*. New York: Grune & Stratton, 1947.

Thompson, L. J. *Reading disability: Development dyslexia*. Springfield, Ill.: Charles C. Thomas, 1966.

Thurstone, T. G. (Ed.). *An evaluation of educating mentally handicapped children in special classes and in regular classes*. Chapel Hill: School of Education, University of North Carolina, 1959.

Towne, R. C., Joiner, L. M., and Schurr, T. *The effects of special classes on the self-concepts of academic ability of the educable mentally retarded: A time series experiment*. Paper presented at the 45th Annual Council for Exceptional Children Convention, St. Louis, Mo., 1967.

Treblas, P. V., McCormick, S. H., and Cooper, J. O. Problems in mainstreaming at the grassroots. *The Directive Teacher* (in press, 1982).

Turnbull, H. The past and future impact of court decisions in special education. *Phi Delta Kappan*, April 1978, 523-526.

Valett, R. E. *Effective teaching: A guide to diagnostic-prescriptive task analysis*. Belmont, Calif.: Fearon, 1970.

VanHouten, R., Hill, S., and Parsons, M. An analysis of a performance feedback system: The effects of timing and feedback, public posting and praise upon academic performance and peer interaction. *Journal of Applied Behavior Analysis*, 1975, *8*(4), 449-457.

Venn, J., Morganstern, L., and Dykes, M. K. Checklists for evaluating the fit and function of orthoses, prostheses, and wheelchairs in the classroom. *Teaching Exceptional Children*, 1979, *11*(2), 51-56.

Washburne, D. A program of individualization. In G. M. Whipple (Ed.), *Adapting the schools to individual differences*, 24th Yearbook of the National Society for the Study of Education, Part 2, Bloomington, Ill.: Public School Publishing Company, 1925, 257-272.

Wechsler, D. Wechsler Intelligence Scale for Children—Revised. New York: The Psychological Corp., 1974.

White, M. A first-grade intervention program for children at risk for reading failure. *Journal of Learning Disabilities*, 1979, *12*(4), 232-237.

Wiederholt, J. L., and Hammill, D. D. Use of the Frostig-Horne perception program in the urban school. *Psychology in the Schools*, 1971, *8*(3), 268-274.

Wolfensberger, W. *The origin and nature of our institutional models*. Syracuse, N. Y.: Human Policy Press, 1975.

Ysseldyke, J. E., and Salvia, J. Diagnostic-precriptive teaching: Two models. *Exceptional Children*, 1974, *41*(3), 181-186.

Name Index

Subject Index

1129